Nick Robinson studied Politics, Philosophy and Economics at Oxford before joining the BBC in 1986. After a decade working behind the cameras – as a producer on programmes ranging from *Crimewatch* to *On the Record* and *Panorama* – he became a reporter and presenter. He is the only person to have been Political Editor of both ITV News and now BBC News – a job he has held since August 2005. As well as appearing on TV and radio, he writes an award-winning blog. Nick lives in North London with his wife and three children.

THE DIVINER.

REPORTER STUDYING A MEMBER'S EXPRESSION AS HE LEAVES THE HOUSE AFTER A SECRET SESSION.

Punch, 3 May 1916

LIVE FROM DOWNING STREET

The Inside Story of Politics, Power
and the Media

Nick Robinson

BANTAM BOOKS

LONDON • TORONTO • SYDNEY • AUCKLAND • JOHANNESBURG

TRANSWORLD PUBLISHERS
61–63 Uxbridge Road, London W5 5SA
A Random House Group Company
www.transworldbooks.co.uk

LIVE FROM DOWNING STREET
A BANTAM BOOK: 9780857500007

First published in Great Britain
in 2012 by Bantam Press
an imprint of Transworld Publishers
Bantam edition published 2013

Addresses for Random House Group Ltd companies outside the UK
can be found at: www.randomhouse.co.uk
The Random House Group Ltd Reg. No. 954009

The Random House Group Limited supports the Forest Stewardship Council®
(FSC®), the leading international forest-certification organisation. Our books
carrying the FSC label are printed on FSC®-certified paper. FSC is the
only forest-certification scheme supported by the leading environmental
organisations, including Greenpeace. Our paper procurement policy
can be found at www.randomhouse.co.uk/environment

Typeset in 11/14pt Erhhardt by Falcon Oast Graphic Art Ltd.
Printed and bound by CPI Group (UK) Ltd, Croydon, CR0 4YY.

4 6 8 10 9 7 5 3

To Pippa, and Alice, Will and Harry, whose evenings,
weekends and holidays have been disrupted,
whose tolerance knows no bounds and whom
I love very dearly.

And in memory of my friends, Will Redhead, and
James Nelson, with whom I wish I could share this.

CONTENTS

ACKNOWLEDGEMENTS

I would never have written this book if it were not for the energy of my agent, Mary Greenham, the inspiration of my literary agent, Ed Victor, the enthusiasm and forbearance of my publisher, Sally Gaminara, the textual massaging and polishing of Caroline North and the tolerance of so many of my colleagues at the BBC.

Broadcast news is a team business in which the people who operate cameras, wield microphones, run studios, edit pictures, sound and words, fix lines and guests never get the credit they deserve. There are far too many people, past and present, to list here but special thanks are due to my PA, Christine Young; my producers, Thea Rogers and Lindsay McCoy; my head of news, Gavin Allen, who helped me juggle day-to-day coverage of the news with writing; and to Sue Inglish, the head of political programmes, and Helen Boaden, the director of BBC News, who gave me the space to do it.

I also owe a huge debt to all those at ITV News from whom I learned so much and who I still miss – in particular, to David Mannion, who both hired and inspired me.

Jonathan Meakin and Jessica Seldon gave invaluable support researching and fact-checking the book and colleagues old and new – Ric Bailey, Malcolm Balen, Bill Bush, Mark Damazer, Martin Rosenbaum, Rob Shepherd, Peter Snowden and Ceri Thomas – were good enough to give their views and insights. Andrew Adonis and the Institute of Government kindly organized seminars to help with my research.

For their expert advice and access to papers I am particularly grateful to Sir David Butler, the father of TV election coverage; Churchill historians Richard Langworth, Professor Paul Addison and Allen Packwood, director of the Churchill Archives Centre at Cambridge University, and his colleague Andrew Riley, archivist of the Thatcher Papers. Also to John Rentoul, Tony Blair's biographer, and to Guy Lodge and Anthony Seldon, Gordon Brown's biographers.

Finally, this book would not have been possible if it hadn't been for Michael Cockerell's pioneering work examining the relationship between television and politics.

Mistakes, omissions and wrong-headed analysis are, of course, mine.

FOREWORD

There is one question I am asked all the time. Not 'What's the prime minister really like?' or even 'Do you actually like politicians?' (incidentally, I do), but 'Why do you stand outside in the rain and cold and dark late at night to do the news?'

Sometimes people are worried about my wellbeing. 'You looked freezing,' they say. Sometimes they're bothered by the distraction of a policeman striding past after a shift change or, as one red-faced copper once confessed, 'so that I can text my mate and say look out for me on the telly'. Sometimes it's because they are hearing not one live report on the events of a big day but snatches of several, like the disembodied voices on the crossed telephone wires of old, as we TV correspondents line up on Downing Street, within touching distance of each other, and shout into our cameras to drown out the broadcasts of our colleagues.

Irrespective of their particular concerns, what those who ask me this question want to know is clear. What on earth is the point of me being out there when I could be sitting with the presenter in a nice warm studio? I sometimes give the practical answer – it's closer to where I work than the newsroom – even after its recent move back to Broadcasting House. Sometimes I explain that TV is as much about pictures as words, and the black door of Number 10 is, of course, the symbol of power in Britain. Just occasionally, though, I admit that for me, at least, there is another reason. It is the reason I have written this book. It's because I can.

My job is to report on what those in power are thinking and doing and on those who attempt to hold them to account in Parliament. I can only do it thanks to a struggle waged over centuries by journalists against politicians for the right to tell the public about the decisions being taken on their behalf – for the right, in other words, to broadcast live from Downing Street.

For many years Parliament didn't allow its debates to be covered at all. Those newspaper men who tried could be thrown in prison. Broadcasters never faced that danger, but they did have to fight for decades for microphones and cameras to be permitted to record the democratic process.

In the early days of radio and television there was a law against reporting anything that MPs had discussed within the previous fortnight or might discuss within the next one. What was dubbed 'controversy' was banned. Prime ministers expected to be able to use the airwaves to speak to the electorate unchallenged and without their opponents having the right to reply. Elections went unreported. Our representatives could be neither seen nor heard by those they expected to vote for them.

At times of national crisis – the general strike, Suez, the wars in the Falklands and Iraq – some prime ministers have sought to take over, others to control, what is broadcast. They have been loath to accept that what is in their interests is not always the same as what is in the national interest. At these and many other times the occupants of Number 10 have complained about what they perceive as bias from broadcasters who declare themselves to be impartial.

For their part, since the advent of radio early in the twentieth century, politicians have had to come to terms with the demands of first the microphone and then the camera. They are now followed by them wherever and whenever they go. Interviews, which once rarely strayed beyond asking those in power whether they had anything to say, are now robust and confrontational. Broadcasting doesn't just reward those able to connect with the people listening or watching at home, it punishes those unable to perform on cue. Being good on the telly is now a necessary, if certainly not a sufficient, quality for national leadership.

When I first joined the BBC in the mid-1980s there were just four television channels and no 24-hour news networks. News was delivered by a box in the corner, a radio or a TV set. There was none on the internet (whatever that was) or mobile phones (which were the size of a brick and almost as heavy). Sky didn't exist and the idea of blogging, tweeting or putting messages on your Facebook wall would have made my head spin.

This book recounts the story of the relationship between the men and women who wield power and those whose job it is to tell the public what they are doing. It focuses on the key milestones in the long and rocky forced marriage between politicians and broadcasters: the prime ministers who pioneered broadcasting live from Downing Street – Baldwin and Macmillan; those who fought back – Churchill, Wilson, Thatcher and Blair; and the leader who could never quite come to terms with it – Brown. It charts the emergence of the charismatic inquisitors of radio and television, from Richard

Dimbleby to Robin Day, David Frost and Brian Walden and, today, David and Jonathan Dimbleby, John Humphrys, Jeremy Paxman, Andrew Marr and Andrew Neil.

It is not a memoir, although it does begin with how and why I became a broadcaster and draws on my experiences as a producer of political TV programmes from the mid-1980s and, a decade later, a political reporter. I have divided the book into two sections to reflect my switch from narrator to player at a time when the media became the multi channel, online, 24/7 creature it is today.

Part I explores the early battle lines drawn between politicians and the press and charts the conflict between Parliament and broadcasters following the birth of first radio and then television. It examines the successes of those who first learned to charm the cameras – and the failures of those who didn't – ending with the Iron Lady's fightback against what she called the media's 'distorted mirror'.

Part II is the story of the New Labour years and Tony Blair's seduction of the media machine he later called the 'feral beast', his bitter and unsuccessful battle to tame it and how it went on to maul his successor, Gordon Brown.

I conclude with 'A final word' addressed to those who believe that 'impartial' broadcasting cannot and should not survive in a world in which anyone can be a reporter and any-one can watch and listen to news produced all over the globe. It is an argument of huge significance for our democracy and one that has taken on greater relevance in the aftermath of revelations about the behaviour of our 'free press'.

Throughout I have tried to convey a sense of how the day-to-day relationship between a reporter and a prime minister works but I believe that what was once private should remain so. Since I have to maintain good working relations with the politicians whose decisions and actions I still report on daily, now is not the time to write in any detail about those who are still active in politics – in the coalition government or the opposition.

From the broadcasting point of view, this account focuses mainly on the BBC and I make no apology for that. It is the BBC that pioneered both radio and television in Britain and for many years was our only broadcaster. As a national institution, paid for by us all, it remains the place where much of the country's conversation takes place, on radio, television and online, and it has always been the politicians' main target for complaints. Nevertheless, as we shall see, it often took competition from ITN, and later Sky, to challenge the BBC's occasional bouts of conservatism and complacency.

Having been a political editor for the past decade, first for ITV News and now the BBC, I have been lucky enough to play a small part in this story. Amid so much change one thing remains constant: the tension between politicians and those who report on them.

Introduction

'A WORD IN THE NATION'S EAR'

'This is London.' Those three words still make the hairs on the back of my neck stand up. Intoned rather than merely spoken at the beginning of every news bulletin on the BBC World Service, they capture for me the thrill of broadcasting: millions of people around the world sitting and listening to what is happening in their part of it conveyed to them from a tiny studio in London. I know how it works but, even in this era of instant, high-quality global communication, it still feels to me like nothing short of a miracle. The reason people listen is, of course, simple: they know they can trust what they're hearing. Journalism can never be the truth and nothing but the truth but the BBC at its best constantly aspires to get as near to the truth as it can that day.

It was my mother's parents – Jewish refugees from Nazi Germany – who taught me to venerate news you could trust. I can picture now my Grandpa Bernard sitting in his apartment holding a radio the size and weight of a paving slab. He would slowly turn the large silver dial, passing from one station to the next in search of the World Service through intermittent blasts of white noise and snatches of German, Russian and French. His half-blind eyes would be closed in concentration. I would sit in reverent silence listening to the voice from London and watching and waiting for what I knew would follow. What, Grandpa would ask me, did I think of the situation in the Middle East? Did I agree with the actions of the British government which had brought people on to the streets again? For a teenager it was a little more challenging than the normal adult fare of 'How's school?' and 'Have you got a girlfriend?' I did my best to give a considered answer. Grandpa would close his eyes once more, as if in deep thought, before, as often as not, replying in his thick Germanic brogue '*No*! I don't zink so.'

This was not, as it first seemed, the conversational equivalent of the death sentence. It was, rather, the signal for me to present my argument and for a lively discussion or debate to begin. Sometimes we would be joined by one of my grandparents' extraordinary array of old friends acquired on their enforced tour of the globe – including a former head of the French Supreme Court and erstwhile executives of Nestlé and National Cash Registers from their days in 'the East', or the man known as 'the Dutch doctor', whose contributions had to be translated from Dutch into German and then into English for me to understand. Although I didn't know it at the time, this was the beginning of my journalistic training.

The book-lined walls of Grandpa Bernard and Granny Susan's apartment in Lausanne, on the shores of Lake Geneva, told their life story and impressed upon me that politics was about so much more than the contrived squabbles that sometimes pass for politics at home. There were books about the Holocaust, which they escaped by fleeing Germany as soon as Hitler was elected; about Shanghai and China, which became a sanctuary for them, along with many others forced to flee Europe; about Japan, their destination when Mao's communists made foreigners less than welcome in Shanghai. Their lives – and the deaths of countless millions who were not so lucky – were shaped and scarred by the political ideas that distorted the twentieth century. Once I asked my grandmother where she thought of as home. 'We have no home,' she told me. Hitler had robbed them of that and so much more besides. Officially 'stateless', they ended their lives in retirement in Switzerland, their final refuge. Whenever I hear people say they find politics boring or the news depressing, I think of how absurd, offensive, even, such a view would have seemed to my grandparents.

My mother's family owed their survival to my grandfather's interest in politics. In the early 1930s, when Hitler was on the rise, Bernard and Susan went to a Nazi rally in Berlin. For a Jewish couple called Rosenberg this was, perhaps, not the wisest of decisions. He told me he'd wanted to see for himself who these people really were. On finding out, he decided that Germany, the country for which he'd fought just a few years earlier, could no longer be considered home.

Millions of words have been written in an attempt to understand how ordinary Germans acquiesced in the mass extermination of the Jews. My family has a letter which, in just a few, illustrates to me one of the reasons: an unwillingness to stand up to and challenge authority and prejudice. It was written by a patient to the doctor who'd treated him for many years. The doctor was my grandfather. The patient explained that, from now on, he would like to enter the surgery by the back door so that he wouldn't be seen. His letter concludes with a phrase expressing the sentiment: 'I'm sure you'll understand.' In other words, I am happy to have a Jew treat me and save my life but I will take no risks myself by being associated with him. It was an attitude that contributed to the deaths of 6 million people and is a lesson which could, so easily, be forgotten unless we remind each new generation of what can and does happen when good men do nothing in the face of evil.

My grandparents did not burden me, as they would have seen it, with tales of the horrors of the Nazis or of war. Thanks to their decisiveness and a good deal of luck, their family escaped the Holocaust. Their stories, like those of so many of their generation, centred on the moments of light in their lives and not on what must have been long stretches of darkness.

Granny Susan used to recount how she'd had to smuggle their money out of the country by sewing it into a padded coat hanger and taking it to Italy by train. Discovery would have brought disaster. She tried to seem relaxed by making conversation with the young woman sitting next to her, who soon confided that her boyfriend, her 'hot water bottle', was very important – he was in the SS. Susan's luck, and her nerve, held and, having got their affairs in as much order as they could, my grandparents collected the coat hanger and boarded a ship bound for China.

A doctor friend of my grandfather's had told him there would be a job for him in a hospital in Manchuria in the north-east, but during the voyage they were warned by telegram that the region was no longer safe. Bernard and Susan had to make a choice between the ship's two other stops, Saigon and Shanghai. They opted for Shanghai, a city known as an international melting pot for people running away from home, everyone from White Russians and

European Jews to Britons who, for whatever reason, felt the need to escape Blighty. Like many of Shanghai's refugees they began with nothing but prospered thanks to their own enterprise, the solidarity of the Jewish community and the opportunities offered by a city buzzing with the energy of twentieth-century Manhattan – or, indeed, twenty-first-century Shanghai.

My granny recalled how they learned of the outbreak of the war through radio. They had left Shanghai for a few days' holiday in Japan when the manager of their hotel rushed into the dining room to interpret in English what he'd just heard on the wireless. 'Chamberlain very sorry but have to declare war,' he told them solemnly. The rather comic translation somewhat undermined the gravity of the announcement. When the hotel guests agreed that they should all head home at once my grandfather turned to my grandmother and asked: 'Tell me, where is our home?' It was clearly no longer the country of their birth. An encounter with a taxi driver confirmed that. Recognizing their German accents, he greeted them with a cheery 'Heil Hitler!'

By the time they returned to Shanghai it was to a city first surrounded and then occupied by the Japanese army. One of the invaders' first acts was to confiscate shortwave radios to cut off people's access to foreign stations. Unwilling to give up the BBC and their only link to what was really happening in the world, the Rosenbergs hid their radio and huddled inside a cupboard to listen to it. My mother still remembers hearing the words 'This is London' and the opening bars of Beethoven's Fifth Symphony, which heralded the news. The rhythm of its first few notes spelled out the letter V in Morse code – dot-dot-dot-dash– a musical reference to Winston Churchill's trademark 'victory' sign. My mother, though just a toddler, was being fed not just news you could trust but a little encrypted dose of British propaganda at the same time.

Just as it has been for her, the BBC news has always been part of the soundtrack to my life. As a child I awoke to the sound of Radio 4's *Today* programme booming out of the bathroom as my dad pumped up the volume to hear it over the noise of his running bath. On returning home from school I would sit on the kitchen table, legs swinging, talking to my mum about my day with *PM* chattering in the background. Our conversations were punctuated by the never-ending saga of Britain on strike in the 1970s. I can still hear the angry voices of the then all-powerful miners' leader Arthur Scargill and my namesake, Red Robbo, the trade unionist who helped to destroy what was left of the British car industry. I remember the hapless tone of prime minister Ted Heath, the avuncular reassurance of Jim Callaghan and the stridency of Margaret Thatcher.

Far more gripping to a schoolboy, though, was the extraordinary courtroom drama of the trial of Jeremy Thorpe, the former Liberal leader. Thorpe was accused, and eventually acquitted, of paying a man to shoot his gay ex-lover (in the event, the hitman ended up shooting his dog). Never before or since has British politics lived through a soap opera like it.

As a child I had my own window on the world in the shape of the first-ever children's news bulletin, *John Craven's Newsround*. Its presenter, editor and inspiration, John Craven – who, in my memory at least, always sported a bright yellow V-neck jumper over his shirt and tie – held the hands of my generation as he took us on a tour of what was happening around the globe. He did it in a way that was simple, engaging but never patronizing.

Each night, like families up and down the land, we had a

regular appointment with the *Nine O'Clock News*. Once a week we would stay up to watch the new TV debate pro-gramme, *Question Time*, chaired by the curious but compelling Robin Day, memorable for his thick, black-rimmed specs, a bewildering range of bow ties, an asthmatic wheeze and what became his catchphrase after introducing the panel: 'There they are, and here we go.'

Ours was not, though, a home of the news-obsessed – my parents weren't journalists, nor were they involved in politics. Like millions of others, they simply took it for granted that you should know what was going on beyond your front door. It was an era in which you couldn't switch on a 24-hour news channel, let alone surf the web, click on an app or tap your mobile to find out what had happened that day. You had to wait until the next bulletin told you. News was all the more exciting as a result.

I was hooked. Yet I did not dream then that I would go on to work with some of the reporters whose words so entranced me and I might never have done so had it not been for our one link with that world. When we tuned into *Today*, we were not merely listening to the day's news and comment but also to Brian, my best friend's dad, talking on the radio. From the age of eight to eighteen I was a regular visitor to Brian Redhead's house, which was on my way home from school. There his son Will and I would sit on stools, eating chocolate cake and drinking milk, and I'd take a look at the *Guardian* and the *Mail* – two papers you rarely see together except in the house of a journalist. Brian, like my grandfather, wanted to know what other people thought. It didn't matter who you were, what you did or how old you were. He believed that wisdom did not reside exclusively – or perhaps, in some instances, at all – in the minds of the great and the good. It was a delight for me to hear him refer to ministers and their opposite numbers as 'berks' while talking excitedly about the insights he'd gained from a conversation with a guard on a train or his neighbourhood butcher who, if memory serves me, also captained the local cricket team.

Brian loved a job which, as he put it, allowed him to 'drop a word in the nation's ear'. I was one of many captivated by his on-air style, a potent mix of terrier-like interviews, caustic asides and affectionate chatter about his cat and the long delays caused by roadworks on the M6 which brought him home from London to the north-west. Some of the ministers in Mrs Thatcher's government were rather less enamoured of him. They even suspected that his jokes about being a member of the mythical organization 'Friends of the M6' were a coded attack on their spending cuts and revealed Brian's true political sympathies. At a time when the north–south divide was widening, Brian spoke up for those who didn't believe the north began at Hampstead Garden Suburb. Reading a weather forecast one morning, telling listeners it would be 'brighter in the north than in the south', he could not resist adding: 'Like the people.'

Brian would tell and retell stories about his clashes with politicians when he and his wife Jenni came to dinner with my parents. My father, a natural Conservative, and Brian, who certainly was not, would work their way through a bottle of whisky while condemning 'the idiots' who, they both agreed, were decimating British manufacturing and impoverishing the north of England. Dad, an engineer by training and later the sales director of a metal company, joined Brian in lamenting the rise of lawyers, accountants and bankers and the decline of people with 'proper jobs who actually make things'. Quite which category journalists belonged to was, sensibly, never discussed. As a teenager, I would return home from parties and be invited to join the debate – if they were not by then snoring boozily in their armchairs.

Years later, when I was asked by a newspaper interviewer about a line of questioning I'd pursued which had upset Tony Blair, I confessed, somewhat bolshily, to being 'northern, arsey and confrontational', a label that has followed me around ever since. Unwittingly, I now realize, I was describing not just myself but the man whose career I chose to follow.

Brian was my childhood inspiration as well as the father of the best friend I still mourn, Will Redhead. Will died along with another friend I still miss, James Nelson, in a terrible car crash which I only just survived. The accident happened in northern France at the beginning of what should have been a tour of Europe. Stop one was to have been my grandparents' home in Lausanne.

After a last meal with Brian and Jenni in their London flat, Will, James and I set off in Will's bright yellow VW Beetle for the coast and the cross-Channel ferry, filled with the sunny optimism and sense of freedom of teenagers who'd just finished their A-Levels and were embarking on a boys' adventure. Little more than an hour after leaving Calais our car was involved in a head-on collision. The Beetle exploded in a ball of fire, killing both my friends instantly. I was trapped in the back of the two-door car, unable to make it to the front through the flames and, despite using all my force, to break any of the windows. I vividly remember concluding that there was, in fact, no way out. Yet somehow I escaped. To this day I do not know how – whether I was thrown out by an explosion or whether I found the strength to smash the glass. What I do know is that I am very lucky to be alive.

My luck did not come to an end on that stretch of road in northern France. Doctors later told me that if the French ambulance crew had taken me to a local hospital instead of a major intensive care unit I would have died. Inhaling so much smoke led my lungs to collapse and I could breathe only with the help of a ventilator. You take it for granted that medics strive to save lives as a matter of course. What I still marvel at is the extra commitment, dedication and love I received in that respiratory intensive care unit in Lille. I will never forget the generosity of the porter who, after I'd emerged from a week unconscious, delivered his tape recorder to my room along, he told me in broken English, with some tapes he thought I might enjoy; or the head nurse who insisted that my parents stayed in her flat rather than pay for a hotel; or my doctor, the charming and amusing Didier Dubois, who told them they could bypass hospital bureaucracy and contact him at any time of the day or night by first calling his brother who, as a family member, would always be put through to him.

After the French medical team had performed their magic I was flown by air ambulance back to Manchester to be transferred to a hospital nearer home where friends and family could visit and where communication did not depend on my schoolboy French or the halting English of the doctors and nurses in Lille. If ever I need to cheer myself up I remember the first words I heard on returning to British soil. They were uttered by a burly ambulance driver who stuck his head through the door of that little Cessna plane on the tarmac at Manchester airport and declared cheerily, 'I'm Gerry from Bury and you're going to be all right.'

I learned a great deal about real life in Manchester's

Withington hospital – no bad thing for a boy brought up in a wealthy, leafy Cheshire village. I learned about life's pressures and absurdities from the man on my burns ward who'd sawed his way through the pipe leading to the gas meter in order to stop the bills clocking up and who had then lit a fag to admire his handiwork. I learned about its tragedies when the nurses asked me to help them convince a mother scarcely older than me that she, too, could recover from her burns. Unspoken between us was the terrible knowledge that what she would never recover from was losing both of her children in the fire that had consumed their home.

I even learned about politics. It was 1983, deep divisions were opening up in Britain and my month in Withington hospital coincided with a wave of strikes in the NHS. Even the nurses walked out, though not those in the Burns Unit, where patients' lives were at risk. One day I asked the feisty and opinionated Glaswegian who cleaned my room every day to explain what the dispute was all about. After regaling me with a catalogue of the crimes of Thatcher and her government, the cuts and the contracting out, she regularly popped her head through my door to add other offences to the list.

Thanks to her, and to the other dedicated hospital staff, Gerry from Bury was proved right. I was 'going to be all right', save for a few scars. I was, though, forced to postpone going to university for a year so that I could pay regular visits to a burns clinic. I could not travel during my enforced gap year and had nothing to do. What filled the hiatus was, by a strange twist, the thing that my grandparents and Brian Redhead had taught me to love: radio.

After the accident, unsure what to do with my time, I wrote to local radio stations asking for some work experience. BBC Radio Manchester agreed that I could come in for two

27

weeks. On my first day the news editor promptly sent me home. 'Where's your tie, laddie?' he boomed. 'What use would you be if the Queen came to Manchester today?' I resisted the temptation to point out that we would probably know by now if Her Majesty was heading our way. As it was, the list of news stories was filled with altogether less significant matters. Nevertheless, it was an early lesson that the first job of any reporter is to find a way to fit in and get on with whoever you are sent to report on, whether that means putting on a tie or changing the way you speak. I am still teased at work and by my kids for adopting a Mancunian accent (don't say 'grarse' as in 'arse', say 'grass' as in 'ass') whenever I pass Watford Junction. I sometimes wince listening back to my reports but I prefer it to the ever-so-faintly patronizing 1950s tones of some reporters forced to talk to 'ordinary people out in the sticks'.

It was local radio that taught me the art of the vox pop: capturing the voice of the people. Vox pops – the short clips of people expressing their views on the day's events as they do their shopping or rush for a train – are a staple part of the daily diet of any newsroom. The quieter the day, the more appetite there is for them to use up airtime. Vox-popping is the media's equivalent of begging. You have to approach people you've never met, who don't want to know you, and persuade them to give up their time and opinions for the amusement of others. They might be asked about great matters of state or, more often than not, about something of no real consequence at all. My first vox pop for BBC Radio Manchester sought to discover why people don't use sun cream (don't ask me – perhaps it was one of those few days when it stopped raining there). My task entailed stopping pretty girls, complimenting them on their tans and asking them whether they'd rubbed cream on their bodies. A result was when they giggled winningly into my tape recorder. It was tough work but someone had to do it.

Curiously, I learned much more about journalism when I left BBC Radio Manchester and went next to their local rival, Piccadilly Radio. I say curiously because Piccadilly was renowned for its pop-music output rather than its news. They were used to kids turning up who wanted to hand out stickers or dreamed of becoming DJs. When I arrived I turned away from the studios and the stars and made a beeline for the newsroom. If I'd turned the other way I might have got to know another local kid, Chris Evans, who, back in 1983, was helping out the station's top DJ, Timmy Mallett. Our paths may have crossed briefly when I was invited to voice one of the characters on the *Timmy on the Tranny* show, on which Evans, in the guise of 'Nobby Nolevel', was a regular. I remain proud to this day of my brief but pivotal role as 'Zak the Zit'.

In those days even commercial pop stations had to produce locally generated news and current affairs in large quantities to hold on to their licences. Piccadilly had a three-hour nightly talk show with the grand title of *The World From the North West*. The task of filling it five nights a week fell to the presenter, Jim Hancock, his producer Ian Walker and, for a few months, me. I might have been just out of school but I was keen, I could talk to people and, above all, I came absolutely free. I'm not sure Piccadilly had ever come across a kid quite like me. One week's work experience soon stretched into month after invaluable month of on-the-job journalistic training.

Jim and Ian could have padded out their programme with phone-ins or blather about what was in the papers, but instead they sent me off round the city streets armed with a Uher, the radio reporter's secret weapon – a portable recorder with clunky metal switches and chunky buttons and dials – and spools of brown recording tape to make mini-documentaries about Manchester's Irish community, Britain's road system and 'the changing face of the family'. I interviewed ministers, ambassadors, businessmen and lots and lots of 'real people', as I soon learned they were patronizingly called by media types. The more interviews I could do the better, as the more time they would soak up. When I listen to those reports now my voice sounds unfamiliar, squeaky and self-consciously Mancunian, and the questions so very, very earnest.

It could all have been so different. The recent movie *24 Hour Party People* is an embarrassing reminder that in the 1980s the world was indeed looking and listening to the north-west. Not, of course, to my worthy radio reports but to the music of Manchester. The Hacienda was fast becoming the most famous nightclub since Liverpool's Cavern, home to the Beatles. It hosted The Smiths three times that year and Madonna's first UK performance the next. I never went, choosing instead the polystyrene rocks and sticky dance floors of the cultural wasteland that was Rumours in nearby Stockport.

Having entirely missed the Manchester scene I took up a place at Oxford which been put on hold after my car accident. My university playground was the Oxford Union Debating Society. The union boasts that thirteen British prime ministers have been members or officers, including William Gladstone, who was one of its first presidents in 1830. Its success as a breeding ground for politicians in the UK and around the world may have something to do with the fact that its debates are run according to the same rules and conventions as the House of Commons. Speakers are not heard in respectful silence and can be interrupted – or intervened on – at any time. This represented an irresistible invitation to a cocky undergraduate and was perfect training for a career challenging politicians. My parents came to watch one debate and reacted with horror when I challenged Denis Healey, the former defence secretary, on his knowledge of NATO. They were relieved and delighted when he told them afterwards that I had been right and he had been wrong. This freedom to interrupt could, of course, work both ways. I still wince at the memory of Helen Suzman, the veteran anti-apartheid campaigner, intervening on a speech I was giving to deliver a crushing correction to an elementary error I had made about southern African politics.

The union not only liberated me from any fear of politicians, it was also where I got my first taste of live broadcasting. On one extraordinary night in March 1985 a student debate about the morality of nuclear weapons was beamed live across Australasia. The prime minister of New Zealand, David Lange, had chosen the union as the forum for a passionate defence of his nuclear-free policy, which led to the exclusion of American and Australian ships from New Zealand waters and risked his country's most vital alliances. In his memoirs, Lange describes it as the most important speech he ever made. I was one of his opponents, which forced me to sit, somewhat reluctantly, with the leader of America's moral majority, the TV evangelist Jerry Falwell, whose presence drew US television to the debate as well.

I can't recall a word I said that night but I do remember the heightened sense of anticipation and interest – the teams gave pre-match interviews strolling around an Oxford quad –

and I will never forget the thrill of taking part in a debate that really mattered, or Lange's kindness to me at dinner afterwards. His passion, wit and grace in arguing for a cause he believed in left a lasting impression on me.

Debating highs were matched by journalistic lows. I tried and failed to set up a student radio station. Campus broadcasting was not common in the 1980s, and I never found my way through the thicket of bureaucracy necessary then but unthinkable now, in an age when the internet lets you broadcast to whom you like, to say what you like and at minimal cost. I did help launch a new student newspaper, portentously entitled *The Sentinel*, whose proprietor was a wealthy American graduate. Its aim was to ape the intelligence, breadth and depth of US newspapers like *The New York Times* and it had, as a result, almost no readers and ran to only one edition.

One of the enormous privileges of going to Oxford is that if you invite interesting and important people to come and speak there they often say yes. ITN's Sandy Gall shared with a group of students his gripping tales of the mujahideen fighting Soviet forces in Afghanistan. If only we'd known then what we know now about how that would turn out. I also met *Newsnight*'s John Tusa when he came to Oxford to make a film about student politics. His producer invited me to London to see the programme being recorded and to watch that evening's edition of *Newsnight* going out. I still recall shuddering as another of its early stars, Donald MacCormick, was told in his ear that the next item had fallen through and he needed to fill for ten further minutes. He had clearly reached the last question of the interview he was on but now had to dream up a whole lot more. Yes, I was horror-struck, but my overwhelming feeling was one of exhilaration.

The visit that influenced me the most, though, was that of

Panorama's Michael Cockerell, the pioneering scholar of television and politics. Cockerell had made a documentary called *The Marketing of Maggie*, which examined what we would now call the spinning of Margaret Thatcher: the voice training, the new hairstyle and the carefully planned photo opportunities. He brought to Oxford never before seen footage of Churchill's TV screen test, to which we shall return later.

On leaving Oxford I applied to both the BBC and ITN to be a trainee journalist. ITN turned me down flat. At the BBC I got as far as the final interview (or what the corporation insists on calling a 'board'). I went in believing that, above all, I needed to make a considered critique of BBC output which I could defend if challenged. I cited the treatment by the *Six O'Clock News* of the space shuttle disaster of February 1986, when, as millions watched in horror, the *Challenger* exploded 73 seconds after take-off, killing all seven astronauts on board, including the first schoolteacher to go into space. Telling the editor of the programme that his coverage of the tragedy had been too long and too mawkish, I ignored all the signals at the board, both verbal and those expressed by body language, that my stridently expressed views were beginning to grate. I suspect that the man from the newsroom had already faced the same criticism and didn't much enjoy hearing it again. Whatever the case, I didn't get the job. Luckily, the night before the application deadline I'd decided that, as a precaution, I'd throw in another form for another BBC traineeship. So it was that I became a trainee TV producer. It wasn't the job I wanted but it was at the place I wanted to be.

At one time a BBC traineeship came with the same kind of status and mystique as being chosen to govern one of Her

Majesty's colonies. Trainees were the men and women hand-picked from thousands to preserve the corporation in all its magnificence to be passed on to another grateful generation. In my era we didn't feel quite so privileged but we still began our careers with a grand tour of the BBC's crown jewels. It was then that I was first able to see, as well as hear, someone utter those three potent words, 'This is London,' that had first sparked my love of broadcasting. At Bush House, the headquarters of the BBC World Service, I peered through a round porthole in the door of a tiny studio. Inside was an equally tiny Tamil man, chattering into a microphone in a language I couldn't recognize, let alone understand. He was, we were told, something of a megastar on the Indian sub-continent, where his programme was listened to by 90 per cent of all Tamil men. The power and the responsibility of his position were awe-inspiring.

Our next stop was equally affecting. We were taken to an old stately home at Caversham, just outside Reading, the headquarters of a unique organization with a dull-sounding title: BBC Monitoring. Inside, in a huge room, were dozens of men and women wearing old black bakelite headphones, hunched over radio sets with huge dials. I was reminded of my grandfather gripping his radio set and searching for the World Service. Each had the job of listening in to a foreign radio station, staying alert for anything noteworthy or surprising and translating any interesting reports they picked up. In one enclave sat those who'd fled East Germany when the Berlin Wall was erected in 1961; in others were refugees from the Hungarian uprising of 1956 or those who had seen the Prague Spring crushed by the Soviet Union in 1968. There were still, if my memory serves me, some veterans whose families had fled Russia after the revolution in 1917.

Each knew not just the language but the dialect and the slang of the country from which they were exiled. Today I can listen to hundreds of radio stations from around the globe on my iPad. Back then, that room was the only spot where you could monitor what ordinary people across the world were hearing. It was a magical place.

Caversham was not there for the fun of it, of course. It had been founded in the early days of the Second World War by a man who, like my grandparents, was a refugee from Berlin. Vladimir Rubinstein spoke Russian, French, German, English and Hebrew more or less perfectly and could get by in a number of other languages. The War Office realized that they could glean as much useful intelligence from domestic radio as from intercepting military communications, so Victor and his team listened in to German, Russian, French and Italian radio broadcasts. Ernst Gombrich, the German Jewish art historian, and the Russian philosopher Victor Frank wore specially extended headsets so that they could play table tennis while one monitored Radio Berlin and the other eavesdropped on Radio Moscow.

Years later, in 1962, when the Cuban missile crisis reached its climax, the Russian president Nikita Khrushchev is said to have broadcast his effective capitulation on a domestic radio channel, knowing full well that it would be monitored at Caversham and relayed instantly to the White House. The year before my visit the monitors at Caversham had listened in for a change to sombre music to confirm that Soviet leader Konstantin Chernenko had finally died.

Our guide that day boasted that all sorts of organizations from around the world, including the Chinese embassy, sub-scribed to the *Summary of World Broadcasts*, the telephone directory-sized report published daily. 'How much do you charge?' I asked, somewhat surprised that we sold this irreplaceable intelligence at all. The answer was £100.

'A day?' I inquired.

'Oh no, a year.'

Only at the BBC and only in Britain could people so undervalue such a unique resource. It sells for rather more than that these days.

My BBC traineeship lasted two years and involved a series of three-month stints on different programmes across the whole range of the BBC's output and outposts. Some you got to choose; others chose you. My first posting was at BBC1's *Crimewatch*. It was a programme I don't think I'd ever watched and I was faintly puzzled as to why anyone would. On arriving in the office I was told to go and buy a tooth-brush: I would be going away for a few days to help make a dramatized reconstruction of the tragic 'Babes in the Wood' murder. Two little girls, Karen Hadaway and Nicola Fellows, aged nine and ten, had been abducted, sexually assaulted and found dead in a park near Brighton. The horrific case was gripping the nation just as the Soham murders did almost sixteen years later. The hope was that our film would jog the memories and the consciences of those who might help to identify their killer.

My job, fresh out of university and with no experience of journalism, let alone policing, was to read all the statements taken by the police in order to propose what we could film that might help the investigation. By three in the morning I had identified a number of areas where the statements appeared to produce contradictory evidence – for example, three people had reported sightings of the girls at the same time but in different places. It might help, I thought, if we could find other witnesses so that a clear timeline could be established. I pointed this out to my producer, who told the police officer in charge. He reacted with amazement, summoning all his officers into the room to hear what I'd 'discovered'. It soon became clear that I was the only person who had actually read all of the statements. The police team had been split into two but Team A had apparently not yet compared its work with Team B's. To this day the murderer of those two girls has not been brought to justice. I wish I could say I was surprised.

There were lighter moments, though they were just as revealing. On the night that one *Crimewatch* programme was broadcast I was one of those manning the phones when viewers called in with information about the crimes featured. Puzzlingly, the phones began to ring before the programme even began. I had been taught exactly how to handle the calls and how to write down what I heard – these were, after all, potential witnesses in serious criminal cases. One call came from a doctor in Worthing who named the person responsible for the crime after seeing the programme trailer. 'Can I ask how you are so sure?' I asked him. 'My wife's a medium,' he told me. Another was from a girl who sounded very angry. She described the assailant in detail. When I inquired how she could be so certain this was the murderer, she memorably replied: ''Cos he's a fucker and I fucking hate him.'

Best of all, though, was the call from a woman who said she could identify one of the men we were seeking.

'I saw him driving the van,' she told me.

'What colour was it?'

'Blue.'

The van in our reconstruction was white.

'Where did you see it?'

'Eastbourne.'

The van had been in Aberdeen.

'What did he look like?'

'He had black hair.'

Our man was ginger.

I asked, ever so politely, 'What makes you think that this is the man we're looking for?'

'He had a funny look.'

I was delighted to be posted to *John Craven's Newsround*, which I'd watched as a child. Writing short scripts that a seven-year-old would understand was perhaps the toughest journalistic challenge I've ever faced. One day in October 1987 I spent many hours writing and rewriting the story of what became known as Black Monday, trying to explain simply not just the stockmarket crash but what the stockmarket was. The Middle East peace process was equally testing. When I was asked to interview a man about tortoises in the *Blue Peter* garden I was grateful for some light relief.

In August of that year news emerged of a horrific massacre in the little town of Hungerford in Berkshire, where a man called Michael Ryan had gunned down sixteen people, including his own mother, and injured another fifteen before turning the gun on himself. These days such dramatic, and thankfully rare, news would immediately be spread on Twitter or the 24-hour news channels, but back then the BBC had a straight choice between breaking it on *Newsround* – the next scheduled bulletin – or asking the TV newsroom to produce a special news flash. I watched in awe as John persuaded his BBC bosses that he should be trusted with covering the massacre rather than allowing the 'grown-up' news to take over his slot. After all, he argued, thousands of children would be watching in any case, having tuned in to see *Newsround*, and he knew how to tell them the story in a way that would limit their distress.

In the general election that year *Newsround* secured a larger audience than the specially extended *Nine O'Clock News*. It's just possible that viewers found its storytelling easier to understand and, frankly, less dull. It was a lesson I've never forgotten: not that you should treat everyone like children, but that if you don't engage people, whatever their age, or you assume too much knowledge, they will quickly switch off.

Another educational experience was Britain's first-ever five-day-a-week chat show, *The Pamela Armstrong Show*, which was broadcast from the BBC's Pebble Mill studios in Birmingham. It was not a programme I'd chosen but it proved again that you often learn the most when working outside your comfort zone. The show had many hours of airtime to fill, a fact that was probably obvious to anyone watching it. Those of us making it, however, had a ball. There was the usual mix of plugs for books, TV shows and plays and 'celebrity' interviews. One of my first jobs was producing a cookery item with the formidable septuagenarian Fanny Cradock, the Delia or Nigella of her day. Fanny was a regular on chat and game shows but had been absent from our screens for some time after the death of her beloved husband Johnnie. Her return was not without its problems. We had been warned that Fanny had always liked a drop of the cooking brandy. What we hadn't anticipated was how alarmingly the pans would shake whenever she picked them up. At the rehearsals, seeing disaster ahead, I suggested to Fanny that the viewers would enjoy it more if we showed her teaching Pamela Armstrong how to cook. She spotted my ruse and protested that she'd never been so insulted in her life. I last saw her being carried off the set by burly security guards.

What filled Fanny's time slot I can't recall. It may have been one of the show's harder-edged items, which included the sorry tale of posties bitten by dogs (I had to find the victims) and prostitutes who refused to use condoms despite the threat of AIDS (you've guessed it: I had to find the prostitutes). *Pamela Armstrong* marked the end of my days as a talk-show producer. As I say, sometimes it is the worst programmes that teach you the most, and I'm sure my colleagues on one so poor it was dropped after its first series would agree: among them were the current head of ITV Entertainment, the editor of *The Archers*, the director of *Miranda*, one of the founders of the Mumsnet website and the man in charge of commissioning all BBC Entertainment shows.

My last stop as a trainee was on the Sunday lunchtime political programme *This Week Next Week*. The editor was a charismatic showman who wore bright red braces and began each week's team meeting by demanding that we bid for interviews with guests ranging from the prime minister to the Pope. On being turned down by Downing Street and, memorably, the Vatican, we all too often ended up with a junior minister at the Department of the Environment. It was here, though, that I got my first taste of the adrenaline rush that comes with a successful political interview.

In March 1988 Margaret Thatcher was struggling behind the scenes with her chancellor, Nigel Lawson, over the control of economic policy and, in particular, his policy of setting interest rates so that the pound would shadow the Deutschmark (these were the days before the creation of the Euro and before politicians lost control of interest rates). When Lawson had to abandon the policy under pressure from the markets his boss ostentatiously uttered unhelpful remarks about the futility of restraining the pound. I researched, planned and plotted the interview he then gave to the host of *This Week Next Week*, Vivian White.

'It wasn't just the press who addressed themselves to the exchange rate in public, it was the prime minister and First Lord of the Treasury herself. Did she devalue your office by speaking about the exchange rate in public as she did?' White asked.

'I don't think she devalued my office,' Lawson answered. 'But I think one needs to be very careful about how one talks about these matters in public.'

'Was she?'

'That incident was unfortunate but that's now behind us.'

The interview proved that politicians couldn't control the pound. It fell 3 pfennigs when the markets opened the following day. The tension between Number 11 and Number 10 was there for all to see. It would lead, eventually, to the chancellor's resignation and the fall of the prime minister. Having experienced at first hand the impact an interview could make I wanted to do more.

This may sound as if, for me, political journalism is about catching out, tripping up or embarrassing a politician. It is not. It is, however, about exposing publicly what many know to exist privately: tension between colleagues, policy contradictions or a failure to have thought through a policy clearly. The job I did then, and to a large extent still do now, is to identify those problems and seek to bring them to light.

The BBC created a new Sunday lunchtime programme, *On the Record*, to do just that. Having completed my two years as a trainee, I applied to join the team and was given my first real job, as an assistant producer. My responsibilities included researching and planning the interviews conducted each week by Jonathan Dimbleby with a leading politician and helping to make short films about topical political issues. I still remember my delight at getting my first scoop which, like so much in journalism, involved asking the right people the right questions and a bucketful of luck.

I was making a film about Labour's approach to Tory trade union laws – a policy review set up by the then party leader, Neil Kinnock, was debating whether to pledge to reverse them, as most union leaders wanted, or to accept them, as he believed was necessary. Knowing none of the figures involved, I scanned the list of members of the review team, looking for a union likely to be sympathetic to the leadership, picked one of its two representatives, dialled his phone number with some trepidation and explained who I was and what I was doing. His response was completely unexpected. 'I suppose you'd like the minutes of all the meetings?'

I laughed nervously, assuming this was my new contact's idea of a joke, and suggested that we might meet for a drink, or even a bite to eat. 'There's no need for that,' he said. 'Just send over a bike and I'll put the lot in a brown envelope.'

It was that simple, though I don't imagine I made that clear to my editor at the time. A few days later the hapless Michael Meacher, then Labour's employment spokesman, sat in our studio watching in horror as my film revealed that the first meeting of his policy review had agreed to scrap all Tory trade union laws, the second had voted to keep them, the third to scrap them . . . and so on, depending on who bothered to turn up to which meeting. He sat with his head in his hands. I looked on with a smile on my face. I can't recall any politician ever being quite so obliging since.

Our studio interviews involved meticulous preparation. They were long – twenty minutes or so – and usually focused on a single subject rather than, as all too often happens nowadays, a shopping list of items from the news. Before briefing Jonathan I would read all the interviewee's recent speeches, talk to officials, colleagues and rivals and get the advice of policy experts. The interview briefs I helped to prepare would go through many different versions before Jonathan tried out different lines of questioning with me and other colleagues standing in for the interviewee. If we could waffle for hours we'd wasted our time. If we were stumped or had to think, rather than trotting out a standard party line, we knew we'd got something worth pursuing. Our aim was to examine an idea, not to engage in gladiatorial combat with a politician or simply to get a clip on that evening's news. In a business where big egos are taken for granted, Jonathan Dimbleby was remarkably tolerant and generous in allowing a twenty-two-year-old novice to attempt first to shred and then to rewrite his questions.

This was a time when politics could scarcely have been more interesting. Labour had started the long process of reform and modernization that would eventually lead to Tony Blair matching Margaret Thatcher's electoral domination. Meanwhile, her government was dividing the country with its radical plan to privatize water, electricity and gas but, above all, with the introduction of the poll tax, and the Conservative party, riven by divisions over Europe, was girding itself to remove the most successful leader it had ever had – a decision that would open wounds which would not heal for many years to come and result in the slow and painful death of John Major's government.

These were also the days when the divisions of postwar Europe ended, Soviet communism failed and the city in which my grandparents grew up was finally reunited. As a student I had visited Berlin and stood on a viewing platform overlooking the wall that had separated not just a city but an entire continent since its erection in 1961. I visited the museum at Checkpoint Charlie which told the heroic and tragic stories of those who'd managed to flee and those who'd been shot in the attempt and left to bleed to death. In November 1989 I was lucky enough to be sent to make a film about the fall of the Berlin Wall. I stood on top of it with thousands of young Germans, singing and cheering and dancing, watched by bemused East German soldiers below. Days before, they would have been under orders to shoot anyone who joined them in what was known as no man's land. I will never forget the moment when those orders were put to the test. Someone jumped. Everyone froze. Nobody could be certain what would happen next. The boy who'd dared to cross the wall held out a hand with a flower in it. The soldiers paused. Then one of them took it and smiled. The wall erupted in cheering and applause. The division of Europe was at an end, the legacy of the Second World War finally over.

At *Panorama*, my next career move, I was able to explore some of the other extraordinary changes taking place in the world as well as to carry on covering the ongoing drama of British politics in the early 1990s. As Britain's longest-running current affairs programme, it had been compulsory viewing for an older generation and regularly provoked huge rows, often about programmes no one had yet seen. During my time there I learned how to handle angry chief executives who felt they and their companies were being traduced, the royal family, whose flunkies were nervous of any debate about the future of the monarchy, and even an interview with a prime minister, to which we will return later, that could never be broadcast in Scotland thanks to a court injunction.

It was also my first exposure to what were euphemistically known as the Troubles in Northern Ireland. I was asked to meet two remarkable people, Colin and Wendy Parry, whose twelve-year-old son had just been blown up by a bomb left in a litter bin on a shopping street in Warrington, not far from my family home. They wanted to know why their son had died and were willing to make a film about it. I sat in their house, often close to tears, as they talked about Tim, and I told them of my own experience of losing my closest friends. I wondered whether it was fair to expose them to the pressures not merely of making a documentary but of confronting people who believed their son's death was a necessary part of the struggle for a free Ireland. Colin and Wendy had never been to Northern Ireland, or to the south, for that matter, and knew nothing of the country's politics. Over the next few weeks they met republicans and loyalists, American fundraisers for the IRA and the president of Ireland. They made a film of insight and quiet dignity which drew the biggest audience ever for a piece on a subject that had millions reaching for the off button.* If I could only ever have made one television programme, that would be the one I'd choose.

Another *Panorama* on Northern Ireland, which asked whether the government ought to be having talks with the IRA, revealed a great deal about how politics really works. Although at the time ministers insisted, as they always do, that they would never speak to terrorists, the suspicion was that an arm's-length dialogue of some kind was already taking

* The Parrys now run the Tim Parry Johnathan Ball Foundation for Peace, which helps young people to confront and reconcile their differences.

place. I advised our reporter to ask the Northern Ireland secretary, Patrick Mayhew, every possible variant of the key question to reduce his wriggle room. The last, as I recall, went something like: 'Have you at any time sanctioned anyone on your behalf, though not necessarily under your control, to make contact with people who might be in touch with the IRA leadership?' Despite our best efforts it appeared to produce nothing. On the eve of the programme going out I received a phone call from the minister's press secretary. We needed to 'freshen up the interview', he said.

I told him this was not a concept I was familiar with, and asked whether what he really meant was that we should do the whole thing again. Guessing what was behind this nebulous requirement, I shouted down the phone: 'You're bloody talking to them, aren't you?'

'Well, all I can tell you is that there is an important development in the story emerging soon.'

'How big is it on the Richter scale?'

'Around a twelve.'

I pointed out that there were only ten points on the Richter scale.

'I know that.'

The *Observer* was about to reveal that the government had indeed been talking, albeit indirectly, to the IRA. We had an entirely new programme to make. We rushed back to the tapes of our interview, assuming that Mayhew had lied to us and as a result might have to resign if it was aired. His final answer to our question had been to declare: 'If, of course, we were to receive a message saying something like "the conflict is over", we would, of course, have to consider . . .' When we had first heard it we thought he was giving himself a get-out in case at some point in the future the IRA changed its policy. In fact, his answer was carefully calibrated to protect his career and save the government from disaster. When Mayhew was interviewed live on our replacement programme he used his 'freshened up' interview to explain that he had received just such a message and that it was his duty to act on it. There are reasons why it sometimes pays politicians to be economical with the truth.

In moving to *Panorama* I had swapped one Dimbleby brother for another. David, the presenter, was the man who interviewed Mayhew live that night and we worked together on many other programmes. In 1994 we flew to South Africa to interview Nelson Mandela on the eve of the nation's first democratic, multi-racial elections.

Although Mandela's release from imprisonment four years earlier and the fall of another evil political system had not been marred by the level of violence many whites feared, there was none the less an atmosphere of deep anxiety in a country that could not really believe it was heading for majority rule. On white radio station phone-ins, I heard the panicky voices of people convinced that the launch of a new line in long-life milk by a supermarket chain proved those with power and money knew a siege was coming. Despite the company's denials, a year's stock sold out in days. So did tents, torches and tinned food. Amid all this, the man who'd been locked up for twenty-seven years remained not merely calm and courteous but serene. It was an enormous privilege to meet him.

Perhaps it is a reflection on my producing abilities that en route David started to quiz me about my career. He told me I was far too young to go into some junior BBC management job – the next obvious move once I'd burned out as a producer – and should instead think about following in his footsteps. Television reporting was, he told me, a career you could carry on doing happily after your hair turned grey. I recall remarking that this was a little bit like my Manchester United hero Eric Cantona advising me to take up football. It was, though, advice for which I will be eternally grateful, because I was gradually beginning to realize that I wanted to be the one asking the questions, not helping someone else to ask them.

In 1995 I was offered the opportunity of a three-month trial as a political correspondent at Westminster. I hadn't worked in a newsroom since that gap year on local radio, and at the time it felt like quite a risk to give up my rung on the management ladder, my private office, my secretarial support and my car parking space. I came very close to returning to them that September after covering the Liberal Democrats' conference in a wet and windy Brighton for *Breakfast News*. I'd spent the week attempting to convince the programme team that I could turn the worthy debates of a party light years away from power into interesting and engaging television. I had expended countless hours trying to devise ways to turn something that was, in truth, neither particularly newsworthy nor visually interesting into an event that might appeal to a viewer buttering a piece of toast or wiping the kids' faces before heading off to work.

Every day my report was reduced to a one-minute summary I could have written in approximately half an hour. No matter, I consoled myself on the last day – at least I've got a proper job to return to. At that moment I was interrupted by my pager. Obeying the message to call the office 'urgently', I was asked: 'Have you got your passport?'

I'd long since learned that the only answer to that is yes, even if – as on this occasion – you then have to ask your wife to arrange for a taxi driver to collect it and make a high-speed dash to meet you in Departures. A minister, I was told, had just attacked the chancellor for his enthusiasm for joining the European single currency. The pound had started to fall. Please would I pack, head to the airport and fly to – at this point I was sure I must have misheard – Bermuda. After half a second's thought I replied that, on balance, and after careful consideration, and despite my regret at leaving the conference and Britain's balmy climate, I would, indeed, be willing to go. So it was that, having flown to a paradise island and located Ken Clarke – who was rather startled to see me walk into the Commonwealth finance ministers' meeting – I found myself standing on the verdant lawn of the governor's mansion, looking out to sea, sipping a cocktail and concluding that I might, after all, give this reporting business a little while longer.

It has been my life ever since. In the run-up to the 1997 election I worked largely on radio, switching to television as chief political correspondent for the BBC's news channel for the 2001 campaign. Next I was hired by ITV News as their political editor, and had the privilege of sitting next to Jonathan Dimbleby in ITV's 2005 election night studio, where he now asked me questions. Finally, I was poached back by the BBC and turned up on their 2010 election night programme sitting beside David.

Sadly, my grandparents did not live to see or hear me reporting on radio and television. Neither did Brian Redhead, who died in 1994. In the aftermath of the car accident that killed his son, it was, understandably, several years before he felt able to resume our relationship – long after I'd joined the BBC. It is only now I am the father of three children that I can hazard a guess at the raw, all-consuming agony and rage he and his wife must have felt at the loss of their child. When I did finally see him again there were no words about what had happened. Instead, he just squeezed my hand and our relationship resumed where it had left off – with talk about 'those idiots' at Westminster and at the BBC and, of course, about the great men and women, too.

PART I

The Battle to Broadcast Live from Downing Street

1740

1

'I SPY STRANGERS'

'Excuse me, sir.' The police officer cleared his throat in that way they do when they want to convey that you are in trouble – serious trouble. This guardian of the law and I were standing in Parliament's Central Lobby, the crossroads between the Commons and the Lords where voters can turn up in the hope of bending the ear of their elected representative. It being just a minute before ten o'clock at night we were, however, alone. Most MPs had long since gone home. The officer was, I noticed, staring intently at my shoes. 'You are aware, aren't you,' he asked sarcastically, 'that the serjeant-at-arms has decreed you may not stand beyond that line?'

I looked down, aghast. It was true. My shoe had indeed strayed across the line on the intricate mosaic floor and thus broken the carefully negotiated agreement between the broadcasters and the Commons authorities. Infuriated by the absurdity of this petty admonishment I began to construct in my head a passionate declaration of my rights as a citizen and a reporter. I never got to deliver it, thanks to the interruption of Huw Edwards in my ear: 'Nick Robinson joins us now, live from the House of Commons . . .'

Few watching at home in the early part of the twenty-first century, had they even been aware of the row about the exact positioning of my shoe, would have recognized it as the latest small skirmish in a long war between Parliament and those whose job is to report on it.* Long before cameras were allowed into the Central Lobby, MPs fought against the idea that anyone else at all should attend their proceedings to record their deliberations. Many of the arguments they deployed have been used many times across centuries to ban or frustrate the reporting of Parliament.

Any visitor to the Commons who witnesses the Speaker's daily procession as it passes through the Central Lobby is struck by the cry: 'Hats off, strangers!' The 'strangers' in question are you and me – namely anyone inside the Palace of Westminster who is not a member of Parliament. For a long time I regarded this as no more than a quaint ceremony rooted in a proper respect for the Speaker, whose pre-decessors stood up for the rights of our elected representatives and resisted the untrammelled power of the monarchy. I have come to realize, though, how revealing the terminology is. The culture of the House of Commons is to regard anyone other than its own members as 'strangers', intruders whose presence is to be resented and resisted if at all possible. It is an attitude founded in the struggle for pre-eminence between Crown and Parliament.

In 1560 the procedures of the Commons stated: 'Every person of the Parliament ought to keep secret and not to dis-close the secrets and things done and spoken in the Parliament house.'[1] Parliament's deliberations were meant to

---

* This was a few years ago. The police and 'men in tights' who run the Commons are now, happily, much more relaxed.

be heard by parliamentarians alone, and for good reason. MPs didn't want the King's men to be able to hear their debates about his latest demands for money or for men to fight his wars. The earliest parliamentary reporters, then, were taking quite a risk. My predecessors could expect far worse than a patronizing ticking-off by a pompous policeman. They could be summoned by the House of Commons and punished for daring to reveal what took place within it. MPs feared that they, in turn, could face arrest if the King got to hear what they had been discussing.

While the British Parliament is one of the oldest continuous representative assemblies in the world, its evolution from its earliest origins – the advisory council established in 1066 by William the Conqueror to help him make laws – was slow and erratic. During the centuries after the signing of the Magna Carta in 1215, under which the King was first required to obtain his council's consent before levying new taxes, it developed into something resembling a parliament and began, in fits and starts, gradually to limit the power of the monarchy.

Before the Civil War, it was a pretty temporary institution: it could be summoned by the sovereign, or dissolved by him, at any time. But the battles between Crown and Parliament in the 1620s, which would eventually culminate in victory over the monarchy, were simply too interesting and too important to remain secret for long. By now the Commons had become a stage on which a daily power struggle was taking place and there was a market for news of its dealings, even though newspapers as we know them today did not yet exist. A printer called Ralph Starkey charged '20 shillings a quire' for lengthy reports on parliamentary proceedings which, thanks to the King's highway, he was able to distribute up and down the land. Scriveners, those rare folk who could both read and write, originated the reports and a team of copyists was employed to reproduce them. These no doubt rather turgid accounts were the start of the news business. They had a wider significance, too: the historian Simon Schama argues that they led to the creation of an informed public opinion beyond the confines of the court and Westminster.

For a while MPs, seeing the propaganda value in people learning about their struggles with the King, tolerated this breach of their rules. However, in 1641 the House ordered that a printed copy of a speech by one MP should be 'burnt publicly by the hands of the common hangman'. The following year the hangman got to set ablaze a whole collection of speeches made by an MP who was expelled for acting 'against the honour and privilege of this house'.[2]

Even after the Civil War the Commons returned to its secretive ways. Ministers took powers to censor what were described as 'the frequent abuses in printing seditious, treasonable, and unlicensed books and pamphlets'. The pamphleteers who, rather like the bloggers of today, had vented their spleen at the political and religious ideas that offended them could do so no more. The Licensing Act of 1662, which regulated both the press and the book trade, saw to that – for a few years, at least.

Come the time of the man we regard as our first prime minister, Sir Robert Walpole, politicians had a new reason for keeping their proceedings secret. They wanted to protect themselves not from an over-mighty sovereign but from the judgement of the people.

These days our leaders may complain about a scathing headline or comment or an unflattering image in a TV report.

When Walpole came to office in 1721 it was graphic and brutal caricatures he had reason to fear. The most famous image of Sir Robert is William Hogarth's *Idol-Worship and the Way to Preferment*, which depicts a huge naked bottom straddling the Treasury, with people lining up to kiss it. No face was shown; none was needed. Everyone knew whose arse you had to kiss in order to get on.

Images of politicians mattered long before the invention of television. Since the early years of the seventeenth century satirical prints had become increasingly popular. Hogarth was the pioneer of graphic satire. He and his successors – notably Cruikshank, who received a royal bribe of £100 to go easy on George III, and Gillray, who famously depicted Pitt the Younger carving up the world with Napoleon – were much harder to control and much more deadly than the writers. They had the unique power to deliver a character assassination or sum up a complex political issue in a single, vicious swipe. By the early nineteenth century, caricatures were being combined with print and for the first time, pictures and words were used together to deliver political comment.

Walpole's official title – First Lord of the Treasury – is still bestowed on today's prime ministers and can be seen on the brass plaque on the front door of the building given to him by a grateful monarch: 10 Downing Street. The office of prime minister in fact exists only by long-established convention and, like Parliament itself, evolved over the years in a haphazard way. At the time, the references to Walpole as 'prime minister' were actually an insult, designed to cast him as a sort of regal teacher's pet, and reflected his dominance of the Cabinet.

However, Walpole did not owe his position solely to the

favour of his monarch. His survival depended on the favours he did for his parliamentary supporters who were, according to one contemporary MP, 'disciplined troops regularly paid'. The prime minister's political army included his own family. He gave his eldest son a post worth £7,000 (a tidy sum in today's money) and a peerage at just twenty-two; his second son got a position worth £3,000 and his third, despite being still at school, was made comptroller of the pipe and clerk of the escheat. No wonder 'every man has his price' is the phrase that will forever be associated with our first prime minister (although, as is the case with so many famous political utterances, there's no proof he ever used those exact words). The satirist John Gay summarized the way politics worked in his *Fables*: 'That statesman has the strongest hold whose tool of politics is gold.'[3]

If Walpole indulged in parliamentary corruption on an industrial scale, few at the time would have raised an eyebrow had it not been for the emergence of a newly popular press. Most MPs regarded their payments as simply the way things were done – just as did many of their successors when they were employing their relatives from the public purse or claiming on their expenses for duck houses, moat-cleaning or dog food.

Parliament's recent expenses scandal was revealed thanks to freedom of information legislation which guaranteed that claims made in secret eventually saw the light of day. MPs reacted by considering changes to the law to exempt their expenses from scrutiny, as well as by wasting vast sums of public money on legal challenges to the rulings under which their claims had been made public. Back in Walpole's day it was not a new law that exposed Westminster to scrutiny but the lapsing of an old one.

The Licensing Act had expired and been renewed several times before it was finally abandoned in 1695, to be replaced in 1709 by the first Copyright Act. Freed from its constraints, news had begun to sell. The first regular daily newspaper, the *Daily Courant*, launched in 1702, was soon followed by a host of rivals in London and around the country claiming to offer the latest on what MPs were up to. Although officially, parliamentary debates were still secret, thinly disguised accounts of proceedings, tolerated by the Commons, helped the *Post-Boy* to compete with the *Post-Man*, the *Flying Post* and the *Evening Post* (the titles of the London papers of the time lacked a certain originality). Walpole responded in the only way he knew how: by buying the support of some papers and by reinforcing the ban on parliamentary reporting.

Walpole scholar Jeremy Black calculates that the prime minister dipped his hand into the public purse to spend £22,000 in one year – equivalent today to more than £2.5 million – subsidizing papers that attacked those who attacked him.[4] On reading the *British Journal*, he probably regarded it as money well spent. This paper took the line that it was only reasonable to call a minister corrupt if Parliament had already done so – which was tantamount to saying that an accused man was guilty only if his fellow conspirators declared him to be so. Another sponsored paper, the *Whitehall Journal*, called for 'the silencing of libellers' and condemned 'grumbling malcontent scribblers'. Comparing the liberty of the press to the freedom to buy 'sulphur, nitrate and arsenic', the paper asserted that such liberty did not extend to using them to blow up the royal family or for mass poisoning.

Walpole's newspapers didn't just fight to protect his reputation, they challenged the right of ordinary people to have a view on politics at all. The splendidly named *Appleby's*

Original Weekly Journal stated on 17 November 1722 that the most loyal subjects were those 'that meddle least in public affairs'. The *Daily Gazetteer* was even more patronizing about one controversy of the day: 'To suppose that a point of this importance ought to be explained in public prints to every little fellow that asks it, is supposing our government [should be] dissolved and the mob ready to sit in judgement on the legislature.'

This was an era in which precious few people had the vote and all too many of those who did were prepared to sell it to the highest bidder. Fear of the mob was a convenient excuse for keeping the public ignorant. They, though, were expected to pay taxes and to send their sons to war and, therefore, had an increasing appetite for news of decisions being taken in their name.

After years of being reluctant to enforce their ban on parliamentary reporting, MPs found an excuse to act. Edward Cave, publisher of the *Gentleman's Magazine*, provided it for them by doing something they regarded as shocking but which would be considered routine today. In 1738 he published a report of what an MP was expected to say in a speech in the Commons. MPs reacted with the sort of fury reserved nowadays for ministers who inform listeners to the *Today* programme of a plan before revealing it in the Commons.

The Commons passed a resolution declaring: 'It is an high indignity to, and a notorious breach of Privilege of this House, for any News-Writer, in Letters or other Papers ... to give therein any Account of the debates, or other Proceedings of this House.' The Commons would, the motion continued, 'proceed with the utmost severity against such offenders'. In the debate Walpole condemned parliamentary reporting as 'forgery of the worst kind'.

> I have read some debates of this House, Sir, in which I have
> been made to speak the very reverse of what I meant. I
> have read others of them wherein all the wit, the learning,
> and the argument has been thrown into one side, and on the
> other nothing but what was low, mean, and ridiculous . . . had
> I been a stranger to proceedings and to the nature of the
> arguments themselves, I must have thought this to be one of
> the most contemptible assemblies on the face of the earth.

This is an elegant way of announcing that it was time to shoot
the messenger. That the struggle between politicians and the
media was – as it is today – about power was made absolutely
plain by Walpole's adversary, the leader of the opposition,
William Pulteney. 'To print or publish the speeches of
gentlemen in this House, even though they are not misrepresented, looks very like making them accountable
without doors for what they say within.'[5]

In other words, the leader of the opposition was asserting
that MPs should not be held accountable to the public. Thus
Walpole's arse was covered – for a while, at least.

Journalists abhor secrecy and relish finding ways to get round
it. We only know the words uttered by our first prime
minister and the leader of the opposition in 1738 thanks to
the efforts of someone prepared to ignore their threats. The
fearless pursuit of truth is a fine journalistic tradition. There
is another, less honourable one: what you don't know, make
up.

For some years in the mid-eighteenth century, parliamentary debates would be reported under fictional cover.

Andrew Sparrow, the modern historian of the parliamentary press gallery, records that the *London Magazine* unveiled a new feature called 'The Proceedings of a Political Club', while the *Gentleman's Magazine* carried reports of 'debates in the Senate of Magna Lilliputia'. These fictional accounts were deemed to be based on fact. However, one of the contributors to the *Gentleman's Magazine*, Samuel Johnson, the celebrated compiler of *The Dictionary of the English Language*, shocked a society dinner party in the 1770s by revealing how loose the connection between reality and reporting actually was.

Having listened to a fellow diner praise the brilliance of a speech delivered by William Pitt the Elder, Dr Johnson confessed that in fact 'I wrote it in a garret in Exeter Street'. His publisher had an arrangement with a Commons doorkeeper, who took a note of the subjects under discussion, the order of the speakers, which side they were on and details of their arguments. So while the *Gentleman's Magazine* was au fait with Pitt's case, the rhetoric they recorded for posterity was entirely Johnson's. The man who famously declared that any man who was tired of London was tired of life was hardly likely to grow weary of the Commons: he told his dinner companions he'd never been there. Perhaps he had his own parliamentary reports in mind when he commented that the press 'affords sufficient information to elate vanity and stiffen obstinacy but too little to enlarge the mind'.

The ban on the reporting of Parliament other than in fictional form continued until a showdown in 1771 between MPs and the 'strangers' determined to report what their elected representatives said and did. The man who provoked it was John Wilkes, a radical MP who championed the right of voters, rather than the House of Commons, to choose who represented them in Parliament. Wilkes was also a trouble-making journalist whose scandal-raking publication *North Briton* was loathed in the Commons. In its first edition Wilkes made a bold declaration: 'The liberty of the press is the birthright of a Briton, and is justly esteemed the firmest bulwark of this country.' Warming to a theme that would scarcely endear him to the political elite, he added that press freedom was 'the terror of all bad ministers; their dark and dangerous designs, or their weakness, inability and duplicity [which] have thus been detected and shewn to the public'. Not surprisingly, in the course of his career Wilkes was repeatedly expelled from Parliament, not to mention outlawed, arrested and shot in a duel after criticizing the King. His supporters defiantly elected him an alderman of London. He later became a sheriff and finally lord mayor.

The catalyst for Wilkes' battle for press freedom was not the uncovering of a great scandal. It was, instead, a report that made a pompous MP feel rather foolish. Colonel George Onslow, despite being rather fond of his own jokes, failed to see the funny side when his oratory was described by Walpole as 'burlesque . . . laughed at for absurdity as frequently as for humour'. The colonel was not amused, either, to be referred to by one reporter as 'little cocking George', an allusion to his enjoyment of cockfighting. He demanded that the printers of this sedition be summoned to the Commons and punished for 'misrepresenting the speeches and reflecting on several members of the House', complaining to his fellow MPs, with no apparent sense of irony: 'Sometimes I am held up as a villain; sometimes I am held up as an idiot; and sometimes as both.'[6]

Onslow was warned – as so many MPs have been over the years – that pursuing his tormentor might prove counterproductive. One MP cautioned the Commons: 'By agreeing to this motion you will only make papers sell better. They will be read with avidity, and believed with credulity.' The colonel – like so many MPs – ignored the warning. The Commons ordered the arrest of the printers of the 'little cocking George' jibe. Wilkes seized the opportunity to stand up to the Commons in defence of the printers and the freedom of the press.

Using his powers as a sheriff, Wilkes arrested the printers before the Commons authorities could get to them, and promptly released them, declaring them innocent on all charges. When MPs responded by sending a messenger to re-arrest the printers, Wilkes and two fellow magistrates had him arrested. The Commons was not going to tolerate this rebellious challenge. It summoned the magistrates, put them on trial and had them sent to the Tower.

An angry mob gathered to protest outside the Commons. They stopped every carriage going in. MPs who backed the ban on the press were manhandled. Even the prime minister, now a hapless fellow called Lord North who'd given his support to 'little cocking George', was pulled from his carriage, which was then demolished. North fled in tears, having suffered the indignity of being hit by a constable's baton in the mêlée and having his hat torn to pieces. He abandoned attempts to enforce the ban on reporting the Commons but did not formally revoke it. For years to come reporters were able to carry out their jobs, but not as a right, and only under parliamentary sufferance.

Several publishers began to try their hand at circulating reports of parliamentary debates. Among them was the *Parliamentary Register* (1775–1813) – an early forerunner of

Hansard, which today offers a comprehensive account of every speech delivered in both Houses.

As for Wilkes, he'd demonstrated that trouble-making journalists can go on to be very effective trouble-making politicians. He built an alternative power base when elected lord mayor of London in 1774. An inspiration, perhaps, for Boris Johnson.

While the principle that debates could be reported without fear of arrest had been established, there were still no arrangements to allow reporters to actually do their jobs. Three years after Wilkes won his battle and Lord North lost his hat at least seven London newspapers regularly sent journalists to cover parliamentary debates. They formed the first-ever press corps – a group of reporters regularly covering the same beat. The most distinguished correspondent of them all was a man known as William 'Memory' Woodfall, who was famous, as his nickname indicates, for being able to remember long chunks of debates. This trick was made necessary by a rule that forbade him and his colleagues from writing down anything they heard until after they had left the public gallery.

Woodfall was rather more honest about the accuracy of his reports than some of his successors. He once warned his readers: 'The public are requested to read the above not as an exact account of the debate on the subject but as a mere skeleton of the arguments used on this occasion'[7] – small print which I am tempted to add to some of my own reports.

As if having to mentally store debates for later re-gurgitation wasn't difficult enough, 'Memory' Woodfall and his colleagues often had trouble remaining in the gallery to hear them in the first place. Any MP crying out 'I spy strangers' could have it cleared instantly without the need for a vote, and the serjeant-at-arms was permitted to take into custody 'any stranger or strangers that he shall see'. This power was used frequently to save the blushes of our old friend Lord North, who was facing another rather more serious defeat: he was losing America to those fighting for her independence. North's supporters were keen to prevent 'strangers' from hearing ministers' reports of the humiliating military defeats being suffered thousands of miles away.

Incidentally, the power to 'spy strangers' still exists. I recall it being used in a stunt by Lib Dem MPs to protest against Tony Blair's government driving through legislation to which they objected. That day in December 2001, the last words audible on the TV pictures coming from the Commons were 'What are we going to do now?' as the Lib Dems realized they'd just voted to switch off the cameras and to eject all those who could report on the reasons for their protest.

By the dawn of the nineteenth century reporters faced a new problem: rather than being thrown out of the Commons while military defeats were being debated, they sometimes never made it into the gallery at all. On 23 May 1803, William Pitt the Younger, the former prime minister who would take office again the following year, led a two-day debate on the latest developments in the long-running war with Napoleon. An invasion by France looked possible, and reporters queued up for the gallery as if for a New Year sale, from 8.30 in the morning until the doors opened just before 3.30 in the afternoon. Still none of them managed to get inside. Pitt, who needed the public to read his wartime rhetoric, was not best pleased.

The Times explained to its readers that the gallery had been filled with the 'friends of members or persons smuggled into the gallery through the body of the House', and that, on the occasions its men did gain access to the Commons, they were 'in constant danger of having a leg or an arm broken'. The *Morning Chronicle* declared:

> It would be much better if the House would forbid the publishing of debates altogether than to render it impossible to report them as they might be. How is it to be expected that persons obliged to struggle in a crowd the whole day should be able to go through the fatigue of writing the debate?[8]

I doubt the Speaker of the Commons cared much about the fatigue of reporters but he did respond to Pitt's frustration. Although in the wake of the French Revolution Pitt had reintroduced widespread censorship and repression, in leading the wars against France, and especially in raising the funds for it, public support was vital to him. Speaker Abbott now ordered the serjeant-at-arms to make special arrangements to ensure that never again would the words spoken in such an important debate fail to reach the public. 'Newswriters' were given seats in the back row of the public gallery. Later they would be given their own press gallery.

One young journalist who benefited from the new arrangement was Charles Dickens – another writer whose career in fiction began in the Commons. Dickens secured a job as a gallery reporter with the *Mirror of Parliament*, which his uncle edited. While the *Mirror of Parliament* (1828–43) was admirably thorough for its time, its publisher, J. H. Barrow, was, perhaps unwisely, in the habit of checking speeches with the MPs who had delivered them, thus giving them the opportunity to remove anything they afterwards regretted having said.

What Dickens thought about his time listening to and reporting on politicians' speeches is made absolutely plain in *David Copperfield*, probably the most autobiographical of his novels, when Copperfield, the narrator, describes his life as a parliamentary reporter: 'Night after night, I record predictions that never come to pass, professions that are never fulfilled, explanations that are only meant to mystify . . . I am sufficiently behind the scenes to know the worth of political life. I am quite an Infidel about it and shall never be converted.'

Dickens bemoaned not only what he was obliged to listen to but also the working conditions in Parliament. He had 'worn my knees by writing on them' in the Commons, which provided no desks; in the Lords, which didn't even provide seats, he complained, 'I have worn my feet by standing in the preposterous pen . . . huddled together like so many sheep.' Like Samuel Johnson before him, he soon concluded that there were better ways to earn a living.

After the House of Commons was almost totally destroyed by fire in 1834 the architect Charles Barry was appointed to build the magnificent new building admired today by locals and tourists alike. His design included a dedicated press gallery.* Thanks to him, I can now sit perched high above the Speaker's chair with a clear view of the green benches of the Commons below. Ever since the press gallery was created, MPs have craned their necks to look up and see who is there, paying attention to and ready, perhaps, to report their words. They have tried to catch the eye of a friendly reporter or, these days, even to send a discreet text message.

---

* Today's press gallery is a replica, as Barry's original was destroyed in the Blitz. However, it was rebuilt to the same design.

Sitting through a debate is quite unlike reading one, or even following it on the radio or TV. Like fans at a football game, we reporters get a much richer experience than those watching at home. The noise can seem overwhelming to those not used to it. The microphones suspended above the heads of MPs are controlled to pick up the voice of whoever is speaking and therefore only a fraction of the ambient noise of the Commons is broadcast. Experienced ministers and their shadows train themselves not to shout above the din, thus making themselves look reasonable in contrast to their unruly opponents. Inexperienced new arrivals on the front bench – including a number of the Lib Dem members who joined the government in 2010 – switch between shouting at the opposite benches and turning to speak to their own supporters, with the result that they are off microphone and can't be heard at all.

To hear the member who is on his or her feet, other MPs often find it necessary to lean back so that their ears are closer to the loudspeakers built into the back of those famous green benches. A newcomer to the press gallery might assume an MP is asleep when in fact he has leaned back and closed his eyes to listen to an argument being made. To some, the racket of the Commons is the sound of a play-ground full of overgrown schoolboys. To me its roar is always revealing. Sometimes it speaks of genuine passion, whether support or fury; at others it is clearly synthetic and orchestrated; occasionally it just represents the boredom of men and women forced to sit through hours of predictable party point-scoring. Distinguishing one from the other is part of the good parliamentary reporter's trade.

It is not just the sound of a debate that is different in the gallery. Sitting high above the Speaker's chair, you can see the whole chamber, just as in a football stadium you can see the whole pitch. Watching those who are not speaking can be as interesting as watching those who are. I look to see which minister nods in instinctive agreement and which is struggling not to betray disagreement. I observe who speaks to whom, and who can't bring themselves to chat to their neighbour. I study backbenchers to see if they have faith in their leader or are wearing the pained expression of those expecting defeat.

Politics, it should always be remembered, is a team sport. Power is given not to individuals but to the red team or the blue – and now, once again, to the yellow team, too. The morale of those teams matters, because the players who do not have the salary or the prestige or the perks of ministerial office must, nevertheless, vote for the team for it to stay in office. They will only do so if they feel good about how it is doing. I made a documentary some years ago on William Hague's troubled time as leader of the Conservative party. I wanted to know how he had survived without being removed by his MPs in the face of Tony Blair's total political dominance. Winston Churchill's grandson Nicholas Soames told me how, week after week, Hague would come to Question Time and 'make a monkey of the prime minister', reassuring Tory MPs that their leader was more than up to the job. He then added wryly that often, only hours later, everything 'would go tits up again'.

Dickens may have concluded that parliamentary reporting was a mug's game but to others the creation of a parliamentary press gallery was a significant milestone for democracy – a concept that was beginning to take root in nineteenth-century

Britain, albeit slowly. In the view of Thomas Macaulay, the great English historian,

> the gallery in which the reporters sit has become a fourth estate of the realm. The publication of the debates, a practice which seemed to the most liberal statesman of the old school full of danger to the great safeguards of public liberty, is now regarded by many persons as a safeguard, tantamount, and more than tantamount, to all the rest together.

It was the Tory Edmund Burke who is thought to have first portrayed the press as a 'fourth estate'. Thomas Carlyle developed the theme: 'There were Three Estates in Parliament; but, in the Reporters' Gallery yonder, there sat a Fourth Estate more important far than they all.'

It was a description, and a complaint, that would be used again and again over the years: the idea that the press mattered more than MPs, peers and bishops who, as the Commons, Lords Temporal and Lords Spiritual, comprise the other three estates in Parliament. However, this was less a victory for journalists than a recognition by politicians in an era of political reform that they had an interest in allowing a wider public to read an accurate report of what they said in the Commons.

By 1829, Hansard had come into being. The radical publisher William Cobbett had been bringing out his *Parliamentary Debates*, printed by Thomas Curson Hansard, since 1802. When Cobbett got into business difficulties, he sold the publication to Hansard, who began to see off the competitors. Since neither Cobbett nor Hansard ever actually sent a reporter to Parliament, relying instead on the accounts of a range of newspapers, the accuracy of the early editions is not entirely to be trusted. However, as Hansard established itself as the leading account of parliamentary debates, the House would eventually decide, in 1889 – perhaps on the basis that if you can't beat them, join them – to subsidize it, ensuring the availability of a permanent, practically verbatim record of front-bench speeches. In 1909, Parliament would take over Hansard altogether, producing two separate volumes, one for each House.

Meanwhile, in 1832, Earl Grey – better known these days for his scented blend of tea than for being prime minister – finally convinced the Commons that the way MPs were elected should smell a little better, too. Grey's Great Reform Act abolished the 'rotten boroughs' which had allowed just 154 individuals to elect 307 members of Parliament – among them the Alexander brothers, who bought the abandoned town of Old Sarum in Wiltshire for £40,000 and installed themselves as its two MPs. Before the Act, the emerging industrial cities of Manchester and Sheffield had no direct representation at all.

The number of people with the vote increased by 40 per cent, though that included none of the working classes, few of the poorer middle classes and, of course, no women (leading many to conclude that the Act wasn't that Great, or even that much of a Reform). However, with an electorate now standing at over 600,000, and with modern parties start-ing to form, politicians needed the press to reach the voters that other methods could no longer reach.

You may be tempted to visualize this as a golden age in relations between the media and politics, in which reporters accurately relayed to the public what was said by their elected representatives, politicians focused purely on substance and not on image and voters pondered on weighty matters of state over a pint at the Dog and Duck. If so, think again.

Successful politicians in the Victorian era knew they had to woo the public – or at least a section of it – and that meant learning how to manipulate the press. Consider the man who became known as the 'people's darling' in the 1850s and 1860s: the triple election-winner Lord Palmerston. He is usually remembered these days as the foreign secretary who invented gunboat diplomacy, but in the context of the relationship between government and media, he should perhaps be acknowledged as the pioneer of political image-making.

A serious, hardworking old man – he was seventy years of age when he became prime minister for the first time – Palmerston did not want the press to focus on his worthy parliamentary speeches about Britain's foreign entanglements. Instead, he gave them what they wanted: a national character who would bring a smile to their readers' faces. They depicted the PM as 'Lord Cupid', a man about town and great seducer of women. It was alleged, with more admiration than outrage, that he had even slipped uninvited into the bedchamber of one of the Queen's ladies-in-waiting at Windsor Castle.

Palmerston seduced the press with the same enthusiasm as the opposite sex. He invited those who'd once been seen as grubby hacks to grand parties thrown by his wife, where they were made to feel part of the social circle of the ruling class. The prime minister took them to one side to show them drafts of speeches he proposed to make and sought their advice on how to rewrite them to make them more interesting. Few voters knew that if Palmerston was a partygoer, he was also a workaholic who could be found at his desk from seven one morning until one o'clock the next, often standing up to stop himself falling asleep.[9] Few ever read that age was taking its toll on the prime minister. This infuriated his opponent, the Conservative Benjamin Disraeli, who was no mean image-shaper himself. Dizzy complained:

> Tho' he is really an imposter, utterly exhausted, and at the best only ginger beer and not champagne . . . with false teeth, which would fall out of his mouth when speaking, if he did not hesitate and halt so in his talk – he is a name which the country resolves to associate with energy, wisdom, and eloquence.

Palmerston's image-making was so successful that when he died the rumour circulated that the old boy's ticker had packed up mid-flagrante with a maid spreadeagled across his billiard table. The truth, rather more boringly, was that he'd been in bed studying the detailed provisions of a foreign treaty.

There was, sadly, never an age of innocence that predated the corrupting influences of spin, sleaze and speculation. But before the invention of radio and television, one more breed of reporter was to become a part of the relationship between politicians and the media: the type of reporter who recorded what he heard inside the Commons but outside the gallery. In other words, the gossip, the intrigue and the rumours.

In the early 1870s, Speaker John Evelyn Denison complained that 'members could not get to the Vote Office or to the refreshment room or to and from the House without being pressed upon and thronged not only by constituents but by members of deputations and other strangers to their excessive inconvenience'. In order to prevent members of the public from wandering into the Members' Lobby, the anteroom just outside the Commons chamber, only those 'strangers' registered on a list kept by the serjeant-at-arms would in future be allowed access to it. Crucially, this list included at least one representative of each newspaper. Its existence spawned this new form of reporting: lobby journalism.

The occupants of the parliamentary press gallery, by now rather grand and self-important, looked down their noses at what they regarded as the journalistic lowlife who reported from 'the lobby'. Gallery reporters were parliamentary spectators and stenographers. They watched and listened to MPs, noting down and summarizing what they heard. They didn't need ever to meet, let alone talk to, the people they were writing about. Members of 'the lobby' changed all that. They hung around outside the Commons chamber, waiting to catch the eye of an MP and have a discreet word with him. They didn't merely record what had been said in debates, they revealed what MPs and ministers were thinking of saying and doing in the future. They took readers into the most powerful club in the land and relayed what had been, until then, heard only by MPs.

From its earliest days 'the lobby' began to operate in precisely the way the Commons had for so long: as a secretive organization with its own bizarre rules. One of the first lobby correspondents, Spencer Leigh Hughes, who went on to become an MP, described it as 'a select club' which insisted on forms of address and jargon 'that would be regarded as excessively official'[10] even between members of the government.

The lobby elected its own officers and controlled the issuing of passes. Journalists were not to approach MPs directly. Like children, they could be seen, but not heard, unless invited to speak. Anything they were told in the lobby was only to be reported on 'lobby terms' – in other words, it was unattributable. Quotes could be used, but not the names of those who'd provided them.

The lobby traded on – and abused – their claim to exclusive access to men of power. Their privileged position was reinforced by a terrorist attack in January 1885, when an Irish bomb plot produced almost simultaneous explosions in the Commons chamber, Westminster Hall and the Tower of London. This convinced the authorities to further limit those allowed anywhere near MPs, to the delight of the lobby correspondents, whose access remained assured and was now even more valuable. The *Standard* pompously declared: 'None will be more pleased than those who have real work to do in the lobby to find it closed in future against the soi-disant leaders of opinion, the miscellaneous button holers and propagandist idlers who haunt the House on important occasions and pester Members with their trivialities.'[11]

That same year, after Gladstone stepped down as prime minister, *The Times* introduced a new heading for reports on what it called the 'political situation'. The Grand Old Man quickly discovered what the 'real work' of lobby journalism often entailed. One day he had to ask a lobby man sitting on the stairs to make way for him. The hack had been pondering what he could write about that day. Now he had his answer. His report began: 'Meeting Mr Gladstone in the lobby this evening I had an interesting conversation with him . . .' In truth the two had barely exchanged a word and the 'conversation' consisted of a list of points he'd lifted from recent speeches by Gladstone. Like most reports politicians complain about, this one was based on several grains of truth but it was nevertheless a confection. Furthermore it was, of course, a breach of lobby rules.

No wonder gallery reporters dismissed their colleagues'

work as 'fiction, supposition and exaggeration', sentiments widely shared by politicians ever since. In the years leading up to the creation of the lobby they had plenty of real drama to recount, thanks to the acerbic clashes between Gladstone and his great rival Disraeli. What a joy it must have been for them to quote Dizzy as saying that Gladstone possessed 'not one single redeeming defect' or to relay his method of assessing the scale of a political cock-up: 'If Gladstone fell into the Thames, that would be a misfortune, and if anybody pulled him out that, I suppose, would be a calamity.'

My favourite Disraeli quotation comes from the moment he was ticked off by the Speaker for using unparliamentary language and asked to withdraw his claim that half the Cabinet were asses. Dizzy replied: 'Mr Speaker, I withdraw. Half the Cabinet are *not* asses.'

However, in the ruthlessly competitive world of news, it was the lobby reporters who saw off those whose job was merely to record the public utterances of MPs – however interesting. It was the lobby's stories that filled and sold newspapers and got people talking. They still do.

My House of Commons security pass bears a large 'L' to signify that I am a member of the lobby. It entitles me to go to twice-daily briefings, although I rarely do: the downside of openness is that it promotes caution, with the result that you rarely learn a great deal from these briefings. My camera may only be allowed behind a designated line in Parliament's public meeting place, the Central Lobby, but when I am not broadcasting I am permitted to pass down the short corridor off it to the place where MPs come to pick up messages left for them in their pigeonholes, to collect the Order Paper setting out that day's business and to see the whips – Parliament's prefects – who tell backbenchers what they should and should not be doing if they want to keep in with their leader. Inside the Members' Lobby stand imposing statues of Margaret Thatcher and Clement Attlee, considered the greatest postwar leaders of their respective parties; guarding the doors of the Commons chamber are Britain's two great war leaders, Lloyd George and Winston Churchill. Their shoes have been rubbed shiny by MPs who think touching them will bring them good luck. The walls are lined with the busts of lesser prime ministers.

Even now that the advent of texting and hand-held computers has made it easy to contact ministers directly, without the risk of their officials knowing, the lobby remains the quickest and most efficient way to test parliamentary mood. On the night of a big vote it's possible to talk to dozens of MPs very quickly. When I was first given a lobby pass I felt like a shy, spotty teenager waiting hopefully on the edge of a dance floor, praying that someone would want to talk to me. These days MPs I know well will stop for a chat and those who know me only from the television screen might stop to complain about the way they or their party are being reported.

There is a small corridor in the Commons press gallery, just below Big Ben, known affectionately as the Burma Road. This is where the Westminster offices of the big newspapers are to be found. In the hours before the newspaper deadlines, spin-doctors and senior politicians can be seen wandering up and down it, touring the offices to inquire about the angles being pursued and adding their own spin to events. Smaller outfits share facilities. When I was political editor of ITV News, my office housed not only my colleagues on *Channel 4 News* but also the London *Evening Standard*, the *Sun*, the Scottish *Daily Record* and the *Eastern Daily Press*, among others. We boasted that there was virtually no story someone in that office didn't know or couldn't find out in minutes. One of the things I missed most about ITV on returning to the BBC was our Westminster office. The BBC has its own, away from the Burma Road and the best lobby gossip.

Today's politicians often condemn the 'tittle-tattle' or 'speculation' which result from reporting on 'lobby terms'. They would no doubt agree with one radical MP of the 1880s, Henry Labouchère, who railed against the 'inventive trash' used by journalists deploying phrases like 'I am enabled on undoubted authority to state', 'I am in a position to inform' and 'the government thinks'. This was, he said, 'disgusting to people of good taste [but] has its effects on millions'.[12] However, many MPs soon came to see the value of using the lobby to give anonymous and deniable briefings.

I cringe slightly if I find myself uttering the phrase 'Downing Street says'. After all, how can a street say anything? Surely only people say things? What's more, when they do, we normally know who it is who is doing the talking. Yet those three words do have meaning, to anyone who regularly follows the news, as a shorthand for the views of the prime minister's official spokesman or woman.

The need for such a person first became clear during the general strike of 1926. It was ministers, not journalists, who wanted someone to speak on the government's behalf. On emerging from Number 10, Cabinet members found themselves harried not only by angry strikers but by lobby correspondents wanting a story. As well, no doubt, as finding it tiresome, these ministers feared that their off-the-cuff comments might prove contradictory. Thus it was decided that the Cabinet secretary should give the lobby what was then called 'guidance' and would now be called 'the line to take'.[13] In return for the privilege of being permitted to wait for their briefing inside Downing Street, the lobby assured ministers that they would treat the briefings confidentially – provided, of course, that they and they alone, and no other journalists, were allowed to attend.[14]

It was another crisis that led to the appointment of the first man to carry out daily briefings on behalf of the prime minister. When Ramsay MacDonald's Labour government collapsed in 1931 journalists were involved in what was described as a 'mass bombardment of the door of Number 10 Downing Street', with 'lobby journalists compelled to take part in much undesirable questioning of Cabinet ministers'. This was the verdict of the lobby's own committee,[15] which pressed successfully for daily, collective, unattributable briefings. A man called George Steward was appointed chief of press and carried out the first of the briefings that Bernard Ingham and Alastair Campbell would go on to make so controversial. Neville Chamberlain, who on becoming prime minister in 1937 was short of friends in Parliament, shored up his position through his press management system. Via his aides, he courted the lobby, flattering them by treating them as insiders.

The chief of press soon became the official, and usually secret, channel of communication between the government and the newspapers. This secrecy enabled journalists to look well informed while ministers put out – all too often unchallenged – their chosen line. The system also allowed a prime minister and his aides to brief the media collectively without the knowledge of the Cabinet. Chamberlain took full advantage of this. Having already seen off one foreign secretary – Anthony Eden resigned as a result of what he viewed as Chamberlain's constant interference in foreign affairs – he continued to bypass Eden's successor, Lord Halifax, who profoundly disagreed with the government line issued to the lobby, of which he knew nothing until he read it in the newspapers.

One veteran lobby correspondent, James Margach of the *Sunday Times*, confessed that he and his colleagues had been 'caught napping' in the run-up to the Second World War. Six days before the Nazis invaded Czechoslovakia in March 1939 no lesser organ than *The Times* reported that 'the international situation seems now to give less anxiety than for some time past'.[16]

It was Lloyd George, a prime minister who had managed the press during the second half of the First World War without the benefit of a full-time spokesman, who provided what is probably the best summary of Downing Street's attitude to the media: 'What you can't square, you squash. What you can't squash, you square.'

For many decades, the lobby operated more like a masonic sect than a body of journalists. New members were handed a maroon-covered set of rules marked 'private and confidential' which included instructions such as: 'Don't talk about lobby meetings before or after they are held, especially in the presence of those not entitled to attend them', and 'Do not "see" anything in the Members' Lobby or any of the private rooms or corridors'. If a lobby correspondent saw an MP who was drunk, say, or fighting with one his colleagues, that information stayed secret. It was the equivalent of the agreement made on many a football or rugby tour that 'what happens on tour stays on tour'.

More seriously, lobby journalists attended government briefings whose very existence used to be officially denied. They were invited to these meetings by means of cryptic notices pinned up on a cupboard in the Commons press gallery. In the 1980s, 'Blue Mantle at 4' indicated that Margaret Thatcher's press Rottweiler – her spokesman, Bernard Ingham – would be briefing at four o'clock. One Cabinet minister's credibility was permanently damaged when Ingham described him at one of these briefings as 'semi-detached'. The story, when it appeared, quoted 'Whitehall sources' or 'sources close to the prime minister' – exactly the sort of code that had so infuriated Henry Labouchère back in the 1880s. Ingham's target, John Biffen, was even ruder about the lobby than Labouchère had been, denouncing it as 'a channel for the transmission of sewage'.

Lobby journalists defended their closed shop, maintaining that the secrecy of the system encouraged more candour and a frank exchange of views, as well as ensuring that every member of the lobby, whether from a local paper, *The Times* or the BBC, was given equal access to government inform-ation. Any other system, they claimed, would lead to exclusive briefings for a select few. Its critics argued that it was a conspiracy against the citizen. It guaranteed the reporter a story no one could check for accuracy and the politician a point of view he or she could overstate with-out the possibility of comeback. The late, great political journalist Anthony Howard compared lobby reporters with prostitutes. 'The fact has to be faced,' he said 'that lobby correspondents do become instruments for politicians' gratification.' In the mid-1980s first the *Independent* and then the *Guardian* announced that they would boycott the lobby in an effort to break the system. They failed.

Alastair Campbell well understood the power of the lobby when he became Tony Blair's press secretary in 1997. As a reporter for the *Mirror* he'd delighted in tormenting John

Major's floundering government, taking particular pride in his observation that the prime minister tucked his shirt into his underpants. Without him Major would have escaped being presented as what the *Guardian* cartoonist Steve Bell called 'a crap Superman' who wore his underpants over his trousers.

Campbell decided to try to break the lobby by opening it up. Briefings by the prime minister's official spokesman were placed on the record so that they could be quoted in full. He invited foreign journalists to attend in the hope of dispersing the journalistic pack and used serious questions about global events to attempt to sweep out what he regarded as the froth, tittle-tattle and trivia of the lobby. He initiated regular prime ministerial news conferences and persuaded Blair to appear for cross-questioning by the chairmen of select committees twice a year. He and Blair concluded that it changed precious little. The culture of lobby journalism continued to rely, in large part, on anonymous sources and on a surprising degree of collaboration between members of the media pack.

Lobby journalists see much more of each other than they do of their colleagues at the newspapers or broadcasters that employ them. They work the same beat, attend the same news conferences, travel on the same trips and they look after each other. A journalist from one paper will often team up with a friend from another to take a politician out to lunch. They do this not simply to make their invitation more appealing, or to spice up the conversation over the crème brûlée, but because it's much harder for a politician to deny a story that has been run by two papers rather than one. It is for the same reason that a correspondent with information of which he is not entirely confident will share it with a colleague on a rival publication. I occasionally hear people suggest a story must be true on the basis that it has appeared in two papers with different political prejudices. If only they knew.

At its worst the lobby has produced a flurry of unverifiable and worthless speculation. It hunts its prey with little mercy and even less sense of perspective. At its best, however, it can provide a vital public service in keeping the electorate informed of the policies, debates and disagreements that those in power would rather stayed secret. Besides, voters no longer have to rely, as they once did, on the reports of others allowed special access to the parliamentary club. Across the centuries, politicians have often regretted allowing journalists into the Commons, and broadcasters would face the same struggle as their press colleagues. Whatever the medium and whatever the era, what has remained constant is the tension between politicians and those who report on what they do.

Sir John Reith

New Statesman, 11 November 1933

2

A TITANIC OPPORTUNITY

It was the invention of radio, and its capacity to inform, educate and entertain the masses, that would trigger the next battle in the conflict.

Initially, however, Guglielmo Marconi, the creator of the 'wireless' and the granddaddy of broadcasting, had a much more modest ambition for his 'wireless telegraphy' machine: simply to make shipping safer by allowing communication from sea to shore. In 1895, frustrated that his invention was not getting the welcome it deserved in his native Italy, he headed to England in search of a better reception. A few years later, in 1912, he found it when the court of inquiry into the sinking of the *Titanic* heard that 'those who have been saved have been saved through one man, Mr Marconi . . . and his marvellous invention'.

Others saw the potential of Marconi's machine, and its ability to transmit signals without the need for wires, to broadcast not merely from ship to shore but to a mass audience. Ironically, given its hostility to the BBC in later years, it was the *Daily Mail* that dreamed up the broadcasting experiment that captured the public's imagination. On 15 June 1920 the paper arranged a special trial broadcast by 'the world's very best artist', Dame Nellie Melba, who travelled to Chelmsford in Essex to sing 'Hello to the World'. Her voice was heard in Newfoundland, recorded at the Eiffel Tower in Paris and listened to by newspaper reporters who wrote excitedly about the 'wizardry' of the wireless.

Not everyone was impressed. The Post Office, which was charged with licensing broadcasts, received complaints about the 'frivolous' use of a 'national service' and warnings that it would interfere with vital communications. But some early broadcasting pioneers could see their way to the future – a future that included news and live broadcasting of Parliament. In 1918 Arthur Burrows, who, four years later, would become the BBC's first director of programmes, wrote an article in the thrillingly entitled *Year Book of Wireless Telegraphy and Telephony*. He observed: 'There appears to be no serious reason why before we are many years older, politicians speaking, say, in Parliament should not be heard simultaneously by wireless in the reporting room of every newspaper office in the United Kingdom.' He was right: there was no serious reason.

In 1922, in the parliamentary debate that created the BBC, the minister responsible – F. G. Kellaway, the postmaster general – also foresaw that 'the possibilities of this service are almost unlimited'. He told the Commons: 'I can see a time when perhaps on this table a receiver will be properly concealed so as not to jar the aesthetic sense of members, and their eloquence will be transmitted to those of their constituents who are prepared to pay for the cost.'[1]

Most MPs laughed. The idea seemed absurd to them and many of their successors. It would, in fact, be another sixty years before MPs could be heard on the radio. Nevertheless, in the years that followed – the age of radio, which lasted until TV took off in the 1950s – the BBC would do much more than report on British public life. It would, in peacetime and in war, define the way the country saw itself.

The BBC was created not by a visionary but by six major manufacturers of radio receivers, including the one Marconi himself had invented, who wanted to sell more of their sets. The companies joined forces and set up the British Broadcasting Company to provide something for people to actually listen to on the receivers they wanted to sell. It aired its first broadcast on 18 October 1922.

The company, a private monopoly, needed Parliament's approval, since the new venture had to be licensed by the Post Office. It was funded by imposing a 10 shilling licence fee on anyone who owned a receiver, half of which went to the BBC. This would help pay for its staff – all four of them. Arthur Burrows was one. His boss, John Reith, was another.

Five years later, Reith, the managing director, would go on to become the first director general of the British Broadcasting Corporation – the public monopoly which replaced the original company. While America's broadcasting revolution was characterized by competition and commercialism, Britain's was marked by the belief, forged in the First World War, that businessmen and government could and should combine in the interests of administrative efficiency. Thus the BBC's first boss was a high-minded Scottish engineer described by the eminent historian A. J. P. Taylor as 'Calvinist by upbringing, harsh and ruthless in character'. His not always benevolent paternalism, and what Reith himself called 'the brute force of monopoly', did a huge amount to shape the broadcasting culture that still exists in Britain today.

Reith, never a modest man, compared himself to William Caxton, the inventor of the printing press in the fifteenth century. In his autobiography *Into the Wind*, he describes how he was given a free hand by the man interviewing him for the job of running the BBC, who told him: 'We're leaving it all to you. You'll be reporting at our monthly meetings and we'll see how you're getting on.'

The BBC's first director general defined its role as 'to bring the best of everything to the greatest number of homes'. From the outset that included politics and news – of a sort. On 15 November 1922 the BBC broadcast the results of a general election. With no more than 30,000 wireless sets in the country, people congregated in the homes of those lucky and wealthy enough to own one to hear the news that Andrew Bonar Law's Conservatives had won, while Labour had made its political breakthrough, outperforming the Liberals for the first time. *The Times* reported that 'listening-in parties were perhaps the most interesting feature of election night'. They might have been interesting, but they came to an abrupt halt at 1am so that the BBC would not rob the morning papers of their headlines.

The day before, Arthur Burrows had read the first-ever radio news bulletin from Marconi House in the Strand. It included details of a speech by Bonar Law and the aftermath of a 'rowdy meeting' involving Winston Churchill, a train robbery, fog in London and 'the latest billiards scores'. Burrows read each bulletin twice, once quickly and once slowly, and sought listeners' opinions on which they preferred. He found it a taxing experience. A couple of years later he wrote: 'I am prepared to assert that there is no more exacting test of physical fitness and nervous condition than the reading of a news bulletin night after night to the

British Isles.' He invited people to imagine having to read a news item about a political crisis in Czechoslovakia littered with 'place names strange to the eye, and looking as though they had fallen accidentally from a child's alphabet box'.

In those early days, the news was preceded by the intonation: 'Copyright of Reuters, the Press Association, Exchange Telegraph and Central News.' When the BBC was created it had been agreed that Burrows and his colleagues would not be permitted to gather their own news, for fear that this would give them an unfair advantage over the news agencies and the newspapers they supplied.

Agencies that collected, wrote and pooled news stories to feed newspapers and magazines – and now broadcasters, too – had been in operation around Europe and in the USA since the nineteenth century. The first, which was to become Agence France Press, was established in Paris in 1835. Ten years on, Associated Press was formed by five newspapers in New York to share the cost of funding dispatches from the Mexican–American War. Reuters followed in London in 1865. The Press Association was set up three years later by a consortium of newspaper proprietors as a co-operative to disseminate news to its members up and down Britain. By the 1920s, news was being gathered and circulated by agencies across the world.

Under the terms of the BBC's agreement, their news bulletins were provided and written by the four agencies they acknowledged and could not be aired before 7pm. The theory was that radio should only be allowed to fill the gap between the last edition of the evening papers and the first of the morning. Just how farcical these early restrictions were was demonstrated when BBC Radio broadcast live from the

Derby in 1926. It was able to capture the drama of thundering hooves and the excitement of the crowd, but that was it. There was no commentary, and anyone interested in knowing which horse had actually won had to wait for their evening paper or the seven o'clock news.

'Eyewitness descriptions' were limited, too, not only in number, but in the range of permitted subjects. BBC reporters did not cover what you and I might today call news. Early examples include accounts of a ride in the cab of an express train and mingling with the holiday crowds in Blackpool. Gripping stuff. 'Talks' were permitted that might touch on the news, but there was no comparison between these carefully scripted, discursive essays about the state of the world and the real thing. The absence of any proper reports meant that when no news came in from the agencies the BBC would, astonishingly, simply announce: 'There is no news tonight.' Unimaginable to those of us brought up on bulletins lasting half an hour whether there are dozens of significant developments in the world or none at all.

It was not just the deal with the news agencies and pressure from the newspapers that prescribed the BBC's very particular tone. It was the influence of John Reith. He decreed that Arthur Burrows and his fellow newsreaders were to remain anonymous – not for them the 'highly individualized announcing in the American style'. A BBC memo defined their job as building up in the public's mind 'a sense of the BBC's collective personality'[2] – in other words, they were to be the voice of the corporation, not 'stars'. So although their strong, warm, dispassionate voices were well known and well loved, the names of the earliest newsreaders were not. Reith recorded in his diaries: 'It is desirable they continue in obscurity . . . the desire for notoriety and recognition sterilizes the seeds from which greatness may spring.'[3] Naturally, however, the press soon worked out who they were and published their names. An announcer had only to cough on air to be inundated with gifts of everything from throat lozenges to woolly underwear.

If newsreaders were sent any attractive knitwear, they wouldn't have been able to sport it at work. These days, while suits and ties are *de rigueur* for their TV colleagues, radio announcers usually dress casually. In the 1920s, however, despite remaining unseen by their audience, they were instructed by Reith to don dinner suits in the evenings, in order to fit in with the other performers. One of them, Stuart Hibberd, explained: 'After all, announcing is a serious, if a new, profession and the wearing of evening dress is an act of courtesy to the artists, many of whom will be similarly dressed.'[4] Even the first outside broadcast engineer was told that he, too, must wear a dickie bow – and he had to pay for it from his own wages.[5]

Those anonymous men delivering the news invisibly in their dinner jackets lent authority to the BBC. It was precisely this anonymity that established the notion of the unvarnished truth, chiselled out, cleaned up and presented to you by people you could trust; people working for an institution committed to informing rather than influencing the public. As Geoffrey Cox, who once worked on those bulletins and later went over to the 'other side' – the newfangled Independent Television News – wrote in his memoirs:

> The technique conveyed a subtle sense that the bulletins were
> the works of high priests of a sacred order devoted to assess-
> ing, analysing and then finally determining The News which
> was then brought from the inner recesses of the temple to be

proclaimed in its purest form, unsullied on its way by contact with vulgar minds.[6]

By 1934, these priests would have their own temple: Broadcasting House, the BBC's first purpose-built head-quarters, often described as an art-deco ocean liner in Portland stone. As well as being architecturally spectacular, the new headquarters was at the cutting edge of technology, boasting twenty-two studios operated from a single control room running the length of the top floor.

When I first went to the radio newsroom at Broadcasting House I found remnants of the atmosphere Reith created. The dinner jackets had gone, of course, but it retained the quiet, contemplative ambience of a library rather than the frantic buzz I expected to find in a newsroom. Stories didn't seem to excite anyone half as much as grammatical inconsistencies did. I remember my irritation, as a young reporter, when the news editor ignored what I regarded as an exclusive to observe laconically: 'You appear to have referred to government in the singular, "the government *is*", in the first paragraph and yet in the plural, "the government *are*", later on.' I now see these men – and they were largely men – as the guardians of Reith's values.

To the delight of millions, BBC radio news still maintains a strong link with the style that secured the corporation's reputation all those years ago. Although Radio 4 addicts can now identify the rich, mellifluous tones of Peter Donaldson and relish the occasional illicit and infectious giggle from the normally serene Charlotte Green, they still have their news delivered by men and women who do not impose their personalities on it. It is all quite a contrast with television news. If radio struggles to compete with the drama and sense of event television can create, it regularly beats its brash cousin when it comes to insight, analysis and intimacy.

Reith wanted to secure for his BBC a place at the heart of the British establishment. He sought to persuade the appropriate authorities to let him broadcast a soundtrack of British public life, with mixed results. In 1923 – the BBC's first full year of broadcasting – radio offered its listeners the opera from Covent Garden, a performance of *Cinderella* and a debate on the proposition that communism would be a danger to the good of the people, as well as the sound of Big Ben's chimes ushering in the New Year, a firm fixture at midnight on 31 December ever since.

However, persuading those in charge to permit events to be broadcast was not always easy. When the BBC's men arrived with their microphones they were often regarded as eavesdroppers and treated with suspicion. Performers feared that the wireless would put them out of a job as no one would feel the need to go to the theatre or to a concert again, and some of the powers that be viewed broadcasting as somehow improper. Plans to air the wedding of the Duke of York, later George VI, were vetoed by the Chapter of Westminster Abbey. Yet the reigning monarch, George V, agreed that his own speech at the British Empire Exhibition at Wembley should be broadcast the following year. The speech was relayed on loudspeakers outside major department stores and the crowds were so large that they stopped the traffic. An estimated 10 million in total heard the King's words in 1924.

You might have thought politicians would see the potential of the wireless, already predicted by others, to broadcast their debates. Not a bit of it. The attitudes that had led to parliamentary reporting being first banned, then restricted and latterly merely tolerated were still deep-rooted. Radio journalists would have to go back to square one and fight the same battles their colleagues in print had won decades earlier.

Reith tried 'every conceivable source'[7] to get permission to broadcast the King's Speech at the State Opening of Parliament. His efforts to woo the royal household and the Cabinet came to naught. Neville Chamberlain – who, as postmaster general, had granted the first operating licence to the British Broadcasting Company – resisted. It would, he believed, set a precedent for broadcasting parliamentary debates 'the prospect of which makes one shudder'.[8] The director general's request for a Budget broadcast by the chancellor, with a reply by his shadow, was turned down flat. Reith was so infuriated by this that he scribbled on the correspondence: 'How absurd. What can we do by way of agitation?' His solution was to bombard ministers with letters. One stated grandly that 'the utility of broadcasting as a medium of enlightenment is prejudiced owing to the ban on such matters'. Indeed it was.

Outside Parliament politicians, in particular prime minister Stanley Baldwin, were less resolute. The BBC broadcast the speeches from the Lord Mayor's Banquet, including Baldwin's, in November 1923 and in the general election campaign the following year, Baldwin, his Labour opponent Ramsay MacDonald and the Liberal leader Herbert Asquith all accepted invitations to appeal to voters over the airwaves. The result was the first-ever election broadcasts.

Yet the three party leaders who agreed to those election transmissions remained insistent that airing their speeches in Parliament was unthinkable. The prime minister told the Commons in 1926 that there was 'a greatly preponderating body of opinion against broadcasting proceedings of the

House'. One MP thanked him 'on behalf of a long-suffering public'. The editor of *Popular Wireless* magazine joked that if parliamentary broadcasts were to take place, 'I presume we shall hear members commence their address to their House with "Mr Loud Speaker".'

Newspaper proprietors did not see the funny side. Having prevented the announcement of sports results and limited news bulletins to the evenings, they feared, unsurprisingly, that broadcasting the business of the Commons would be another blow to the viability of the press. One of them, Lord Riddell, accused the supporters of the idea of 'trying to take the bread out of our mouths'. What would MPs these days give, one wonders, for a battle over who should be allowed to report on their debates?

The shackles imposed on the BBC by Parliament extended beyond a refusal to air its debates. It was not until 1940 that the corporation was even permitted to send a reporter to sit in the Commons press gallery. In 1932, according to a note in the BBC's files, the Speaker, after extensive consultation with the prime minister and others, declared that 'it was decided unanimously that it was undesirable to have an account of the proceedings in the House broadcast daily by a BBC representative in the press gallery'.[9] It is just possible that the course of history might have been altered if people had been able to hear Parliament's powerful and divisive debates about the economic crisis of the early 1930s and appeasement in the face of the rise of fascism. But exile from Parliament was not enough to defuse the power of radio to shape the country's perceptions of its political leaders.

Stanley Baldwin was the first to appreciate that the 'box in the corner' gave him direct access to practically every voter in the country. Britain was gradually evolving into a mass democracy. At the start of the First World War, fewer than 8 million men had the vote. By the eve of the second, the electorate would quadruple. There would be 31 million potential voters – not only all men aged twenty-one or over but women, too.

The new age of radio reflected the spread of enfranchisement. In 1922, when Baldwin came to power and the BBC was created, only 22,000 radio licences were issued. By 1938, the year after he finally left office, there were 8.5 million, allowing 98 per cent of the country's population to tune into the BBC. People all over Britain were picking it up, to start with on primitive crystal receivers, often home-made, with the help of a 'cat's whisker' – a fine wire that was adjusted until it made a good contact with the crystal – and earphones, and later on more sophisticated sets sold in polished wood casings or state-of-the-art moulded Bakelite.

The election broadcasts of 1924 revealed Baldwin's grasp of how radio could enable him to reach mass audiences and, paradoxically, appear at the same time to be speaking personally to individual voters in their own front rooms. Whereas his opponents, MacDonald and Asquith, simply asked for a microphone to be brought to one of their regular election meetings, Baldwin took Reith's advice and made his broadcast from a studio. The results were telling. MacDonald strode about the stage, as he always did, which meant that his BBC audience heard only the occasional fragment of what he was saying, when he happened to stride close enough to the microphone. Asquith treated the mic as if it were just another member of the crowd packed into the hall, leaving listeners at home feeling harangued.[10] John Reith commented in his diaries: 'It was a mistake to append an invisible audience

98

of millions to a visible audience of two to three thousand.'[11]

The prime minister, meanwhile, addressed the electorate from his quiet studio using a specially written script. Just as he might have done if he'd been sitting with a single voter in his parlour, Baldwin paused mid-sentence to light his pipe. The press comment after the broadcasts focused on the sound of a match being struck and the sense it created of a man at ease with himself. To help him set the right tone, he had brought Mrs Baldwin along to the studio and placed her on a chair in front of him. According to one account,

> she sat there placidly knitting, with appraising ears open and alert while he talked to the microphone. He wanted to get the right atmosphere; he realized that most women . . . would probably be doing much the same sort of thing as his wife in the studio – knitting calmly.[12]

Baldwin had taken to heart the need to communicate with an audience not of millions or thousands but of one or two. He was the first prime minister to escape the confines of Downing Street, Parliament and the public meeting to speak to people one-to-one, using the airwaves to soothe them with his fireside chats. He had a lot of soothing to do: in his three terms in office in the 1920s and 1930s, in the wake of the horrors of the First World War, he faced an extraordinary series of crises, from a general strike, the Wall Street crash and the rise of fascism in Europe to the King's abdication.

The prime minister recognized that his political success depended on coming to understand this new medium. In an era light years away from the invention of focus groups, he was eager to inform himself about who listened to the wireless, how and when, to help him target his audience. In a letter to John Reith he wrote: 'I want to classify my potential listeners, e.g. what proportion may be working class? Does wireless go to the workman, or is the workman listener an exception, or would he be likely to listen at a club or a pub?'[13] Some years later he explained his broadcasting style to a friend.

> Workmen probably haven't had the advantages in education of some of our people . . . It is not only unfair but it is unmannerly to be sarcastic to them. Furthermore, I always try to speak slowly for the reason that people can't take it in when you speak quickly. When I broadcast I always go along at a crawling pace so that people can not only hear plainly but can take it in as I go along.[14]

As many political leaders would go on to discover, broadcasting could be a useful antidote to the antipathy of the press. Baldwin, the quiet, uncharismatic, accidental prime minister (he was first handed the premiership when Bonar Law was forced to resign through illness), was regarded as dull and spineless by the newspaper magnates of the day and hounded by Lords Rothermere and Beaverbrook, who almost succeeded in having him ousted as Tory party leader. Baldwin denounced them in terms which would still sting today: 'What the proprietorship of these papers is aiming at is power, and power without responsibility – the prerogative of the harlot through the ages.'[15]

His relationship with the 'box in the corner' was not confined to affairs of state. A BBC recording still exists of one of his radio talks, introduced by an announcer declaring portentously: 'It is our privilege to give you the opportunity to listen for twenty minutes to the Rt Hon. Stanley Baldwin MP.

Mr Baldwin, who is speaking from the Cabinet room at 10 Downing Street in London, will talk to you about the English character.' The word 'character' was pronounced 'carreecktar'.

There then follows a deep and resonant voice – the first belonging to a political leader to have become familiar to contemporary listeners – remarking that it is 'a good thing to take stock of our national characteristics'. Before turning his attention to the history of village communities, Baldwin shares the searing observation: 'No people grumble more than we do. I do myself, every day. But though I grumble, I do not worry and I keep cheerful, and the more difficult times are, the more cheerful we become.'

It all sounds banal and quaint to modern ears but this lengthy talk had a carefully calculated political purpose. At a time of huge upheaval, Baldwin wanted to create a reassuring portrait of national life that would help to stabilize the country and counter the rise of the Labour party, which had experienced its first-ever taste of government, albeit without a majority, immediately after Baldwin's inaugural term as prime minister. Baldwin's biographer, Philip Williamson, says that talking about the countryside was his way of evoking an arcadian stability and harmony to counter what was seen as the very urban nature of socialism.[16]

It is easy to picture Baldwin lighting his pipe and ruminating on England's bucolic charms from studio ED, his favourite, on the third floor of the new Broadcasting House. It had been designed to give the feel of a study or library, with bookshelves, a fireplace and a false window. His evident sense of comfort here, and the calm, cosy atmosphere, were in turn transmitted to an audience of voters increasingly fearful of the rapid and alarming changes taking place in the outside world.

The key to Baldwin's broadcasting success is that he never resented radio. Instead he embraced the possibilities it offered and harnessed its power. The same is true of every prime minister since who has been a skilled communicator. His principal opponent, Ramsay MacDonald, was a great supporter of the BBC and indeed of John Reith, but failed to engage with radio on a functional level, declaring that he was 'against all this booming' and preferred to be left alone.[17]

At a private dinner in March 1925 prime minister Baldwin and his friend John Reith sparred about which of them was the more powerful. Baldwin cited a recent occasion when, en route to an engagement, his car had been waved through and allowed to drive up the wrong side of Piccadilly to bypass the traffic. Reith was unimpressed. He boasted that he could pick up the telephone in his study, give two simple orders and his voice would be transmitted to the homes of several million people around the country. The PM was obliged to concede that he had been trumped.

On 30 April 1926 John Reith interrupted Jack Payne's late-night dance music programme with some important breaking news: a dispute in the mines had spread right across industry bringing the country grinding to a halt. Baldwin described the general strike, which would last nine long days, as 'a challenge to Parliament' and 'the road to anarchy and ruin'. The strike stopped the printing presses of most national newspapers and, for the first time, people were entirely dependent for information on BBC broadcasts.

While the general strike secured the BBC's national status, it also provoked the first of many divisive rows about the company's reporting of political events. Reith insisted that for the duration he allowed only 'authentic impartial news' to be broadcast. His claim was disputed on both sides.

Many assume that the BBC was instructed to be impartial when it was founded. In fact the word 'impartiality' did not feature on what was, in effect, its birth certificate – the Wireless Broadcasting Licence of 1923 – which simply demanded that it 'transmit efficiently' a daily programme 'of broadcast matter to the reasonable satisfaction of the Postmaster General'. Nor would the word appear in its first Royal Charter, granted in 1927.

The BBC *chose* to be impartial thanks, in part, to the high-minded aspiration of its founder and in part to his cold-headed calculation about how best to shield his monopolistic organization from political and commercial attack. From the very start John Reith saw the BBC as a means by which people could have 'all the facts . . . presented to them, in such a way that it is possible for them to make up their own minds'. He also knew that the future of his fledgling institution depended on the approval of politicians, who feared it could abuse its monopoly to broadcast propaganda, and was alert to the fact that the postmaster general had the power to revoke the licence at any time.

Reith saw impartiality as a remedy for the failures of a one-sided press. In 1924 he had written a book in which he set out his philosophy.

Suppose a speech of first-rate importance on some vital and highly controversial subject is delivered. It may be agreeable to the policy of half the newspapers of the nation and distasteful to the other half. To a large part of the country it may be represented as indicating a way of salvation; another large part may hardly have their attention drawn to it at all. Today, however, the whole country can hear it, and hear it direct from the lips of the exponent![18]

In law, the government could order the BBC to broadcast whatever it liked and, if necessary, take full control of it. Long before the strike, ministers had made preparations to use the BBC as 'an aid to the state'. A memo written in May 1923 stressed 'the unique facilities for the purposes of communication' now available 'during a state of emergency'. Henceforth it would be possible, according to the memo, for 'the highest authorities to speak over the broadcast and to use their influence to quell panic'.[19]

The news agencies removed their restrictions so that the BBC could write its own bulletins and broadcast five times a day, from 10am until 9.30pm. Those who didn't have a radio receiver travelled to places that did. The *Brighton Herald* reported large crowds in Gallier's electrical shop, there not for the bargains but to hear the broadcast news. In Brentford and Chiswick Town Hall six shorthand typists were employed to type out BBC bulletins, which were posted outside. London clubs bought wireless sets for the first time to keep their members informed. So, too, did the House of Lords, where copies of each BBC news bulletin were circulated not only among their lordships but to newspaper journalists in the press gallery.

The government was divided – as Reith discovered when he was summoned to see the prime minister at the beginning of the strike. Years afterwards he recalled Stanley Baldwin pacing up and down the Cabinet room, smoking a pipe as he made 'a passionate appeal that the government should leave the BBC alone and trust to me – I suppose that's what it came down to'. Baldwin told him there were 'grumbles that

Cabinet weren't happy about this . . . in particular Churchill didn't like it'. As a former journalist, Winston Churchill, chancellor of the exchequer at the time, had also been put in charge of government propaganda. He did more than merely grumble, arguing with a passion equal to Reith's that the BBC should be used to present the government's case, supplementing the *British Gazette*, a newspaper he edited and managed from 11 Downing Street. He declared that it was 'monstrous not to use such an instrument [radio] to the best possible advantage'.

Churchill, like so many of his successors, believed that the BBC should take the government's side when the nation's future was at stake. He told John Reith later that he had 'no right to be impartial between the fire and the fire brigade'. In years to come he would refer to the BBC as the 'enemy within'. The irony was that the BBC had indeed taken the government's side, while managing to maintain the impression of being impartial.

Reith saw no contradiction in upholding the journalistic objectivity of the BBC and helping his friend the prime minister. In the middle of the strike Baldwin broadcast to the nation from an armchair in Reith's own house. Some of the strongest words he used were, in fact, written and inserted by the man from the BBC, as Reith noted in his diary:

> [Baldwin] gave me his manuscript asking me what I thought of 'this tripe' and to make any comments. He said he thought of ending with something personal, and I said yes, something about trusting him. Then I said, 'What about this – I am a man of peace; I am longing and working and praying for peace; but I will not compromise the dignity of

the British constitution.' He said, 'Excellent; write it down if you have a legible hand.'

Baldwin changed just one word: 'compromise' became 'surrender'. Reith made another amendment even as the prime minister was speaking. He wasn't happy with the word 'dignity'. 'The PM had reached the second last page but I took the last from under his hand and wrote "safety and security". When he came to this, he paused but almost imperceptibly.'[20]

By contrast, when Ramsay MacDonald submitted a speech to Reith, the government refused to allow it to be broadcast. It would be a long time before the opposition's right to reply was established. The result, as so often in the future, was anger on both sides of the House. While Churchill was furious that the BBC would not be coerced into functioning as the mouthpiece of government, many on the left thought that was precisely what it had become. The *British Worker*, a trade-union newspaper, instructed its readers not to rely on the BBC. One Labour MP, Ellen Wilkinson, declared: 'The attitude of the BBC during the crisis caused pain and indignation to many subscribers.' Everywhere she went, she said, 'the complaints were bitter that a national service subscribed to by every class should be giving only one side during the dispute. Personally, I feel like asking the postmaster general for my licence fee back.'

The Labour leader and trade unionists were not the only ones denied a broadcasting platform. A peace appeal by the archbishop of Canterbury and other churchmen was delayed for five crucial days after the prime minister made it clear that he did not want it to be aired. Reith remembered drily that he found himself in 'a nice position . . . between Premier and Primate'. He chose to back the premier, telling the primate: 'We have maintained a certain degree of independence hitherto . . . it would therefore be inadvisable for us to do anything that was particularly embarrassing to the government, by reason of the fact that it might lead to the other decisions we're hoping to obviate.' In other words, he wanted to avoid the BBC being taken over by the government.

Reith's stance was not governed solely by his desire to preserve the BBC or his friendship with the prime minister. 'Assuming the BBC is for the people, and that the Government is for the people, it follows that the BBC must be for the Government in this crisis too,' he wrote. A BBC memo entitled 'Suggestions for the Policy of the Broadcasting Service during the Emergency' concluded: 'As the Government are sure that they are right both on the facts of the dispute and on the constitutional issues, any steps which we may take to communicate the truth dispassionately should be to the advantage of the Government.'[21]

On 12 May 1926 it was Reith who announced the end of the strikes. He was reading the news at one o'clock when a piece of paper was pushed in front of him telling him that the strike was over. 'Get this confirmed by 10 Downing St,' he scribbled on it. Ten minutes later, with that confirmation secured, he told the country that 'at a meeting with the prime minister at 10 Downing St, Mr Pugh announced on behalf of the General Council of the TUC that the general strike is terminating today'. In what might be regarded as just a little bit of editorializing, the BBC's boss then read out the words of the nation's favourite hymn, 'Jerusalem', to celebrate the end of the strike that had posed a threat to the tranquillity and stability of England's green and pleasant land.

The general strike had established radio as the country's

primary source of news – particularly during a national crisis. It had also demonstrated that at such times the BBC would face simultaneous accusations of failing to stand up for the national interest and kowtowing to the establishment. Some on the left dubbed it the 'British Falsehood Corporation'. Politicians on the right saw the value of what one of those who sat at Baldwin's Cabinet table and helped restrain Churchill called 'this semi-independent body'. Sir Samuel Hoare concluded: 'I think very wisely we decided to leave the BBC.' Speaking in a BBC radio documentary some years later, he explained: 'We knew the BBC would take into account what the government would say.' Reith was seeking to prove that he could exercise power with responsibility, in contrast to the press barons. The question of how the BBC should strike this balance would be asked again and again – during the Suez crisis, the Falklands War, coverage of the troubles in Northern Ireland and, of course, over Iraq.

A few months after the end of the general strike, John Reith was knighted and the British Broadcasting Company was converted into the British Broadcasting Corporation. The innovative idea of a public corporation was Reith's, born of his commitment to public-service broadcasting. The BBC as we know it today was created on 1 January 1927 by Royal Charter, which brought this unique organization into being by 'the exercise of our Royal Personage'. It was established this way to ensure that it was not 'a creature of Parliament and connected with political activity'.[22] Britain had turned its back on the commercial and competitive route being followed by the American media and the state control of much of what was broadcast in Europe. It had chosen, instead, a peculiar British compromise: it was a broadcaster licensed by government, funded by a compulsory tax but not run by politicians.

The corporation was initially told that in accordance with Clause 4 of its licence, it had to abstain from 'statements expressing the opinion of the Corporation on matters of public policy' and from 'speeches or lectures containing statements on political, religious or industrial controversy'.[23] The BBC even set up its own controversy committee to examine what did and did not fall under the ban.

The new BBC was, however, liberated from some of the limitations placed on the old one. It was, for example, given the freedom 'to collect news of and information relating to current events in any part of the world'. And in March 1928 the government agreed that, while the broadcaster still could not express an editorial opinion, it could now broadcast non-news programmes on matters of 'political, religious or industrial controversy'.

Sir John Reith was not a man to push this 'freedom' too far. In the debate about whether to turn the BBC into a public corporation he conveniently ignored the furore over the coverage of the general strike, reassuring politicians that his broadcasting company had 'never, I think, broadcast anything controversial . . . whether or not they are prevented from doing it, they obviously would not do it'.[24] It is hard now to imagine any broadcasting executive, let alone a news man, boasting that his organization had at all times avoided controversy. This, though, was the way Reith ensured the survival of his beloved BBC.

One example is instructive. The Labour party arranged a dinner to celebrate the seventieth birthday of George Bernard Shaw on 26 July 1926. The BBC was keen to broadcast the great man's speech but wanted an undertaking from

Shaw that he would avoid controversy, a request that was both naïve and futile. Shaw's response was to the point:

> Tell the B.B.C. and the 'authorities' what they know very well already: that my speech, like all my speeches, will consist from beginning to end of violently controversial arguments on questions of public policy, and that the only undertaking I will give is to use my own best judgment as to what I ought or ought not to say. If any authority pretends to be a better judge, the public will be glad to know his or her name.

This was not what Reith wanted to hear. He asked the postmaster general for his advice and was told to cancel the broadcast. Shaw had to make do with an audience of 120 dinner guests rather than a radio audience of millions.[25]

Reith's main way of steering clear of controversy was to aim for political balance. He did this by subcontracting the choice of political speakers heard on the BBC. The leadership of each party could choose who broadcast on its behalf and thus who should not be heard. It was an approach that guaranteed exposure for the opinions of ministers and their shadows, even when there was little disagreement between them, while dissident voices were silenced. Winston Churchill and David Lloyd George jointly complained that they were being prevented from broadcasting their views simply because they were not party loyalists.

Churchill was invited to speak, but rarely on the subjects he wanted to talk about. His frustration grew so great that in 1929 he offered the BBC £100 to allow him to make a single broadcast warning against dominion status for India. When his offer was rejected he complained that the corporation was 'debarring public men from access to a public who wish to hear'. In a Commons debate in February 1933 Churchill vented his frustration at the straitjacket that constricted the political debate on both the left and the right. 'These well-meaning gentlemen of the British Broadcasting Corporation have absolutely no qualifications and no claim to represent British public opinion . . . It would be far better to have sharply contrasted views in succession, in alternation, than to have this pontifical anonymous mugwumpery with which we have been dosed so long' – a delicious description of what the early BBC offered up to its listeners.

Radio was fast becoming as influential as the press and beginning to reach people no newspaper could reach. Between 1930 and 1939 the number of radio licences issued tripled from 3 million to almost 9 million. Yet in these years, when his voice could have made such an impression on the public consciousness, Churchill was heard only rarely on the BBC. He spoke on just ten occasions in ten years, and two of these were appeals for charitable causes. Bizarrely, the man who would go on to inspire a nation through radio was obliged to learn how to use it in another country, the United States. He made his first American broadcast on 8 May 1932. 'They tell me I may be speaking to 30 millions of Americans. I'm not at all alarmed. On the contrary I feel quite at home.'[26]

That July, on discovering that the BBC still would not allow him to speak to the people of his own country, he wrote an angry letter to the foreign secretary, Sir John Simon: 'Surely such a government containing so many statesmen, and supported by such overwhelming majorities, has no need to fear independent expressions of opinion upon the controversies of the day?'

On St George's Day 1933, three months after Hitler rose to power, the BBC did broadcast a speech by Churchill, given to the Royal Society of St George. It was, ostensibly at least, not about the Nazi threat. It began with a poke at his old adversary, the BBC's director general. 'We can picture Sir John Reith with the perspiration mantling on his lofty brow, with his hand on the control switch, wondering, as I utter every word, whether it will not be his duty to protect his innocent subscribers from some irreverent thing I may say about Mr Gandhi, or about the Bolsheviks, or even about St George and the Dragon. But let me reassure him. I have much more serious topics to discuss.' That sarcasm masked the fact that Churchill would go on to imagine how St George might have dealt with the threat posed by his mythical foe in the era of appeasement: 'He would propose a conference with the dragon – it would be a round table conference, no doubt. So much more convenient for the dragon's tail. He would make a trade agreement with the dragon. He would lend the dragon a lot of money . . . Finally, St George would be photographed with the dragon.'

Churchill was finally invited to address listeners directly by giving a talk as part of the BBC's *Causes of War* series in 1934. He used this opportunity to warn of the danger of wishing war away and ignoring German rearmament.

There is a nation which has abandoned all its liberties in order to augment its collective strength. There is a nation which, with all its strength and virtue, is in the grip of a group of ruthless men, preaching a gospel of intolerance and racial pride, unrestrained by law, by Parliament, or by public opinion . . . they are rearming with the utmost speed, and ready to their hands is the new lamentable weapon of the air, against which our navy is no defence, and before which women and children, the weak and frail, the pacifist and the

jingo, the warrior and the civilian, the front-line trenches and
the cottage home, all lie in equal and impartial peril.

That broadcast, which led to complaints of 'gratuitous
attacks' on Germany, demonstrated the impact Churchill
could have had in warning the country against appeasement.
It was not to be. This was his last radio appearance on the
subject before the outbreak of war.

The following year he finally got to broadcast on his other
great cause, India, but in the second half of the decade he was
more frequently heard on foreign stations than on the BBC,
speaking at least four times on American networks. Between
April 1937 and 1939 his views on what was happening in the
world were heard by American audiences but not at home.[27]

There is no written evidence that Churchill asked the BBC
for the opportunity to speak out against appeasement.
However, he did complain to a young BBC producer who
visited him at Chartwell, his country house, on the day after
Neville Chamberlain returned home from signing his agreement with Hitler in Munich and declared 'peace for our
time'. A memo records their meeting. They spent hours discussing the Nazi threat and 'Churchill complained that he
had been very badly treated in the matter of political broadcasts and that he was always muzzled by the BBC . . . He
went on to say that he would be even more muzzled in the
future, since the work of the BBC seemed to have passed
under the control of the Government.'[28]

The producer was called Guy Burgess. So it was that, on 1
October 1938, the man who would become his country's most
famous traitor tried to reassure the man who would become
its saviour that the BBC was not biased.

Two weeks later Churchill broadcast again to America at

the invitation of NBC. The force of his words is a reminder of what listeners to the BBC were denied.

> We must arm. Britain must arm. America must arm. If, through an earnest desire for peace, we have placed ourselves at a disadvantage, we must make up for it by redoubled exertions, and, if necessary, by fortitude in suffering . . . Is this a call to war? Does anyone pretend that preparation for resistance to aggression is unleashing war? I declare it to be the sole guarantee of peace.

There is, however, written evidence of Reith's willingness to help the government to appease Nazi Germany. In March 1938 the BBC was warned to do nothing to spoil a visit by the Nazi foreign minister, Herr von Ribbentrop. John Reith was summoned to see the foreign secretary, who asked him to drop a programme discussing German demands for a return of their lost colonies. Reith not only did as he was asked, he also chose not to reveal that he'd come under ministerial pressure. The sole explanation given for the cancellation of the programme was that the timing was 'inopportune'. On the night before it should have gone out, Reith attended a party at the German Embassy with Ribbentrop. He wrote in his diary: 'I made myself very agreeable to lots of people and quite enjoyed myself. I told Ribbentrop and the Embassy counsellor to tell Hitler that the BBC was not anti-Nazi. And I invited them to have my opposite number come over to us. I said I would put up the flag for him.' Two days later, Hitler marched his troops into Austria.

As war grew closer the BBC was not deaf to the anger of the anti-appeasers. In April 1939 the chairman of the governors,

R. C. Norman, wrote to the postmaster general, the minister responsible for broadcasting, to protest about the constraints on the corporation.

> The vast audience of thirty millions who listen to the wire-less in this country are deprived of the opportunity of getting such an education in the most vital controversial questions as it is in the sole power of broadcasting to offer . . . It cannot be right that their fellow countrymen should have no oppor-tunity at such a time of hearing statesmen of the standing and quality of Mr Lloyd George, Mr Churchill and Mr Eden – to name only a few.

The government attitude was summed up in a civil servant's note stating that the question 'boils down to the fairly simple one of whether or not it is desirable for speeches to be made on Foreign Policy in opposition to the government', which would, the note continued, 'be irresponsible and mischievous'. The conclusion was inevitable: the muzzle would remain.

The way Churchill was handled is a powerful warning of the dangers of the BBC believing it is being balanced by excluding the voices of those who do not represent conventional wisdom. His absence from the airwaves was not solely the result of the BBC's rules or his own party's mistrust of him. John Reith had always disliked him and ended up loathing him. After the war he remarked: 'A whole lot of people could have done it better and more cheaply.'[29] Even when Churchill was dead Reith refused to walk past his commemorative plaque in the floor of Westminster Abbey. The feeling had been mutual. Churchill referred to the puritanical Scot who towered over him as 'that Wuthering Height' and wrote snarlingly of Reith: 'I absolutely hate him.'

These two gigantic egos were always likely to collide spectacularly. Both men had enormous self-belief and very little self-doubt. At the time of Chamberlain's agreement with Hitler at Munich, Reith wrote in his diary: 'I suppose it is too late to get to any position such as I should have. I ought of course to be dictator.'[30] This was a personality clash with policy consequences. Churchill never forgot the rows over the general strike or forgave the BBC for what he saw as the censorship of his views in the run-up to the war.* He came to believe that the corporation was full of communist sympathizers. Years later he would exact his revenge.

There were, of course, other reasons for the BBC's failure to bring home the dangers of the rise of fascism in Europe. It did not have its own foreign correspondents, for a start, and without such reporters there was very little on-the-spot broadcasting of the extraordinary events of the 1930s which would lead to the loss of so many lives and have such far-reaching consequences for so many of those who survived.

Geoffrey Cox, who worked in the BBC newsroom at that time, recalled having to listen to German or Italian fascist radio to monitor what was happening in Europe. 'No British voice sought to describe or interpret these scenes,'[31] he wrote. Or almost no British voice: Cox noted that there was, in fact, one heard when Hitler seized Austria under the Anschluss. It was the voice of the man from the *Daily Mail*, who stood by the führer's side on the balcony of the town hall in Linz and told German radio of the delight he felt.

---

* As Reith retired in 1938, he cannot be personally blamed for Churchill's failure to broadcast after Munich, although his policy on party political balance, continued by his successor, would have been a factor.

We now know that the man from the *Mail* was far from alone in his Nazi sympathies, even if few others displayed them so grotesquely. Shortly after Hitler seized control of the Reichstag in March 1933, Reith wrote in his diary: 'I am certain that the Nazis will clean things up and put Germany on the way to being a real power in Europe again ... They are being ruthless and most determined.' The diary reveals that he even approved of the Nazis' attitude to popular music: 'Germany has banned hot jazz and I'm sorry that we should be behind in dealing with this filthy product of modernity.'

Reith's daughter Marista Leishman has written a biography of her father which confirms that he celebrated both Hitler and his policies. She describes a lunch between the director general and Guglielmo Marconi, the inventor of radio, in 1935. 'He told Marconi how much he had always admired Mussolini for having "achieved high democratic purpose by means which, though not democratic, were the only possible ones".'[32] Marconi might well have agreed since he was by then a member of Mussolini's Fascist Grand Council in Italy.

Even as late as 1938 the director general of the BBC was recording his private regard for the 'efficiency' of the German invasion of Czechoslovakia. Luckily for the BBC, for Britain and for Reith's own reputation, his personal opinions do not appear to have shaped the corporation's pre-war news reporting and he resigned that year, before the outbreak of the hostilities that cemented the standing of the institution he'd done so much to create. It should be noted, however, that despite the views he expressed in the 1930s, he went on to serve the government with distinction during the war, under both Chamberlain and Churchill, as minister first of information, then transport, then works, before joining the Royal Navy and playing a key role in organizing the D-Day liberation of France.

The man who would, during the war years, bring the events of Europe back home for the BBC was Richard Dimbleby, father of David and Jonathan. As a young 'topical talks assistant' he had stretched the rules limiting 'eyewitness descriptions' and pioneered modern broadcast reporting. In 1936 he was sent to cover the fire that devoured Crystal Palace. Dimbleby and his sound engineer linked a microphone to a nearby phone line so that he could report live for the news. The following year he was again heard live on BBC Radio's *Ten O'Clock News*. Dimbleby, who understood that broadcasting was about drama as well as facts, told the audience he had 'one foot in France and one foot in Spain' as he described the retreat of the defeated Spanish Republican Army. With the outbreak of war he would become the voice of the BBC and ensure that never again did the corporation merely elegantly read out other reporters' accounts of what was happening in the world.

In the early years it was for its presentation of the news, not its own first-hand reporting, that the BBC had become respected. A memo to BBC news staff in its final days as a private company summed up its ambition: 'It would be enough for people to say "If it came through the BBC it is so." '[33]

The creation of the BBC Empire Service, the forerunner of the World Service, in 1932, the abdication crisis of 1936 and the coronation of George VI in 1937 had secured for the BBC a massive audience. It had attained its goal of becoming the most trusted purveyor of news in the world. The Second World War was what sealed that status. Things could easily, however, have been very different.

In the mid-1930s, John Reith had secretly agreed that in the event of war the BBC would go 'out of commission'. Happily, this plan was scuppered by others at the corporation when they discovered it,[34] and on 3 September 1939, prime minister Neville Chamberlain announced over the airwaves that Britain was in 'a state of war' with Germany – a broadcast heard not just at home but by people around the world, including the hotel manager in Japan who related it to my grandparents.

In the days leading up to the declaration of war, chancellor of the exchequer Sir John Simon called the BBC to demand that cuts be made to news reports of a Commons debate in which Chamberlain was accused of appeasement,[35] while the prime minister considered stopping broadcasting altogether for the duration since it was thought that people would not bother to listen.

The government couldn't have been more wrong. People were hungry for news. With newsprint rationed, papers were scarce; in any case, everyone knew someone fighting on the front line and they did not want to wait for the papers to find out what was happening. The BBC's news operation expanded rapidly. Soon half the adult UK population was listening to the *Nine O'Clock News*. Indeed, it seems to have been a priority: water company records suggest that people tended to delay 'spending a penny' or putting the kettle on until after the news.

It was during the war that BBC newsreaders would be named for the first time ('Here is the news and this is Alvar Lidell' – or Stuart Hibberd or Freddie Grisewood – 'reading it . . .') but only to ensure listeners would smell a rat in the event that the Germans stormed Broadcasting House, took over the microphones and placed men with well-trained and appropriately clipped accents to present Nazi propaganda in the guise of 'the news'. It emerged years later that the Germans had indeed carefully schooled substitute announcers to speak just like Lidell and his colleagues for precisely that purpose.[36]

However, Lidell and the others continued to present the news in evening dress, despite being often obliged to sleep in a toilet next to their studio. Broadcasting House was not spared the air raids and twice suffered bomb damage. In 1940, it was hit by a delayed-action bomb which exploded as staff tried to move it. Seven people were killed. Listeners heard the muffled crump of the blast as announcer Bruce Belfrage read the nine o'clock news. Belfrage paused. A whispered 'Are you all right?' was audible over the airwaves before he continued, covered in dust, making no comment on the disaster. How very British. How very BBC.

After Winston Churchill became prime minister, on 10 May 1940, vast numbers listened to his extraordinary wartime broadcasts, which are unlikely ever to be matched for their impact. Families huddled around their sets to listen to the words of their war leader. Churchill claimed that all he did was to give voice to the national mood of defiance: 'The people's will was resolute and remorseless, I only expressed it. I had the luck to be called upon to give the roar.'

Some luck. Some roar. Even now, the sound of that deep, gravelly voice warning of the need for 'blood, toil, tears and sweat' or vowing to 'fight them on the beaches' makes the hairs on the back of my neck stand on end. But many of the recordings of those speeches preserved today were made after the event. At the time, people often had to rely on a radio announcer reading out the text of speeches Churchill had given in Parliament, except on the occasions when the great man could be prevailed upon to repeat them for the benefit of the audience at home.

His first prime ministerial broadcast to the nation was made nine days after he took office, on Trinity Sunday, 19 May. He called upon the British people to 'arm yourselves, and be ye men of valour, and be in readiness for the conflict'. Britain and France, he declared, had

> advanced to rescue not only Europe but mankind from the foulest and most soul-destroying tyranny which has ever darkened and stained the pages of history. Behind them – behind us – behind the armies and fleets of Britain and France – gather a group of shattered states and bludgeoned races: the Czechs, the Poles, the Norwegians, the Danes, the Dutch, the Belgians – upon all of whom the long night of barbarism will descend, unbroken even by a star of hope, unless we conquer, as conquer we must; as conquer we shall.

A Home Office report on public opinion conducted the following day, while registering some adverse comments about the delivery, found that the anxiously awaited speech was considered 'courageous and hopeful'. BBC research showed that 51 per cent of the population had heard it. The numbers increased with every subsequent broadcast.

The prime minister's speech to the House of Commons on the afternoon of 18 June 1940 has become one of his most famous. It gave the Battle of Britain its name and ended with a phrase that became shorthand for the country's resolve: 'their finest hour'. The speech was, though, much more than a battle cry. It brought MPs up to date with the latest developments in the war and lasted thirty-six minutes. The prime minister had to be bullied by the information minister,

Harold Nicolson, into repeating it almost word for word in a broadcast to the nation at nine o'clock that evening. He was rewarded with an audience estimated to have represented 60 per cent of the population.

The man who showed the prime minister to the microphone was Robert Wood, a BBC engineer and pioneer of outside broadcasting. He had already given sterling service to the great and the good by helping Edward VIII with his abdication broadcast and George VI to overcome his stutter to speak to the people via the BBC on his coronation. Wood noted in his memoirs how Churchill psyched himself up to go on air. When advised that he should wait first for the bongs of Big Ben and then to be introduced by an announcer, Churchill boomed at Wood: 'Why Big Ben? I am speaking. The world is waiting for me, not Big Ben.'

Before one broadcast Churchill asked Wood to stop one of the studio's antique clocks, which could be heard ticking in the background, on the grounds that it sounded 'like bloody jackboots, and I won't have them marching in Downing Street'. No wonder Wood concluded: 'He was a devil to work for but a treat to work with.'[37]

Churchill could have been saved the need to record speeches he'd already made to MPs if Parliament had agreed to microphones being installed in the Commons. He could also have avoided allegations (untrue, as it turns out) that the voice the nation heard was not always his own but sometimes that of Larry the Lamb – or, rather, of the actor Norman Shelley, who played the children's character and also did a pretty good Churchill impression.

Parliament had one opportunity to relax the rules at the request of our wartime leader. It came after the prime minister suffered a minor heart attack during a visit to the

White House in December 1941. On returning home, he asked the Commons to consider 'electrical recording' of his next parliamentary speech to save him the effort of going to Broadcasting House to give it a second time after a tiring transatlantic crossing. 'I have been constantly asked to repeat the speech I have delivered in the House over the broadcast later,' he complained to MPs in January 1942. 'This imposes a very heavy strain, and is, moreover, unsatisfactory from the point of view of delivery.' He had a suggestion for them:

> It has been represented to me that in the Dominions and in the United States there are very large numbers of people who would like to listen to a record of the actual speech or parts of it rather than to a news summary, such as are usually compiled – very well compiled – by the British Broadcasting Corporation ... I should hope, therefore, that the House might be disposed from time to time to grant me or any successor I may have during the war this indulgence.

The War Cabinet, under the chairmanship of his deputy, Clement Attlee, had already considered this idea in Churchill's absence and turned it down flat. The Cabinet minute concluded: 'The broadcast of Parliament generally was strongly deprecated.'[38] Churchill had hoped that the Commons might take a different view, but they did not. One sympathetic MP* asked him to 'bear in mind that Parliament, of its nature, is not a platform but a representative assembly intended to express the whole will of the nation'. Churchill knew when he was

---

* Leslie Hore-Belisha, the inventor, as transport minister, of the Belisha beacon and the driving test.

beaten. He told MPs he would not 'take it amiss in any way' if they refused. They did.

Thus, throughout the war and for a long time to come, the public had to be content with long extracts of crucial Commons debates read out by radio announcers. The BBC archives reveal that listeners to the six o'clock bulletin on 10 June 1941, for example, would have heard a solitary announcer intoning the words of ten MPs who took part in the debate on the fall of Crete.[39] There was no description or commentary on the mood of the House, no variety of voices, no concession to the poor old listener at all.

After the war, *Today in Parliament* was created to give a fuller account of the day's deliberations in the Commons and Lords, but although the programme had more time to summarize MPs' speeches it was no freer to evoke the theatre of parliamentary debate. The first edition was broadcast on 9 October 1945 after Labour's extraordinary postwar land-slide election victory. Mark D'Arcy, the historian of what is known affectionately in the BBC as '*TIP*', notes that it began with a rather flat opening sentence: 'The House of Commons reassembled in strength this afternoon, to get down to the serious business of the session.'

After three editions the director general rebuked the team, warning them that expressions like 'tartly' and 'pointedly' should not percolate into their reports since 'they are both comment and the beginning of a sketch'. Later, the DG would tell *TIP* (the BBC loves acronyms) not to include MPs' 'undistinguished wisecracks' in their summaries.[40]

In spite of the frustrations and constraints the war had firmly established the BBC as a trusted voice both at home and abroad. Moreover, it had freed the BBC to do its own reporting rather than merely summarizing news gathered for it by agencies. Yet while Churchill's status and reputation had been established during the war in large part by radio, it had not converted him into a friend of the corporation.

In his diaries John Reith, the BBC's founding father, records a Cabinet meeting in November 1940 during which the corporation came under fire: 'Churchill spoke with great bitterness: an enemy within the gates; continually causing trouble; doing more harm than good; something drastic must be done about them . . .'

Something drastic had not been done but, as the age of what Churchill would describe as 'that thing they call TeeVee' approached, nor was the BBC any closer to being allowed to cover Parliament or politics properly.

"Look how Conservative freedom WORKS!"

Daily Mirror, 8 August 1955

3

'WHY DO WE NEED THIS PEEP SHOW?'

It is hard now to conceive of a world without television. Yet when it arrived in the 1920s only a few grasped the possibilities of an invention that had been talked about for a century and which, if it had not been for a young Scot, we might still be calling radiovision or the telephonoscope or seeing by wireless – or, indeed, any one of a string of other more improbable names.

Before turning his attention to transmitting moving images, John Logie Baird had tried his hand at creating the air-soled shoe, a haemorrhoid cream and a rustless glass razor (a project he abandoned after cutting himself badly). In 1926, the year that saw people huddled around crystal radio sets to hear news of the general strike, Baird gave the world's first demonstration of a working television system to members of the Royal Institution and a reporter from *The Times* at his laboratory in London. His first 'televisor' bore little relation to today's 50-inch HD flat screens. It was described as having 'the ingenuity of Heath Robinson and a touch of Robinson Crusoe' and consisted of an old tea chest, a darning needle, an empty biscuit box and a projection lamp whose bull's-eye lenses were bought from a bicycle shop at a cost of £4 apiece.[1]

The inventor of radio, Guglielmo Marconi, declared in 1928 that the prospect of watchable television was a long way off. Another radio pioneer, Sir Oliver Lodge, agreed that developing the technology might take another century. Yet thanks to electronic advances in America and elsewhere, the journey from Baird's early apparatus of sealing wax and string to the feasibility of a nationwide television service was remarkably rapid – even if, with just thirty lines making up the picture compared with hundreds today, the images were far from clear.

Baird ran experimental broadcasts using the BBC's transmitter and in 1930, a 'televisor' was installed at 10 Downing Street, where the prime minister, Ramsay MacDonald, became one of the first people to watch TV. Having viewed Gracie Fields singing 'Nowt for Owt' and a Pirandello play, *The Man with the Flower in his Mouth*, MacDonald wrote to his fellow Scot: 'When I look at the transmissions I feel that the most wonderful miracle was being done under my eye. You have put something in my room which shall never let me forget how strange is this world – and how unknown.'[2]

In 1932 the BBC opened a television studio in the basement of Broadcasting House and began to make its own programmes, transmitting daily to the several thousand enthusiasts who had bought Baird 'televisors'. Four years later, the corporation was licensed to expand its role to 'the representation by telegraph in transitory visible form of persons or objects in movement or at rest' – a parliamentary draftsman's definition of what we call TV. Ramsay MacDonald may have considered it a miracle but it never occurred to him, or to any other politician at the time, that it could and should allow the governed to observe and to judge for themselves those who governed them.

BBC TV was officially launched on 2 November 1936 from Alexandra Palace, set on a 400-foot high ridge in north London. It began with a bulletin of *British Movietone News*, one of the cinema newsreels, followed by a selection of programmes including *Picture Page*, a talk show billed as a 'magazine of topical and general interest' which involved the sort of faked viewer participation that would get the BBC into serious trouble decades later. A woman on a telephone switchboard would pretend to receive calls from viewers asking to see a particular celebrity who just happened to be standing by to walk into the studio. This early service ran for just two hours a day, between three and four o'clock in the afternoon and nine and ten in the evening, and was received by only 20,000 viewers in London and the home counties. But it laid the foundations for what was destined to become the principal means of communicating ideas to the public.

The BBC's own director general was, however, rather less enamoured of the new invention than the prime minister. John Reith loved radio, where carefully chosen and precisely enunciated words were everything. He mistrusted not only television's emphasis on pictures but the people who made them, most of whom hailed from the frivolous worlds of music hall, theatre and movies. The BBC historian Asa Briggs believes Reith saw television as a threat to society: 'He thought it would really corrupt and ruin the nation and you can't go much further than that.' One of his farewell gifts when he left the BBC in 1938 was a television set. He said he would never look at it.

The first staff to work at the new hilltop studios at Ally Pally, as it would soon be dubbed, were known within the BBC as the 'fools on the hill'. Among them was a young former radio 'talks' producer named Grace Wyndham Goldie, the inspiration for the heroine of the BBC TV drama *The Hour*, who was to become one of the most significant figures in the relationship between politicians and television. Over two decades she pioneered TV coverage of elections, introduced a weekly interview programme called *Press Conference* and took charge of *Panorama*, *Tonight* and *Monitor*. Her boss acknowledged the importance of her influence in a letter. 'By God,' he wrote, 'you have changed the whole future of politics in Britain.'

In her memoirs Goldie recalls being asked why she wanted to move to Ally Pally, given that 'television won't last. It's a flash in the pan.' She summarizes the culture prevalent at the time:

> Television could be brushed aside; it was not a medium to be taken seriously; pantomime horses and chorus girls were its natural ingredients; it was not suitable for news and current affairs, let alone for important statements of policy . . . and certainly not for such major occasions as the presentation of the results of a general election. All these were matters which must be dealt with in words not vision.[3]

It's an attitude of which the top echelons of the BBC have never entirely rid themselves. Although television is now recognized as the dominant medium and receives the lion's share of resources there is still a view among some senior figures that it is not really a 'grown-up' way of talking about matters of any weight. This view has long been shared by the nation's politicians.

The BBC was not the first broadcaster to provide a regular public TV service. The British had been beaten to it in 1935 by Nazi Germany, which founded its service with the aim of 'imprinting the image of the führer in the hearts of the German people'. That goal was chillingly achieved when the Berlin Olympics of 1936, the first to be shown live on TV, were broadcast by the German Post Office. The Nazis kept their service going for most of the war and, it has been claimed, were making plans to beam propaganda to big screens in cities across the country before their progress was halted by the Allies.

In sharp contrast, as we have seen, Britain's prime minister, Neville Chamberlain, considered closing down the whole of the BBC for the duration of the war. In the event, radio broadcasting did continue and proved vital, but maintaining a television service for such a tiny minority was unquestionably a luxury the country could not afford. Even so, its users might have expected some notice of its suspension. As it was, on 1 September 1939, a couple of days before war was declared, the television transmitters were abruptly switched off without explanation. The last thing viewers would see for seven years, it turned out, was Mickey Mouse. The immediate shutdown had been ordered by the government for fear that TV transmitters could be used by enemy planes as homing beacons.

Only one prime ministerial television appearance was made before the war. It was an historic moment, and not just for the BBC. Outside broadcast cameras had been sent to Heston aerodrome to await Chamberlain's return from his talks with Hitler in Munich. They recorded him waving his piece of paper, signed by himself and the Nazi leader, and giving his infamous promise of 'peace for our time'. What viewers did not hear was Richard Dimbleby muttering to his BBC colleagues: 'I wish that were true.'[4]

It was not until June 1946 that the television service resumed, with the cheery greeting: 'Here we are after a lapse of nearly seven years, ready to start again, and of course we are terribly thrilled and excited.' The schedule kicked off with the Mickey Mouse cartoon that had brought an end to TV broadcasting in 1939. The audience still consisted of a mere 25,000 middle-class households in the south of England: television would not reach the Midlands and the north before the late 1940s and early 1950s.

For many years BBC TV did not provide a television news service. Viewers were treated to a recording of a radio news bulletin presented by the customary anonymous announcer, under orders to read out the news of a natural disaster or a significant political development in precisely the same detached, monotonal voice he used for the football results. All that appeared on the screen was a single photograph of Big Ben. Movietone's light, bright newsreels continued to be screened on TV but the BBC regarded them as 'entertainment'. The director general appointed in 1944, William Haley, was much more interested in launching his beloved Third Service, the forerunner of Radio 3, than he was in television or in news. Haley, who would go on to edit *The Times*, asserted that it was 'no part of the BBC's function to become another newspaper. News is only a small fraction of the BBC's activities and output.'

When sent a proposal for an illustrated news programme combining radio news bulletins with a few pictures for the benefit of TV viewers, Haley told his staff that this idea should be resisted, 'otherwise the necessity would arise to subordinate the primary function of news to the needs of visual presentation. Any such subordination would prejudice all sorts of values on which the BBC's great reputation for news has been founded.' On the notion of using television to discuss politics he was equally clear: 'I think there are many other things we should concentrate on developing in television before we get around to political discussions.'[5]

Eventually, in 1948, Haley (now Sir William) succumbed to pressure to allow television to develop its own equivalent of the cinema newsreels. Silent pictures were accompanied by jolly music – 'Comic Cuts', 'Peanut Polka' or 'Joy Ride', for example – and uplifting commentary. *Television Newsreel* was hugely popular but it was hardly what you'd call news. It was so lacking in topicality that the same edition ran twice in a week. Still classified as entertainment, it was not even made by the news department.

It was to be another six years before a proper TV news bulletin was launched. It took the prospect of competition to spur the corporation into action, and even then, the bulletins were proper only up to a point, since the BBC had signed up to a bizarre limitation on its coverage of what was happening in politics and on the international stage. Imagine a world in which you could learn from the news about matters of war and peace, life and death, prosperity and hardship and yet watch or hear no discussion or debate about them at all. That was the effect of the deal the BBC had made in 1944 with a wartime coalition government led by a Conservative, Winston Churchill, who loathed TV and liked the BBC little more, and his Labour deputy, Clement Attlee, who took no interest in the media at all.

This restriction was known as the fourteen-day rule, since it prevented the BBC (and later the fledgling ITV, too) from broadcasting discussions on any subject that was due to be debated in Parliament within a fortnight. It was to last for thirteen years. The news – such as it was – could report what was said in Parliament but no MP could be interviewed about it and no one who was not an MP could comment on it. Debate about public life was to be limited to Parliament, which still refused to admit microphones, let alone cameras, to record its deliberations.

At first this 'rule' was not even written down, for reasons made clear in an extraordinary letter from a minister in Attlee's postwar government: 'The principles to be adopted [by the BBC] must depend upon good sense and goodwill, and it is as impossible to formulate exhaustive principles on paper as it is, for instance, impossible to define what conduct is unbefitting to an officer and a gentleman.'[6] This was a politician – and a *Labour* politician at that – telling the BBC to behave like good chaps by censoring themselves, and the BBC quite happily acquiescing.

General elections, too, were off limits for the BBC, which avoided the risk of being seen to take sides by aiming to 'broadcast nothing . . . which might be held to influence the voter'. There were also fears that under some interpretations of the Representation of the People Act 1949 – the law that governs elections and the limits on what candidates can spend – TV coverage could be seen as illegal campaign spending. Between elections, both TV and radio news simply ignored stories which commanded front-page newspaper headlines if they focused on disagreements within parties or criticisms of individual politicians.

The result of these two self-imposed constraints was to neuter political debate. The elections of 1945, 1950 and 1951 were not mentioned on the BBC at all, either on news bulletins or discussion programmes. Save for the introduction of TV party election broadcasts in 1951 these contests were fought in much the same way as those contested by Stanley Baldwin in the 1920s and 1930s, with leaders travelling the country to speak at mass meetings.

When Churchill gave a speech during the 1950 campaign about the future of the atom bomb it was entirely ignored by the BBC, leading one observer to condemn 'neutrality carried to the lengths of castration'.[7] In the following year's election campaign his eve-of-poll oration was a riposte to allegations that he and his party were warmongers – what became known as his 'finger-on-the-trigger' speech. This was not covered by the BBC, either.

With matters of controversy almost entirely confined to official election or party political broadcasts, the big political parties were able to control not only what was spoken about but who did the speaking. Responding to complaints that Churchill had been silenced prior to the war, the BBC agreed to an 'aide memoire' in 1947 reserving for itself the right 'to invite to the microphone a member of either House of out-standing national eminence who may have become detached from any party'.[8] For the next decade, despite fierce debates within both major parties, this right was never exercised.

By 1950 a new controller of television had won a battle to create a TV discussion programme called *In the News*. The title was rather ironic given that the fourteen-day rule and restraints on election broadcasting meant they could not dis-cuss politics at the time it actually was in the news. Nevertheless it proved popular and its regular panellists – a rebel Tory MP, Bob Boothby, Labour left-winger and future leader Michael Foot, an independent MP called W. J. Brown and the famous Oxford don A. J. P. Taylor – became known as the Famous Four. The political parties reacted just as they do today when independently minded MPs are invited on to *Question Time*. They demanded that they, not TV producers, should choose who represented their parties. Among the rising stars picked by Labour was a young man called Jim Callaghan, while the Conservatives, unusually, offered a woman, by the name of Margaret Thatcher.

As the programme grew in confidence its chairman, Dingle Foot, became increasingly angry about the bizarre limitations imposed on him and his panel. They all railed at the 'lunatic restriction' which prevented them from discussing on one edition the development of the hydrogen bomb, which was going to be raised in Parliament in the next fortnight. A. J. P. Taylor said the case 'raised greater issues than John Wilkes' had when he fought for the right to report parliamentary debates over 150 years earlier. Michael Foot urged the BBC 'to break this law' and proposed that, if need be, the director general should be willing to be 'dispatched to the Tower'. Even the press – who had once fought to limit what the BBC could do – came to the corporation's aid.

The protests were in vain. The Commons responded by reinforcing the fourteen-day rule, setting it out in writing where before it had been merely an understanding. In Parliament Churchill warned – as many MPs have before and since – that the BBC might replace the Commons as the principal national forum for debate. 'It would be shocking to have debates in this House forestalled time after time by expressions of persons who had not the status or responsibility of members of Parliament,' he argued. 'The bringing on of exciting debates in these vast, new robot organizations of television and BBC broadcasting . . . [would have] very deleterious effects.'

Labour's Clement Attlee also backed the restriction. He predicted: 'There might come a time when major measures were introduced by a minister, not first in this House, but first on the wireless.' Were he alive today, Attlee would no doubt cite the *Today* programme as evidence of just how right he'd been. And he went on to describe television as 'an instrument the use of which has to be watched extremely carefully'.

If television was becoming increasingly popular, it had no friends within the establishment. Churchill, who had used radio to inspire, reassure and rally a nation in wartime, never took to this 'robot organization', asking, 'Why do we need this peep show?' There are plenty of images from this period of the great man chomping on his cigar but if a camera got too close he simply walked past it or raised his hand to cover the lens. His private secretary, Sir John Colville, recalled that 'he hated the lights, he hated the glare, and he hated the heat'.[9]

Since the man to whom he lost office in 1945, Clement Attlee, showed little if any interest in creating, let alone burnishing, his own image, television didn't impinge on his consciousness whatsoever. The indifference shown by this low-key, laid-back antithesis of the modern politician was due in part to his awareness that 'I have none of the qualities which create publicity'. As *Tribune*, the political paper, put it: 'He seems determined to make a trumpet sound like a tin whistle . . . He brings to the fierce struggle of politics the tepid enthusiasm of a lazy summer afternoon at a cricket match.'

Peter Hennessy, Britain's premier contemporary historian, describes Attlee as having 'all the presence of a gerbil . . . on the Richter scale of charismatic leadership the needle did not flicker'. So slight was the impression the prime minister made that it was said when he once bumped into someone with whom he'd been at school, the man asked him what he was up to these days. Churchill is alleged to have joked: 'One day an empty taxi drew up and Mr Attlee got out.'

Attlee wasn't just uninterested in how the news covered him, he wasn't much interested in the business of news at all. This created huge problems for his press secretary, Francis Williams, who was called upon to comment on breaking news and found that Downing Street, unlike every newsroom in the country, did not have a machine to print out the latest bulletins from the Press Association. He persuaded Attlee to install one directly outside the Cabinet room by telling him that it would allow him to follow how Middlesex were doing at Lord's. Some time later the prime minister remarked, apparently in astonishment, that the tape from which he was reading the cricket scores was 'pinging out the Cabinet minutes!' He was oblivious of the fact that Williams had just briefed the Press Association and the press on the Cabinet's deliberations.

Grace Wyndham Goldie recalls inviting the prime minister to watch an evening of television with his wife at the BBC's studios at Lime Grove.

> He sat, obstinately silent and disapproving, watching, with some of us in attendance, television output on a monitor . . .
> At the end he briefly compared the BBC television service unfavourably with the excellent work done by the Workers' Educational Association and departed as coldly as he had come.[10]

Despite the hostility of Attlee and Churchill, other politicians were beginning to see the value of television – providing, naturally, they could use it on their own terms to communicate directly with potential voters.

Before the 1951 general election campaign politics was blacked out on news bulletins and *In the News* was taken off the air. However, the parties now agreed to an innovation for which voters are still cursing them today. Ever since, the words 'There now follows a . . .' have been taken as a cue by millions to make a cup of tea or pop to the loo. Party election broadcasts were coming to television.

Those pioneering PEBs may have been painful to watch at the time but they are a treat now. The Liberals went first and chose an octogenarian, Lord Samuel, to speak live to camera for fifteen minutes. In truth he scarcely made eye contact with the lens since he was reading from a script. However, his broadcast was memorable for another reason. The producer, Grace Wyndham Goldie, had asked him for a copy of his speech so she'd know when to fade out his microphone and the pictures at the end. He refused, arguing that he wouldn't stick to the precise words on the page. She then suggested he said 'Good night' to indicate when he'd finished but Lord Samuel didn't want to do that, either. Instead he decided he would put his notes down on the table at the conclusion of his talk. A minute or two after his allotted time he paused, having lost his place, and Goldie, seeing that his notes were on the table, faded him out. As a result his concluding thoughts were never seen or heard.

The Tories were rather more professional. Churchill, of course, had no interest in making their broadcast and selected his deputy, Anthony Eden, for the job. Eden proposed that he should be interviewed – or rather appear to be interviewed – by an experienced TV presenter. The party turned to Leslie Mitchell, a familiar face on television screens since before the war. Mitchell began his interview by introducing himself as 'an unbiased member of the electorate', thanking Mr Eden for agreeing to answer his questions and inviting him to choose what he would like to discuss. 'Well now, Mr Eden, with your very considerable experience of international affairs, it is quite obvious that I should start by asking you something about the international situation today – or perhaps you would prefer to talk about home?'

Eden went on to speak about domestic challenges before an apparently fearless Mitchell inquired: 'I wonder, Sir, whether I may introduce a question which I am sure will infuriate you?' The Conservative party, he suggested, had been seen as 'a warmongering party'. Eden reacted appropriately, declaring: 'I do resent that question.'

The press loved it. As David Cameron would show decades later, journalists are easily wowed by the idea of a politician speaking without notes. The *Daily Express* trumpeted: 'Hail to Anthony Eden, the scriptless wonder.' In fact the entire broadcast had been rehearsed word for word, including the impertinent question and the shocked reply. The two men had sat down with a tape recorder, working out who should say what and in what order.

In the first of many examples of broadcasters and politicians jumping from one side of the fence to the other – a trend that would carry on for many years to come – Labour used a former minister turned BBC broadcaster, Christopher Mayhew, for its election broadcast. He was determined to counter Tory charges that the Attlee government had presided over huge price rises. He held up a graph to counter what he claimed was misleading Tory propaganda put out by 'criminals'. It sparked talk in the papers about an election 'battle of the graphs', which the BBC was, of course, prevented from reporting or explaining to its viewers and listeners.

When the Conservatives won the 1951 election Churchill became prime minister for the second time. In the next four years he did not give a single television interview. Despite his obvious antipathy to TV, this was the period when it began to flourish – thanks, largely, to the princess who became Queen.

The crowning of Queen Elizabeth II in 1953 was, of course, going to be a massive national event, and one which saw a surge in the sale of television sets. Over 2 million licences were issued that year, compared with the mere 25,000 held when transmissions restarted after the war. In 1937 the coronation of the Queen's father, George VI, had been one of television's first outside broadcasts, though the cameras had been kept outside Westminster Abbey. This time the BBC wanted its cameras inside the abbey so that the Queen would be crowned live on TV. The prime minister, the archbishop of Canterbury and the earl marshal, who were all on the coronation arrangements committee, were united in the view that cameras should not be permitted. It would be vulgar, intrusive and stressful for the young Queen. She, however, did not agree.

Churchill was told in no uncertain terms by his monarch that the coronation should be seen by as many people as possible. He returned from Buckingham Palace declaring that since she was the one being crowned and it was what she wanted, 'it shall be so'. But the prime minister ordered that the cameras must be positioned at a distance from her so that 'no more intimate view be given than [should] be available to the average person seated within the abbey'. The BBC respected the ruling that cameras should be at least 30 feet away but frustrated its purpose by using very long lenses that allowed people to see the Queen in close-up.

The numbers who did far exceeded those who actually

possessed TV sets. Twenty million – 56 per cent of the adult population – watched the coronation service on television. Over 10 million saw it in other people's houses and 1.5 million in public places – cinemas, halls and pubs. Britain had been brought together by the BBC just as it had been during the general strike and the war. The difference, of course, was that this was a feelgood event and one that united rather than divided the country. Television had been placed at the heart of national life by a queen who defied political advice and who showed she had a clearer idea of popular sentiment than those who claimed to represent the public.

The world of politics was ever so slowly coming to terms with the fact that the box in the corner that mattered was now more likely to be a television set than a wireless. On Grace Wyndham Goldie's programme, *Press Conference*, launched in 1952, three newspaper journalists cross-questioned a leading politician. Their first guest was the chancellor, 'Rab' Butler, the first holder of that office to appear on TV following his Budget. His decision changed the balance of power between politicians and broadcasters. He could have demanded what was known as a 'ministerial' – a speech straight to camera as used in party election broadcasts. He chose instead to answer unscripted questions live without notice of exactly what he would be asked.

The following year saw the birth of *Panorama*, though back then it did not make the hard-hitting films I worked on in the 1990s. Initially it was a studio-based magazine programme, a bit like *The One Show* today, with discussions on weighty matters such as the poor wearing quality of nylons. It would go on, though, with Richard Dimbleby as its presenter, to become a national institution watched by one in four adults. As a 'radio talks' reporter Dimbleby had been the first to do live news broadcasting; now he and his team pushed the boundaries again, establishing the innovative format of reporters speaking to camera at a time when their news colleagues were still making radio bulletins with pictures attached.

That same year, 1953, the first party political broadcasts outside election campaigns were screened. Naturally, Churchill ignored them and invited one of his party's rising stars, Harold Macmillan – who, as prime minister, would go on to master television technique – to deputize for him. Churchill did speak for the cameras that year, although perhaps unsurprisingly, given his feelings about the BBC, he did it for the American networks. On board the *Queen Mary*, headed for New York harbour on an official visit, Churchill stood with his wife, daughter and son-in-law and conceded self-consciously:

> This television has come to take its place in the world. As rather an old-fashioned person, I have not been one of its principal champions but I don't think it needs any champions; it can make its own way. And it's a wonderful thing indeed to think that every expression on my face at this moment may be viewed by millions of people throughout the United States.

Showing that he'd lost none of his sense of timing, the old master communicator paused before adding: 'I just hope the raw material is as good as the means of distribution.'

The coronation convinced Churchill that TV was good for moments of national celebration. One such occasion was his own eightieth birthday in 1954, which was marked by his first and last special TV appearance in Britain. In addition to filming the formal celebrations – speeches in Westminster Hall, the presentation of a portrait and dinner at Buckingham Palace – the BBC planned a special commemorative programme. Grace Wyndham Goldie came up with the idea of a *This Is Your Life*-style tribute in which family, friends and fellow statesmen would record messages to be played into a studio where Churchill was watching. Goldie prepared three alternative endings to the programme: 'one for a situation in which Churchill neither watched nor spoke; one in which he was seen but did not speak and one in which he would be seen and also reply'.

In the event Churchill sat, she recalled, 'like an ancient tortoise withdrawn into itself and unaware of its surroundings . . . [and] gazed blankly at the television set'. At the end of the programme, however, he suddenly came to life 'like a statue from the Stone Age taking on humanity', and spoke to camera: 'I have been entranced by the thrilling panorama you presented to me . . . I am grateful that modern science has enabled me upon my birthday to receive in this amazing manner their friendly greetings and good wishes.'[11]

If it had not been for my BBC colleague Michael Cockerell's research for his brilliant 1980s documentary on the history of politics and television we might never have seen another recording of Churchill on TV. Cockerell and his production team unearthed a secret screen test which Churchill had disliked so much he ordered all copies to be destroyed. Happily, not quite all of them were. Dressed in black jacket and spotted bow tie, the great man growls into a microphone suspended over his head: 'I have come here not to talk to you and certainly not to enable you to spread the tale all over the place, but just to enable me to see what are the conditions under which this thing they call TeeVee is going to make its way in the world.' Revealing his distaste, if not contempt, for the medium that would soon come to dominate coverage of politics, he asserts:

> I am sorry, I must admit, to have to descend to this level, but we all have to keep pace with modern improvements ... There is no point in refusing to move with the age and therefore I have consented to come and have this exhibition, which is for one person and one person only. And only one person is to judge what is to be done with this. I am that person. There you are, here you see me: there is no other in this business.

When the recording was played back for him Churchill hated what he saw. It is easy to mock his unwillingness to come to terms with television but, as he was about so many other things, he might have been right: his grand oratorical style was unsuited to TV, particularly in peacetime. Both radio and television favoured politicians like Stanley Baldwin, who were capable of making a personal connection with individual listeners and viewers, rather than those with a tendency to declaim or growl.

On 5 April 1955 my predecessor E. R. Thompson, the BBC's first parliamentary correspondent, delivered the first-ever live TV news report. The occasion was the announcement that Winston Churchill was retiring to be replaced as prime minister by Sir Anthony Eden. The end of the political career of Britain's wartime leader and the appointment of a new one might have provided an excuse for the odd dramatic rhetorical flourish or burst of excitement. Even a little hyperbole might have been forgivable. That is not, though, how things were done in those days. Thompson, a pleasingly balding man, sat in the BBC's Alexandra Palace studios and began his report with the words: 'The following announcement was issued by Buckingham Palace . . .'

He then proceeded to read out the formal court circular notice confirming that Her Majesty had accepted Churchill's resignation and that his successor had kissed the monarch's hand and accepted her invitation to become First Lord of the Treasury. Thompson then introduced a short film of Sir Anthony's 'great day', in which the country was told that he was wearing morning attire and that 'photographers captured his famous smile'. That was as animated as it got – about as lively as a disco in an old people's home. There was no mention of Eden's policies, no attempt to interview him, no analysis of what his arrival in Downing Street might mean.

Churchill had unwittingly done the BBC a favour by resigning during a newspaper strike so that the corporation had the story to itself. Not for much longer, though, would the BBC be the only news provider to cover any story. Some years earlier Churchill had taken a decision which would change television for good. He had decided to break the monopoly that his old enemy John Reith had considered so vital for the health of broadcasting. He did so in the face of Reith's hysterical warning that commercial television would be as disastrous for Britain as 'dog racing, smallpox and bubonic plague'. Indeed, that wild overstatement seems to have helped overcome Churchill's initial doubts about the need to establish a competitor to the BBC. The grand old man explained his conversion to his doctor, Lord Moran: 'For eleven years they kept me off the air. They prevented me from expressing views that proved to be right. Their behaviour has been tyrannical.'

Not for the last time the BBC was being punished by a prime minister who could not and would not forget how they had mistreated him two decades earlier.

Not for the first time Churchill was to be proved right and Reith completely wrong. The legacy of their bitter personal feud was the end of the BBC's monopoly and the creation of a brand-new TV channel.

Concerns about the monopoly had been rumbling since soon after the television service was resumed in 1946 and were not silenced by the conclusions of the Beveridge committee, formed in 1949 to examine the future of broadcasting, which came down firmly in favour of maintaining the status quo. The campaign for an independent television channel gained momentum and secured government support in 1953. Control of television, Parliament decided, 'should not remain in the hands of a single authority, however excellent it may be'. Most people agreed in principle; what caused huge controversy was the recommendation that a second channel should be a commercial enterprise, funded by on-screen advertising – an idea seen by many as the exploitation of the masses for profit. It is hard to appreciate, in these days of multiple channels and multiple media, the degree to which opinion was polarized and the strength of the passions the debate aroused.

As a result the passage of the Bill through Parliament was turbulent, to say the least, but finally, on 30 July 1954, the Television Act became law and the government established the Independent Television Authority (ITA) to put licences out to tender and grant the franchises for broadcasting commercial television to the regions. Independent Television – ITV – was launched in the London area in 1955, reaching the Midlands the following year and the north of England in

1957. It was run largely by former BBC men disillusioned with the corporation and eager to embrace a new opportunity. Despite Reith's pessimistic predictions they brought his values with them, while rejecting the extreme caution that by now characterized the BBC, leading to stagnation and a sense that it was becoming imprisoned in its own past.

At first only a quarter of a million homes had access to ITV. Nevertheless, the competition it provided helped to end the censorship of political debate in Britain and to lay the foundations of modern TV news. The days when politicians felt able to ask broadcasters to act like 'an officer and a gentleman' by not intruding on decisions that should be left to parliamentarians would be soon gone. So, too, was the notion that it was perfectly acceptable to provide TV viewers with news bulletins made for listeners to the wireless.

The BBC newsreader Robert Dougall describes in his memoirs how the head of BBC News, obsessed with guarding the reputation built up during the war, pursued a line of 'hyper caution'. It produced bulletins that were 'colourless, long-winded and dull'.[12]

The prevailing culture is illustrated by the experience of a former Fleet Street journalist who joined the BBC before fleeing to Independent Television News (ITN) to become its first news editor. In 1949 Arthur Clifford broke a major story when he obtained confirmation from the Foreign Office that a British frigate, HMS *Amethyst*, was coming under Chinese shellfire in the Yangtse river. The newspapers raced to follow it up. Clifford was summoned by the BBC's editor of news who, far from congratulating him, insisted that this must never happen again and carpeted him for ignoring the way the BBC did things. Although Clifford's story had been verified by the government, the rules stated that any BBC report must first be confirmed by three news agencies. He was informed that his annual increment would not be withheld but told firmly that 'enthusiasm does not constitute journalistic ability'.[13]

Before ITN showed them how it should be done the BBC had made an effort to modernize television news. They came up with something only a committee could have designed: half painfully dull, barely illustrated radio news bulletin and half chirpy but insubstantial newsreel film. *BBC News and Newsreel* had, indeed, been dreamed up in part by the BBC newsroom and in part by the television service, with scant collaboration: the two departments loathed each other in the way only rival sections of a large organization can.

The first edition of the new hybrid hit the screens on 5 July 1954, less than four weeks before the new Television Act came into force, its title circling an image of the transmission mast at Alexandra Palace. As the jaunty theme tune faded out the disembodied, unidentified but unmistakably clipped voice of radio's John Snagge could be heard listing the key points of the news. They were illustrated by the occasional still and crude caption ('Indo-China. Truce talks near Hanoi', 'Princess Margaret visits Lancashire'). Snagge was not allowed to appear, lest his expression betray a reaction or opinion on the news he was reading out. Next came 'the latest films'. In one a reporter asked 'a representative of those who go to the butcher's to do the family shopping' to describe the impact of the end of rationing. A Miss Warren of Herne Hill said it meant she could dash to the shops to buy a steak if she suddenly had someone else to feed when entertaining. The camera lingered silently on a juicy piece of rump just in case viewers had missed the point.

The whole concoction was deeply unsatisfying. It was as if

today someone tried to mould a programme by combining the matiness of the breakfast telly sofa with the restrained authority of Radio 4's *Six O'Clock News*. A critic in the BBC's own journal, *The Listener*, commented that the more she saw of television news, 'the more I like my newspaper'. The BBC's interviewing style also came under the lash: 'Its interviewers are apt to behave like footmen in the presence of public personages.'

ITV's news bulletins, by contrast, were made by ITN, a separate company whose first editor-in-chief was another poacher-turned-gamekeeper, the former Labour minister Aidan Crawley. He went to America to see how news was broadcast there and came back with the daring idea that it should be presented by people the viewer could see as well as hear – newscasters, as opposed to mere newsreaders – and whose names they would be allowed to know. In other words, men and, yes, women too, who wrote what they read out and helped to select and shape the news that was reported.

ITN's first hiring was a young, aggressive former barrister called Robin Day. When he met the studio director at ITN she took one look at this former president of the Oxford Union in his heavy, horn-rimmed spectacles and asked, 'Who the hell are you?'

'I am a newscaster,' he replied.

'God almighty, can't they do better than that?'

In truth they couldn't have done any better. First at ITN, and then at the BBC – as a reporter on *Panorama*, presenter of Radio 4's *World at One* and the first chairman of BBC1's *Question Time* – Day revolutionized TV's coverage of British politics and pioneered an interviewing technique which challenged rather than flattered. In the place of courteous inquiries to ministers as to whether there was anything they might like to say to a grateful nation, Day used his inquisitorial skills to get answers for those who gave politicians their jobs. It's easy to see why he felt a 'revolutionary thrill'[14] in those early ITN days.

When the BBC heard what ITN was up to it did what it would do again and again over the years when faced with a successful competitor – copy it. Just eighteen days before Robin Day and his colleagues went on air, BBC TV brought its newsreaders out on to the screen – although, bizarrely, it did not go as far as naming them, with the result that they suddenly appeared in the corner of the nation's sitting rooms and then went away again without ever introducing themselves. They were not allowed, either, to use the newfangled teleprompter – in those days simply a mechanical device with the script printed on a paper scroll. So for much of the time, BBC TV news meant nameless men looking down at their scripts rather than into the eyes of their new viewers. It could not and did not last. Fifteen months later the BBC followed ITN in identifying its newsreaders and letting them use all the new tools of the TV trade.

Even after the ITN revolution TV news bulletins on both channels were very different from those of today. As yet there were no satellites to deliver live broadcasting from anywhere at the drop of a hat; no lightweight cameras recording sound as well as pictures; no sophisticated graphics and, of course, no colour.

Bulletins were, partly as a result of these limitations, much shorter than they are now, around ten to twelve minutes long. Largely silent film had to be brought to the studio – in the case of international news, this meant shipping it back from abroad – and developed before commentary, sound effects and, perhaps, music were added. Foreign reports did not carry the voice of the reporter: they were read out by the studio presenter or a specialist 'commentary reader'. Journalists never spoke to camera and appeared only occasionally when asking a question.

To make his regular one- or two-minute reports on what was being said in Parliament the BBC's man, E. R. Thompson, had to make the journey from Westminster to Alexandra Palace by cab. He used the time to commit his lines to memory by reading them out loud, leading his driver to believe that 'he'd got a nut on board'. On one occasion he was asked to read someone else's script for a film about Anthony Eden at just a few minutes' notice. As he went on air, barely having had the chance of a run-through, the cue light that told him when to read his next line failed. Someone from the newsroom had to lie under the desk and tug his trouser leg at the appropriate moments. As he faced this ordeal he heard a voice out of the darkness: 'I wouldn't be that man Thompson for a million pounds!'[15]

The first reporter ever to broadcast live from Westminster was Thompson's assistant, Roland Fox. He used a tiny purpose-built studio near the Palace of Westminster. Once, when the studio lights blew in the middle of his piece, he was left to continue his live report in total blackness. Fortunately, he knew his lines so he just kept going until he'd finished.

For many years to come most political reports on BBC TV news would be provided by a man sitting in that little studio, staring into a camera and reading from an autocue he controlled with a foot pedal. He would merely give a short précis of who had said what, which, given how much there was to summarize, required real skill. But with cameras banned from the Commons there were rarely any pictures, and reports were largely free of commentary, analysis and explanation – an extraordinary deficiency in an era of wars, protests, the exposure of Russian spies and the arrival of rock and roll. John Reith would have been proud. I would have hated it.

The BBC employed just two men – Thompson and Fox – to cover politics then. Today they employ dozens. They worked out of a small telephone booth off Parliament's Central Lobby. Once a Tory MP with the splendid name of Sir Waldron Smithers wrenched open the door as Fox was phoning through a story to his news desk and shouted: 'Tell them they're all a lot of commies!' Smithers, it should be noted, was inclined to see reds under most beds. He regularly called for the Commons to set up a 'committee on un-British activities' to conduct McCarthyite witch hunts on this side of the Atlantic.

Soon a more mainstream Conservative would be complaining about 'those communists at the BBC'.[16] Churchill's successor as prime minister, Sir Anthony Eden, the first to seem comfortable with television, was to fight a bitter battle with the BBC after they refused to back him over his decision to launch a controversial and divisive war. To modern ears, it all has a very familiar ring. Eden had every reason to be comfortable with television. He was suave, good-looking and a quarter of a century younger than Churchill. He was even a leader of fashion. The hat he wore, a Homburg, became so trendy that it was known as 'the Anthony Eden'.

Eden wanted his own mandate and had called a snap election within a week of succeeding Churchill. He said that he 'attached the first importance to television as a medium'. No wonder: by 1955 a third of the population had their own sets. All the old rules which censored political debate were still in place and ITN was not yet up and running. The BBC refrained from reporting the campaign itself and comedians were warned not to make jokes about it. A Conservative party memo told ministers that 'during an election period the corporation is extremely careful to avoid broadcasting any political matter which might have an influence or bearing on the result of polling'. This, it went on, was 'an admirable policy'.

What Eden actually meant was that he attached 'the first importance' to propaganda broadcasts. As foreign secretary he had demanded the right to make a ministerial broadcast with no reply from the opposition. He was furious when the BBC had instead offered him the chance to be questioned on the new *Press Conference* programme. During the election the rules and conventions of the day allowed him to design the broadcasts on which he appeared. Eden had been the star of the Conservative's first party election broadcast four years earlier; now he had the chance to use full-length programmes – one half-hour and two fifteen-minute broadcasts – to woo the British people.

Once again the Conservatives were nothing if not professional. The Conservatives' final PEB was an early variant of the modern Downing Street news conference. Eden, flanked by his chancellor, foreign secretary and a clutch of other ministers, faced questions from ten invited newspaper editors. 'We haven't, of course, the least idea what the questions are going to be,' Eden assured viewers before adding with a smile: 'I only hope we shall know the answers.' Since most of the editors were from Tory-backing newspapers that claim lacks credibility.

The Conservatives had, however, thought of this and to forestall such criticisms they had included the editor of the Labour-supporting *Daily Mirror*, one of Fleet Street's most famous figures, Hugh Cudlipp. He asked Eden what sort of Toryism the country would get if he obtained a large majority – the prewar Toryism of the welfare state or that of the slums, massive unemployment and neglected housing and defence? 'I hope and believe an intelligent, progressive Toryism,' Eden smiled. Cudlipp, who knew how to tackle politicians in print, didn't take the opportunity to point out that this hardly answered his question. It was a reminder that interrogating politicians on television requires a particular knack that even some of the very best journalists, whether from print or TV, simply do not possess.

The broadcast was another impressive television performance by Eden – in stark contrast to Clement Attlee's doomed attempt to enter the television age. Anthony Wedgwood Benn, one of Labour's rising stars, produced his party's election broadcasts that year. A long while later, as plain Tony Benn, the figurehead of his party's left wing, he would routinely condemn the politics of what he called 'pershonality' and insist that what mattered were the 'isshoos'. Not then, though. In 1955 he had his veteran leader filmed sitting with his wife in a studio mock-up of their sitting room. The fire was lit, despite the fact that it was mid-May, and a tame interviewer lobbed pre-planned softball questions.

'Mr Attlee, you are off tomorrow on your 1,200-mile tour by motor car. That means you must still have some faith, in spite of television, in the old-fashioned public meeting.'

Mr Attlee sucked his pipe and brought forth this great revelation:

Um, I think there's a good deal, you know, to the public meeting. After all, a candidate likes to see his audience. And I think the electors like to see their candidates. And after all, too, you can't heckle on television, while you can at a public meeting. I had an extremely good one at Blaydon the other night.

Benn recalls that this was as good as it got. Even on his own terms, on the eve of an election, Attlee was incapable of using television to sell himself. The twenty-eight questions prepared for the quarter-of-an-hour broadcast were exhausted after five minutes.[17] 'He was monosyllabic,' Benn told me. 'Conversation is mostly like a game of tennis, but with Attlee it was like feeding a dog a biscuit.'

Attlee was by then seventy-two and had led his party, now hopelessly divided, for twenty-one years. Eden won the election easily.

A little over a year into his premiership Eden took a massive political and military gamble. He reached a secret agreement with France to support a military assault by Israel on the forces of Egypt's nationalist leader, Colonel Nasser – a man Eden presented as the Hitler of the Arab world. Nasser had seized control of the strategically vital Suez Canal, which links the Mediterranean and the Indian Ocean. It was seen then as essential for transporting British and Commonwealth troops around the Empire and accessing oil from the Persian Gulf. Eden claimed that the world could not afford to appease another dictator.

Suez was to be the first crisis of the television era when what began as a military success turned into a political disaster. It marked the end of the British Empire, led to the ignominious resignation of the prime minister and would become a milestone in the relationship between broadcasters and the government.

On 8 August 1956 Eden asked to make a prime ministerial broadcast on television – the first ever. Radio 'ministerials' had been common but Eden's predecessors had rejected the chance to do them on TV. Attlee had believed that they would turn politicians into entertainers while Churchill objected to the idea that if he broadcast the opposition should get the right of reply. Eden, however, had been inspired by what he'd heard from the American president and French prime minister, both of whom regularly made television broadcasts. He wanted to match Churchill's stirring wartime performances. As his press secretary, a former BBC man called William Clark, put it: 'He wanted to use television as a new instrument and new weapon of national unity and purpose.'

To deliver his broadcast, Eden went to Lime Grove studios, a rabbit warren of winding corridors, metal ladders and steaming pipes. When I took Norman Tebbit into a studio there he joked that he'd not been in a place like it since he'd visited a Hong Kong sweatshop. On that night in 1956 it was certainly steamy. The BBC producer Grace Wyndham Goldie laid on iced champagne but she wrote in her memoirs of feeling ashamed that

> the BBC had not been able to provide the prime minister with more suitable surroundings in which to make so momentous a broadcast . . . there was no air conditioning yet the windows had to be kept closed and heavily curtained because trains ran past outside them every few minutes. In the August heat the small rooms were stifling and since there was no lift they could be reached only by climbing three flights of concrete stairs lit by naked hanging bulbs.[18]

Things did not improve. Eden had always appeared on television without his spectacles, having learned his scripts off by heart. Now, however, the situation was too delicate to risk a stumble or an ad lib. The prime minister had come with a script produced in large type but he still couldn't read it properly and was obliged, reluctantly, to put on his glasses. He believed, according to his press secretary, that 'those communists in the BBC' were deliberately shining the studio lights in his eyes.

Eden warned of the 'very grave situation' and told the country that if Colonel Nasser's action succeeded 'each one of us would be at the mercy of one man [for] the supplies upon which we live. We could never accept that. With dictators you always have to pay a higher price later on, for their appetite grows with feeding.'

The Labour party, which had been against intervention from the outset, was not offered the chance to respond. Ministerial broadcasts were controlled by the unhelpfully ambiguous aide memoire drawn up in 1947 after talks between the BBC and the political parties, where it was agreed that such broadcasts should not be controversial and should be confined to explaining legislation approved by Parliament or appealing for public co-operation. The aide memoire stated: 'It will be incumbent on ministers to be as impartial as possible and in the ordinary way there would be no question of a reply by the opposition.' If the opposition thought the government broadcaster had crossed the accepted boundaries, it would be open to them to ask the government to give them the opportunity to reply, with the BBC 'exercising its own judgement' if the parties could not agree.

Eden was outraged when, soon after he addressed the

country, the BBC turned down an offer from the prime minister of Australia, Robert Menzies, who was visiting the UK, to make another television broadcast. The BBC was concerned about balance. Since the foreign secretary, Selwyn Lloyd, had also delivered a 'ministerial' and Menzies was publicly supporting Eden, this would have been the third in a row backing the government's position. The prime minister called the chairman of the BBC governors to protest. The chairman, Alex Cadogan, was a man with a clear conflict of interest. Not only had he been the top civil servant at the Foreign Office when Eden had been foreign secretary, he was also the British government's appointee on the board of the Suez Canal Company. He allowed the Menzies broadcast.

During the dispute William Clark called Grace Wyndham Goldie to say that the prime minister found the corporation's behaviour 'quite intolerable' and to express his fear 'that in his anger the prime minister might take some drastic action which will be permanently harmful to the BBC'.[19] It was the clearest of threats and not an idle one. Clark would later tell the BBC that Eden had ordered the drawing up of 'an instrument which would take over the BBC altogether and subject it wholly to the will of the government'. He had witnessed the prime minister ordering the lord chancellor 'to see what the government could do to get what they wanted on to the BBC'. Harold Macmillan, the man who would take over from Eden after Suez, then met the director general of the BBC and noted in his diaries afterwards: 'Personally, I doubt if we shall get through all this without taking back the old war powers.'[20] The BBC was not taken over but later Eden cut half a million pounds from funds for the World Service, or what was then called the Overseas Service.

The rows did not stop there. The BBC invited an Egyptian

officer, Salah Salem, to talk on a radio broadcast which, thanks to the Overseas (now the World) Service, could be heard in the region. Eden wrote to the chairman of the BBC board of governors to complain that it gave 'a deplorably misleading picture of British opinion as uncertain and hesitant'. On this occasion the BBC stuck to its decision.

Eden had negotiated a secret military pact with France and Israel to invade Egypt and seize back control of the canal. He'd done so without consulting the American president, the United Nations or Parliament. In late October 1956, Israeli troops were parachuted into Egypt while British and French forces prepared to occupy key points on the canal and to bomb military targets in readiness for landing their own ground troops. On 3 November Eden made another broadcast to the nation: 'There are times for courage, times for action. And this is one of them . . . to prevent the horror and devastation of a larger war.'

The new Labour leader, Hugh Gaitskell, chose to invoke his right of response to the prime minister's broadcast. The BBC informed him that under the terms of the aide memoire this was something he should first try to agree with the government. On doing so he was told that since the prime minister did not regard his own broadcast as particularly controversial he would not agree to a reply. Gaitskell was furious. Eventually he persuaded the BBC that he should be allowed to become the first-ever British politician to make a broadcast opposing his own government's intervention in a foreign conflict. 'Make no mistake about it – this is war: the bombing, the softening up, the attacks on radio stations . . . opposed by the world, in defiance of the world. It is not a police action; there is no law behind it. We have taken the law into our own hands.'

Gaitskell saved his most damning message until the end:

> I don't believe that the present prime minister can carry out
> this policy. I bear him no ill will . . . But his policy this last
> week has been disastrous . . . Only one thing can save the rep-
> utation and the honour of our country – Parliament must
> repudiate the government's policy. The prime minister
> must resign.

Gaitskell's broadcast, on Sunday 4 November, was heard
not just in his own country but, despite the pleading of
Eden's press secretary, all over the Middle East as well,
thanks to the BBC Arabic service. His words were powerful
but his was not the critical voice. After the Soviet Union
offered Egypt its support, the USA, concerned about any
expansion of communist influence, demanded the with-
drawal of all foreign forces. The next morning a ceasefire was
declared. The troops would be removed and by January 1957
the prime minister had, indeed, resigned.

Eden had found that the 'new instrument' he'd wanted so
badly to make use of had been turned against him. He deeply
resented the BBC's failure to rally to his side. Tory MPs
claimed that its coverage had been inaccurate, one-sided and
disloyal – charges that would be heard again during the
Falklands War and the invasion of Iraq.

The BBC had resisted government pressure – most of the
time. It had maintained its independence – just. It had gained
credit for telling the truth to audiences around the world.
Grace Wyndham Goldie concluded: 'Suez is a salutary warning of the lengths to which a political party may go when in
power to prevent the broadcasting of any opinions but its
own.'[21] If the world had reacted differently the BBC as we
know it might no longer exist.

Suez did at least lead to the scrapping of the absurd

fourteen-day restriction. Like all bad laws it simply became unenforceable, as was made abundantly clear on the Friday night following Eden's first broadcast. By then British jets had bombed targets in Egypt, the House of Commons had been suspended in uproar and at the United Nations the government had vetoed a ceasefire: the focus, you might imagine, of the main forum for debate outside Parliament – BBC Radio's *Any Questions?* However, the country's premier panel discussion programme began with an unusual announcement by its much-loved presenter, Freddie Grisewood: 'Now, before we have the first question, I must point out that the question which very many of our audience has handed in to be discussed cannot be dealt with in this programme because of the fourteen-day rule.'

His explanation was interrupted by a cry of 'That's monstrous!' The panellists – two of them members of Parliament – were unimpressed. 'This really makes the whole programme absolutely ridiculous,' one said, triggering thunderous applause. Another declared: 'I must say that I cannot understand why I, as a journalist, am allowed to write and discuss this in a newspaper but I cannot talk about it on the radio. It seems to me the most nonsensical rule.' To which, in a classic example of English understatement, one added: 'It is quite silly.'

The protests made it difficult for the programme to get going at all. When it did the first question could not have been better chosen to highlight the censorship the ban imposed: 'Does the panel consider carpets in the home to be a necessity or a luxury?'

One reply, which prompted much laughter, was that 'carpets are in the home in order to put the opposition on for their ridiculous attitude to Suez'. The programme was abruptly taken off the air and resumed only when the panel had 'calmed down'.[22] Among the other comments that breached the ban was this elaborate attempt to raise the burning issue of the day: 'We're all under the illusion that Britain has invaded Egypt. I want to talk about the other invasion which has been ignored, which is that Britain has invaded a country called Ruritania.'

In general the BBC had done its best to circumvent the rule during the crisis. *The Economist* praised them for 'progressively allowing the distinction between fact and comments to be blurred . . . let them go on blurring it'. The government agreed to suspend the rule for six months. It stayed suspended and was eventually repealed.

The country had been led into war by a prime minister elected without any radio or news coverage of his campaign, without facing a single unscripted question on television, without voters being able to see or hear Parliament debate the issue in the House of Commons and with discussion programmes prohibited from discussing the one thing listeners and viewers wanted to hear discussed.

The demise of the fourteen-day rule was a small but significant victory for broadcasting in its own long war of attrition with the politicians.

'We're trying to appease Wilson'

Daily Mirror, 5 October 1965

4

'THE HOT, PITILESS, PROBING EYE'

Television entered its teenage years in the late 1950s. It became questioning, disrespectful and rebellious. It experimented with raucous debate, outspoken drama, searing satire and provocative current affairs, though most politicians would not have noticed.

If an MP owned a television at all, which was unlikely, he would refer to it as a 'receiver'. When he switched it on he would choose between just two channels, BBC and ITV, and the picture would be in black and white. To watch a programme he would have to be in at the right time – there was no way to record anything you missed – and to change channel he'd have to get out of his chair and turn the dial. And if news was what he wanted, he'd almost certainly switch off the television altogether and tune in instead to the wireless to listen to the Home Service of the BBC at nine o'clock.

However, in the twelve years between the end of the Second World War and Suez, television had begun to find its way into more and more front rooms in more and more homes. By 1957, 7 million households had a set. There were still – just – more licences issued for radio alone, 7.5 million, but this would be the last year in which that was the case.

Broadcasters had, thus far, steered clear of controversy when instructed to do so; they had left debate to the 'grown-ups' in the House of Commons; they had treated elections as a private ritual between elector and elected into which reporters should not intrude; they had behaved with deference to those in power.

They were now becoming increasingly reluctant to do as they were told. Suez had highlighted the failings of a ruling elite used to taking decisions in secret and without challenge. Competition from TV's cheeky newcomer ITV had shaken up the BBC. Besides, what was good enough for the generation who were content to swing with Glenn Miller was not nearly exciting enough for those who wanted to rock and roll with Elvis.

The era in which politicians thought they could control the young upstart was over. The future would belong to those who could charm the cameras; those who accepted that if you couldn't beat them, your only option was to join them. Two prime ministers called Harold, one Tory, one Labour, were to show the way forward – for better and for worse.

The first Harold of the new television age was the last prime minister to have been born in the reign of Queen Victoria, the last to have fought in the First World War and the last to sport a moustache. He was someone who admitted that he had rarely, if ever, watched television himself. He was a man who looked and sounded, even in the late 1950s, as if he'd come from another century. When Harold Macmillan had free time he spent it shooting in the country or staying at home and reading Trollope. When he spoke he used

Edwardian English: 'off' was 'orff', 'lost' became 'lorst', 'girl' emerged as 'gel' or 'gal'.[1] Parliament was pronounced with four syllables: 'Parl–ee–a–ment'.

Yet Anthony Eden's successor adapted to and mastered the challenge posed by TV, even joking with his audience about how uncomfortable it was. He began one Conservative party broadcast by showing viewers all the TV paraphernalia needed to enable him to speak to them. 'So there you are, you can see what it is like. The camera's hot, probing eye, these monstrous machines and their attendants – a kind of twentieth-century torture chamber, that's what it is. But I must try to forget about that, and imagine that you are sitting here in the room with me.'

Macmillan swapped his baggy old suits for new ones from Savile Row. He had his teeth fixed and his moustache trimmed. He self-consciously cultivated an image to handle the new demands of TV which, during his time in office, would start to cover elections properly for the first time, to ask searching instead of supine questions and to discuss the issues of the day when viewers wanted to hear about them rather than when politicians decreed.

The story of how Harold Macmillan became prime minister at the beginning of 1957 reveals, however, just how embryonic the relationship between politics and broadcasting remained. Macmillan made it into Number 10 thanks not to an election – not a single MP, never mind a party member or ordinary elector, cast a vote for him – but after Lord 'Bobbety' Salisbury, the lord president of the council and 5th Marquess of Salisbury, consulted fellow members of the Cabinet and invited them to choose between 'Wab or Hawold'. The outgoing prime minister, Eden, would have chosen 'Wab' – Rab Butler – had he been consulted, but he wasn't, and the Cabinet chose 'Hawold'. No one carried out a poll or organized a focus group, let alone arranged for a TV debate between the rival candidates.

On the evening he was selected for the highest job in the land the new prime minister decided to celebrate with his chief whip, Ted Heath, by dining at his favourite club. When Macmillan headed home he was shocked to find that 'our way was barred by all the usual paraphernalia of press and television to which I had not yet become accustomed. I thought that my guest and I were entitled to a bottle of champagne and some game pie.' The old world had come face to face with the new, although the days of cameras outside the front doors of politicians' homes and the shouts of 'Are you going to resign?' still lay a long way in the future.

Macmillan didn't expect to be in power long, so great had been the convulsion caused by Suez and so deep the national humiliation. He told the Queen that his new administration might last just six weeks. Within days of moving into Downing Street he decided to make a national television broadcast to try to reassure the country that their best days were not behind them. 'Britain is great,' he told viewers, 'and will stay great.' Like his predecessor, Macmillan believed it was his right to broadcast whenever he thought it appropriate. He also talked about, though never acted upon, the idea of regular presidential-style news conferences of the sort that Tony Blair went on to introduce. Nevertheless, Macmillan opened himself up in a way that had been unthinkable before.

Today all politicians expect to be 'doorstepped' when walking into or out of any building. They are prepared to have a camera thrust in their face and to be asked difficult questions. Not in 1957. In an age when air travel was expanding as fast as television, the VIP lounge at what was then called London (now Heathrow) airport was where reporters and their cameras could catch up with globetrotting dignitaries. Anyone willing to talk would be filmed standing in front of an 'improbable background of patterned curtains which gave it the look of a pretentious seaside boarding house'.[2]

A year after Macmillan moved into Number 10, in January 1958, he found himself in front of those curtains facing questions about the resignation of not one minister but his entire Treasury team – the chancellor and both of his deputies – who objected to his approach to spending. He reacted with an air of studied insouciance.

> It is always a matter of regret from the personal point of view when divergences arise between colleagues, but it is the team that matters and not the individual, and I am quite happy about the strength and the power of the team. So, I thought the best thing to do was to settle up these little local difficulties and then turn to the wider vision of the Commonwealth.

It took some nerve to dismiss such major ructions in the government as 'little local difficulties', not least when the prime minister was about to depart on a tour of the Commonwealth lasting a staggering six weeks. Macmillan had shown how to deal with a political crisis: look confident for the cameras and pretend to shrug it off.

He would, though, also be the first prime minister to discover that getting away from home doesn't put you beyond the reach of difficult questions when the television cameras are on your trail. Macmillan spoke for all his successors when he complained once in a speech:

Television and jet aeroplanes . . . are the things that have made the life of a modern prime minister almost impossible because it is in airports that television chooses to lurk. You go by sea, you go by road, you go by rail, nobody bothers you very much. If you go by air, there it is – that hot, pitiless, probing eye. After fourteen hours of travel you get off the aeroplane, wanting only a shave and a bath – oh no, you are cornered. The lights in your eyes, the cameras whizzing. You put up your hand to shade your eyes and the next day there you are in the *Daily Clarion* looking weary, old, worried, over a caption which implies you're past it. Alternatively, you pull yourself together and you try looking young and buoyant. You say something which you think will be apposite and enlightening and what happens? Why, in the editing your carefully chosen phrases are all boiled down to fifty seconds and focused on the aggressive question to which you fumbled the answer. You can't win.[3]

Where Macmillan did win was in beating television at its own game. In 1959 he laid on a TV show no broadcaster could resist by persuading his old wartime chum President (formerly General) Eisenhower to come to Britain. He went to the airport to meet his friend and the two of them rode back to Downing Street in an open-top car with the number plate USA1. The journey through cheering crowds took two hours – twice the normal time – allowing Eisenhower to stand and acknowledge the British public as Macmillan sat regally alongside him. The tableau conveyed the unmistakable message that the transatlantic bond severed by Suez had been restored.

The show did not stop there. The BBC's cameras had been invited into Downing Street to film the two leaders chatting before dinner. They sat companionably in armchairs, both dressed in dinner jackets. The prime minister welcomed the president and the 'frank talks' they were having. Eisenhower told 'all those good people out there' that 'we are mighty glad to be back visiting again this lovely country'. After twenty minutes of talking about their two lovely countries and their relations with Russia they rose to their feet to head to dinner. The camera showed a footman opening a door for them, revealing their guests, who included Sir Winston Churchill. It was a brilliant finale to a carefully planned piece of propaganda. The prime minister and the president had earlier spent hours with the BBC rehearsing what became known as the 'Mac 'n' Ike show'.

Every prime minister since has tried to bottle the magic of the special relationship and use it as an electoral elixir. There have been many memorable images – Thatcher and Reagan dancing, Blair and Bush joshing about sharing toothpaste, Cameron and Obama flipping burgers and watching basketball – but none of them has ever pulled it off as spectacularly as Macmillan did with the Mac 'n' Ike show. His timing was perfect as well: a week later, he called a general election.

In 1959 Harold Macmillan faced a serious challenge from a younger 'man with a plan', Labour's Hugh Gaitskell. Asking for an unprecedented third consecutive Conservative term in office was no easy task after the disaster of Suez and in what was to be the first modern TV election.

As we have seen, during previous elections, while the politicians had been devising ways to harness the power of the box, the growing television audiences had been denied political news and debate in the name of impartiality. Democracy was dragged into the television age only thanks to an extraordinary summit staged secretly at Nuffield College, Oxford one weekend in January 1958. It brought together the

Tory home secretary, Rab Butler, and chief whip Ted Heath; Labour's Hugh Gaitskell and Anthony Wedgwood Benn; the Liberal leader, Jo Grimond, and the director generals of both the BBC and the Independent Television Authority.

They agreed that, if discovered, they would tell the press they were discussing 'problems of public information in a democracy'. This deliberately bland description was designed to conceal the significance of what was on their agenda. The political academic and granddaddy of TV election coverage, David – now Sir David – Butler, confronted the politicians and broadcasters with a direct challenge to what he called their policy of 'comprehensive omission'. He told them that if 'honest impartiality' meant avoiding anything that could possibly have 'even an indirect impact on the outcome' of an election, 'suicide would be the only route to impartiality'.[4]

Perhaps surprisingly, the politicians proved to be 'more buccaneering', in Rab Butler's words, than the broadcasters. Some at the summit urged caution; others said the only choice was between 'a blackout and a spotlight'. As so often in the history of television and politics, it was the buccaneers who would be proved right.

Weeks after the summit a by-election was called in the Lancashire town of Rochdale. The BBC announced that it would continue with its policy of not covering the campaign at all – a policy of journalistic suicide. Broadcast executives still feared they could be imprisoned for breaching the Representation of the People Act, which spelled out the limits on campaign expenditure. Although the law made it clear that newspaper coverage would not count as a campaign expense, no one had thought to include television at the time the legislation was drawn up.

ITN decided to take the risk. They sent their reporter George Fitch to interview 'the man and woman in the street'. A bus conductor was asked for his views about international affairs. 'Well,' he mused, 'the atom bomb seems to have something in it.'[5] Thus was born the political vox pop, a staple of TV election reports ever since.

Even ITN stopped short of interviewing the candidates themselves. Granada TV, the ITV station in the north-west of England, was bolder: it staged a debate between them. This produced a record turnout – over 80 per cent – on polling day and the *Daily Mail* declared: 'Television is established as the new hub of the hustings.'

No one went to jail and shortly afterwards the law was changed, reassuring broadcasters that covering elections was not illegal.

In the wake of the battle of Rochdale, then, the 1959 general election was on course to be the first to be properly reported. Provided, of course, things went to plan. They did not. Michael Brunson, former political editor of ITN, once described TV news as 10 per cent journalism and 90 per cent logistics. The first week of the first-ever television election was a textbook example of what he meant. ITN's coverage was almost wrecked by logistical problems or, to give them their proper name, cock-ups.

On the opening night of his re-election campaign prime minister Harold Macmillan was seen and heard delivering a witty speech in front of hundreds of cheering supporters at Manchester's Free Trade Hall. His challenger, Hugh Gaitskell, was, by contrast, merely shown silently scurrying along a station platform in London. In the days when cans of film had to be carried by road to the nearest TV studio to be processed before being piped down to London for editing, the problem was one of location. Macmillan had been speaking a walk away from a TV studio whereas the ITN cameraman who filmed Gaitskell's speech in Cardiff had to race his footage to Bristol. He did not make it in time. Labour, who'd always taken the view that commercial TV meant Conservative TV, were not best pleased.

The following night ITN promised to make up for this disaster. Two cameras and special TV lights were installed for the Labour leader's speech just down the road in Battersea. Unfortunately, they overloaded the electrical circuit and blew the lights in the entire building. Gaitskell carried on by candlelight, but his effort didn't make for usable television.

By the third night of the campaign ITN's editor, Geoffrey Cox, knew he had to get it right. Imagine his reaction when he was told that the dispatch rider carrying the footage of Gaitskell had skidded on ice, the can of film had broken open and the contents were ruined. Cox did the only thing he could do: he phoned a friend.[6] The head of BBC News, a former colleague, agreed to help by lending him some of the corporation's footage. He was, no doubt, keen to ensure for everyone's benefit that the first televised election wasn't the last.

Before becoming prime minister Macmillan had starred in his party's early election broadcasts, once being sent, after interminable run-throughs, to rest on a bunk bed in a darkened room before the live transmission. He complained that it reminded him of being in the trenches during the First World War. Having emerged unscathed he soon proved that an old dog could learn new tricks. For the final PEB of the 1959 election campaign he posed in front of a grand desk next to a large globe: the elder statesman musing about Britain's place in the world. 'Look at this globe. How sad it is to feel that it's divided into the two great groups – communists and the free world; East and West.'

Almost 5 million people watched the broadcast, including Labour's veteran warrior Nye Bevan, who was sitting in his sister's house in Tredegar. He turned to her and said: 'You know, we've lost the election.' He was right. Macmillan secured not just victory but a hundred-seat majority. The prime minister who had been lampooned in a cartoon portraying him as 'Supermac', a flying superhero in a cape, had simply embraced the image as a compliment. This old, shambling Edwardian gent had not simply survived television's torture chamber, he had used it to make his political opponents suffer. Not bad going for a man who joked at a dinner for TV's twenty-fifth anniversary:

> I hardly ever see a television programme. Now, that is not just the stock boast of those who like to feel intellectually superior. On the contrary, I say it with a feeling of resentment and deprivation. Not for me the joys of half-hours with Hancock. No Dixon. No Maigret. No Chiselbury. No Lone Ranger. No Lenny the Lion. It isn't actually that we can't afford a set at Number 10, but the trouble is my employers never actually give me an evening off.[7]

It's a far cry from political leaders these days, most of whom have at least pretended to be familiar with those facing elimination from this week's X Factor or Strictly.

Even if the prime minister wasn't a viewer of Dixon of Dock Green, television was coming of age. In 1958 the number of applications for radio licences (under 6.5 million) had been surpassed for the first time by the demand for those covering both TV and radio – just over 8 million.[8] That figure would climb to over 9, then over 10, then over 11 million in the next three years. By 1962 more than half the population cited TV as their main news source.

There was, though, still a long way to go in the creation of a televised democracy. In the 1959 election there had been no TV interviews with party leaders and the BBC, ever wary of provoking a row, took off air its popular nightly current-affairs programme *Tonight* and banned politicians from appearing on *Panorama* and *Press Conference*. Furthermore, the House of Commons seemed no closer to admitting cameras or microphones.

Robin Day at ITN continued to try to escape from the straitjacket politicians had forced upon broadcasters. In 1956 he had brought alive the crucial debate over Suez in an unscripted seven-minute report – about five times the length of a typical 'live' report on the news today. He would rewrite the straight factual parliamentary reports sometimes drafted for him by ITN's sub-editors and put his own stamp on them. When the minister of health announced that two known cancer-producing agents had been found in tobacco smoke, Day personalized his script: 'After lunch today I stubbed out a cigarette and went into the House of Commons press gallery to hear – with some apprehension – what the minister of health had to say about smoking and cancer.'[9]

None of this could, of course, be a substitute for witnessing the debate itself; for hearing the arguments at first hand, for seeing ministers and their shadows sitting glumly or shaking their heads or shouting at their opponents; for the 'hear-hears' of MPs or the 'order, order!' of the Speaker trying to calm proceedings. MPs could have followed the lead given to them by Her Majesty the Queen who, in 1958, agreed to allow the BBC to film the State Opening of Parliament and the

Queen's Speech in which she hailed this new openness.

> Today, for the first time, this ceremony is being watched not
> only by those who are present in this chamber, but by many
> millions of my subjects . . . Outwardly they will see the
> pageantry and the symbols of authority and state; but in their
> hearts they will surely respond to the spirit of hope and
> purpose which inspires our parliamentary tradition.

This experiment was enough to convince some that televising
Parliament was the way forward. Among them was one of
the Labour party's giants, Nye Bevan. In the debate on the
following year's Queen's Speech, he warned his colleagues of
the 'considerable gulf growing between this House and the
nation . . . There is a lessening interest in our discussions. We
are not reaching the country to the extent that we did.'

Having tried and ultimately failed to preserve the Commons
as the sole forum for national debate, MPs were now struggling
to recapture the ground they'd lost to the broadcasters. Bevan
proposed that 'we should seriously consider re-establishing
intelligent communication between the House of Commons
and the electorate as a whole'.

He argued, wrongly as it turned out, that allowing cameras
in would end 'the most humiliating state of affairs' whereby
TV and radio producers – or what he called 'unrepresent-
ative persons' – were able to pick and choose which
politicians and which political views were heard. (Since news
bulletins are only half an hour long, TV and radio folk
carried on picking which politicians to broadcast even after
microphones and cameras were finally admitted.) The
Hansard report of what turned out to be Bevan's last speech
before his death from cancer reveals that his call for a serious

investigation into the technical possibilities of televising parliamentary proceedings was greeted with the shout 'Oh no, Nye.'

When scandal rocked Macmillan's government in 1963 demands for cameras in Parliament increased and grew louder. The secretary for war, John Profumo, was alleged to have shared a bed with a call girl who'd also slept with the Soviet defence attaché. The Profumo affair was threatening to bring down the prime minister but, as with Suez, radio listeners and TV viewers were unable to follow the debate about the minister's behaviour at first hand. Robin Day was forced to present a TV programme in the rain from outside Parliament on College Green. These days the green is often filled with tents and platforms on big parliamentary occasions – the Budget, the Queen's Speech and so on – to enable the media to interview politicians and other commentators as well as relaying to the public MPs' speeches in the Commons. Back then the interviews were all they had.

An angry Robin Day wrote a pamphlet making the case for televising Parliament. He argued for a nightly TV equivalent of Hansard, which would, he claimed, 'develop into the most influential forum of public affairs on television'. He was flattering MPs and underplaying the significant role he himself already had in national life.

His argument did not convince Labour's chief whip, Herbert Bowden, who described the idea of screening Parliament as 'frightening' and predicted that 'the whole atmosphere of the chamber would change'. For example, Bowden reasoned, 'when an important statement is imminent we are often apprehensive and giggle and behave rather like schoolgirls . . . it is right that members of Parliament should react in that way'.

It was a novel and brave argument to make: that Parliament must, at all costs, preserve the right of MPs to giggle like schoolgirls, unseen and unheard by their constituents.

Day's pamphlet ended with a question: 'How long will it be before television takes its inevitable and rightful place in the Press Gallery? It cannot be long now.' It was, in fact, to be another two and a half decades.

Politicians aren't like most of us. Now, as fifty years ago, they don't watch much, if any, television. Few people attracted to the long hours of campaigning, debating and manoeuvring have the time or the inclination to spend their evenings in front of soaps, sitcoms or talent shows. When they do watch TV they tend to pick news, current affairs or documentaries. The result is that, all too often, they complain about some perceived slight on a current-affairs programme while completely ignoring the more popular output that has a far more significant influence on the public.

The early 1960s saw the birth of TV soap opera and satire – both capable of shaping opinion as much, if not more, than news and current affairs. The *Daily Mirror*'s verdict on the first episode of ITV's *Coronation Street* in 1960 was that it was 'doomed from the outset'. A year later it was Britain's top-rated show and by 1964 it had more than 20 million regular viewers. Over half a century later it is still pulling them in. *That Was the Week That Was*, the BBC's first and best-ever satirical TV show, was on our screens for only a little over a year between November 1962 and December 1963. It had a much smaller audience than the *Street* but together they captured the spirit of the times: rebellious, non-deferential and anti-establishment. Harold Macmillan and his Tory successor, Alec Douglas-Home, were swept aside by that spirit. Another Harold, Labour's new leader, Harold Wilson, came to embody it.

That Was the Week That Was, or *TW3*, as it became known, was fronted by an angry young man called David Frost. David, who was to become a pillar of the establishment himself, recalled how the show tapped into 'a feeling of impatience, a feeling of wanting something like a demolition job . . . a feeling of the country wanting a change. Macmillan was in the forefront of what people felt they'd had enough of.'[10]

The programme mocked the prime minister and what it saw as his delusion that Britain was still great. In the week when the US secretary of state, Dean Acheson, made his famous claim that Britain had lost its Empire but had yet to find a role, *TW3* ran a parody of Macmillan phoning President Kennedy in the White House. 'About this Acheson thing, Jack . . . It's Harold here. Harold Macmillan. M-a-c-m . . .' The message couldn't have been clearer: Macmillan and Britain were irrelevant. The fact that the prime minister had, in fact, built a good relationship with America's new young president, who called him 'Uncle Harold', was lost on the electorate.

As the Profumo affair sapped the government of its authority at home, on the international stage the humiliation of Suez was followed by De Gaulle's veto of Britain's application to join the EU. Macmillan retired believing, wrongly, that he was terminally ill. *TW3* marked his exit with the prime minister, impersonated by the comic Willie Rushton, singing 'The Party's Over'.

The Tories now faced a new opponent: the first-ever political leader not merely to learn the techniques of television or to smarten himself up to appear on it but to forge an image especially for television. His name was Harold Wilson.

When Wilson became leader of the opposition in 1963 he calculated, as Tony Blair did three decades later, that he could use television to overcome the prejudice of the right-wing press. 'Most of the press were against us. And if the right-wing press were tempted to say about me, "This is a terrible man, looks like an ogre, his voice is terrible," then you go on television and the people say, "Oh look, he is an ordinary chap like the rest of us." '[11]

It was not hard to appear ordinary next to Macmillan, who allowed himself to be filmed shooting grouse, surrounded by dogs, ladies in headscarves and staff driving Land Rovers, and who looked and sounded as if he'd never left the grouse moors. However, Wilson and his advisers were not content simply to rely on the ready-made contrast between him and his aristocratic Tory opponents. In the words of the influential Labour thinker and political diarist Richard Crossman, they set about 'creating a political image'. Wilson once told the Irish prime minister: 'A political leader should try to look, particularly on television, like a family doctor – the kind of man who inspires trust by his appearance as well as by his soothing words.'[12]

Wilson's early attempts to look like a family doctor were marred by his habit of raising his fist to make a point. On television it appeared very threatening. His closest adviser, Marcia Williams (later Baroness Falkender), concluded that something must be done but instead of simply telling him to stop she provided him with a prop: a pipe which he could grasp in his fist, transforming his belligerent hand-waving into a gesture that seemed somehow reassuring. Wilson was, in fact, a cigar-smoker but, thanks to Marcia, he was only ever seen in public with a pipe. It had other uses, too. In interviews he could fill it or light it or tap it as a way of defusing tension or buying himself time. Williams recalled:

> He knows when he lights his pipe that he is lighting his pipe
> to make a relaxed break in the performance. He often rubs his
> nose to give himself a chance to think out the end of the
> sentence he has already begun. But the image which comes
> across is completely clear; it was and is the image of the
> extraordinary ordinary man: the first in this country people
> had seen reach the top in politics.[13]

So powerful a symbol did Wilson's TV prop become that
Labour would go on to produce election posters bearing
nothing but the image of a smoking pipe.

The extraordinary ordinary man's image was carefully
cultivated. Wilson, the son of an industrial chemist from
Huddersfield, wanted the electorate to know that you could
take the boy out of Yorkshire but not Yorkshire out of the
boy. So he kept his accent, unlike many grammar-school boys
who won scholarships to Oxford. He drank beer and smoked
his pipe in public while drinking brandy and smoking cigars
in private. He boasted that he liked HP Sauce and preferred
his salmon tinned to smoked. For a profile on *Panorama* he
was filmed mending a bike in the front room. Asked what he
watched on TV, his answer was, of course, *Coronation Street*.
In an era when foreign holidays were beginning to become
affordable for the masses, the Wilson family were filmed
spending their holidays in the Scilly Isles, just off Cornwall.

Wilson was, in truth, not quite as ordinary as he made out.
His politically active father had taken him to have his photograph taken in front of Number 10 Downing Street at the
age of eight. At twenty-one he had been one of Oxford
University's youngest dons of the twentieth century; by

thirty-one he had been appointed president of the board of trade by Clement Attlee, becoming the twentieth century's youngest Cabinet minister. He was, though, learning from the mistakes made by his predecessor Hugh Gaitskell, another academic, whom he criticized for 'adopting more the manner of an Oxford don explaining economic theory' than 'seeking to identify himself in homely terms with the electorate'.[14]

Wilson wanted to be seen not just as ordinary but as modern, in contrast to the old-fashioned, out-of-touch Tories who'd been in power for thirteen years. One symbol of that modernity was his Gannex raincoat which, according to Marcia Williams, 'stood out because it was different from anything [people had] ever seen a leading politician wear'. Made in Yorkshire by a friend, Joseph Kagan, later ennobled by Wilson, the Gannex became so fashionable that it was soon being sported by leaders around the world, from Chairman Mao to the Queen.

The new leader of the opposition was soon hailed by the media as a 'British Kennedy'. It was quite a compliment since the young president had dazzled not just America but the rest of the world, too. On a visit to the White House soon after he became Labour leader, Wilson tried to reinforce the link, declaring: 'I think there is a worldwide feeling, not so much for young men as such but for young ideas . . . some of the older gentlemen are perhaps not so well fitted to that.'[15]

Kennedy, Wilson later said, had 'shifted the whole idea to a younger generation', ending the tradition that leaders should be in their sixties, which showed, he added tartly, that you could have 'a head of government not half dead'.[16] Wilson and his team of advisers studied the techniques used in J.F.K.'s 1960 election campaign, examined their crafting of what would now be called soundbites and aped his rhetoric. The British political establishment's long infatuation with American campaign techniques had begun. Ever since, campaign strategists, speechwriters and ad men have pored over the commercials, the speeches, and the photo opportunities of US elections in enormous detail in the hope of smuggling whatever they can into their own plans without anyone accusing them of plagiarism.

In the run-up to the 1964 election Wilson posed with four young men who were destined to become almost as famous as J.F.K. He presented the Beatles with an award from the Variety Club of Great Britain and was seen on television joking with the Fab Four. Paul McCartney, thanking the organizers for the silver heart he'd been awarded, remarked: 'I still think you should have given one to good old Mr Wilson.'

A Labour election rally at Wembley was sprinkled with a little bit of television glamour thanks to the presence of the actress Vanessa Redgrave and Harry H. Corbett, star of the BBC comedy hit *Steptoe and Son*. Wilson closed the rally with a speech that drew inspiration from J.F.K., offering voters a choice between 'standing still, clinging to the tired philosophy of a day that is gone or moving forward . . . to a dynamic, expanding, confident and, above all, purposive Britain'.

Wilson had come to regard the television camera as 'my friend, not my enemy'. Politicians who lack self-confidence in front of the camera resent its requirements – the need to speak in crisp soundbites; to look down the lens, not at their notes; to walk towards or stand in particular spots. All of these Wilson mastered. He demonstrated a particular talent for delivering his message exactly on cue for television audiences when news bulletins switched live to one of his campaign speeches.

In those days news viewers were likely to be offered more of a soundmeal than a soundbite – several minutes of live orating from a party leader at a public meeting. Wilson quickly developed a technique for maximizing the impact of his airtime. Beginning his speech long before the news was ready for him, he would saunter through a few points, encouraging hecklers with his slow pace and entertaining the crowd with his sharp ripostes, until the cameras were turned on. He had an arrangement with the TV producers travelling with him. If he was unable to see a clock or the red light on top of the cameras, or to spot a signal from his own aides, they would throw a handkerchief in the air to signal that they were cutting to his speech. Immediately he would abandon his gentle knockabout with the crowd to stare down the lens, adopt a tone of gravitas and serve up his pre-prepared message to the unsuspecting viewers.

In his memoirs ITN's editor Geoffrey Cox is full of admiration for the way the Labour leader handled the demands of live television. '[When] our titles came up on the screen Harold Wilson's whole manner changed. He dropped the attitude of the jesting debater and, almost as if he had changed his very garb, became in a flash the serious statesman.'[17]

Wilson's Tory opponent in the 1964 election was hopelessly unsuited to the job of leading a country restless for change. The 14th Earl of Home hadn't, initially at least, even wanted the job. After Harold Macmillan's sudden retirement through illness, he, too, had been picked to do it by the Conservatives' 'magic circle' – the old boys' club who chose leaders in the days before party elections and, just as significantly, blocked those they didn't like. Home had to disclaim his peerage in order to leave the House of Lords and enter the Commons as plain old Sir Alec Douglas-Home. For two weeks he was prime minister but not a member of either House as he waited to be elected to the Commons in a by-election in a safe Tory seat left vacant by the death of its MP.

Home became another target for a demolition job by *That Was the Week That Was*, and David Frost was even more savage to him than he had been to Macmillan. He dressed up as Home's Victorian predecessor, Benjamin Disraeli, to deliver this scathing verdict on the new prime minister.

> Your acceptance of the Queen's commission to form an administration has proved and will prove an unmitigated catastrophe for the Conservative party, the constitution, for the nation and for yourself. The art of statesmanship consists as much in foreseeing as in doing. You, my lord, in your sixty years have foreseen nothing. As you yourself have confessed in the past, you lack many of the basic qualifications for political leadership at this time. You know little of economics, little of all the manifold, complex needs of a country that has become tired in a technological age and nothing of the lives of the ordinary people who must now, without consent, submit as your subjects. You have foreseen nothing; you are qualified to do only . . . nothing.

Today television comedy carries its fair share of sneers and putdowns but it is hard to imagine an attack so pointed, so direct or indeed, so political being aired today. *TW3* didn't survive for much longer. The BBC's director general knew it spelled trouble and took it off the air well in advance of the 1964 election. The damage to Sir Alec, however, had been done.

Home could not match Wilson's ease with the camera. He would never have thought of adopting the Labour leader's 'tricks of the trade', let alone been capable of pulling them off. His world was that of the gentlemen's club, the dinner jacket and the wireless. Years later he told Michael Cockerell: 'I never dreamed of holding the position of prime minister. Had I done so, much as I would have detested the exercise, I would have taken the trouble to master the techniques of television.'[18]

For a short while Home played up his naïveté and lack of television nous, trying to make a virtue of it in comparing himself favourably with the tricksy Harold Wilson. In his first broadcast as prime minister he declared: 'No one need expect any stunts from me – just plain speaking.' He and his advisers kidded themselves that the public would equate dull and wooden with plain-speaking and straight. It was the same comforting but hopelessly optimistic view taken by some of those close to John 'I am what I am' Major and 'Not flash, just Gordon' Brown.

Home's problem was not simply that he was no TV natural but also that he had what these days would jokingly be called a good face for radio. One side was partially paralysed and the rest tended to freeze when he spoke direct to camera. The prime minister once asked a TV make-up artist whether she could make him look better than he normally did on TV. 'I look rather scraggy, like a ghost,' he complained.

She replied that no she could not and, when pressed, explained rather uncharitably: 'You have a head like a skull.'

'Does not everyone have a head like a skull?'

'No.'

One of Home's favourite jokes on the campaign trail was to

tell the crowd he was glad they'd come to see him in person so he could show them that 'I'm not exactly what they make you look like on a TV screen'. His aides dragged him from one campaign stop to the next in the belief – perhaps in the hope – that if enough people saw him in the flesh the country would discount his staid, old-fashioned, uncharismatic television image. It was, of course, a delusion but election campaigns often see optimism triumph over realism. At one rally the TV cameras lingered on a banner that read: 'Who exhumed you?' Perhaps they should have seen that as an omen.

Yet the race remained too close to call even in the final week. Both leaders, remembering the impact Macmillan had made in 1959, placed huge significance on their final election broadcasts – which, back then, could secure vast audiences. Even by this stage Sir Alec had no experience with what used to be called a teleprompter. The TV professional hired to produce the broadcast was determined that the prime minister would speak directly to viewers without having to look down at his notes. The producer decided that no man could learn a fifteen-minute script by heart so instead Sir Alec memorized and recorded his speech in a series of two-minute chunks with the joins covered by editing shots. This painstaking process took two whole days – and it was still a failure.

Wilson, on the other hand, had mastered the technique and ended his broadcast with a final powerful appeal: 'If the past belongs to the Tories, the future belongs to us – all of us.'

The Labour leader was still far from certain of victory and panicked when he saw the TV listings for election day. The BBC had scheduled its most popular programme, *Steptoe and Son*, just an hour before the close of polls. Wilson feared that watching Harry H. Corbett could prove more appealing to traditional Labour voters than leaving the sofa to go out and vote for Harold Wilson.

Confronted by the horrifying prospect of the TV star he'd chosen to speak at his election rally unwittingly robbing him of victory, Wilson called the BBC's director general, Sir Hugh Carleton Greene. He implied that this was part of a 'BBC plot'[19] and broke an agreement that no 'particularly glamorous programmes' should be aired which might distract voters from performing their democratic duty. Greene asked him what he suggested was broadcast instead. The reply was 'Oedipus Rex'. Although the BBC didn't take his advice to air a Greek tragedy it did agree to put *Steptoe* back by an hour, a move which, Wilson told Greene, 'may be worth a dozen or so seats to me'.

If he was right that one decision alone was enough to deliver Labour's win. Election night 1964 was a long and anxious one for Harold Wilson. With the result still far from certain he was interviewed on the BBC's election results programme and asked how he felt things were going. 'I think I wouldn't go further than to say the results are moderately encouraging.'

'Well, do you feel like a prime minister?' asked the enterprising BBC reporter.

Wilson was even quicker-witted. 'Quite honestly, I feel like a drink,' he replied.

With a slender parliamentary majority of four – which in the months to come would be reduced to just one – he would need many more drinks to get through the difficult times ahead.

The eve-of-election row with the BBC was one small sign of the turbulence to come. In opposition Harold Wilson had grown used to being given favourable coverage and getting his way with broadcasters. He liked television and television liked him, but all that was to change when he became prime minister. Like so many of his successors, he took it personally when the news focused on the bad rather than the good. Hugh Carleton Greene observed: 'Harold Wilson thought he had money in the bank with the BBC but when it came to cash the cheque, it bounced.'[20]

Wilson's chief whip, Edward Short, revealed in his memoirs that the prime minister frequently phoned in with complaints about BBC programmes, in particular the newspaper review broadcast on the *Today* programme, which he called 'a daily party political programme on behalf of the Conservatives'[21] – a view later to be echoed by Alastair Campbell on Tony Blair's behalf.

Some of Wilson's accusations of bias over the years that followed were bizarre. Newsreaders on Radio 1, the BBC's pop-music station established in 1967, were, he believed, delivering 'news items with an anti-Labour bias'. The BBC was deliberately excluding his wife Mary from their pictures so as to avoid embarrassing the new opposition leader, Edward Heath, a bachelor. He even passed on a letter from a constituent complaining that the corporation did not show enough programmes about angling.

Most of his views were kept private at the time, recorded only by the diarists of the Wilson era. Tony Benn noted 'a twenty-minute rant about the bias of the BBC against him personally';[22] Dick Crossman 'an extraordinary outburst about the wicked political bias of the BBC compared with the honesty of commercial television'.[23] Crossman said of Wilson: 'He is obsessed with the BBC, and this and his obsession with leaks are his most outstanding weaknesses as leader.'[24]

There were occasionally public shows of Wilson's sensitivity. Acknowledging the applause of his party before delivering a conference speech he declared: 'Thank you for what the BBC, if they are true to their normal form, will tonight describe as a hostile reception.'

Wilson's transition from opposition to government had convinced him that he should no longer be treated as a mere politician or party leader. As the nation's premier, he was entitled to respect and deference. Like so many British prime ministers, he compared himself with the leaders of our closest ally, the United States, and our nearest rival, France. He came to envy the status of their presidents, forgetting, of course, that they were both directly elected heads of state whereas the British prime minister is the head of government – a position held or lost according to the whim of his party.

What Wilson particularly envied was a president's right to broadcast to his people without the prospect of a balancing speech being granted to the leader of the opposition. After Eden's row with the BBC over its decision to allow Gaitskell to respond on Suez, the rules had been changed. The BBC now had complete discretion over whether to 'invite' the prime minister to address the nation (in reality to accede to his request) and whether such a broadcast merited a response. The guardian of the rules was Grace Wyndham Goldie, who insisted: 'The right of reply is a national safeguard against a kind of dictatorship and a hogging of the microphone by the leader of the party in power.'

With another election certain before too long the BBC had to be sensitive to the danger that they were being used by Wilson to shore up his precarious political position. On his first day in office he was invited to deliver a 'ministerial' and sought to reassure the country that he could govern with a wafer-thin majority. A few days afterwards he was given another, to explain his decision to put a surcharge on imports. When *Panorama* requested an interview a couple of months later to *ask* the prime minister about the government's emergency economic measures, he refused, offering instead to broadcast an appeal direct from the programme without anwering any questions – a 'ministerial' in disguise. The BBC declined. Wilson was furious.

He protested that his government was being given fewer ministerial broadcasts than its Conservative predecessors. Opposition leader Edward Heath mocked him, pointing out that most of the Conservative broadcasts had been made on the radio and many had simply been to urge people to post early for Christmas. In Wilson's first eighteen months in power he made six ministerial broadcasts and was inter-viewed five times on *Panorama*.[25]

The satirist John Bird parodied him addressing the nation: 'It's more than a day since I last spoke to you. I'm sure you are wondering what I did since teatime yesterday.' The *Daily Mirror*'s cartoonist, Franklin, produced an image of Ted Heath being tortured on a rack by the BBC under the caption: 'We're trying to appease Wilson.'

Wilson was the first prime minister to set for himself the ambition that all today's political leaders now share. He wanted to be a constant presence on TV but at a time and in a place of his choosing without the distraction of awkward questions. In other words, he wanted to broadcast regular televised press releases. He clashed with a BBC slowly freeing itself from the mindset that political broadcasting was whatever politicians were happy to see or hear broadcast. However, it still occasionally allowed itself to be taken for a ride.

On the eve of Ted Heath's first conference as Conservative

leader in October 1965, Wilson demanded and was granted a ministerial broadcast. Its ostensible purpose was an appeal to the Rhodesian prime minister, Ian Smith – at the time almost as big a figure in British politics as he was in his own country – who had been threatening for some weeks to unilaterally declare independence from Britain. Its real purpose was to use the power of his office to drag the media spotlight away from his opponent.

The prime minister's spin-doctor (who then bore the more reassuring job title of press adviser) boasted that as a result 'no one was interested in what the Conservatives were going to say'. Wilson knew that he was robbing Heath of his last good chance to dominate the headlines before an election the prime minister had already secretly planned for the following spring. Just to make sure, though, he flew to Balmoral to see the Queen on the day after the broadcast. Speculation that he might be about to ask her to dissolve Parliament wiped out another day on which the Tories expected to have the news to themselves. It was a trick that a future Labour leader, Gordon Brown, would try to emulate by visiting troops in Iraq on the first day of the Conservative conference of 2007.

Perhaps inevitably, when Wilson did actually call the 1966 election tension with the BBC escalated. He had subjects he wanted to avoid at all costs: Europe, or the Common Market as it was then known, and relations with the unions. The BBC's newly liberated and confident journalists were equally determined to ensure that those were the two issues Wilson did address.

Wilson was stung when the BBC started referring to him not as prime minister but as the leader of the Labour party, in line with their previous practice at elections. What was more, they pushed hard for a televised leaders' debate modelled on the one staged between Kennedy and Nixon in 1960. They made the mistake of taking Wilson at his word. Publicly he expressed enthusiasm for a TV showdown. In reality he had no intention of doing anything that might elevate the status of his opponent.

When the leader of the Labour party took his customary interest in the election night TV schedules the BBC was ready for him. He asked the director general to move the hit spy thriller *The Man from U.N.C.L.E.* Greene refused. This time, though, Wilson's future didn't depend on the corporation's acquiescence. He was re-elected with a majority not of four but of only four short of a hundred – a landslide. The prime minister now had real power to wield, something he was not slow to recognize.

On the morning after his stunning victory Wilson decided to teach the BBC 'a lesson they won't forget in a hurry'. He had agreed to give his first interview since the confirmation of the result live from the train bringing him back to London from his constituency. This had never been done before, and even these days it would pose a few technical challenges, as anyone who has tried making a call from a train can testify. It involved installing a specially built studio in one of the train carriages and identifying one precise point on the route, in Buckinghamshire, where a receiving dish could be positioned to overlook the railway track. But Wilson didn't merely refuse to do the interview. He poured salt into the BBC's wounds by seeking out the man from ITN and giving him an exclusive taped interview instead.

Journalists don't take defeat lying down. The BBC sent their new recruit from ITV current affairs, Desmond Wilcox, to Euston station to meet Wilson off the train, instructing him to stand apart from other BBC staff. They were hoping

Wilson would not have remembered that Wilcox had switched sides and would give him an interview as well. The ploy worked, though, of course, once Downing Street discovered what had happened it did nothing for the warmth of their relations with the corporation. Not long afterwards the BBC's chairman and director general were summoned to see the prime minister at Number 10. So secret was the meeting that they were slipped in via the Cabinet office rather than through the front door. Wilson told them that he had been persuaded to 'break off relations with the BBC' by what he described as the corporation's manoeuvrings. The DG felt forced to deny that he was presiding over any sort of 'Tory plot' at the BBC.

Handling Wilson must have required more than a degree of patience. Few politicians since Machiavelli had been as poorly placed to accuse other people of 'manoeuvring'. He loved the twists and turns of the political game, or what he used to call 'the circus'. He used to chuckle with his aides over a cigar and a brandy, comparing his ups and downs to the storyline of a detective novel. Real life, as so often, was much less plausible than fiction.

Every good detective story has to have a dame. In the story of Harold Wilson she was Marcia Williams. The influence and the power of Wilson's private and political secretary and gatekeeper terrified even the prime minister, not to mention fellow members of his 'kitchen cabinet', who believed she had some secret hold on him (rumours of an affair have persisted though have never been substantiated). So nervous of Marcia were Wilson, his senior ministers and civil servants that they conducted some of their most important private conversations in the gents' loo a few steps from the Cabinet room, the only place where they felt safe from her all-seeing eye.

Every good detective story needs a crime, too, and, hard though it is to believe, Wilson's personal doctor, Joe Stone, did talk of committing one, in order to solve the 'Marcia problem'. Both Wilson's press secretary, Joe Haines, and his close adviser Bernard Donoghue claim that the doctor spoke of a plan to 'dispose of her' or 'put her down'. But since they made these allegations after Joe Stone's (unsuspicious) death, he was never given the opportunity either to deny them or to insist that he had only been joking.

When politicians complain that reporters are obsessed with gossip, tittle-tattle and speculation, that story is a salutary reminder that often we don't know the half of what really goes on.

Another reason why Wilson liked to hold discussions in the gents' was his fear that he was being spied on by the security services. Shirley Williams once told me about a remarkable encounter she had with the prime minister when she first joined the Cabinet. 'Harold always thought that there was a bug in the Cabinet room . . . He said, "That's to hear our conversations." He pointed to something in the ceiling and it might have been a microphone – God knows what it was. He thought it was a bug. I went out of there thinking, the prime minister's paranoic.'[26]

'Paranoid' is a word often used about Wilson, even by those who admired him. Of course, as the saying goes, just because you're paranoid, it doesn't mean they're not out to get you, and years later evidence did emerge that a section of the intelligence service had, indeed, been trying to do him down. The longer he was in office, the more Wilson became obsessed with the idea that the whole establishment was plotting his downfall. And the BBC was, in his mind, very much part of that establishment.

In contrast the prime minister made it clear that he loved what he called 'our channel', ITV, with its 'absolutely scrupulous impartiality'. Some on the left had been deeply suspicious of the idea of a commercial channel from the out-set, assuming that any profit-making broadcaster must automatically be Tory inclined. Not Wilson. He liked ITV not just because he believed it dealt fairly with him but also because it was watched by 'our people'– the working-class voters who formed Labour's base.

Denying the BBC interviews and access was one way of putting the corporation in its place. There was another: squeezing its finances. When, in 1966, the BBC asked for an increase in the licence fee – it hadn't gone up for a decade and inflation was eroding its real value – Wilson refused. Furthermore, he initially backed the plans of the minister responsible for the BBC to force the Light Programme, later succeeded by Radio 2, to take some advertising and to set up a new corporation to run what eventually became Radio 1. He knew both ideas were anathema to the BBC.[27]

That minister was Tony Benn. A former BBC producer, he went on, like many ex-members of staff, to become one of the corporation's fiercest critics. In a speech in 1968, sanctioned by Wilson, he attacked its 'enormous accumu-lation of power' and the 'constitutional monarchs who preside in the palatial Broadcasting House'. He argued that a few hundred executives were being permitted to shape public opinion and decide who broadcasted what. As so often, Benn's analysis had more than a grain of truth in it but, as so often, his conclusion revealed his – and Wilson's – real objective: 'Broadcasting is really too important to be left to the broadcasters.'

Tony Benn pursued his theme with me years later when he turned the tables on a series of TV interviewers by inter-rogating them for a Channel 4 programme. He was, as he always is, polite, respectful and inquiring. However, I thought he somewhat gave the game away when he told me off camera that his favourite interviews were with Al Jazeera, the Arabic news channel, which had given him two hours to set out his views on the Iraq War.

Benn and Wilson never did take over the BBC – they knew it would be too divisive and too controversial to try – but their threats had an impact. A cartoon of the time showed the director general holding a pot of paint and adding to the letters BBC to spell out 'Be Bloody Careful'. They did not, however, stop a huge expansion of the corporation: 1967 saw the launch of four new radio stations and the first television channel in Europe to broadcast regularly in colour.

Radio 1 was created as the BBC's answer to the flourishing offshore pirate radio stations that had been attracting listeners in their millions and which were about to be out-lawed. The Light Programme was renamed Radio 2 and concentrated on easy-listening music and light entertainment while the Third Programme and Music Programme were merged to become Radio 3. Finally Radio 4, the successor to the Home Service, was devoted to the spoken word, and coverage of news and current affairs was beefed up. The *Today* programme, previously broadcast in two twenty-minute editions after the seven and eight o'clock news bulletins, was turned into a single two-hour morning pro-gramme. *The World at One* would be followed in the afternoons by the new *PM*.

BBC2 was created after an official report chastised ITV for

its populism and authorized the BBC to set up a second television channel to bring programmes of depth and substance to the masses. At both Broadcasting House and the new Television Centre in Shepherds Bush, the world's first and biggest purpose-built TV studios, the BBC's coat-of-arms proclaimed 'Nation shall speak peace unto nation'. The prime minister seemed to interpret this motto as 'Wilson shall speak unto the nation'. It is ironic, given his theories about BBC 'manoeuvrings', that the single broadcast that damaged his reputation irreparably was one over which he, and not the corporation, had total control.

For more than three years Wilson and his government had fought to resist what others regarded as the inevitable: the devaluation of the pound. On 18 November 1967 he was forced to admit that the fight was at an end. The Bank of England had spent £200 million trying to shore up the pound from its gold and dollar reserves and the government had spent enormous amounts of political capital over the previous few weeks dismissing increasingly feverish speculation.

Wilson, who once described himself as 'an optimist who carries a raincoat', was not a man to admit defeat. Choosing to inform the country of his decision via television before announcing it in Parliament two days later, he ignored advice from his aides and opted to present it not as a failure but as a success and an opportunity.[28] It would, he said, tackle the 'root cause' of Britain's economic problems, allowing the country to 'break out from the straitjacket' of boom-and-bust economics.

However, there was one passage in particular that would haunt him for ever. Telling the people that they must 'face a new situation', he said: 'From now on the pound abroad is worth 14 per cent or so less in terms of other currency. That doesn't mean, of course, that the pound here in Britain, in your pocket or purse or in your bank, has been devalued.'

It was a classic piece of political positioning. The prime minister was explaining that he had devalued the pound but that, somehow, miraculously, he had managed to do so without devaluing the pound in *your* pocket or purse. His political purpose was clear: he wanted to forestall sudden demands for higher wages. To be fair to him, he did admit later in his broadcast that devaluation meant Britain would have to pay more for its imports and prices were sure to rise, but this caveat came too late. Wilson's key message of reassurance – the 'pound in your pocket' claim – was, taken on its own, fatally misleading.

Any decision to devalue is one of those which makes liars of politicians. Revealing that they are even thinking about it will move markets. So until the moment they are resolved to do it they are obliged to be 'economical with the truth'. John Major encountered the same problem in 1993 when deciding to leave the European Exchange Rate Mechanism. It's a dilemma officials can also face when debating whether to issue a major health warning. The public is, though, not very forgiving when people do the opposite of what they said they would do without then admitting it and apologizing for eating their own words.

When Ted Heath made his reply he accused Wilson of failing to protect the people's money and to keep his word. Heath pointed out that twenty times in the previous thirty-seven months Wilson had denied that he was planning to devalue. As ever, the satirists were even less generous. One mused on the signs that tell you when someone is lying. In some people, he said, it was a nervous tic near the eye, in others a vein on the neck that stood out. 'What's the telltale sign with Harold Wilson?' he asked his audience. 'When you see his lips moving.'

Wilson was apoplectic. He demanded a public apology and threatened to sue for libel not just the BBC but its boss as well. He had personally hired Lord Hill as chairman some months earlier for the express purpose of taming the organization he loathed and ensuring that it stopped behaving like an 'independent empire'.[29] He'd poached Hill from the ITA, boasting that the appointment would 'leave the BBC on its beam end'.[30] Though a Tory – indeed, a former member of Macmillan's Cabinet – Hill was among the 'trade union' of ex-politicians on which Wilson thought he could rely to appreciate his concerns and act on them. He was wrong. Hill had indeed switched sides: he now saw things from the perspective of the BBC. He met the prime minister in his Commons office for a tense summit and persuaded him that suing the man he'd hired would look absurd, not to mention thin-skinned.

After yet another row in 1969 Hill was called into Number 10 for a dressing-down. The official minutes of the meeting record Wilson complaining about 'an endemic situation which was sheer political bias'. Hill assured him there was no conspiracy against him. Wilson accepted this, but only up to a point. He did not accept that the BBC wasn't biased, only that there was no conspiracy, since, he pointed out, conspiracies had to be organized.

Marcia Williams wrote in her memoirs that before one campaign event the BBC had called to tell her they were setting up a 'scaffold for Harold to use'. The remark 'caused amusement, even if we were irritated by the daily necessity of watching every newscast and keeping a continual eye on what the BBC was doing'.[31]

The prime minister, meanwhile, was distraught that the man he'd brought in to impose order on the BBC had gone native. Hill had, in fact, perfectly understood the myopia of his old trade, politics, when dealing with his new one, broadcasting. Years later he said: 'The point about politicians is . . . they regard something that is impartial as biased against them and something that is biased in their favour as beautifully impartial.'

Quite so.

Politicians, of course, can punish those they see as biased – with a row, by threatening their source of funding and by denying them access. At different times Wilson responded with all three. He could not forgive the joke that you could tell he was lying because his lips were moving. He decided to have the last laugh. Wilson's lips were not seen moving on any BBC programme – except for the main news bulletins – for the next fourteen months.

ITV, though, were to be given access beyond their wildest dreams.

'Hello, good evening and welcome to 10 Downing Street,' chirruped David Frost at the beginning of *The Prime Minister and Mrs Wilson at Home*. The programme had the look and feel of *Through the Keyhole*, the game show Frost hosted two decades later. Television's angry young man had switched camps – not just from the BBC to its commercial rival but also from those challenging the powerful to those buttering them up. Prompted by their 'interviewer', Harold and Mary Wilson chatted about how they'd first met, their holidays and their admiration for each other, punctuated by occasional cries of 'How fascinating!' from Frost. Wilson spoke of his wife and family being 'an essential release, relief and inspiration'. There was no need to point out that his

Tory opponent, Ted Heath, had neither wife nor family.

The stars of ITV's hit soap *Coronation Street* were also recruited to bolster the prime minister's working-class credentials. Wilson was filmed on the doorstep of Number 10 with the *Street*'s salt-of-the-earth heroines Elsie Tanner and Annie Walker. In the run-up to the 1970 election he visited the programme's set and sang a duet with the nation's favourite battleaxe, Ena Sharples.

A brilliant campaign, sympathetic television coverage, positive opinion polls and bookmakers' odds of 33-1 all pointed to certain victory. The electorate, however, chose to pay more attention to the grim economic news and elected Heath. Labour had tried to portray the Tories as the failed relics of a bygone age, dubbing them 'yesterday's men' in a controversial advertising campaign. Wilson was soon to find that label being attached to himself and his former Cabinet colleagues by the BBC, triggering a row that made all that had come before seem almost trivial.

Not since Clement Attlee had there been a prime minister less interested in image-building than Ted Heath. After the election, the team of television and advertising professionals who'd helped him to win it were sidelined. During his first hundred days in office the new occupant of Number 10 did not appear on television at all and even cancelled the rental on Wilson's TV set.[32]

When he did decide to use the small screen to speak to the nation he emulated the style of France's President de Gaulle, summoning the press and the cameras for a grand televised address. Heath may not have had the Elysée Palace but he did have the magnificent Lancaster House, with its own Louis XIV interiors, just down the Mall from Buckingham Palace –

a residence so splendid that Queen Victoria is said to have remarked to its owner on one visit, 'I have come from my House to your Palace.' This did little to convince a sceptical electorate that Heath was a man of the people.

Heath had his fair share of clashes with those who cross-examined him on television during his brief but turbulent period in office between 1970 and 1974. He no doubt had Robin Day in mind when he described an interviewer as someone who 'has to make clear to everybody that he is much cleverer than the politician he is interviewing'. However, he rarely complained and did not boycott programmes that upset him, unlike Harold Wilson.

It is testimony to the level of acrimony between Harold Wilson and the BBC that one of the most serious bust-ups in the history of the relationship between politicians and broadcasters occurred when he was in opposition, nursing the wounds of his election beating. The BBC poured salt into those wounds when it decided to make a documentary about how the party's leading figures were coping with defeat. It did not tell them that the programme would be called *Yesterday's Men*, that it would feature satirical songs and cartoons by the brilliant but unforgiving Gerald Scarfe, or that its focus would be on the dent to their ambition and wallets.

The *Radio Times* billing described a profile of half a dozen ministers 'given their cards . . . in an election which upset all the pundits', revealing 'what it's like to be out of office and, in some cases, short of money, prestige, glamour and a chauffeur-driven car'.[33]

Unaware of the programme-makers' plans, Wilson was at first delighted with the filming of his Christmas holidays in the Scilly Isles, where he was seen playing golf, singing 'On Ilkley Moor Baht 'At' in the pub and reading a lesson in church. This, though, was to be no reworking of ITV's sac-charine *The Prime Minister and Mrs Wilson at Home*. The programme's presenter, a young David Dimbleby, was to be a little more challenging than David Frost had been. So much so that Harold Wilson walked out of his interview, demand-ing that the BBC cut the offending section and pledging never to be interviewed by Dimbleby again.

Wilson's rage had been unleashed by a sarcastic question about whether the profits from publishing his memoirs, reported to have been between £100,000 and £250,000, had been of some consolation after he lost office. Wilson was livid. 'Why do you come snooping with these questions? ...You are just repeating press gossip ... This last question and answer are not to be recorded ... I think it is disgraceful – I have never heard such a question. If this film is used or this is leaked then there is going to be a hell of a row.'

It was, of course, leaked and there was a hell of a row, described by the show's editor as 'the biggest and most furious that a television programme in the English language has ever provoked'. Wilson threatened an injunction and libel actions. After a time the BBC buckled and agreed to cut some of the interview. What really damaged the corporation, though, was not the decision itself but how it had been taken. The BBC's governors, who are meant to safeguard its independ-ence, had, for the first time ever, insisted on watching a programme before it was transmitted and had ordered changes. Instead of defending the management and inquiring afterwards into whether they'd carried out their jobs properly, the governors had taken over editorial control at the prompting of a political leader.

The BBC, as it would after other conflicts to come,

asserted that it had learned the necessary lessons and would now carry on without fear or favour. However, the Annan commission into broadcasting found that the rumpus had induced 'caution, lack of direction, touchiness and unsteadiness' at the corporation.

Wilson, meanwhile, went on to disprove the programme's title by defeating Heath in the two elections of 1974. The road to his fourth victory was paved with yet more complaints about the BBC and more evidence of paranoia. He even complained about the show he'd used to promote his first-ever bid for power, *Steptoe and Son*. When the scriptwriters gave his namesake, Harold Steptoe, a girlfriend called Marcia, he was convinced that the BBC were implying he was having an affair with his closest adviser.

On 16 March 1976 Wilson secured his 'greatest political triumph' over the media. It was to be his last. BBC Radio News reported that day: 'We have just heard from our staff at Westminster that the prime minister, Mr Harold Wilson, has resigned. He feels he has been leader of the Labour party for long enough.'

This came as a bolt from the blue. When the prime minister broke the news to the Cabinet, it stunned most of them, let alone the reporters, commentators and pundits, all of whom had been kept in the dark. Wilson's adviser Bernard – now Lord – Donoghue told me that his main objective in deciding how and when to announce his decision had been to defeat the media. Wilson claimed that he was physically and mentally drained and that it had in any case always been his intention to call it a day at sixty. It is not known whether he might already have been aware of the earliest symptoms of the Alzheimer's disease that began to become apparent a few years after his resignation.

At a farewell news conference he referred back to his constructed image of himself as the nation's family doctor: 'They don't need me to stay on as a doctor or a healer.' He then looked round the pack of cameramen and reporters and declared, in priestly tones, 'I forgive you all.'

As Labour leader Wilson had won the people's trust again and again and again and again. His four election victories would not have been possible without his mastery of television.

He was far from the only Labour prime minister to believe that the BBC was biased against him. His successor, Jim Callaghan, shared that view, and Gordon Brown's relationship with the corporation was never easy. When Callaghan paid tribute to a retiring director general, Ian Trethowan, he described him as exactly the sort of person who rose at the BBC, someone 'with a strong sense of principle and [who is] determined a Conservative government is going to win'.

Tom McNally, Callaghan's political adviser and now, ironically, a Lib Dem minister in a Tory-led government, concluded: 'There is always a feeling with Labour governments that the BBC is doing them down, misrepresenting them, angling it against them.'[34]

Wilson was in the vanguard of a new relationship between prime ministers and broadcasters, who now found themselves locked together in a loveless marriage. He sought to control television by one minute giving broadcasters what they so desperately wanted and the next by denying them, alternating between charming them and bullying them. It took a lady to take this approach to the next stage.

No. 613
Friday
14 June '85

40p

14 June 1985

5

THE LADY WHO WAS
FOR TURNING

The raw material wasn't at all promising: an austere appearance, a shrill, upper-class voice and a speaking style that was both bossy and hectoring. One TV reviewer described it as 'the condescending, explanatory whine which treats the squirming interlocutor as an eight-year-old child with personality deficiencies'.[1]

The woman who would dominate our screens for more than a decade, and do her best to dictate what was on them, hated TV and, at first, TV seemed to hate her. Margaret Thatcher was a lone Tory woman who stood out from the sea of grey men. As a mother of two, she should have been able to reach those parts of the electorate that other Conservatives could not reach. As her party's spokesman on education in the 1970 election which pitted Edward Heath against Harold Wilson, she should have been a gift to the admen making the Tories' election broadcasts. She should have been, but she was not. Filmed in a children's playground with happy kids romping in the background, she seemed rather less happy. One of those involved in the filming said Mrs Thatcher looked as if she was afraid one of the children was about to be sick on her dress. In the event she was cut out of the broadcast because of her 'posh voice and false smile. She was ill at ease and looked out of touch.'[2]

In the years that followed Thatcher would change her clothes, her hair, her teeth, her voice and even her manner of delivery. A voice coach from the National Theatre gave her humming exercises and taught her to modify her breathing and to speak from the front of the mouth, not the back of the throat. In a decade she managed to reduce the pitch of her voice by 46 Hz – half the average difference between men's and women's voices.[3]

She was prepared to change anything – except, that is, her beliefs, her values and her policies. The woman who was fanatical about the free market was willing to be repackaged, rebranded and sold like a soap powder. In an era when Tony Blair has paid the price for spin and David Cameron was accused of having his photograph airbrushed, it is hard to imagine a prime minister agreeing, as Mrs Thatcher would do, to appear on a programme called *The Image Makers* and talk unapologetically about what she'd done.

> If you have a good thing to sell, use every single capacity you can to sell it. It is no earthly use having a good thing and no one hearing about it . . . No one can give you an image you don't possess. I think my hair is a little better because it's less fussy. You know that when you're nervous as a woman your voice goes all high-pitched and what you learn is, bring it down, bring it down.

It would be unthinkable today for Cameron to say, 'I wear jeans to make me look less posh and comb over my bald spot,' or Ed Miliband to announce, 'I had my nose sorted not just to deal with apnoea but with a voice some people find annoying.'

Mrs Thatcher's first image-maker was Gordon Reece, one of the admen who'd worked with her in 1970. He had seen something beneath the awkward exterior, the off-putting appearance and the grating voice. More importantly, he'd carried out research which showed that the voters saw something else, too: sincerity and conviction. Reece became Thatcher's TV coach. He helped her to rehearse her television appearances again and again; he made her watch herself on tape until she got it right; he accompanied her to TV studios to keep her calm. Mrs Thatcher had one quality needed by any politician who wants to conquer television: a willingness to learn. She had an answer for those who said she'd reinvented herself to suit the cameras: 'It may sound grittily honourable to refuse to make any concessions but such an attitude . . . is most likely to betray a lack of seriousness about winning power.'[4]

By the time Edward Heath and Harold Wilson had their final showdown in the two elections of 1974 Margaret Thatcher was ready for a starring role. Now her party's environment spokesman, she was actually more prominent in the Conservatives' election broadcasts than Heath himself. That was something he would regret.

The year after Heath was ousted from Downing Street he found himself ousted as party leader, too. Tory leaders were no longer selected by the 'magic circle' of party grandees but elected by Conservative MPs. Though Heath himself had been the first to be chosen in this way he still behaved like the chief whip who had joined Harold Macmillan for a celebratory slice of game pie and champagne after Supermac became prime minister. He believed in privately wooing the electorate. Mrs Thatcher, the outsider who few in the Tory high command took seriously, decided to wow them publicly.

Bravely, she agreed to be filmed for a profile entitled 'Why I Want to be Leader' on ITV's campaigning current-affairs programme *World in Action*. It was a common assumption that the left-leaning production team believed simply putting her on screen would destroy her chances. Nothing could have been further from the truth. Seen chatting sympathetically with workers at a refuse dump and praising their 'quiet dignity', she impressed colleagues used to and frustrated by Heath's cold stiffness. One backbencher thought the broadcast was worth twenty votes. Given that she beat the former prime minister by eleven, even something short of that was more than enough. Heath, who would never forgive her for defeating him, sniffed that when he'd been elected leader ten years before 'we didn't carry on in great television and radio campaigns'.[5] He was not the first man to complain that she had beaten him by not playing by their rules, and he wouldn't be the last.

Thatcher became leader not just by choosing when to appear on TV but when not to do so. After wiping the floor with Heath she still had to overcome four new candidates for the job in a second ballot of Tory MPs. This time, though, she was the clear favourite. On the eve of the ballot, she pulled out of the BBC's *Panorama*, on which she'd agreed to be interviewed alongside her rivals. Reece calculated that absenting herself from the company of four squabbling grey men would only enhance her standing. She did as she was advised, the other candidates appeared on the programme without her, Reece was proved right and Thatcher was unstoppable.

It was not Thatcher or Reece who came up with the epithet that captured the image she embodied. It was a young soldier in the Soviet Union, working as a journalist for the Red Army's newspaper *Red Star* – not a paper widely quoted in the UK until it reported, in January 1976, the call of the new leader of the opposition in Britain for her country to 'wake up' to the Soviet threat. The Russian reporter, Yuri Gavrilov, dubbed her the 'Iron Lady'.

Gavrilov says he was simply making a historical comparison between Mrs Thatcher and Germany's 'Iron Chancellor', Otto von Bismarck. Years later, he told the *Daily Mail*: 'I always found her attractive as a woman. If I hadn't, maybe I would have used a harsher label to describe her. She was possessed with a kind of aristocratic beauty.'[6]

It was typical of her willingness to forge an image that, far from dismissing the nickname as an insult coined by the enemy, Mrs Thatcher embraced it as a compliment, telling Conservatives in her local Finchley constituency:

> I stand before you tonight in my Red Star chiffon evening gown, [laughter, applause] my face softly made up and my fair hair gently waved, [laughter] the Iron Lady of the western world. A Cold War warrior, an amazon philistine, even a Peking plotter. Well, am I any of these things? [No!] Well, yes, if that's how they . . . [laughter] Yes, I am an Iron Lady. After all, it wasn't a bad thing to be an Iron Duke. Yes, if that's how they wish to interpret my defence of values and freedoms fundamental to our way of life.[7]

At the first Prime Minister's Questions (PMQs) after the label was applied a Tory backbencher taunted Harold Wilson that it was better to have an Iron Lady than 'a plasticine man'.

In the future she would do everything she could to reinforce her new image. Everything, that is, except one. As prime minister she vetoed proposals for a pint pot with an Iron Lady shown on one side and the Iron Duke on the other. Fearful, perhaps, of appearing on a million tea towels and teacups, she wrote her firm instructions on a Downing Street memo: 'No permission to be given at all for any goods of any kind.'[8]

Mrs Thatcher and her TV advisers wanted to emphasize the Lady and not just the Iron. They arranged for her to be filmed shopping, cooking and talking about clothes and make-up to underline her femininity and booked appearances on non-political TV programmes where she could show her humanity. On *Jim'll Fix It*, the popular Saturday evening family show, she met a group of schoolchildren who'd asked the host, Jimmy Savile, to 'fix it' for them to meet Mrs Thatcher. 'When I was small I didn't think there could be a woman prime minister,' she told one of them. 'But we hope you're going to fix that, Jimmy!'

The man who would become notorious after his death as the nation's most prolific child-abuser had, in life, been one of its best-loved entertainers and charity fundraisers. He was remarkably close to Mrs Thatcher, lunching with her and her husband Denis at Chequers and celebrating countless New Year's Eves with the Thatchers. In her final year in office she finally overcame the official mutterings about Mr Savile – 'a strange and complex man' – and secured for him the knighthood he craved. The Cabinet secretary, Lord Armstrong, had warned that 'he has made no attempt to deny the accounts in the press about his private life'. This referred not to child abuse but to Savile's sexual conquests which, at the time, were assumed to be legal if distasteful.

*

It didn't take Jim or a television programme to assist Mrs Thatcher in proving her youthful self wrong. It was good, old-fashioned radio that helped fix it for her. Just a few months after she became leader of the opposition in 1975 MPs finally voted to allow the people to hear their representatives speaking in the Commons. Hear, not see: the radio microphones were to be let in, initially on an experimental basis for four weeks.

TV cameras were still considered a step too far, and were rejected by a margin of twelve votes. It would not be until April 1978 that regular radio transmissions began. Nevertheless, the four-week trial provided Mrs Thatcher with an important new platform, albeit a temporary one, on which to prosecute her case against the government.

In the first Prime Minister's Questions ever heard outside the House of Commons, on 10 June 1975, Mrs Thatcher taunted Harold Wilson, asserting that, thanks to soaring inflation, 'the value of the Wilson pound in the pocket has fallen faster than ever before and is now worth less than 80p'. *The Economist* commented: 'She exploited the broadcasting of Parliament . . . by repeatedly prodding Mr Wilson and Mr Healey to do something about the rate of inflation; she realized they knew about it, but the performance heartened her supporters.'

Grandly and, as it turned out, in vain, the magazine went on to warn: 'She should ration her scoring of cheap points over the prime minister at Question Time. It may excite the fourth-form element on her back benches but, if it is overdone or highlights trivial issues, it will not impress the BBC's listening millions.'

When Harold Wilson retired as prime minister in April

1976 the Jim she now needed to fix it for her to get to Number 10 was his replacement, Jim Callaghan. The new occupant at Downing Street was comfortable with television and television was comfortable with him. As a young politician he'd featured regularly as a panellist on *In the News* before going on to hold the three great offices of state: home secretary, foreign secretary and chancellor of the exchequer.

On his first day as prime minister Callaghan ended a direct broadcast with a reassuring smile and an invitation to the people to 'join me, join all of us in a national effort to uphold our values and standards'. 'Sunny Jim', as he became known, took questions from TV viewers around the country on BBC1's early-evening *Nationwide* programme, chatting with them and using their first names. It was a performance his rather less sunny opponent struggled to match. However, even the most confident TV performers can misjudge the public mood. Callaghan was to do so not once but twice, fatally undermining his authority and that of his government.

Despite the difficulties of governing during a period of high inflation and rising unemployment, by the autumn of 1978 Labour were ahead in most opinion polls and Callaghan was expected to announce a general election. His decision to delay proved to be a massive misjudgement. The prime minister convinced his colleagues, his backers in the trade unions and the media that he was on the brink of calling an early election – one it was widely thought he might just win. He made a television broadcast which spelled out why he might do so – the economy was improving and there was 'blue sky ahead' – before revealing in the last twenty seconds that he'd decided not to. It was a disastrous miscalculation. Labour's electoral prospects would only get worse and all those who'd been misled into believing polling day was imminent resented it. All the more extraordinary, then, that Gordon Brown would make the same mistake three decades later.

In the months that followed Callaghan lost his struggle to control union demands for higher pay in the face of rising inflation and unemployment. The widespread strikes of the so-called 'winter of discontent' produced television pictures, used again and again in Tory propaganda, of rubbish piled high in the streets and the gates of cemeteries barred as the dead lay unburied. The impact of these images was under-scored by Callaghan's second TV howler.

Early in 1979 he flew to the Caribbean island of Guadeloupe for a summit of world leaders. TV news reports of the prime minister's sojourn in a resort where the sun shone, the sea sparkled and the beaches were white were always going to prove a little hard to take for people freezing at home and waiting for the next strike. On his return he was met at the airport by a phalanx of cameras and reporters. Having joked about having gone for a swim in the Caribbean, he turned on a journalist who asked him how he planned to tackle the 'mounting chaos' in the country.

'Well, that's a judgement that you are making. I promise you that if you look at it from outside, and perhaps you're taking rather a parochial view at the moment, I don't think that other people in the world would share the view that there is mounting chaos.'

The *Sun* finessed that display of prime ministerial in-souciance into the headline 'Crisis? What Crisis?' These were words he'd never used but they stuck. David Cameron did not forget this lesson. When he travelled to a Mexican beach resort for a G20 summit in the summer of 2012 his spin-doctors made sure that he was only ever filmed indoors, with the views of the pool and the beach covered by a blue summit backdrop. His advisers told him that the water might look tempting but he was not, under any circumstances, to go for a swim.

It was not, however, the winter of discontent, the state of the economy or even Sunny Jim's Caribbean complacency that undid his government. It was, instead, a failed attempt to create a parliament for Scotland and an assembly for Wales. A House of Commons defeat on devolution was followed, in March 1979, by defeat on a motion of no-confidence by a single vote, forcing Callaghan to call an election.

Mrs Thatcher was now taking full advantage of the millions listening to her assaults on the government in Parliament. The leader of the opposition declaimed:

> The essence of the motion is that the government have failed the nation, that they have lost credibility, and that it is time for them to go . . . our citizens expect and are not getting an ordered or orderly society. They expect the rubbish to be cleared, the schools to be open and the hospitals to be functioning. They are not. They expect each man and woman to rise to his obligations in an orderly and decent way. They expect bargains to be kept between trade unions and employers. Finally, they expect ministers to support them in those views.

She rammed her message home in a TV broadcast she made in reply to one by the prime minister. Her terse conclusion was 'Enough is enough.' Gordon Reece made her rehearse those three words repeatedly to make sure her voice went down, not up, on the final 'enough'.

He spelled out his view of TV in a revealing memo to her.

'Television can change people's hearts and we should use it that way.'[9] In the 1979 general election Mrs Thatcher, under Reece's tutelage, did everything she could to use television to 'change people's hearts'. She did not dismiss TV cameramen as mere spectators of the dialogue between her and the voters. They were, instead, treated as 'the most important people on this campaign'. Everything was done with them in mind. It was the electorate that had become the spectators. A familiar tactic now, novel then.

The Tory leader tasted tea, sorted chocolates, stitched overalls, sampled butter, tested a heart-monitoring machine, carried a shopping basket, bought the Sunday joint, chatted about the price of bread and brandished a broom for the cameras.[10] One image, though, will for ever stay in the minds of those who saw it: the Iron Lady posing in a field with a new-born calf. She was meant to be gently cradling it but holding it still for fifteen long minutes for the cameras was easier said than done. Her husband, Denis, evidently feared she might strangle it. He was heard muttering, 'If we're not careful we're going to have a dead calf on our hands.'

Jim Callaghan complained, just as Ted Heath had done after the Tory leadership election, that this was, somehow, not playing by the rules. 'If you want her to be photographed holding a calf the wrong way round, she'll oblige. But ask them to discuss the issues and all you get is a deathly silence. The truth is, in this election the Tories are being sold like Daz or Omo.'

The Conservatives were to prove rather sensitive to the charge that their leader was being marketed like soap. After winning the election Mrs Thatcher would hire a man from the nation's soap-makers, Lever Brothers, to work in her policy unit. A memo was sent to the Downing Street press office advising them how to handle the appointment of Norman Strauss – 'Try to avoid being too specific about Mr Strauss's job' – to prevent any suggestion that he would be 'doing detergent marketing for the Conservative government'.[11]

Mrs Thatcher's election campaign, soon dubbed 'Thatchertours', became the model for all future successful election campaigns. Reporters soon realized that they were not being invited to ask questions, to hear new policy or, indeed, to report on anything much at all. They were merely being used to transmit a carefully contrived image to the millions watching at home. Ever since, election campaigns have consisted of a series of carefully controlled photo opportunities and precious little real contact with the electorate. Those of us who cover them sometimes delude ourselves that if we point out that something is a photo opportunity we will dull its impact or subvert its purpose. Not a bit of it. The reason the phrase 'a picture speaks a thousand words' is such a cliché is because, like most clichés, it happens to be true.

Gordon Reece played one other crucial role in securing the Tory victory. Just as he had in the Conservative leadership contest, he told Mrs Thatcher not to risk her front-runner status by debating with her opponent. Callaghan was ready to cross swords and the Tory press enthused: 'Take him on, Maggie!', but she wanted to keep the spotlight on the government's troubles. It would be more than three decades before Britain saw US-style leadership debates on television.

On 4 May 1979, Mrs Thatcher stood on the steps of Number 10 to declare that, as Britain's first woman prime minister, she would be inspired by the words of St Francis of Assisi: 'Where there is discord, may we bring harmony.

Where there is error, may we bring truth. Where there is doubt, may we bring faith. And where there is despair, may we bring hope.'

The Thatcher years were, in fact, to be marked by a good deal of discord, doubt and despair. There was to be all too little in the way of shared truth. It was a recipe for fraught relations between Mrs Thatcher and those at the BBC who were most definitely not considered to be 'one of us'.

At the end of 1979 the prime minister wrote a thank-you letter to the staff in her private office for their Christmas gift, a radio, which revealed a great deal about her attitude to the BBC. 'Thank you a thousand times for solving a perpetual family feud as to who should have the radio by providing us with another one. Now we can all listen to the *Today* programme and all complain to the BBC!'[12]

In office Mrs Thatcher's approach to the media would be shaped by her successful election campaign. She would focus on the mass-market tabloid papers and TV news bulletins, steering clear of the powerful current-affairs programmes like the BBC's *Panorama* and ITV's *This Week*, despite their remonstrations. 'Theirs is a wailing worth putting up with,' Reece assured her.[13]

The Thatcher household already had one vigorous complainer about the BBC: the prime minister's husband, Denis. His private views on the corporation, and much else besides, were often more lurid even than those parodied by *Private Eye* in their famous 'Dear Bill' letters. On one occasion he told the producer of a BBC TV phone-in programme that his wife had been 'stitched up by bloody BBC poofs and Trots'.

In the days before breakfast television the big evening current-affairs programmes got the big political interviews. Mrs Thatcher was determined not to give her first as prime minister to the BBC. In normal times this would have caused her no inconvenience at all. She would simply have appeared on the only other channel then available, ITV. However, these were not normal times, as anyone tuning into the commercial station on 10 August 1979 discovered. Viewers were greeted by a blue screen carrying the following message in white type: 'We are sorry that programmes have been interrupted. There is an industrial dispute. Transmissions will start again as soon as possible.'

They did not start again for a staggering seventy-five days – the longest broadcasting strike in history. During that time the prime minister's advisers presented her with a bid to be interviewed by Robin Day on *Panorama* and the option of an interview with the BBC's political editor. On the memo, which has been released by the Thatcher archives, she has added her short but unambiguous verdict on both possibilities: 'No.' In another note Gordon Reece fleshes out why. 'Their interviewers are hostile. They are more than reluctant to meet us halfway in our requests for such things as OBs.'

He was referring to the outside broadcasts that allowed Mrs Thatcher to be interviewed on home turf at Downing Street or Chequers. The BBC preferred her to come to them. If she gave her first big interview to ITV, Reece added, 'This will leave the BBC angry . . . [but] it would serve notice on the BBC that they are *one* of the broadcasting services and not the self-appointed tribunes of the people.'[14]

Sure enough, Mrs Thatcher's first interview was given to her favourite interviewer, Brian Walden, on ITV's *Weekend World*. It is testimony to the depth of her dislike of the BBC that she was prepared to wait for ITV's strike to finish, even though, as the legacy of years of inefficiency, over-manning and weak management, the very idea of such a strike being justified would have been anathema to her.

Carl von Clausewitz, the Prussian military theorist, famously observed that 'war is the continuation of politics by other means'. As prime minister, Margaret Thatcher behaved as if politics were a continuation of war. She spoke of battles, not debates; enemies, not opponents; victories, not successes. Since she saw herself as fighting for the national interest she demanded to know who was with her and who against. If you were not 'one of us' you were, at best, a bystander in the struggle between what was right and what was wrong and, at worst, one of those she dubbed 'the enemy within'.

In the Thatcher years most of the press could be relied upon not simply to take her side but to cheer her on. Broadcasters were another matter. Like previous prime ministers she despaired of their unwillingness to bat for Britain when, in her eyes, the national interest was at stake. Churchill had complained during the general strike that the BBC should not be neutral between what he dubbed the fire and the fireman. Eden had raged that the corporation should take his side in his fight with Egypt's dictator Colonel Nasser. Margaret Thatcher would echo their anger when she went to war with the unions, in the Falklands and after riots set Britain's streets ablaze. Her fury with the BBC was first sparked, though, by its coverage of Britain's long-running battle against Irish terrorism.

Just two months after Mrs Thatcher came to power, the BBC current-affairs programme *Tonight* interviewed a masked gunman from INLA, the Irish National Liberation Army. This was the organization which, weeks before the general election, had murdered Airey Neave, the Tory MP who had run her leadership campaign and headed her private office. The programme itself passed without much comment, as is often the case with broadcasts later said to have generated huge numbers of complaints. The trigger for the row on this occasion was a letter from Neave's widow to the *Daily Telegraph*. 'I am appalled that it was ever transmitted,' the new prime minister told the Commons. 'I believe that it reflects gravely upon the judgement of the BBC and those responsible for the decision.'

In the autumn, very soon after the IRA killed Lord Mountbatten, the Duke of Edinburgh's uncle, and three others fishing with him on holiday in Ireland, *Panorama* poured salt in the wound. They made a programme assessing the strength of support for the IRA. They filmed, as a result of a tip-off, a dozen or so masked gunmen setting up a road-block in the village of Carrickmore in the 'bandit country' of County Tyrone. According to an Army statement, the security forces had the border area under control. The footage was never shown but news of what had taken place found its way into a newspaper. That day, at Question Time, the prime minister told MPs: 'The home secretary and I think it is time the BBC put its own house in order.'

Others were less restrained – they talked of 'treasonable activity' and wrongly alleged that the *Panorama* team had colluded with the IRA to manufacture the incident. The press now turned on the Beeb. Mrs Thatcher's new press secretary, the self-consciously gruff, plain-speaking and irascible Yorkshireman Bernard Ingham, presented her with his daily summary of what was in the papers. 'Blunderama' led his list of headlines, alongside others featuring words like 'treason', 'outrage' and 'dupes'.[15]

The Cabinet, which happened to be meeting that day, had a new item on its agenda: 'Presentation of news and current events'. The minutes, now in the public domain, are so bland as to be misleading. They note the prime minister advising her colleagues of the need for 'constant pressure upon the media to observe acceptable standards of accuracy and balance'.[16] They do not note that the home secretary was sent out of the room on a mission: to ensure that the BBC governors, who also happened to be meeting at the same time, were left in no doubt about the depth of the prime minister's fury.[17]

An internal inquiry was announced and the editor of the programme, Roger Bolton, was sacked, only to be reinstated after staff protests. In a little twist of fate, Bolton, one of broadcasting's great survivors, now presents *Feedback*, the programme which invites Radio 4 listeners to complain about the BBC and its output.

Mrs Thatcher went on to challenge broadcasters to reconcile their 'freedom' with 'responsibility' and to have 'due regard for the effects your activities have on the quality of society'. She was addressing political journalists at a dinner to celebrate the centenary of the parliamentary press gallery in 1981. 'There can be no escape from that responsibility in the concept of detachment and balance,' she lectured. 'None of us can be detached from the quality of the society in which he lives nor be balanced when the issue at stake is freedom.'

Her speech was not just about the coverage of terrorism. It was delivered in the immediate aftermath of riots sparked by racial tensions and urban deprivation that had filled the nation's TV screens with images of Britain's inner cities burning. Some blamed television for encouraging copycat behaviour. In advance of the speech, Bernard Ingham sent his boss a memo containing advice 'I feel very strongly about' – so much so that he underlined it. 'You cannot afford to get across the media . . . <u>You should not get yourself into the position of apparently advocating censorship</u> . . . <u>worry with them, not at them</u>.'

Perhaps that was why she concluded with what she claimed were the views of an unnamed TV journalist to whom she'd spoken. They may well have been her own views, thinly disguised, just as Ingham had suggested.

> If the television of the western world uses its freedom continually to show all that is worst in our society while the centrally controlled television of the communist world and the dictatorships show only what is judged as advantageous to them and suppress everything else, how are the uncommitted to judge between us? How can they fail to misjudge if they view matters only through a distorted mirror?

It was the Falklands War that highlighted the gulf in perspectives between broadcasters and politicians; between those who see it as their duty to report what is really happening and those who hold that the country's interests should always come first. Naturally, politicians believe that they are best placed to determine what the country's interests actually are. Along with Suez, the Falklands War was the only dry run the BBC would have for the battle with Tony Blair over Iraq.

This was no war of national survival. Though provoked by an invasion it was, nevertheless, a war of choice. Not every leader would have fought it. Mrs Thatcher was certain that Britain's standing in the world depended on retaking the Falkland Islands from the Argentine forces sent there by the country's military junta. She was certain that a principle was at stake – that dictators should not be allowed to invade other sovereign territory. Furthermore, she knew that if she did nothing her government was doomed.

When the prime minister announced the dispatch of a naval task force she echoed words Churchill had kept on his desk throughout the Second World War. She told the BBC and ITN: 'There is no possibility of defeat. I am talking about succeeding in a very quiet, I hope, British way.'

Privately, she feared that defeat could come from a loss of national will caused by images of soldiers dying and being maimed in a conflict many thousands of miles away. In other words, a repeat of what had happened to the Americans in Vietnam. This, remember, was just seven years after the fall of Saigon. Thus television would be used to bolster the propaganda war but it would be heavily controlled: scripts would be censored, pictures would be held back and news would be released only when it suited the prime minister. Reporters could not make their own way to the Falklands. They travelled with the task force under its rules or not at all.

So it was that when British forces landed on the tiny island of South Georgia the announcement of that symbolic first victory was delayed by four hours and timed for midway through ITN's peaktime Sunday evening news. It was made not in the South Atlantic but from Downing Street. The prime minister marched out of the door of Number 10 accompanied by the defence secretary, John Nott, who had, she said, 'some very good news and I thought you would like to hear it at once'. John Nott then read the signal from the task force commander which had been received hours earlier. 'Be pleased to inform Her Majesty that the white ensign flies alongside the Union Jack in South Georgia. God save the Queen.'

As Mrs Thatcher headed back inside reporters shouted

out questions about what would happen next. She turned on them and barked: 'Just rejoice at that news and congratulate our forces and the marines.' The role of television, as she saw it, was to highlight the good news, not to focus on the bad, and certainly not to ask awkward questions.

The BBC felt that it was its duty not to rejoice at British victories but to report on the view from Buenos Aires as well as that from London and to reflect the fact that some MPs and members of the public objected to the government's policy. A memo was sent to BBC News staff instructing them not to use the word 'our' when they meant 'British'. This was in response to concerns about a news headline that stated: 'We have warned the Argentinians to stay clear of our fleet.' One BBC executive cautioned that such language could make the corporation sound like 'a mouthpiece of government'. 'We are not Britain. We are the BBC,'[18] he asserted. On *Newsnight* Peter Snow compared the credibility of official communiqués from the Argentinians and 'the British'. Mrs Thatcher loathed this 'treachery'. As far as she was concerned, there was only one side – ours.

Early skirmishes with the BBC developed into a full-scale battle only once flag-waving cries of defiance gave way to the true horrors of war: young lives lost or blighted by appalling injuries. On 4 May 1982 an Exocet missile destroyed the HMS *Sheffield*, the first British battleship to be sunk since the Second World War, revealing how vulnerable the task force was. This was the moment Mrs Thatcher had dreaded. It was followed within days by a *Panorama* programme which interviewed Argentina's representative at the UN and reported on doubts among some MPs on both sides of the House. Mrs Thatcher had watched the programme 'transfixed', according to Bernard Ingham. She and her cheerleaders felt they were now fighting the BBC as well as the Argentinians.

The next day the *Sun* screamed: 'Storm at *Panorama*'s despicable Argy bias'. At PMQs, one Tory MP denounced 'enemy propaganda amounting to a sort of treachery'. Mrs Thatcher said she shared 'the deep concern' that had been expressed. 'I know how strongly many people feel that the case for our country is not being put with sufficient vigour on certain – I do not say all – BBC programmes.' She went on to quote an assurance from the corporation's chairman that 'the BBC is not and cannot be neutral between our own country and an aggressor'.[19] She did not quote the rest of what George Howard had said: 'We are not in the business of black propaganda or distortion of the truth. All we can do is proclaim the truth so far as we can.'

One MP suggested that Mrs Thatcher ought to 'take the hint' and stop her political 'intimidation' of the media, to which she replied: 'It is our pride that we have no censorship. That is the essence of a free country. But we expect the case for freedom to be put by those who are responsible for doing so.'[20]

This distinction was one Mrs Thatcher often made. She appeared not to recognize that censorship does not simply involve the use of the law to limit what reporters can say. It can come about through pressure, bullying and intimidation. And the control of television footage coming back from the South Atlantic did amount to censorship, of a particularly old-fashioned kind.

It took a staggering twenty-two days to bring pictures of the sinking of the HMS *Sheffield* back to London, even though those on board the task force were able to watch videos of the cup final within forty-eight hours of it being played. The images were, one TV executive complained, 'almost like the Dead Sea Scrolls when we got them'.[21] The BBC and ITN believed they were being denied the use of satellites which could have had the pictures home within hours. The Navy had leased American satellite bandwidth for its communications but insisted that it was not sufficient to accommodate the BBC and ITN as well. Sir Bernard Ingham conceded in an interview I did with him recently that he had been told it might have been possible to get pictures back if the Americans had 'tilted their satellite' but that he 'drew the line' at going to the prime minister in the middle of a war to ask her to call the American president to make that request.

Censorship was not confined to pictures. The Ministry of Defence sometimes approved one journalist's dispatch while sitting on another simply because they didn't like its tone. Michael Nicholson's report for ITN on the landings at Bluff Cove – which spoke of 'a day of extraordinary heroism'– was cleared. However, the late, great Brian Hanrahan of the BBC had his report held back. It spoke of 'a timely reminder that the Argentinan air force is still to be reckoned with'.[22] Even Hanrahan's iconic commentary from the war – 'I counted them out and I counted them back' – was challenged for giving potentially useful evidence to the enemy by confirming that they had failed to destroy any British planes.

The Falklands might have been fought in the age of television but it turned out to be the last radio war. The news of the fall of Goose Green, a critical battle, was read out in the anonymous tones of a BBC announcer just as such news had been during the Second World War. Journalist Robert Fox wrote his report in pencil after being helicoptered off the battlefield and on to a ship. Signallers then tap-tapped his words back to London. The technology of 1942 still dominated in the year 1982.

Sir Bernard Ingham is totally unapologetic. 'So far as censorship is concerned, I remain as unsqueamish about it today as I was in 1982. Journalists who are affronted by this can put it down to my age. I have an old-fashioned view that wars, if they must be fought, are there to be won.'[23]

On 14 June 1982, after the fall of Port Stanley, Downing Street imposed a complete news blackout on reporters in the Falklands which lasted nine hours. The prime minister was delaying her announcement to the Commons that the Argentine forces were now flying white flags so that ITN's *News at Ten* would broadcast it live. Once again, viewers of the BBC's *Nine O'Clock News* would have to wait until the next day. On returning to Downing Street, Mrs Thatcher was filmed mingling with jubilant supporters singing 'Rule Britannia'. She declared: 'We knew what we had to do and we went about it and did it. Great Britain is great again.'

Where Anthony Eden had failed in Suez, Margaret Thatcher believed that she had succeeded. Watching and learning was a young Labour party candidate who had been selected to stand in a by-election in the safe Tory seat of Beaconsfield. His name was Tony Blair. The election had taken place the day before the invasion of the Falklands. Reflecting Labour's national position, he had said that he supported sending the task force but 'at the same time I want a negotiated settlement . . . we need to compromise on certain things. I don't think that ultimately the wishes of the Falkland Islanders must determine our position.'

Blair had lost not just the by-election but his deposit and Labour's vote share had halved. The lesson some believe he absorbed that day was that wars are popular and so too, in the right circumstances, are battles with the BBC.

For Mrs Thatcher, electoral triumph followed military

triumph. In the 1983 general election the Conservatives invited Brian Hanrahan to cover the prime minister's campaign tour. The BBC declined. It was one last attempt to manipulate television to enhance the Falklands factor. It was hardly necessary: she won by a landslide.

Long after the conflict with Argentina was over the war with the IRA was still no closer to being won. Indeed, on 12 October 1984, Irish terrorists came extraordinarily close to murdering the prime minister and members of her Cabinet. In the early hours of the morning a bomb tore apart the Grand Hotel in Brighton, where Mrs Thatcher and most of her ministers were staying for the Conservative party conference. Viewers of the new breakfast television awoke to see extraordinary pictures of the front of the hotel ripped open by a massive explosion. Survivors picked their way through the rubble and the cameras filmed the operation in progress to release Norman Tebbit, the trade and industry secretary, who was trapped in the rubble, agony etched on his face. At four in the morning – a little over an hour after the blast – Mrs Thatcher had given an interview to the BBC's political editor, John Cole, insisting that the conference would start on schedule and go ahead as planned.

The bomb failed in its principal objective, to kill Thatcher or any of her government ministers, but five others died and Tebbit's wife, Margaret, was left permanently disabled. The IRA issued a chilling statement: 'Today we were unlucky, but remember, we only have to be lucky once; you will have to be lucky always. Give Ireland peace and there will be no war.'

Margaret Thatcher responded with a statement of personal and national defiance, addressing her party and, a few hours later, the country. 'The fact that we are gathered here now – shocked, but composed and determined – is a sign not only that this attack has failed, but that all attempts to destroy democracy by terrorism will fail.' The woman who had once been so awkward on television had learned to use the medium to send a powerful message around the world. She was now resolved to deny terrorists the same freedom.

What she didn't know was that at the time the BBC was preparing a profile of a man long thought to have been the IRA's chief of staff, Martin McGuinness. His interview for the *Real Lives* programme was far from the only one he had given – he was, after all, an elected representative of a legal party, Sinn Féin, and so drew a salary paid by the British tax-payer. That was not how Mrs Thatcher saw it. Her home secretary, Leon Brittan, called for the programme to be dropped. The BBC's board of management rejected the request and urged the board of governors to back them, to withstand political pressure and to stand up for the corpor-ation's independence. Their plea was ignored. The governors' routine response to complaints was that if a problem came to light after a programme went out and it could not be cleared up by the usual complaints process they would intervene. Not this time. They did something they had only done once before, under pressure from Harold Wilson over *Yesterday's Men*: they demanded to see a programme before it was shown. Then they decided to ban it.

The board of governors had been hand-picked by the prime minister. Over the decades ministers have sometimes deliberately chosen a chairman of a different political persuasion from their own or, if not, balanced the board with a vice-chairman and other governors who held an opposite viewpoint. Not Mrs Thatcher. She was interested in chang-ing national institutions, not preserving them. At the time of the *Real Lives* controversy the BBC chairman was Stuart Young, brother of one of Thatcher's staunchest Cabinet allies, David Young. The vice-chairman was Sir William Rees-Mogg, who had stood for Parliament as a Conservative MP. Other governors included Daphne Park, a former MI6 officer who later became a Conservative peer, and Malcolm McAlpine, brother of Mrs Thatcher's Conservative party treasurer Alistair McAlpine. Even the traditional slot reserved for a trade unionist was filled by a man on the right of the union movement, Sir John Boyd. Their decision split the BBC as no decision has since.

On the night *Real Lives* was pulled (it was screened eventually, with minor changes) Mrs Thatcher appeared on *Newsnight* and insisted that while she did not believe in censorship, 'Let me be quite clear; I do say things to the media. I do request them.' In a speech the following year, 1985, it was evident that Mrs Thatcher's approach was developing beyond requesting things. 'We must try to find ways to starve the terrorist and the hijacker of the oxygen of publicity on which they depend,' she stated.

Her analysis was simple: without publicity, terrorists would find that the impact of their violence was minimized.

> They see how acts of violence and horror dominate the newspaper columns and television screens of the free world. They see how that coverage creates a natural wave of sympathy for the victims and pressure to end their plight no matter what the consequence. And the terrorists exploit it. Violence and atrocity command attention. We must not play into their hands.[24]

Censorship, pure and simple, was to follow.

It sounded innocuous enough and it was presented as such by the ever-reasonable home secretary, Douglas Hurd, when he announced on 19 October 1988 'a restriction on direct appearances by those who use or support violence'. Hurd stressed that he was not imposing 'a restriction on reporting' and was making 'no criticism' of broadcasters. Nevertheless it was a ban on airing interviews with the elected represent-atives of perfectly legal political parties, among them Sinn Féin and its loyalist counterpart the UDA. Britain had seen nothing like it since the Second World War.

The ban allowed pictures of interviews with the likes of Martin McGuinness and Sinn Féin president Gerry Adams to be broadcast, but not their voices. Hurd justified it on the grounds that appearances by those making excuses for terrorism caused 'widespread offence to viewers and listeners', offered terrorists 'support and sustenance' and that the time had come 'to deny this easy platform to those who use it to propagate terrorism'.

The ban looked tough, made those who believed terrorists should be ignored feel better and appears to have been a sub-stitute for other measures which Mrs Thatcher's ministers would have advised her against, such as the internment of terrorist suspects or the banning of Sinn Féin. Mrs Thatcher spoke of it in the Commons with all the conviction Douglas Hurd lacked. 'I well remember the letter that I received from the mother of a soldier who has been murdered. Referring to the electronic media, she stated: "They talk about the freedom of the press and the media. Where is the freedom of my son?"'

Broadcasters got round the ban by using actors to speak the words of the gagged Sinn Féin politicians. This made the men who played Gerry Adams and Martin McGuinness a lot of money, and did nothing to deny the IRA's cheerleaders the oxygen of publicity. Under IRA rules, prisoners were no longer members so, bizarrely, one *Panorama* programme was able to broadcast convicted terrorists speaking in their own voices without contravening the ban.

On Margaret Thatcher's first visit to the Home Office in 1979 she is said to have asked: 'What are we going to do about the BBC?'[25] It's a question she never tired of posing but one to which she never found an answer.

The BBC was dubbed at various times by senior Tories the Bashing Britain Corporation, the Stateless Persons Broadcasting Corporation and the Anti-British Broadcasting Corporation. Although the Thatcher years produced endless rows, although she appointed a chairman to 'get in there and sort the place out, and in days not months',[26] although she bent over backwards to do favours for ITV and to snub the BBC, Mrs Thatcher never actually did any lasting damage to the institution.

As well as stacking the board of governors, she appointed one chairman specifically because he supported advertising on the BBC. He changed his mind. She selected a committee she expected to recommend what he had failed to back. They decided against the idea. She exerted enormous pressure to see a director general she loathed sacked. He eventually was. She bullied and complained and sneered, yet still the BBC rolled on.

After the flak taken by Stuart Young, the Peacock committee and Alasdair Milne respectively, many on the BBC's staff believed that the last director general of the Thatcher era, John Birt (another executive poached from ITV) had been brought in to do her bidding; to tame its journalists and to cut costs by forcing different parts of the corporation to compete with each other in a new internal market. Birt did indeed restructure the BBC and was hated by many of his own staff as a result. A dreadful internal communicator, prone to using management-speak, he nevertheless not only rescued the corporation from threats of a government sell-off, he also proved to be a brilliant external strategist who massively expanded the BBC's reach into digital television, the internet and 24-hour news.

These were my early days as a TV current-affairs producer. The BBC at that juncture resembled the warring factions of Monty Python's *Life of Brian*, in which the People's Popular Front of Judea was determined to fight the Popular People's Front of Judea instead of joining forces to confront their common enemy, the Romans. The filmmakers of current affairs detested being forced to work with the 'hit-and-run merchants' from news and scoffed and sneered at the ideas of the new 'Birtists' – disciples of his 'mission to explain', which insisted that analysis had to come before the demands of good pictures or compelling storytelling. Most had arrived with Birt from the programme he'd created at London Weekend Television, *Weekend World*. They adopted and promoted me, so I became a Birtist. Looking back, the war – and at times it really felt like one – seems absurd. Both sides were serious about journalism and cared about the BBC. Both ignored the fact that they would soon face a common adversary: the threat posed to serious broadcasting by the advent of multi-channel TV, much greater consumer choice and the desperate search for ratings.

Just as a previous Tory government, Winston Churchill's, had set up ITV to compete with the BBC, Mrs Thatcher's launched another channel. Channel 4, which began broadcasting in 1982, was charged with providing edgier programming than its established competitors. Once again ITN, who produced *Channel 4 News*, showed how to innovate and to rewrite the rules of television news.

A year later, families who'd always been glued to their radios at breakfast time were given the chance to switch on the telly instead. Breakfast TV had been regarded for many years as somehow unBritish by a media elite brought up on Radio 4's *Today* programme. It arrived a full three decades after it had become a fixture of American television, importing its style from across the Atlantic. The aim was to offer a light, bright start to the day in which a mix of news and features was delivered by friendly presenters in jumpers and open-necked shirts sitting on sofas. Frank Bough and Selina Scott hosted the BBC's *Breakfast Time*, while its ITV rival, produced by the newly formed TV-am, was fronted by broadcasting stars including Michael Parkinson and Anna Ford.

TV-am's other star name, Sir David Frost, the pioneer in the 1960s of satirical television with *That Was the Week That Was*, created a new, more informal Sunday morning show which would change political broadcasting for ever. He invented the sofa interview – or rather, imported it from the States – and in so doing gave politicians a softer, altogether more comfortable alternative to the more robust interrogations of *Panorama*, *This Week* or the Sunday lunchtime programmes. John Birt took his old friend Frost and his programme to the BBC and unwittingly hobbled those committed to more serious interviewing.

Ironically, Margaret Thatcher who, like Harold Wilson, much preferred ITV to the BBC, was to do it great damage. In 1990, the law was changed to allocate ITV franchises by blind auction rather than awarding them on merit or potential.

One consequence was that ITV and the news programmes she liked were robbed of the money they needed to compete. The Broadcasting Act, passed in her last year in office, deregulated ITV, allowing the channel, some years later, to scrap the most successful news programme Britain had, and still has, ever seen: ITN's *News at Ten*. It is a decision from which the company has never fully recovered and one that gave the BBC even more influence than before.

Although the 1990 Act also approved the setting up of a fifth analogue channel (Channel 5 would not be launched for another seven years) and paved the way for multi-channel satellite TV, it was only her decision to allow the international media tycoon Rupert Murdoch to move into satellite broadcasting that kept alive her hope that the BBC's dominance of British broadcasting could be broken – but that would come much too late to benefit her.

After the Falklands, the Brighton bomb and the struggle with the doubters in her own party, there was one more fight awaiting the Iron Lady – to overcome the 'enemy within'. The National Union of Mineworkers had helped to destroy Ted Heath's government and had compelled Mrs Thatcher to blink in her earliest years in government rather than gamble on a confrontation she would have lost. In 1984, though, she was ready – not just with significant coal stocks to minimize the impact on industry of a strike and with the police primed to break picket lines, by force if necessary, but also with a meticulously planned media strategy. The government had a simple, powerful narrative: the country could not afford to subsidize uneconomic coal mines, however devastating the impact of closure would be on the communities affected, and militant trade unionism had to be defeated once and for all.

Arthur Scargill, the NUM's militant leader, replaced

Argentina's General Galtieri as the man to be beaten. He had, it was said, denied miners the chance to vote on a strike and was set on challenging the rule of law by encouraging violence on the picket lines. My old colleague Nicholas Jones, who was the BBC's industrial correspondent at the time, has compared the media's coverage of the strike to that of the wars that would follow several years later. Journalists only felt safe on one side of the conflict – behind the police lines and not in mining communities, which were often hostile to reporters – and thus carried reports dominated by the violence of the strikers and the heroism of those willing to take the risk of returning to work. Jones argues that had he and other reporters done more to challenge the underlying merits of the government's case, a negotiated settlement might have been possible.[27] As it was, once again, Margaret Thatcher's victory was total.

Now, some believed, the Iron Lady was afraid of nothing. There was, though, one thing she – like all politicians – always feared: defeat in an election. As a result she wanted to broadcast, like Harold Wilson before her, only on her own terms. She wanted to be interviewed on the day she wanted, in the studio she wanted, with the interviewer she wanted. Her aides had drawn up an 'enemies list' of those she wouldn't accept and another list of her preferences. Serious interviews were supplemented with softer access programmes: the PM making breakfast in the kitchen of her Downing Street flat, talking emotionally about her father or even, once, offering tips on cooking her favourite fish.

There was one place she was not seen by the general public throughout most of her premiership: in Parliament. While radio microphones now transmitted sound from the House of Commons, the prime minister remained invisible to

'And the result is just in from…' Election results were first broadcast in November 1922. 'Listening-in parties' were held as only 30,000 homes had a 'wireless' and the stylish headphones needed to hear the transmission.

The first master of the microphone: Stanley Baldwin. The prime minister invited his wife to sit in the radio studio knitting to remind him to chat to those listening at home and not to deliver a speech, as his rivals did.

BREAKING NEWS

The BBC built a reputation for delivering news you could trust at moments of national crisis. During the general strike in 1926, huge crowds gathered for public broadcasts of the BBC – the only source of information since no newspapers were able to print (**below**). Prime minister Neville Chamberlain's return from talks in Munich with 'Herr Hitler' in September 1938, with his promise of 'peace for our time', was BBC TV's first broadcast of a live news event (**beneath**). What viewers didn't hear was Richard Dimbleby muttering: 'I wish that were true.'

Winston Churchill's wartime radio broadcasts – this was his first, in October 1939 – were weapons of national resistance, but his prewar warnings about appeasement went unheard and he never forgave the BBC.

Churchill's successor, Anthony Eden (**left**), failed to rouse the nation to back war in Suez in 1956. He blamed 'those communists at the BBC' for shining lights in his eyes, forcing him to wear glasses to broadcast. After a bitter battle with the corporation, proper TV political coverage was pioneered by Grace Wyndham Goldie (**below**), praised by her boss for changing 'the whole future of politics in Britain'.

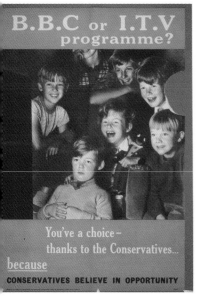

In the late 1950s TV became what Harold Macmillan dubbed 'a torture chamber' for politicians thanks, in part, to the creation of a brand-new channel, ITV, which, as this Tory election advert (**above**) boasted, gave viewers a choice for the first time. ITV's rising star, Robin Day, seen here grilling Macmillan (**above right**), invented the robust political interview. **Below**: Jolted out of its complacency, the BBC responded in the early 1960s with political satire, notably *That Was the Week That Was*, fronted by David Frost (*left*), then the scourge of the establishment.

Politicians preferred their own softer TV vehicles, such as 'the Mac 'n' Ike show' – prime minister Macmillan and US president Eisenhower appearing live from Downing Street in August 1958 (**above**) – and *Portrait of a Man*, in which Labour's new leader Harold Wilson was filmed relaxing at home (**left**) for 'our channel', ITV.

Wilson rarely smiled when at the BBC, as he demonstrates in the *Panorama* studio (**below**) with Richard Dimbleby and Robin Day (who had switched channels).

HOW TV MADE AND BROKE MAGGIE

Margaret Thatcher supplied television with what it craved: powerful images and on-screen drama. When she cradled a calf on her election tour in 1979 (**left**), her focus was the cameras, not the voters. Husband Denis muttered: 'If we're not careful we're going to have a dead calf on our hands.' Thatcher's TV interviews were always highly charged: the Iron Lady was the first to outwit the self-styled 'grand inquisitor' Robin Day (**below**).

Below: Mrs Thatcher thrived on 'the oxygen of publicity' while castigating broadcasters for supplying it to her foes. She repeatedly condemned the BBC's coverage of Irish terrorism but when an IRA bomb destroyed the Brighton hotel where she was staying in 1984 she sought out the BBC's camera to insist the Tory conference would go on.

Thatcher's downfall was the final episode of a long-running political soap opera. In October 1989 her favourite interviewer, LWT's Brian Walden (**above**), told her she came over as someone '"slightly off her trolley" – authoritarian, domineering, refusing to listen to anybody else'. Sir Geoffrey Howe (**left**) delivered the fatal blow just over a year later. His Commons speech had a huge impact because it was broadcast live on TV, captured by the cameras Mrs Thatcher had fought unsuccessfully to keep out of the Commons.

'We're leaving Downing Street for the last time after eleven and a half wonderful years.' The Iron Lady's tearful departure from Number 10.

THE MAN WHO INSPIRED ME

Brian Redhead loved 'dropping a word in the nation's ear' as presenter of BBC Radio 4's *Today*, which he helped turn into the country's most influential programme in the 1980s and early 1990s. Brian said that the key to being a good journalist was being 'nosy'. He believed in both the value of politics and the importance of challenging politicians. He was also the father of Will, the best friend I still miss.

viewers of television news. Her speeches were instead accompanied by a still photograph of the Commons chamber. In fact, by allowing cameras to film their proceedings, it was the House of Lords that finally led the way. In 1983 peers had voted for another experiment (they'd tried it once before in 1968) and two years later the cameras arrived in the upper chamber. However, there remained considerable resistance to the idea in the Commons.

By 1985, twenty-one years had passed since a select committee had recommended a television trial and nineteen since MPs had first held a private experiment with radio coverage. At long last, six decades after the invention of television, MPs debated again whether it might now be time to let the cameras in. It was to be a 'free vote' – one in which, in theory at least, MPs would decide for themselves rather than being expected to follow the instructions of their party.

Uncharacteristically, Mrs Thatcher was in two minds about what to do. Gordon Reece told her the cameras would play to her strengths. At first she seemed to agree and the press were briefed that they would have her blessing. Then she began to have doubts, perhaps remembering Reece's earlier advice about always denying your opponents a platform. Just as she had vetoed TV debates with Jim Callaghan and her rivals for the Tory leadership, she now opted to deprive her latest opponent of the oxygen of publicity. Labour's Neil Kinnock had just received rave reviews for his brave party conference speech condemning supporters of the Militant Tendency. Mrs Thatcher decided she had no desire to give such a powerful orator a twice-weekly televised opportunity to look her equal.

The word went out in the Commons tea rooms that the PM did not want the cameras. The whips reminded MPs that the House of Lords had unhelpfully provided TV news with clips of the government's critics. The former Tory prime minister Harold Macmillan, for example, had memorably condemned privatization as 'selling off the family silver'. Still Mrs Thatcher did not publicly state a view but she was seen smiling when the result was announced: the Commons said no to the cameras once again, by the same margin, twelve votes, as they had a decade earlier.

After the 1987 general election, MPs decided to debate the issue for the eleventh time in twenty-two years. This time the prime minister left her party in no doubt as to her own opinion. She told BBC News: 'I've thought about it very deeply. The Commons is a small, intimate chamber; those heavy lights, the heat, I think it would be dreadful.' Privately she warned her supporters that television would lead to demonstrations being staged for the cameras and that left-wing, anti-establishment MPs might take the opportunity to out Britain's security chiefs, whose identities at that time were as secret as their organizations. Even the position of the sun was cited as a reason to say no. It was pointed out that during Prime Minister's Questions it would shine on the opposition benches, leaving the government benches in the dark. Whether it was assumed voters would see this as God's blessing on Labour was not made clear.

Her opponents smelled fear, sensing that she preferred to be seen 'as above the dust of battle, loftily speaking for the nation'* or facing questions from 'complacent interviewers made pliable by knighthoods or the promise of knighthoods'.† At PMQs Mrs Thatcher claimed she was thinking not of herself but of the Commons. 'My concern is quite

* Former Tory leader of the Commons John Biffen.
† Shadow leader of the Commons Frank Dobson.

simply this: my concern is very much for the good reputation of this House.'

At this point Labour MPs began jeering, 'Frit! Frit!', throwing back at her a word she had used contemptuously against them in accusing them of cowardice. Neil Kinnock then took up the attack: 'For centuries we have had this place reported . . . What reasonable cause can be given for not reporting and broadcasting this House with moving pictures? What is the prime minister afraid of?' The answer was quite a lot.

The House of Commons voted to defy the lady. The result – a much larger than expected majority of fifty-four backing the cameras – was greeted with wild cheers. The first-ever televised Prime Minister's Questions followed on 28 November 1989. Mrs Thatcher was given an hour to rehearse in front of the new cameras, with the assistance of a TV monitor set up beside the dispatch box. She was wearing new make-up that was kinder to her face under the lights and her notes had been prepared in larger, easier-to-read type so that she wouldn't have to keep putting on her glasses. Nevertheless that first session showed the dangers of this new accessibility. Though she produced a confident performance she was seen shuffling through her papers, destroying the impression given to radio listeners that she carried all the relevant facts in her head. Despite the bigger type she still had to reach for her glasses to read out key quotes.

What was worse, though, was that it wasn't just Mrs Thatcher who could now be scrutinized by the electorate, but also the expressions of any MPs within shot. A Tory back-bencher, Michael Carttiss, no doubt thought he was being helpful when he highlighted the open revolt among Tory

MPs against her continued leadership. Pledging that he was no rebel, he roared: 'My constituents – and the people of this country – demand that she remains!'

'I'm quite sure,' replied Mrs Thatcher, 'that he and his constituents are both quite right.'

As Tory MPs bellowed, their deputy leader, Sir Geoffrey Howe, could be seen on camera smiling, his arms crossed. A year later the prime minister would be driven from office after he spelled out his own views on her leadership in front of those same cameras.

The loss of political authority accumulates like snow before an avalanche. It is impossible to know exactly where or when the slide will come, but you had better be sure that it will.

Mrs Thatcher's problems began to accumulate years before she was forced from office, even before her third and convincing general election win in 1987. It was the previous year that Michael Heseltine had stalked out of a Cabinet meeting and marched off down Downing Street, taking the film crews stationed outside Number 10 by surprise. They barely had time to switch on their cameras before he told them he had resigned as secretary of state for defence. From that moment on the prime minister had been facing two oppositions: Labour and a growing faction in her own party who had simply had enough of her, of her views, of their own marginalization or often of all three. Heseltine's complaints about her style of governing were fuelled by a series of unforced errors on television, the medium she'd striven so hard to conquer.

At the beginning of the 1987 campaign my predecessor John Cole had asked Mrs Thatcher if this would be her last election.

I would hope not – this is only the third term we are asking for. There is quite a long way to go. We are going to be rather lucky to be living at a time when you get the turn of the thousand years and we really ought to set Britain's course for the next century as well as this . . . Yes, I hope to go on and on.

There is of course no way, as Tony Blair was to find, of answering this question without causing a fuss. Say yes and you instantly become a lame duck and trigger a contest for the next leader. Say no and you will be accused of being power-obsessed. However, to talk of ruling into the next millennium, still some thirteen years away, was hubris on a gargantuan scale.

On the Tories' Achilles' heel – the NHS – she defended her use of private health insurance by explaining at a Conservative news conference that she insured herself 'to enable me to go into hospital on the day I want, at the time I want, and with a doctor I want'. This was perfectly true, but scarcely calculated to reassure those who could not afford that luxury. And hours before polling day, in an interview with David Dimbleby, she was asked why she didn't show more sympathy for the unemployed and underprivileged. 'Please, if people just drool and drivel [that] they care, I turn round and say, "Right, I also look round and see what you actually do."'

Dimbleby instantly picked up on the phrase 'drool and dri-vel'. 'Is that what you think saying you care about people's plight amounts to?'

Mrs Thatcher suddenly realized what she'd said and four times said sorry in her next two answers. The interview ended with a question about what she'd learned during the campaign. An unusually contrite prime minister replied:

'Perhaps you have taught me one [lesson]. It's not actually enough to do things which result in caring, you also have to talk about it.'

Despite the drooling and drivelling, and despite a slick Labour television campaign choreographed by Peter Mandelson, a former *Weekend World* producer hired by Labour a couple of years earlier as director of communications, Margaret Thatcher won by another landslide in the 1987 election. Yet Maggie, the leader praised for her robustness, now found herself condemned for her stubbornness and unwillingness to listen. It was a problem summed up in three letters: TBW – That Bloody Woman. Politicians' strengths can all too quickly become their weaknesses, but personal failings would never have been enough on their own to prompt the defenestration of the most successful political leader since Churchill. Policies would see to that.

It was at this point, the end of Mrs Thatcher's reign, that I got my first proper job in television. I started work in 1988 as a producer for the BBC's new Sunday lunchtime political programme *On the Record*, which highlighted the deep rifts within the Conservative party. Week in, week out I examined the policy problems that would lead to Mrs Thatcher's demise and spoke to disaffected Tory MPs. One leading Conservative backbencher jokingly referred to me as the BBC's 'ambulance-chaser', since whenever there was a political accident involving the government, and there were many of those in the late 1980s, I followed not far behind.

It was, however, long before the implementation of the deeply unpopular poll tax, as everyone except Mrs Thatcher called her community charge, that I produced a film predicting its impact. I invited a specialist in local government finance to estimate how much the new flat-rate tax for local services would cost people on a street in Buxton in Derbyshire where rates, under the old system, were low. I filmed a Tory councillor walking from house to house discovering, to her mounting horror, how much more the Smiths or the Joneses would have to fork out. She reacted with predictable disquiet to the news that many less well-off families would face bills of hundreds of pounds more than they had been paying before. If Margaret Thatcher had watched our programme she could have saved herself an awful lot of trouble.

As the poll tax undermined the prime minister's support in the country a row over economic management corroded Cabinet unity. She appointed an economic adviser, Alan Walters, who she knew disagreed fundamentally with her chancellor, Nigel Lawson. Number 10 wanted to let the pound float freely while the Treasury argued that it should join the European Exchange Rate Mechanism. Happily for journalists, neither side could resist airing their differences in public. While Mrs Thatcher stuck to her favourite Sunday interviewers, David Frost and Brian Walden, Nigel Lawson was happy to appear with Jonathan Dimbleby on *On the Record*.

In June 1989 Jonathan asked the chancellor what might have appeared to be a stock interview question: would he complete another two years as chancellor before the next general election? We on the programme, however, were unsure how Lawson might answer it. We thought we understood what he was thinking and we certainly knew he wasn't someone who flannelled or obfuscated. Most politicians would have responded by saying there was nothing to be gained from 'pointless speculation' or 'that's a matter for the prime minister and not for me'. Lawson, however, said it would depend in part on the prime minister and in part on himself. Pressed on whether he would be available if the prime minister wanted him to continue, he replied: 'You will have to wait and see.' His message to his boss was clear: I will only stay on my terms. The interview fuelled speculation that Lawson might quit if he didn't get his way, which is precisely what he did that October.

Underlying the bust-up between Thatcher and Lawson was the mother of all Tory splits: Europe. My editor at *On the Record*, David Aaronovitch, now a columnist on *The Times*, still generously reminds me of a memo I wrote in 1988 predicting that Europe would divide the Conservatives as emphatically as the Corn Laws had 140 years earlier. It was, of course, someone else's insight, obtained over a good lunch. If I could remember who said it to me I'd buy them another.

Behind the scenes in early 1990 Tory MPs were talking endlessly about whether they should move against their leader. However, none of them was prepared to do so publicly. *On the Record* spoke to no fewer than a hundred Conservative MPs (off the record, of course) in our quest to find someone who would. Eventually, a student on work experience, a striking young black woman who admitted she was a member of the Socialist Workers' Party, told me she'd unearthed an MP willing to call for Thatcher to quit. If she was an unlikely person to track down a disgruntled Tory backbencher missed by a vast pack of political journalists, the late Barry Porter MP was an unlikely candidate to lead a rebellion. He was best known for being pretty right wing and pretty fond of his food and drink. I was so nervous that he would not repeat on camera what was said to be his private view that I advised our reporter, John Rentoul (now the *Independent on Sunday*'s star political columnist), to offer him a stiff drink and wind him up a bit.

After a large Scotch arrived John asked Porter about Europe. Porter praised his leader's resolve. John asked him about the poll tax. Porter replied that 'the community charge put the community in charge', a stock line only a Tory loyalist would have uttered. I was in despair. John was running out of questions which might needle a Tory rebel. What, he asked with little conviction, is your advice to Margaret Thatcher? Barry Porter took a deep breath and delivered his verdict on his leader.

> I have supported Margaret Thatcher throughout the last ten years of this government. Having said that, Sir Len Hutton does not still play for England, Stanley Matthews does not play football for England. People do what they can do for a period of time and then the time comes when it is proper to hang up their boots, pads, or whatever else . . . I would like to say to the prime minister, 'Thank you and goodbye and enjoy yourself.'

It was the perfect soundbite. After the camera was turned off Porter told us he'd been growing increasingly anxious that we weren't going to get round to asking him about Thatcher at all. He had scripted and rehearsed his call for her to go the night before, in consultation with other independent-minded Tory MPs at a boozy dinner held by the Curry Club, set up in mocking defiance of Edwina Currie, the former health minister who'd infuriated her colleagues by telling the country what they ought to eat.

It was another sporting metaphor delivered on TV by another unlikely candidate that finally finished Mrs Thatcher off. The patience of Sir Geoffrey Howe, the longest-serving member of the Thatcher government, had been exhausted by her approach to Europe, which she had summed up pithily and provocatively in the three words 'No, no, no'.

Howe told stunned MPs in his resignation speech on 13 November 1990 that the prime minister had totally undermined those negotiating on the government's behalf in Europe. 'It is rather like sending your opening batsmen to the crease only for them to find, the moment the first balls are bowled, that their bats have been broken before the game by the team captain.'

Had it been delivered just a year earlier, no one but those present in the Commons that day would have been able to see the effect of this attack. Everyone else would have missed the sight of Mrs Thatcher as the blows landed – arms folded, muttering to herself and ignored by both John Major and Ken Baker, sitting on either side of her. Howe concluded with a coded call for the Cabinet to turn on their leader. 'I have done what I believe to be right for my party and my country. The time has come for others to consider their own response to the tragic conflict of loyalties with which I have myself wrestled for perhaps too long.'

If that speech and its audience had not been seen in offices, homes and newsrooms up and down the country it might have had only a fraction of the impact it did. As it was, many of those watching realized that what they had just witnessed on live television was a political coup, and this time there was nothing the Iron Lady could do to stop it. On 28 November Margaret Thatcher walked out of Number 10, looked into the cameras waiting for her there and, with tears in her eyes, bade farewell to Downing Street for the last time.

The tumbler of whisky, the finely coiffed hair, that oh-so-familiar low timbre as Lady Thatcher, as she was by then, recalled telling George Bush not to go wobbly. Those are my memories of my last meeting with her. I'd been granted an audience as political editor at ITV (a privilege I would not be granted when I moved to the BBC) and hoped to persuade her to do one final interview. I had, though, asked her very clearly about the current president, George Bush junior, not senior. Still fluent on the past she was, by then, faltering and uncertain on the present. When I raised current British politics her loyal servant and protector, Mark Worthington, put his hand on her knee and said, 'We don't talk about these things, do we, Lady T?' It was a shock to see the corrosion of a mind once so sharp.

For years afterwards I, along with every other BBC correspondent, worried about how we would handle the reporting of the death of a woman whose achievements were unique but who had an unrivalled capacity to divide people. Some colleagues carried a sheaf of crib notes with them wherever they went in case they were the one who happened to be on duty when the news broke. I told myself that I really ought to do the same. I remembered that I had not, in fact, got round to doing so when my mobile rang at home on the last day of a holiday. I was half undressed as I was changing out of my jeans into a suit to travel to Paris to film the prime minister on a visit to the Elysée Palace.

'She's died. Lady Thatcher,' my news editor told me.

'Not funny,' I replied.

When I realized it was not a joke I ran down the stairs, simultaneously pulling on a fresh pair of trousers, shouting to the children not to make a noise and to bring me a glass of water and something to eat as Dad would be broadcasting from the basement for a long while. 'You'll be on air in a few seconds,' said the voice in my headphones. 'Oh, God, why didn't you prepare for this?' said the voice in my head. Then, as Martha Kearney's comforting tones started to introduce me on the *World at One*, it dawned on me that I'd been preparing for it for my entire adult life.

Pointing out that Mrs Thatcher had been a figure both loved and loathed in equal measure proved to be a pretty un-controversial observation. Even her most ardent supporters were aware of and, indeed, drew strength from the hatred of her enemies. What was more problematic was capturing that in a TV news report. I was determined that my piece should not be over-reverential or shorn of political content. I expected all the political leaders to be restrained and respect-ful but was equally sure that one politician or another on the left would come forward with a more critical view. By six o'clock nobody had. However, a producer who'd gone to the gates of Downing Street had come back with some sponta-neous reactions from passers-by – some sad, others unaffected emotionally and one who angrily remarked that he was glad she was dead as 'she destroyed my town'. Faced with a loom-ing deadline, I had to choose between having no critical voice – which would annoy those watching whose emotion that day was certainly not grief – or one I knew would offend those who thought it shameful to speak ill of anyone who'd just died, let alone somebody they regarded as one of their coun-try's greatest-ever leaders. I included the angry voice. Predictably, the *Mail* and the *Telegraph* reported the outrage at this and the pictures I used the following day of left-wing activists dancing in the streets.

Many at the BBC dread moments like this when we are caught between two deeply held and bitterly opposing world views. Fine judgements are involved. They are what people like me are paid to make.

Days later I sat next to David Dimbleby in a glass bubble overlooking the steps of St Paul's Cathedral, watching a funeral procession the like of which had not been seen since the death of Winston Churchill. Extensive preparations had been made for protests but so far scarcely any had been seen or heard. When the coffin emerged after the service to be carried down the steps a roaring sound rose up from the assembled throng. 'Get the cameras on to the crowd!' I shouted as it became clear that this was not booing or jeering but, instead, Mrs Thatcher's most loyal supporters cheering her on her final journey. It was a send-off I doubt she would even have dreamed of. It is, as she said on the day she left office, 'a funny old world'.

The Times, 11 August 2000

6

'ANYTHING ELSE YOU'D
CARE TO SAY, PRIME
MINISTER?'

If you dream of standing one day on that step in front of the most famous door in the world and calling Downing Street home you need to be pretty thick-skinned. You will face questioning, if you haven't already, not just about your policies and plans, your suitability for high office and your personal integrity but, potentially, about your sexuality and your use of drink, recreational drugs or prescription medication. Those asking those questions will do so with the assumed authority of the tribunes of the people, insisting on the public's 'right to know'. You will be judged not on your answers alone, but also on how you reply – your facial expression, your body language and the tone you use – or, just as importantly, how you avoid replying. That is the modern rite of passage for any aspirant political leader.

It is all so very different from how it was even a little over half a century ago. The contrast between today's routine aggressive interviewing of politicians and yesterday's subdued deference is as stark as the difference between Dame Vera

Lynn and Beyoncé. Before we go on to examine the evolution of broadcast interviews from tame inquiry to fearsome interrogation, via the occasional cosy chat on a sofa, let us look back for a moment at the way politicians were questioned back then.

Imagine, in today's world, the leader of the opposition being caught on the hop on a foreign trip when the prime minister calls a snap general election. He or she might want to respond at home on British soil, having talked with and consulted his or her party. However, the politician knows that unless the TV reporters and cameras get the news clips they need – and fast – questions will be shouted at him (or her) as he walks into or out of any building or car the cameras can get close to. He will also face a reporter 'going live', standing just a few feet in front of him while endeavouring to explain why he has said what he's just said and analysing what he didn't say.

In 1955, Labour's Clement Attlee found himself in precisely this situation. He was on a lecture tour of the United States when Anthony Eden called an election days after he'd replaced Winston Churchill at Number 10. In those days, of course, with no technology for beaming pictures back from America, reporters had to wait at London airport in the hope of getting a word with the great and the good. Thus, on his return, Attlee was greeted by a man from the BBC, who conducted an interview which made history, but for all the wrong reasons.

He began with a cheery greeting, presumably in an attempt to ingratiate himself with Britain's famously taciturn former prime minister.

'Good morning, Mr Attlee. We hope you've had a good journey?'

'Yes, excellent,' came the jaunty and encouraging reply. The intrepid reporter pressed on.

'Can you, now you're back having cut back your lecture tour, tell us something of how you view the election prospects?'

At first Attlee was helpful. 'We shall go into them for a good fight . . . we've a very good chance of winning . . . we shall go in confidently – we always do.'

Given that this was the Labour leader's first opportunity to speak to the nation since people had learned they'd soon be going to the polls, our reporter justifiably assumed that more might follow. When it didn't, he asked: 'And on what will Labour take its stand?'

Which is where the problems began.

'Well, that we'll be announcing shortly.'

Determined not to be put off by this curt response, our prototype Paxman ploughed on. 'What are your immediate plans, Mr Attlee?'

'My immediate plans are to go down to a committee and decide just that thing.' By this stage Attlee's voice betrays more than a little irritation.

The Beeb's man had one last try. 'Anything else you'd care to say about the coming election?'

Attlee's reply was clear, concise and, above all, definitive.

'No.'

It evidently never occurred to Clement Attlee that this was a broadcasting opportunity to be seized and it never occurred to his interviewer to demand fuller replies. This now hilarious *pas de deux* reflects the fact that politicians saw TV and radio as spectators, not players. Neither Attlee nor Winston Churchill ever gave what we would regard these days as an interview. They expected to have their speeches reported and to face questioning only by fellow members of Parliament, not mere journalists.

A parody by George Scott in the *Manchester Guardian* perfectly captures a typical interview of the day – one to which many modern politicians no doubt dream of returning.

Q: Sir, would you say your visit to Timbuktu was worthwhile?

A: Oh yes, I would definitely say my trip had been worthwhile. Yes, definitely.

Q: Ah, good. Could you say what topics were discussed, sir?

A: No, I'm afraid I could not do that. These talks were of a highly confidential nature, you understand, and you wouldn't expect me to reveal anything which might prejudice our future relations.

Q: No, of course not, sir. Well, sir, you must be very tired after your talks and your journey – may I ask, sir, if you are going to take it easy for a while now, a holiday perhaps?

A: Ah, if only one could. But you know, a minister in Her Majesty's government can never take it easy, never rest, not really, you know. They're waiting for me now.

Q: Well, thank you very much, sir.

A: Thank you very much.

Everyone in the Westminster club knew the rules and no one contemplated rewriting them. It would take the arrival of a rowdy newcomer to do that.

It was the creation in 1955 of commercial television and the hiring by ITN of the young Robin Day that changed the political interview for ever. Day invented the tough, robust and challenging interrogation familiar to us today, although later even he came to believe that things had gone too far.

His appointment as one of ITN's first newscasters had been resisted by the ITV companies themselves, who equated a TV 'personality' with good looks and matey charm. Day hardly fitted that mould and his first day on air was not well received. The waspish Bernard Levin, then writing TV reviews for the *Manchester Guardian*, was unimpressed. 'Mr Day was, to put it mildly, far too eager to please. You cannot sell people the news, as sound radio learned many years ago, when it banned "tendentious inflection".'

Day, however, enjoyed the adrenaline rush of gladiatorial combat and his genius turned out to be not 'selling' the news but making it, using the skills he'd honed as a barrister to cross-examine politicians. In 1958, at the age of thirty-four, he conducted the first substantial one-to-one interview of a prime minister shown on television. The fact that he had the temerity to ask Harold Macmillan the question all the papers were gossiping about – whether he would dump his unpopular foreign secretary, Selwyn Lloyd – provoked disquiet in the press.

There was angst in the *Daily Telegraph*. 'Should the Prime Minister have been asked what he thought of his own Foreign Secretary, before a camera that showed every flicker of the eyelid? Some say Yes; some say No. Who is to draw a line at which the effort to entertain stops?' The diarist of the *Observer*, Pendennis, wondered: 'Will the television screen bypass the House of Commons, or even (dread thought) the press? This is the kind of question that has been sending a shiver down what's left of Fleet Street's spine.' Cassandra, the *Daily Mirror*'s columnist, was furious that the interview might have forced Macmillan to save a man who many wanted to see sacked.

What else could he say about his colleague? How could he suddenly reject him? . . . Mr Robin Day has been responsible for prolonging in office a man who probably doesn't want the job and is demonstrably incapable of doing it. The idiot's lantern is getting too big for its ugly gleam.

So what was the searing challenge that led to so much concern; the inquiry Macmillan refers to in his memoirs as 'a somewhat truculent question from one of the new class of cross-examiners which has since become so popular'? This is what Robin Day asked.

'What do you say, Prime Minister, to the criticism which has been made, especially in Conservative newspapers, about Mr Selwyn Lloyd, the foreign secretary?'

When Macmillan replied that if he didn't think his foreign secretary was any good he would have 'made a change', Day followed up by inquiring: 'Is it correct, as reported in one paper, that he would like, in fact, to give up the job of foreign secretary?'

It was hardly, from the perspective of the twenty-first century, revolutionary, but it was a long way from asking the prime minister whether he had anything to say and being content with 'No.' The ugly gleam of the idiot's lantern was here to stay.

As we have seen, in the decade that followed respect for the political establishment was corroded by national humiliation over Suez, the embarrassment of the Profumo affair, the shame of the exposure of Philby, Maclean and Burgess as spies and the impotence demonstrated by the devaluation of the pound. At the same time television was growing in confidence, casting off the rules and restrictions of the past and recognizing that it was its duty to hold the powerful to account. The age of deference was truly dead. While politicians were mocked and wounded on satirical programmes like *That Was the Week That Was*, they were being tested and challenged as never before by a new cadre of interviewers.

MPs developed their own techniques to parry the assaults of these newly self-assured inquisitors. Some were more successful than others. When the Tory minister Lord Hailsham was quizzed about the Profumo scandal by Bob Mackensie he tried patronizing him by addressing him as 'Young "Mackenzie"' and telling him not to be silly. Only one of them looked silly, and it wasn't Mackensie. Labour's Harold Wilson opted instead for flattery and friendliness with men like Robin Day. He set out to charm his tormentor, chummily calling him 'Robin', and to charm the audience at the same time.

The interviewers responded by becoming sharper still. Initially Robin Day, and many of his colleagues who had been MPs themselves, justified their challenges on the basis that they were much milder than those lobbed about in the bearpit of the House of Commons. But before long they were posing questions that would have been unimaginable on the green benches. In 1966, when the Tory leader Ted Heath's ratings were particularly poor, Day asked him: 'How low does your credibility have to go before you consider yourself a liability to the party you lead?' With his reply, Heath originated what has become the stock answer to questions about poll ratings. 'Well, popularity isn't everything. What matters is doing what you believe to be right.'

Day made Heath's adversary, Harold Wilson, sweat, too, when he inquired: 'In view of your past record of lies and broken promises, do you really expect the electorate to place any reliance on your word?' He enraged Wilson during the 1970 election by asking whether the miners' strike was justified now that the Pay Board was considering their claim. The prime minister responded by alleging that Day was doing the Tories' job for them. 'I think the nation is growing a little tired of these questions from Mr Heath, for clearly political purposes, now peddled by you, inspired by the old principle of have you stopped beating your wife.' When he went on to describe these as 'trick questions', Day protested that he was being accused of bias.

'Don't be so sensitive,' retorted Wilson. 'Good heavens, you ought to be in politics. You mustn't behave like a child about it.'

Even 'Sunny Jim' Callaghan's patience was tested by Day's persistence in one interview.

'Robin, leave it.'

'I've not started yet.'

'Not started? I beg of you, don't.'

The ultimate answer to a Day grilling was simply to end the interview. The most memorable walkout of the television era came in the 1980s when Margaret Thatcher's defence secretary, Sir John Nott, was facing questions about planned cuts to the Royal Navy. Day suggested that the criticisms of the naval establishment might matter more than the opinions of what he called provocatively a 'here today, gone tomorrow politician'. Nott, here for the question, was gone straight after it left Day's mouth. He stood up, removed the microphone from his lapel and strode off the set, making it abundantly clear that he thought it ridiculous.

Nott had nothing to lose, having already announced that he was retiring from politics. Afterwards he said he 'simply got bored'. He was rewarded with the biggest sack of fan mail of his life. Many of the letters applauded him for finally teaching these ghastly interviewers how to behave. Looking back on a seventeen-year career on the political front line, he commented ruefully: 'You're only remembered for one thing in politics and I'm remembered for that.'

Only one person consistently outwitted the self-styled 'grand inquisitor' without resorting to storming out, and that was Nott's boss, the Iron Lady herself. In an interview with Margaret Thatcher during the 1987 general election, Day pleaded helplessly for the opportunity to get a word in. 'We're not having a party political broadcast. We're having an interview, which must depend on me asking some questions occasionally.'

Mrs Thatcher replied imperiously that she was answering his last question and ploughed remorselessly on, leading one TV critic to remark that Day had been 'crushed with the effortlessness of a beautifully coiffured steamroller . . . flattening a blancmange'. Day claimed that he was a prisoner of his generation, which believed in the need to deal with a woman politician differently since the audience would expect her to be treated with greater courtesy. Mrs Thatcher had developed the technique of coming to an interview with something to say regardless of what she was asked. He joked that he had a foolproof plan for their next encounter, which was to start by inquiring, 'Prime Minister, what is your answer to my first question?'

It was Day who established a new televised national forum for debate: BBC1's *Question Time*, a format inspired by radio's *Any Questions?*, which began a few months after Thatcher moved into Number 10. It was originally intended only for a short run but remains, more than thirty years later, as successful as ever under the chairmanship of David Dimbleby.

As a junior researcher on the BBC's Budget programme in the 1980s, I once had the great privilege of working with Robin Day. By then Sir Robin, the grand old man of political broadcasting had the task of interviewing a panel of senior politicians in a studio on College Green overlooking Parliament. He demonstrated the spirit that made him such a fearsome interviewer when he heard the message in his ear suggesting it was time for him to wind up. He theatrically removed his earpiece, held it up for all to see before placing it on the table in front of him and continued with his next question. The programme moved on when, and only when, he was ready. I'm looking forward to the day I have the courage to do that.

The 1980s saw the rise of the long, forensic, analytical interview. Sunday lunchtime became the time and ITV's *Weekend World* the place for politicians to be put through their intellectual paces for half an hour or more in inquisitions that were carefully researched, plotted and rehearsed to reveal the thinking behind a political idea or to force a politician to confront and resolve its inherent contradictions.

The face of *Weekend World* and its intellectual driving force was Brian Walden, a Labour MP who had resigned his seat to take up the job. Walden, like Robin Day, defied the standard requirements of a television 'personality'. His voice, which came to define the programme, was high-pitched, lacked the capacity to pronounce the letter 'r' and carried a distinct Brummie twang ('Pwime Minister, I'm weally going to have to push you on this . . .').

His studio presence was founded not on aggression but on intellect. John Birt, who worked with Walden at London Weekend Television before becoming director general of the BBC, recalls:

> *Weekend World* interviews were meticulously planned, like
> chess games. We were not in the hardball school of interview-
> ing, throwing quickfire, aggressive questions to unbalance or
> discomfort the interviewee – an interviewing technique
> which puts a high premium on the most basic of all political
> skills: dodging the question ... We moved away from the
> notion that there are risk-free 'right' answers, accepting that
> all political options have downsides. This approach was far
> harder for politicians to dodge. Evasion became much more
> clearly exposed.

Walden's interview plans looked, he used to say, 'like the
charts of the kings of England'. Every question had four
branches for four possible answers, yes, no, don't know and
won't say, and every answer pointed to a separate new
question. The basis of this approach was the belief that
politicians could be led into laying bare more than perhaps
they intended or wanted to. It assumed that, given time – and
Walden's interviews had lots of time – interviewees would set
out rather than conceal their thinking.

His approach was also rooted in sympathy for rather than
hostility to the Thatcher project. Walden had fallen out of
love with the party he'd once served. In 1976, while still an
MP, he had offered to vote with the Conservatives to bring
down a Labour government he believed was failing the
country. When he moved on to television, Thatcher was his
first interviewee; she also gave him her first interview after
becoming prime minister. Their mutual respect was obvious
from the opening sentence of his introduction. 'Britain enters
the eighties under the most radical leadership the country has
known for a generation ... Mrs Thatcher has been trying to
put this plan into effect for eight months now and so far it's

proved far more workable than many people expected, on some fronts.'

Instead of challenging her strategy Walden pressed her as to why she didn't carry it to its logical conclusion. He asked her why her government's policies for tackling the unions were so timid – aware, no doubt, that she was frustrated by the slowness of reform. 'You'll need to go a lot further than this if you intend to get to terms with the realities of trade union power . . .'

At one point, when the prime minister apologized for being too long-winded, her interviewer told her, 'No, no, no, no, very valuable, and very shrewd.'

It was a modus operandi that infuriated those who hated Mrs Thatcher and all she stood for, but again and again it proved revealing. In that first interview with the new prime minister Walden extracted the admission that her policies would increase inequality.

'A more unequal society, you think, is actually better for prosperity?'

'A more opportunity [sic] society,' she countered, 'which enables the able to earn more. For example, I don't expect to be paid as much as you are, Mr Walden . . .'

'But it does mean more inequality, does it not?'

'It does mean more . . . yes, indeed, if opportunity and talent is unequally distributed, then allowing people to exercise that talent and opportunity means more inequality, but it means you drag up the poor people, because there are the resources to do so. No one would remember the Good Samaritan if he'd only had good intentions. He had money as well.'

Margaret Thatcher's favourite interviewer put her at her ease and brought forth prime ministerial performances that excited not just Walden but the watching political world. Critics accused them of forming a mutual admiration society, a charge that was put to a stern and memorable test during the crisis that marked the beginning of the end for Thatcher's premiership.

Days after Nigel Lawson resigned as chancellor in 1989 the prime minister was due to be interviewed by Walden. There was much speculation in broadcasting circles as to whether she would withdraw or he would pull his punches. Both predictions turned out to be wrong. Thatcher had come to praise the economic management of the man she'd once described as 'unassailable' and to insist that the government was as strong as ever. What she didn't want to talk about was why she'd fallen out so catastrophically with her own chancellor.

'Why did Nigel resign?' prodded Walden. 'You say he knew that he was unassailable, he knew that you loved him and that everything that he did was marvellous, but he resigned. Now people are going to want to know why.'

'I think that is a question you must put to him and not to me . . . it was quite clear that he had made up his mind and there was nothing I could do to dissuade him, quite clear; that was just a fact of life and I have to accept it. More you must ask of him. He went with great dignity.'

The expression on her face was priceless when Walden replied casually, 'He is coming on next week so I will have the chance.' She sat there, stunned, as he summed up what she had told him so far. 'You do not accept blame for the resignation of the chancellor of the exchequer; you do not know why he resigned . . . you do not accept that the other resignations from your government, or the other sackings from your government, have arisen because you cannot handle strong men, because you like strong men and you like argument.' But all this was merely the preamble to a question Margaret Thatcher had never been asked in her life.

> Let me put this to you, Prime Minister . . . It may be the case that in private you will have a lusty argument and you will listen to other people's opinions and that you are only too happy to accept a suggestion if it is correct, but you never come over in public like that, ever. You come over as being someone who one of your backbenchers said is 'slightly off her trolley' – authoritarian, domineering, refusing to listen to anybody else. Why can't you publicly project what you have just told me is your private character?

No one before or since ever told Mrs Thatcher she was 'off her trolley'. She was visibly shocked. 'Brian, if anyone is coming over as domineering in this interview, it is you, hammering things out instead of just talking about them in a conversational way.' Yet at the end of what proved to be a bruising fifty-five minutes she wanted to go on, and on, and on.

'Prime Minister, I must stop you there,' said Walden.

'No, you must not!'

'I must! Thank you very much indeed.'

Mrs Thatcher was determined to have the last word. 'Strong leadership will continue!' she cried.

Some believe Walden had been goaded into his tough approach by the predictions that he would go soft on Mrs Thatcher. Whatever the case, it was the most captivating interview I have ever seen and a reminder that politicians and interviewers, however much they admire one another or however cosy their relationship may seem, are not on the same side.

* * *

As a young producer on *On the Record*, the BBC's attempt to compete with *Weekend World*, I watched those Walden interviews in awe and with envy. Our programme was John Birt's creation and he'd hired many of his old *Weekend World* team to help him fulfil his brief to revolutionize BBC News and current affairs. I was fresh out of university, new to the BBC and fascinated by politics which, at that time, combined big and controversial ideas – about economic management, privatization, Europe and much more besides – with the drama of the slow political deaths of first Margaret Thatcher and then John Major.

Our presenter, Jonathan Dimbleby, prepared just as meticulously as Walden. He shared his interest in and appetite for ideas and was surrounded by a formidable team of people who have gone on to great success elsewhere. As well as David Aaronovitch and John Rentoul, there was Gerard Baker, deputy editor of the *Wall Street Journal*, Martha Kearney of *World at One*, and colleagues like Glenwyn Benson and David Jordan who would later hold senior positions within the BBC.

Our reward came not merely from seeing our interview quoted extensively on news bulletins and in the newspapers but from following a line of argument not previously pursued. So, for example, when Douglas Hurd, foreign secretary in the 1990s, appeared on *On the Record* to defend the EU treaty agreed by John Major in Maastricht, he came prepared to counter opposition charges that Britain was abandoning working people by opting out of the social chapter. We decided that the more interesting line of questioning was to challenge him from the Eurosceptic viewpoint – that is, to ask whether he had signed up to another turn of the integrationist ratchet.

Michael Heseltine was the programme's star turn and he knew it. Ever since walking out of Margaret Thatcher's Cabinet Hezza had been 'box office', adding around half a million extra viewers to our normal viewing figures and taking them above 2 million. Aware of his value to us, Heseltine refused to interrupt his Sunday to travel to the BBC's studios and instead invited us to send an outside broadcast unit to his imposing estate in Northamptonshire. I soon realized that this was not merely a way of conserving his weekend; it was also a ploy to ensure that the interview would be staged on his home turf, where he felt comfortable. Beforehand the statuesque Heseltine would come in and offer cushions to the somewhat more diminutive Dimbleby. Ostensibly he was being thoughtful. In reality it was a power play designed to unsettle his interrogator. Heseltine, incidentally, was interviewed for *On the Record* on the same lunchtime as Margaret Thatcher was being asked at *Weekend World* whether she was off her trolley.

One of Labour's cleverest and sharpest politicians was the late Robin Cook. As shadow health spokesman in the run-up to the 1992 election he effortlessly scored goals for his team by attacking the Tories on the NHS. He was very rarely asked to set out his own policy in any detail. In advance of an interview with him I spent a great deal of time talking to experts at health think-tanks. They were united in believing that Cook and his party had very little idea how they'd run the health service if they came to power. It was an analysis Tony Blair later came to share and to deeply regret. At the end of a programme which revealed this rather important hole in the party's readiness to form a government, I continued the discussion with Cook over a glass of wine in the green room at Television Centre. 'What do we need a new health policy for?' he asked me. 'We're thirty-three points ahead of the Tories on health.' That was an interview that clearly justified the long-form, carefully researched, forensic treatment.

Before the advent of Sunday politics programmes, *Panorama* had for many years been the BBC's showcase for lengthy studio interviews. Prime ministers Wilson, Heath and Thatcher all faced Robin Day regularly on the programme. I joined it in the early 1990s to produce interviews and studio discussions with Day's successor, David Dimbleby.

Dimbleby made a fatal error when he interviewed Tony Blair as opposition leader during the 1997 election. He was just too good.

David decided to put the New Labour marketing campaign to the test. He set out his stall from the outset. 'Mr Blair, in this election you're asking the electorate to put their trust in you, the new Blair. Isn't there a problem that there is an old Blair, who believed quite different things, which makes it rather difficult for people to trust the new one?'

He quoted the young Blair talking of 'hobnail boots trampling on the rights of trade unionists' and backing unilateral nuclear disarmament and asked him whether he'd been wrong. The Labour leader, reluctant to pick a fight in the middle of an election with those in his party who didn't like the direction he was taking, replied repeatedly with variations on the same theme: 'These days are past and gone and there's no point in going back over them.'

Dimbleby pressed on. 'Your new ally, Rupert Murdoch, was right to take on at Wapping the print unions and was Labour wrong to support the unions against him?'

'Look, these days are past.'

It was, one paper reported, 'a sub-psychiatric examination of the intellectual basis of [Tony Blair's] reinvention of himself and his party since 1994'.[1] The Labour leader coped, but his eyes revealed his pain at having his attention drawn to the gulf between what he'd once said and what he was saying now. The interview infuriated many party supporters who'd grown used to their champion being treated with the deference they felt was due to a prime minister in waiting. It was Dimbleby's manner as much as his line of questioning that angered them. Peering over his half-moon spectacles at someone who, he reminded the audience, was a young man, he addressed the Labour leader as 'Mr Blair' and not 'Tony', as some were already doing. Tom Sutcliffe, the *Independent*'s TV reviewer, commented: 'Dimbleby adopted the faintly sarcastic tone of a bank manager who has already decided not to approve a loan but is making his client go through the hoops anyway.'

When Tony Blair became prime minister he decided that one appearance before the bank manager was enough. He was not in any case interested in the old-fashioned, long-form political interview and *Panorama* was not the only such programme he shunned. Too many at the BBC, myself included, had forgotten that it takes two to tango. Politicians have to be willing to step on to the studio floor. The broadcaster cannot simply demand their presence: he has to entice, to charm, to woo. We had forgotten, too, that there were now plenty of alternative television opportunities available to politicians. The creation of 24-hour news channels – Sky in 1989 and the BBC's in 1997 – provided a platform for the instant, news-making soundbite, while breakfast TV tempted interviewees with a comfortable sofa and gentler questions.

* * *

272

By the time New Labour came to power, the long analytical interview was in crisis, and not long after Blair's 1997 grilling *Panorama* stopped doing studio interviews altogether. *Panorama*'s loss was to be *Question Time*'s gain as David took over that programme and restored it to the status it had enjoyed under Robin Day.

New Labour was being advised on how to professionalize its communication by Peter Mandelson, whose emphasis was on message discipline, 'the line to take' to reach out to a new audience, rather than on Socratic dialogue. He encouraged his boss to appear on non-political programmes and chat shows reaped the benefit. Tony Blair's memoirs reveal that he regarded his appearance on the *Des O'Connor Show* in 1996 as one of the most significant interviews he did before becoming prime minister. When Blair wanted to get a message to the electorate, though, his first choice was *Breakfast with Frost*, the Sunday morning programme (launched originally as *Frost on Sunday* by TV-am), that made the friendly sofa chat with a politician an indispensable part of British political life for a staggering twenty-two years.

No interviewer will ever assemble a CV to rival David Frost's. He is the only person to have interviewed eight British prime ministers (Harold Wilson, Edward Heath, James Callaghan, Margaret Thatcher, John Major, Tony Blair, Gordon Brown and David Cameron) and seven US presidents (Richard Nixon, Gerald Ford, Jimmy Carter, Ronald Reagan, George Bush, Bill Clinton and George W. Bush). His post-impeachment interviews with Nixon didn't just make history for the near-apology they elicited over Watergate – 'I let down my friends, I let down the country, I let down our system of government' – they also attracted the largest-ever audience for a TV interview, 45 million, a record that stood until 1999, when it was broken by Barbara Walters' rather less significant interrogation of Monica Lewinsky, 'that woman' with whom Bill Clinton did 'not have sexual relations'.

Frost was, perhaps, the first interviewer to deploy the calmly repeated question to embarrass an interviewee into exposing what he'd rather keep private. Aware that Ted Heath was no fan of his rival, Harold Wilson, Frost once asked the Tory leader: 'Do you like him?' not once or twice but three times. An evasive Heath began by wriggling, insisting this wasn't the real question, and ended by supplying the awkward but intriguing answer 'That will have to remain to be seen.'

Frost's critics have often viewed his approach as too chummy, too saccharine and too easy for those sharing the sofa with him. Politicians, on the other hand, have frequently said they have found his interviews the most dangerous of them all. So it's all the more surprising, you might think, that in the 1980s and 1990s party leaders and a growing number of other politicians voted with their bottoms, choosing to sit alongside the man they claimed to fear rather than to lock eyeballs with Messrs Walden, Dimbleby, Dimbleby, Paxman or Humphrys.

Defenders of Frost's style argue that it was by putting his interviewees at ease that he persuaded them to relax, open up and share more than they meant to. During the 1987 general election campaign the unguarded words of Labour leader Neil Kinnock on Frost's sofa were a gift to Mrs Thatcher. Frost suggested to Kinnock that his policy of unilateral nuclear disarmament represented a choice between surrender and extermination. Kinnock replied that in the event of war Britain would have 'to use the resources you've got to make any occupation totally untenable'. By even entertaining the possibility of Britain being occupied by Soviet forces, he put his head into the lion's mouth. The Tories produced a campaign poster showing a soldier with his hands in the air under the slogan 'Labour's policy on arms'.

Frost always insisted that his conversational style extracted more from interviewees than the more abrasive style of rivals who 'huff and puff'. 'If you can enter into a real conversation you get more of the real person. It pays to change the subject quite quickly so that it's not too predictable, then you get something more special, more newsworthy.' Speaking not long before his death he said he'd be happy to have put on his coffin words of praise from Kinnock's successor, the late John Smith: 'You can put just as testing a question in a relaxed way as you can in a hectoring way . . . You have a way of asking beguiling questions with potentially lethal consequences.'[2]

Frost totally unsettled Tony Blair in the run-up to the Iraq War when he leaned forward and inquired hesitantly about his relationship with President Bush. 'Both you and he are great, greatly men of faith and so on . . . I mean, do you pray together?'

'Pray together?'

'Mmm.'

'How do you mean?'

'Do you say prayers together for peace, you and the president?'

'Well, we don't say prayers together, no, but I'm sure he in his way hopes for peace and I hope for peace too.'

Tellingly, there was a row when Jeremy Paxman asked a variant of the same question the following year.

Frost was the great impresario of the television age. Throughout his career he understood that before discussing what to ask an interviewee, let alone deciding what style of questioning to use, you have to secure his agreement to appear. He showed enterprise, courage and sheer chutzpah in persuading Richard Nixon to be interviewed by him rather than by an American journalist; he had, though, already ingratiated himself with the former president by producing a Christmas entertainment special from the White House in 1970, to which he took his mum. He buttered up British prime ministers in the same way: relaxing at home with the Wilsons, flattering Mrs Thatcher on her tenth anniversary, genially orchestrating the first-ever joint interview with President Clinton and Prime Minister Blair. The bonhomie, the anecdotes, the legendary annual Frost party, at which the great mix with the good and the merely famous, are all part of what transformed him from scourge of the establishment to the amiable host whose sofa they loved to grace. However far he rose, Frosty retained a boyish excitement about events and seemed to want no part in the backstage bitching common in his industry. I once delivered a lecture about the media and politics at Oxford University in which I was more than a little dismissive of the rise of the cosy breakfast-time interview. Only afterwards did I realize that Sir David had been in the audience. He congratulated me on the thoughtfulness of my speech. There will never be another like him.

The TV sofa may have helped kill the analytical interview but, confounding many expectations, it did nothing to dent the dominance of one programme, not on television but on the good, old-fashioned, steam-powered radio. *Today* was first heard on the BBC's Home Service on 28 October 1957. If it hadn't been for the good sense of its senior producer, Isa Benzie, it might have been called *Morning Miscellany* or *Listen While You Dress* or even, rather splendidly, *Background to Shaving*. However, Miss Benzie was aware that her listeners would be involved in a variety of activities at that time of day. One of her memos records: 'The audience, to me, is typically on its feet, dressing, making packed lunches, cooking and eating – certainly before I am. Gentlemen still able to enjoy a leisurely breakfast table may be catered for – if necessary – later on.'[3]

The programme was designed to be 'a collection of brief items all of which can be said to have topical interest to the average intelligent reader of morning newspapers'.[4] Matters 'likely to find a place' on the twice-daily editions of *Today*, running for twenty minutes after both the seven and eight o'clock news bulletins, were:

Notices of new theatrical, opera, cinema productions.
Various OBs under the general heading 'Going to Work Today'.
Reviews of gramophone record releases.
Items about dress, fashion, cooking, shopping and – if exceptional – weather.
Medical notes – usually suggested by items in the news.
Notes about significant anniversaries.

In other words, no politics whatsoever. It would be many years before *Today* was regarded as the home of the political interview and 8.10am became a time when no one interested in public affairs could afford not to tune in. It was after Brian Redhead joined John Timpson in *Today*'s studio that the programme earned its place in the nation's heart and grew to be politically influential. Redhead, the chippy, self-proclaimed 'bighead' and proud representative of the north, formed an unlikely partnership with Timpson, the avuncular, slippers-

and–pipe man from the comfortable home counties. A former newspaper editor, Redhead, who loved being on the inside track, was the perfect complement to a colleague who seemed to find politics rather dull. One reviewer remarked that 'they have "chemistry", they "bounce off" one another. Redhead is the irritant, Timpson is the emollient. Four million listeners can't be wrong.'[5]

The Times noted with pleasure how the old boys broadcasting on the old medium trounced the brash new television celebs who were 'not to know that the consumers of breakfast broadcasting preferred cardigans, comfortable middle age to self–regarding, tinselled celebrities'. To his frequent observation that if you wanted to drop a word in the nation's ear you went on *Today*, Redhead added: 'If you want to whistle in the wind you appear on breakfast TV.'

Ministers in Margaret Thatcher's government thought it was they – and not radio presenters – who should be dropping a word in the nation's ear. They became convinced, whether Redhead was asking questions about job losses in manufacturing or joking about being a member of the 'M6 club', that he was somehow subtly attempting to sway the audience. Jeffrey Archer used to delight Tory audiences by declaring that the 'Bashing Britain Corporation' would never employ a presenter called Brian Bluehead. In 1987 the chancellor, Nigel Lawson, went much further in an interview after his Budget, when Redhead suggested that the fall in unemployment was down to special measures and job clubs in which people played games. Lawson's response was explosive:

Well, you have been a supporter of the Labour party all your life, Brian, so I expect you to say something like that. You

really shouldn't sneer at the job clubs, which are giving real
hope to the long-term unemployed, getting them out of the
depressed state of mind many of them are in, and they are
going on to get real jobs.

Redhead was equally incensed. 'Do you think we should
have a one-minute silence now in this interview, one for you
to apologize for daring to suggest that you know how I vote,
and secondly, perhaps, in memory of monetarism, which you
have now discarded?'

The editor of the *Today* programme, Jenny Abramsky,
dropped her pen in shock, terrified that Redhead might indeed
commit the ultimate radio crime by going silent. Happily for
all concerned, although Lawson didn't apologize, he refrained
from escalating the row. 'I see no cause for a one-minute
silence,' he replied. 'Monetarism, as you call it, is not discarded.' Looking back later, he still insisted that Redhead's
'lack of professionalism' revealed 'his own political viewpoint'.

It was the one-liners and the need to have the last word
that, understandably, riled many Conservatives. They delighted
many other listeners. Redhead once introduced an item about
the Boat Race by saying: 'There was a time when such an
important occasion divided the nation. Now we leave that to
the Tory party.'

Having talked about politics often with Brian throughout
much of that period I have a pretty good idea of what he did
and didn't believe. He was not a Labour supporter at that
time, let alone all his life. Indeed, in the same year as he
clashed with Lawson, he told our local Conservative MP,
Nicholas Winterton, that he'd voted for him, marking the
ballot paper 'This is a personal vote, not for the Conservative
party'. However, Lawson had correctly detected that he was

no fan of Mrs Thatcher's economic policies. His dismay at the destruction of manufacturing industries that was impoverishing the north was shared by many beyond the home counties and, incidentally, by a number of senior Conservatives. It was this, not political bias, that coloured Brian's questions. Political bias is very often in the ear of the beholder.

Margaret Thatcher's ministers never used their most powerful weapon against *Today*: a simple refusal to appear. It was not just because, for all Brian's jibes, they knew he and the other presenters took what the government was doing seriously. It was also because they were sure *she* would be listening. This belief was confirmed when Mrs Thatcher phoned in from Downing Street one morning in 1988 when she heard breaking news on the programme. Owing to a terrible earthquake in Armenia, Mikhail Gorbachev had flown home from New York and cancelled his scheduled trip to the UK. The Downing Street duty press officer had some difficulty convincing the production team that it really was the prime minister on the line and not a hoax caller.

'I heard it on your news briefing,' she explained when she was finally allowed on air. 'It was the first indication we had. Then I heard later that you didn't know if I knew, so I thought I'd better phone . . . when there's trouble like that, home is the place to be.'

The presenter that morning, who had thirty-five seconds' warning of the first-ever prime ministerial phone-in, was John Humphrys, appointed in 1986 to replace John Timpson. Humphrys had joined *Today* after five years as anchor of the BBC's flagship *Nine O'Clock News* – a decision that baffled most of his TV colleagues, who couldn't imagine voluntarily giving up so much nightly exposure to take a job on the radio. His explanation was telling: 'You could put a blue-faced baboon on the news and in ten years he would become top of the list as a national celebrity.' Almost a quarter of a century later, it doesn't look like such a bad career move.

After Brian Redhead's untimely death in 1994, Humphrys was joined by Jim Naughtie and 'John and Jim' became the *Today* programme's new dynamic duo. John was now the 'irritant', Jim the 'emollient'. Jim, once the *Guardian*'s man in the lobby, is the political insider, steeped in Westminster, where he remains well connected. John, the chippy outsider educated at the university of life, is still inspired daily by his late father to pick a fight with the powers that be.

> He was an uneducated man, but he was very clever, and immensely bitter about the establishment. He had a chip on his shoulder a mile high. A tough guy and very bitter about the way life had treated him . . . What I got from him was 'You're as good as any man. Just because you haven't been to university' – and I didn't go to university – 'it doesn't mean you're not as good as the next guy.' That's always stayed with me.[6]

When they no longer had Redhead to complain about Humphrys drew the politicians' fire. Jonathan Aitken, the chief secretary in John Major's government, claimed in a speech that Humphrys had 'poisoned the well of democratic debate'. The fact that Aitken was later jailed for perjury and perverting the course of justice somewhat diminishes the power of the attack with the benefit of hindsight. However, at the time it was deadly serious. 'I was terrified,' admitted Humphrys, talking on *Desert Island Discs* in 2008.

> I actually thought my career, such as it was, had come to an end at the *Today* programme, because if others in the

Cabinet had taken the same view and did not want to be interviewed by me – and that was the implied threat, a stated threat, in the Aitken speech – I couldn't continue to present the *Today* programme. That would be an end to it.

The reason it wasn't is that other senior ministers made it clear they rejected Aitken's claim. Among them was his boss, the chancellor, Ken Clarke, who had suffered no fewer than thirty-two interruptions from Humphrys in a *Today* interview which had infuriated the Tories. The next time Clarke appeared on the programme John handed him a calculator to 'count up my interruptions'. Clarke replied cheerfully: 'I've never been able to work one of these things.'

To celebrate *Today*'s twentieth anniversary, the tables were turned and Clarke came on to the programme to interview Humphrys. In reply to Clarke's first question he did his best to explain why he often felt he had no choice but to interrupt.

May I just say, before I answer that question, that I've come in here today to deliver my bit of propaganda, which is what you lot do all the time. You come in here with the intention of delivering a particular message. Now, that may or may not have anything to do with the questions to which the listeners want answers. And it's our job . . . er, you're not going to interrupt me now, are you?

The defence offered by many politicians, usually in private rather than public, is that they should, as elected representatives, be allowed to get their key point across as well as dealing with whatever question they're being asked. The difficulty of doing so was dubbed the 'Humphrys problem' by New Labour very soon after they came to power. The phrase was used in a letter of complaint from their director of communications, David Hill, to the BBC. It followed an interview with Harriet Harman, Tony Blair's first and hapless social security secretary, in which her plan to cut the benefits of single parents was described by Humphrys as 'Alice in Wonderland stuff'. The letter, inevitably, was leaked.

> The John Humphrys problem has assumed new proportions after this morning's interview with Harriet Harman. In response we have had a council of war and are now seriously considering whether, as a party, we will suspend co-operation when you make bids through us for Government ministers. Individual Government Departments will continue to make their own minds up but we will now give very careful thought to any bid to us, in order to make absolutely sure that your listeners are not going to be subjected to a repeat of the ridiculous exchange this morning.

Labour insisted that they were not objecting to any criticism but to Humphrys 'becoming dismissive', an echo of John Nott's anger at being disparaged as a 'here today, gone tomorrow' politician by Robin Day.

The fuss about the 'Humphrys problem' came, ironically, only weeks after Tony Blair and David Hill had hand-picked him as the interviewer they wanted to get them out of a hole. Blair had been elected thanks, in part, to attacks on Tory sleaze, but now his image as a new prime minister leading a 'whiter than white' government was threatened by the revelation that Labour had accepted a donation of £1,000,000 from Formula One's Bernie Ecclestone just before exempting the sport from a ban on tobacco sponsorship.

By 1997, Humphrys was also presenting *On the Record* on Sunday mornings, Jonathan Dimbleby having moved to ITV. The prime minister decided he had to deliver a *mea culpa* on television and chose Humphrys for the job. Blair, plastered in so much make-up that he risked comparisons with a pantomime dame, pleaded that he'd been 'hurt and upset' by much that had been written about him before making this direct appeal to a nation that had only recently embraced him at the polls: 'I think most people who have dealt with me think I am a pretty straight sort of guy, and I am . . . I would never, ever, do something wrong or improper or change a policy because someone supported or donated money to the party. I didn't in this case.'

Although the interview got Blair off the hook he never appeared again on *On the Record*. The programme had been used to prove that he could survive fifteen rounds with one of broadcasting's big beasts. The next time he needed to do that he would choose Jeremy Paxman instead.

Paxman has prowled BBC2's *Newsnight* studio in search of fresh meat since 1989. Interviewees have learned to their cost that a mere look of boredom or disbelief can be as devastating as a strike from a Paxman paw. It is what makes him feared, revered and resented.

Newsnight began life in the 1970s as a late-evening news bulletin before its format was changed in 1980 to provide the current familiar mix of studio interviews, discussions, news and analysis. Paxman, is, in many ways, the inheritor of Robin Day's mantle. However, they are different in one important respect: Day liked politicians. Indeed, he tried to become one, resigning from ITN to run for Parliament as a Liberal in 1959. Four years of questioning others from the sidelines about big decisions had left him feeling both guilty and unsatisfied about not playing his own part in actually making them. Paxman appears to see politicians as almost another species. In his entertaining book *The Political Animal*, he tries to get to the root of what makes someone become a politician, approaching his subject like a modern version of those Victorian explorers who travelled to Bongbongoland in khaki and a pith helmet and returned to describe the 'funny little people' who lived there. The book begins: 'My first encounter with one of this curious tribe came at school . . . I thought he was mad.'

Jeremy knows, of course, that he is far from alone. Many of his viewers do not regard politicians as merely mad, they believe they are bad, too. Paxman once seemed to suggest that he agreed with that assessment: 'When he started as a young man on *The Times*, Louis Heren was given a piece of advice by an old hack. He was told that you should always ask yourself when talking to a politician, "Why is this lying bastard lying to me?" I think this is quite a sound principle from which to operate.'[7]

It is a comment he's come to regret and he has since stressed that 'I most emphatically do not believe that they [politicians] are all crooks. Or, even, that they are all dishonest.'[8] Jeremy might have had fewer problems if he had originally quoted the counsel given to Louis Heren in full: 'When a politician tells you something *in confidence*, always ask yourself "Why is this lying bastard lying to me?"' It is perfectly reasonable to mistrust information given to you by a politician who insists on remaining anonymous. Regarding all of them as 'lying bastards', on the other hand, stretches scepticism a little too far for my taste.

Some credit another former *Times* man, Claud Cockburn, as the originator of this line. A radical journalist who reported on and then fought in the Spanish Civil War, Cockburn was also adjudged the winner of a competition among hacks to come up with the ultimate accurate yet boring headline. 'Small Earthquake in Chile – Not Many Dead' is still used in newsrooms to this day to describe any particularly dull story.

It is, no doubt, because so many agree with Heren, Cockburn and Paxman that *Newsnight* viewers chose as their favourite moment of the programme's first twenty years Jeremy's now famous interview with Michael Howard. While a lot of them can recall with glee how many times Paxo asked Howard the same question – in case you've forgotten, it was fourteen – few remember what the question was or what the interview was about. 'Did you threaten to overrule him?' was the apparently innocuous inquiry put to the home secretary about his dispute with the head of the prisons service, Derek Lewis.

What was most revealing in this exchange was Howard's visible discomfort and not what he said, but what he did not say – just as it had been when David Frost put one question repeatedly to Ted Heath. Paxman, who is, believe it or not, rather shy in private, has claimed that his most famous moment came because he couldn't think of anything else to ask. Derek Lewis was, by coincidence, also the focus of one of Jeremy's more controversial questions. He asked Howard's prisons minister, the celebrated spinster Anne Widdecombe, whether she was 'in love' with the prisons boss.

Paxman defends his technique as necessary when dealing with 'speak-your-weight machines' and says that getting past prepared answers 'very often involves trying to find a way of wrong-footing them. They're expecting you to come from the left, you come from the right. You might use a bit of humour, anything to get behind the carapace.'9

This approach may have made Jeremy a pin-up with television audiences but it hasn't always won him the backing of his bosses. John Birt used a major speech when he was director general of the BBC to condemn 'interviewers who feel more self-important than the subject matter in hand' and employ what he called the 'rabbit punch' question to unsettle the interviewee. He called on broadcasters to remember that politicians, unlike them, had an electoral mandate and to consider their impact on the democratic process.

> The balance is swinging towards disputation and away from reflection. The media today resound with acrimony, allegations of incompetence, demands for resignations. In the era of the soundbite and the tabloid, a stray remark, a poorly judged phrase on a Sunday morning programme – a repeated evasion, a careful nuance, a finely drawn distinction – can build up by Tuesday into a cacophony of disputation and a political crisis.[10]

Birt's targets were widely assumed to be the BBC's terrible twins, Humphrys and Paxman. In fact, the director general wrote what he described as a 'billet-doux' to Humphrys – a note of 'warm reassurance' that 'whatever the papers may have said, he was the last person on my mind'.[11] Paxman, then, appears to have been the one in his sights.

Other senior BBC executives have, over the years, echoed Labour's concerns about the 'Humphrys problem' but have never moved against either of their star performers. They know the public howl of outrage that would follow if they did. After John Birt's speech, the BBC consulted the public about 'courtesy in interviews'. The results showed that while some may find interruptions frustrating, most either liked the rough stuff or believed it was necessary to get at the truth.

So it is left to politicians to try to cut presenters down to size. Soon after becoming Conservative leader, David Cameron decided to do just that, arriving at the *Newsnight* studio with a series of prepared put-downs. Jeremy Paxman unwittingly prepared the ground for the politician's fight-back by beginning with a classic rabbit punch: 'David Cameron, do you know what a pink pussy is?'

He didn't.

'Do you know what a slippery nipple is?'

He knew that one. It was a drink.

Not just any drink, Paxman countered. Jugs of this cheap but intoxicating booze were being sold at knockdown prices in bars owned by a company on whose board Cameron sat. It was the cue the new boy was waiting for. 'This is the trouble with these interviews, Jeremy. You come in, you sit someone down and treat them like they are some cross between a fake or a hypocrite and you give no time for anyone to answer their questions.' Later he added: 'Why don't we have an agreement? Give me two sentences and then you can interrupt.'

It was a rare example of a politician successfully turning the tables on the interrogator. Ever since, however, David Cameron has been very reluctant to involve himself in a rematch.

I confess that there are times when I have shouted at the radio or the telly in frustration at an interruption too far, or because I have felt that a politician has something more interesting to say than he or she is being given the chance to articulate. Far more often, however, John and Jeremy's interviews and, latterly, Andrew Neil's as well, have left me enthralled by a sense of theatre, stimulated by the intellectual jousting and relieved that a politician is being held properly to account.

* * *

What Attlee would have made of questions about pink pussies and slippery nipples one can only imagine. What has changed since his day is not just the way interviews are conducted but what it is deemed acceptable to ask about. Two highly personal questions posed in the last decade have raised the issue of what should and should not be off limits.

In 2002 Jeremy Paxman asked the Liberal Democrat leader, Charles Kennedy, about his fondness for drink. This, remember, was five years before Kennedy resigned, admitting that he had a drink problem. Paxman began by remarking that when he'd told politicians he was interviewing Mr Kennedy they'd replied, 'I hope he's sober.' Mr Kennedy retorted that this was a 'Westminster hothouse' slur and that his re-election showed his MPs trusted his political judgement. Paxman pressed on. 'How much do you drink?'

'Moderately, socially, as you well know.'

'You don't drink privately?'

'What do you mean, privately?'

'By yourself, a bottle of whisky late at night?' Paxman suggested.

'No, I do not, no.'

This exchange drew complaints not from Kennedy, who, of course, knew the truth, but from others. Labour's Robin Cook warned the BBC against trying to compete with 'the bottom end of the market'. Paxman was put under some pressure to apologize, which he duly did: 'I have always found Charles Kennedy an affable chap. I am sorry if any offence has been caused. Maybe there was one question too many on drink.'

When Kennedy eventually revealed that he was indeed fond not just of a drink or two but rather more than that, many viewers complained that the media in the Westminster village who were aware of this fact had deliberately concealed it. Proof once again that you are damned if you do and damned if you don't.

Andrew Marr who, since the retirement of David Frost, has made the BBC's Sunday morning sofa his own, has sought to steer a new course between the matiness of his predecessor and the sometimes sterile ferocity of Paxman and Humphrys. However, even he strayed into sensitive territory with a question to Gordon Brown in September 2009. Commenting that if Brown were an American president the public would know all about his medical history, and pointing out that he had recently been asked by an American interviewer whether he was at risk of going blind, Marr said: 'Let me ask you about something else everybody has been talking about – a lot of people . . . use prescription painkillers and pills to help them get through. Are you one of those?'

'No. I think this is the sort of questioning that is –'

'It's a fair question, I think.'

'– is all too often entering the lexicon of British politics.'

Marr touched on the journalistic instinct that had led him to put the question. 'I think the reason you were asked is because people were wondering whether that would be a reason for standing down at some point.'

Brown took this as a cue to speak about his eye injury and to insist that, though he did have to have regular checks, he was perfectly capable of continuing to do the job of prime minister.

'What about my other question?' Marr persisted.

'I answered your other question,' replied Brown. 'Although I have problems with my eyes and it has been very difficult over the years, I think people understand that you can do a job and you can work hard. And I think it would be a terrible indictment of our political system if you thought that because someone had this medical issue they couldn't do the job.'

Downing Street soon denounced the line of questioning taken, which stemmed, they said, from rumours on a right-wing, anti-Brown blog that had unhelpfully posted a congratulatory message to the interviewer: 'Bravo Marr'. Andrew has always insisted that it had nothing to do with the internet but had arisen from a conversation he'd had with Lord Owen. Owen had written a book about politicians' health, arguing very strongly that we were far too fastidious in this country compared to the Americans, who expect to know all the ins and outs of their president's physical and mental condition. At the time, more and more complaints from ministers about Brown's temper and erratic behaviour were also being heard. Marr now says he doesn't think it was 'my finest hour, to be honest' and that he wouldn't 'do that one again'. It would have been wiser to ask Brown about his behaviour – a problem that, like Kennedy's drinking, was the talk of Westminster and yet one most of us, myself included, had been too squeamish to ask about.

For years challenging interviews belonged on current-affairs programmes and not on TV news bulletins. With the decline in audiences for such programmes, leading politicians showing less interest in the long-form interview and as television news has expanded, the role of the interview in news has increased. In 1995, I moved from current affairs to news, and to the business end of the microphone, first as a reporter, largely on radio, then on TV as well, initially as chief political correspondent of the BBC's new 24-hour news channel. I now had the opportunity to ask the questions rather than helping others to plot theirs. I regard it as one of the great privileges of my job, and see it as a duty to try to make my questions count.

I don't believe it is the work of TV news reporters to simply harvest and display a series of carefully market-researched, well-rehearsed and partisan soundbites. Asking one question, whether at a news conference or a 'doorstep' (when a politician is simply confronted with a camera, as Clement Attlee was at London airport), is, of course, different from planning a whole interview but, if the question is chosen well, it can challenge, encapsulate the concerns of many of those watching and, above all, force a politician to think before answering.

It is a style that has not always won me friends. When I became BBC political editor in 2005 my appointment was attacked by the *Guardian*'s Polly Toynbee, who described me as

> a man seen as a Rottweiler of the lobby: relentlessly aggressive, abrasive and sometimes downright rude, admired for his take-no-prisoners onslaught on politicians ... The BBC's big political beasts – John Humphrys, Jeremy Paxman, Andrew Neil and now Nick Robinson – all treat politics and politicians in more or less the same way: with naked contempt. Default mode is to regard all politicians as liars. If they are only laying out some prosaic but important policy, then the only way the viewer/listener might possibly be saved from boredom is by assault and battery on them.

I was more surprised than upset by this. As a producer and reporter I'd been regarded as something of a 'pointy head' rather than a populist. My training, as I've recounted, had been on long analytical interviews about policy. Whenever asked privately about politicians I tend to defend them as a group. I don't regard all politicians as the same. I don't think they're all in it for themselves. I don't believe that you can't trust a word they say. Clearly, though, that's not how it seemed to Polly or, I must assume, to those who agreed with her. So I have had to ask myself, have I changed, or has something else?

The answer is both. The way politics is conducted has changed dramatically over the past couple of decades; the media have changed beyond recognition and, inevitably, I – and others who broadcast about politics – have adapted to those changes.

Politicians still want to use TV and radio, as they always have, to broadcast directly and unmediated to the electorate. Baldwin, Churchill and Eden expected to do this via ministerial broadcasts. Wilson and Thatcher used a combination of in-depth interviews, soft features and soundbites on the news. Since the explosion in the number of television channels and the arrival of rolling news politicians have discovered that more is in fact less. With audiences fragmented, there are fewer and fewer opportunities to reach large numbers of people at once and news has become a monster roaring to be fed twenty-four hours of every day. They can find themselves literally overwhelmed by the media's demands and have reacted by seeking to impose strict controls on their appearances.

Spin-doctors have learned how to exercise the power they have. They trade access – giving it to those who behave well, in their eyes, and denying it to those who don't. They try to set conditions on where and when interviews are done, how many questions can be asked, and even which subjects can be discussed. Andrew Neil, the presenter of the *Daily Politics* and *Sunday Politics* programmes, brilliantly subverted this attempt to manage media exposure when introducing a discussion with David Cameron. He informed his viewers that he'd been told he had to do it standing up, outside, not inside, and that it could last five minutes and not a second longer (an order he ignored).

The result of this struggle for control is too often sterility. Handling an interview and avoiding answering the question has become such an art form that it is now the subject of academic study. Peter Bull of York University has observed and identified thirty-five different evasive tactics employed by politicians (in addition to merely ignoring the question). They range from labelling a question 'hypothetical' or 'speculative' to casting doubt on the veracity of a quotation, questioning its context and insisting that they're 'not aware' of the specific issue they're being asked about. Interviewers have responded with the surprise attack, the ploy of repeating the question or feigned disdain or disbelief. Both sides now prepare as if for battle, concentrating too little on content and too much on how to outwit 'the opponent'.

Before he became prime minister Gordon Brown was regarded as a model political communicator. In fact, as chancellor he avoided long interviews, appearing only five times in a decade on *On the Record* and its successor, *The Politics Show*. He never did *Question Time*. Brown would occasionally turn up on the sofa or in the *Today* programme studio but his focus was on producing a perfect stream of TV news soundbites. They came in two flavours: aggressively partisan or reassuringly managerial. As a young news reporter I used to joke that if you asked Gordon what his name was he would reply by condemning twenty-two Tory tax rises or pledging prudence.

When I was asked to write a paper for the BBC on how to tackle this 'soundbite culture', I proposed that instead of clipping out a few pithy seconds – usually the ones the politician had pre-cooked – we should have the courage to run the questions as well as the answers to expose what they were up to. The proposal was ignored but I adopted this approach when I had the chance to conduct interviews myself. It did not, as we shall see, make for the easiest of relationships.

It seems to me that both sides are losing out. Politicians feel that they cannot find the space to communicate their message at any length or to explore ideas before they have reached firm conclusions. Broadcasters feel that politicians are not willing to open themselves up to scrutiny.

Broadcasters need to accept that there are times when simply asking a politician what he or she is planning to do or is currently thinking is not soft. Politicians need to accept that interviews are just that – questions that deserve proper answers, not merely a rehearsal of a pre-prepared 'line to take'.

No one should be nostalgic for the days when an interviewer asked a prime minister, 'Is there anything else you'd care to say?'

PART II

A Dispatch from
the Front Line

Independent, 6 August 1997

7

TONY TAMES THE BEAST

'**B**ye. I don't think we'll miss you.'

Those were the last words uttered as Tony Blair bade farewell to Downing Street in 2007 after more than ten years as prime minister. They were said not by him but by his wife, Cherie. Pausing before getting into the chauffeur-driven Daimler that would take them on one last journey to Buckingham Palace, she looked long and hard at the towering wall of reporters and cameramen there to record the end of the Blair era. Her parting shot was not whispered or muttered under her breath but offered up as a final judgement by someone well used to summing up in court. I can't have been the only one there that day who felt as if her words were directed at me.

Earlier I had bumped into Cherie and three of her four children in Parliament's Central Lobby as they waited to be escorted to the public gallery to watch Tony Blair's final bow at Prime Minister's Questions. 'I hope you enjoy the day,' I said cheerily to a family I'd got to know a little over the years. The children smiled. Their mother did not. Cherie wasn't one to hide her feelings. By contrast, a few minutes later in the Commons the master craftsman of the soundbite brought his remarkable decade in office to a close with a quiver in his voice. 'I wish everyone, friend or foe, well. That is that. The end.'

Blair had wanted those to be his final words on leaving office. We had been told he would not add to them when he left Downing Street for the last time. Thus it was his wife who wrote the epitaph to the tempestuous relationship between a prime minister and large sections of the media who began as friends and ended as foes. Her husband's final months in office had been dogged by the three Ss – spin, sleaze and splits – thanks to unresolved questions about the Iraq War, fresh claims about cash for honours and his long-running and debilitating rows with his successor, Gordon Brown.

What started as an unhealthy infatuation between the media and Blair ended – equally unhealthily – in contempt. The man who had risen to power partly on the strength of his TV appearances ended up presiding over a conflict with the BBC more damaging than any seen since Suez. The prime minister who had put so much time and effort into wooing journalists, so many of whom had been on his side for so long, left office complaining about how they had treated him and alleging that the fourth estate 'saps the country's confidence and self-belief; it undermines its assessment of itself, its institutions; and above all, it reduces our capacity to take the right decisions, in the right spirit, for our future'. It was, he said, a 'feral beast' that 'tears people and reputations to bits'.

By the time the Blair era drew to an end, I had moved from the operations room to the trenches in the battles between politicians and broadcasters. So for the rest of this story, the narrator is also one of the protagonists – no longer a spectator, but one of the troops on the front line.

My career change had come at a time of massive change in the news media. As we've seen, while current affairs was in decline, news was burgeoning, in terms of volume, if not quality, as never before. As we've also seen, every prime minister has had cause to despair of the media. Tony Blair was, though, the first to live with a beast so large, and one that prowled twenty-four hours a day, seven days a week. In 1997, the year he became prime minister, two thirds of homes with TVs – over 15 million – still had only four channels or had just acquired a fifth, thanks to the arrival of the newly created Channel 5. Within a year Sky would offer its customers 140 channels to choose from. News on the internet was in its infancy, and the press barons were years away from realizing that the web was a place where newspapers could be read. The 2001 election was the first in which Sky and the BBC competed minute by minute and hour by hour for 'breaking news' on their 24-hour news channels.

I charted Tony Blair's protracted and painful departure as the BBC's political editor, a role I'd previously been fulfilling for ITV. It's the job I continue to do for the BBC today, and it's one that requires you to be at different times an analyst, a sketch-writer and an interviewer and at all times, and above all, a reporter. Which is why I am often to be found standing outside in the dark and the cold and the rain. Downing Street, Parliament and my newsroom at Millbank, just down the road, are my office. Television Centre and Broadcasting House are places I visit only rarely. In that sense I work like a foreign correspondent, reporting not from a country but from the 'Westminster village'.

Even with the advent of family-friendly hours in the Commons politics tends to happen at night, when votes are held, party meetings staged and plots hatched in Parliament's lobbies, bars and restaurants. Details of what's in the next morning's papers begin to filter through just before the *Ten O'Clock News*. Politicians offer themselves up for late interviews to reshape the way the story will be told. I am a notorious 'deadline merchant', often finishing the editing of my report just minutes and sometimes only seconds before it is played on air.

I usually work out what I'm going to say (which is not, to answer a question I'm often asked, displayed on an autocue or written for me by someone else) as I run down the road to make it on air in time. The last thing I want is to have to factor in a journey to west London, which can take up to an hour.

I could, of course, sit in a studio in Westminster and be interviewed 'down the line'. TV fashion dictates otherwise. Producers like live TV, not just because it creates the impression that events are unfolding there and then. It is also the one elastic bit of a news bulletin they can cut or extend at the last minute if a taped report comes in too long, too short or not at all. Provided you stop talking when someone shouts 'Wrap!' through your earpiece, most news editors are quite happy. Early in my career I discovered that if you asked a news editor what your 'two-way' was about, he or she would usually answer, 'It's about a minute.'

'Two-ways', the TV jargon for a presenter interviewing a reporter, usually go without too much of a hitch but occasionally when you're cold or distracted or tired your memory can freeze or your tongue can do things that your brain didn't really intend. Some years ago I was trying to convey a degree of scepticism about a claim that David Cameron was 'relaxed' about having to sack a member of his frontbench team. I lost the brief thinking time I'd normally have as there was a problem with the link to TV Centre and my crew was shouting into phones, pulling at wires and constantly asking me if I could hear now. As a result I hadn't come up with an apt phrase or metaphor and found myself saying: 'If he's relaxed, then I'm a . . . a . . . pineapple.' I looked about as surprised as everybody watching at what had just popped out of my mouth.

Once off air I realized where this surreal and baffling comparison had come from. It had been planted in my head by my youngest son, Harry, who had spent breakfast toying with his latest amusing primary-school insult. It's fortunate that only part of it had permeated my subconscious. That morning he'd called me a 'pineapple windybottom'. No, I've no idea why, either, but it was a brief phase and it soon passed.

My predecessor, Andrew Marr, turned the two-way into a news highlight for many viewers but even he once got slightly lost while conjuring up one of his celebrated and colourful metaphors to explain how that day's news had been shaken up. 'It's as if,' he began, 'someone had poked a stick into a . . .' – with characteristic gusto he began to wave an imaginary stick – 'into a . . .' What it was that the stick was poked into the viewer never discovered. It was, I believe, a hornet's nest that he couldn't quite call to mind.

The BBC's early political reporters were allowed no such freedom to conjure with metaphors about pineapples or hornets' nests. They were obliged to stick to a script and not allowed to comment on the news in any way. Conrad Voss Bark, the BBC's parliamentary correspondent in the 1950s, got into trouble with his bosses for describing a statement by the

Conservative home secretary Rab Butler as 'non-committal' – not the most damning of descriptions. His career was saved when Butler defended him, declaring that he had indeed intended to be just that.

Another alternative to braving the elements might be to try to persuade my bosses to drop the late-night 'lives' from Downing Street. The reason I don't comes back to what the job of a political editor is fundamentally about. We're expected to know what those in power are thinking and to find out you need access. Sometimes that means a call or a text message or a lunch meeting with a contact, but being around to bump into the right people in the right place at the right time is also vital. Stand on Downing Street for a short while and you'll meet officials, ministers and anyone else who is visiting the prime minister. There is a back entrance, a route through the Cabinet office and even a tunnel leading from the Ministry of Defence to Number 10, but most people use the front door and over the years I've had many enlightening conversations with those walking past as I wait to go on air.

Before Mrs Thatcher's time in office anyone could walk up Downing Street. In her early years, her husband Denis used to get a black cab to the door of Number 10. However, the threat of terrorism led to the installation of giant gates at the end of the street, now furnished with airport-style security, and only those of us with the right pass or an invitation can gain access to the street.

My counterparts in America are based inside the White House itself in a cramped, sweaty, dark corner of the West Wing. Every so often the president's staff come up with a proposal for new, spacious, air-conditioned, luxury accommodation somewhere else. The correspondents always say no thanks. They know that their ability to do their jobs depends on access; on wandering into the office of the press secretary or a chance meeting with a White House staffer in a corridor.

When I began working as a reporter the media were invited into Number 10 (albeit via a side door) for a regular briefing by Tony Blair's press secretary, Alastair Campbell. After he moved the briefing to another location, political reporters only got to walk the corridors of power when invited to do so. It was a deliberate gambit to limit political reporters' claims to special access. I once suggested that it would be helpful if those of us forced to stand on the street for hours on end for 24-hour news channels or to cover a reshuffle could have access to a loo. The Downing Street official I spoke to replied with a smirk that if he agreed to this he would be making us welcome, and he had no intention of doing that. After all, we were at liberty to broadcast from somewhere else.

My day does, in fact, often begin with broadcasting from somewhere else – my basement at home in Highbury. That is because it often begins with a report for Radio 4's *Today*, which remains compulsory listening for politicians and opinion-formers.

I can broadcast from my study thanks to what once seemed like the magic of ISDN – a digital phone line whose quality is good enough for broadcasting. Soon these lines will go the way of the typewriter, the fax machine and so much else, to be replaced by a computer or iPhone hooked up to the internet. I plan to retire long before technology allows you to appear on TV from your home. My early-morning reports are only made possible by a supply of tea and toast from my family and the fact that I can do them before shaving or dressing – an image best not dwelled on.

My task most mornings is to 'set up' the interview of the

day, a piece of broadcasting jargon nervy politicians find less than reassuring, or to give a form of instant post-match analysis. If a story is developing this entails early texts and phone calls over the breakfast table. Things do not always go to plan. When negotiations were taking place over the formation of the coalition government in the days after the 2010 election, I spoke to one of those involved and relayed to Radio 4 listeners what I'd been told were the latest calculations. Minutes later the same individual came on air and denounced what he'd just told me as 'inaccurate speculation'.

Broadcasting from home has other perils. I once interviewed the American senator George Mitchell for a programme I was making about the Northern Ireland peace process. At the only time he was free my wife was away and I was looking after two toddlers single-handedly. I told Alice and Will to play quietly while Daddy did some work on the radio, sat down with my headphones on and my questions ready and waited for my interviewee to come on the line for our allocated five-minute slot, sandwiched between various other media interviews. As word came through from Washington that Senator Mitchell would be with me very soon, in north London I became aware of a rattling sound from upstairs, then a knocking and finally muffled voices. 'Daddy,' I thought I could hear my children saying, 'we're locked in.'

At that moment there was a voice in my headphones. 'Good morning, Mr Robinson.'

'Good morning, Senator,' I replied as the knocking sounds reached a crescendo. There was now no mistaking my children's complaint. 'DADDY! We are *LOCKED IN*!' It was clear that they had abandoned their strategy of quiet pleading and were trying to break their way out. I did the only thing possible in the circumstances. I started the interview, knowing how important my guest was and how little time I would have with him. I did not, however, allow for the fact that George Mitchell was a thoughtful man who paused occasionally to pick his words about 'the Troubles' carefully. On the recording of our interview those pauses were filled by the sound of my own troubles in Highbury. It took the studio manager several hours to clean up the tape. My children are still recovering.

After appearing on the radio, or on days with quieter starts, my first destination is usually 4 Millbank – home not just to the BBC's Westminster newsroom but to ITN, Sky and a number of foreign broadcasters. Changing employers from BBC to ITV to BBC again has not meant changing my workplace. I walk into the same building, but up to a different floor. I still have an office in the Commons press gallery, just on a different level. Millbank, which runs from Parliament along the north bank of the Thames, is best known these days for the student riot during which the windows of the Tory headquarters were smashed. The Conservatives now occupy the same tower block that lent its name to New Labour's 'Millbank machine'. Between our building and theirs are the spooks of MI5.

The area was known in the nineteenth century for its prison, which held up to 1,000 inmates awaiting transportation to the colonies. Charles Dickens wrote in *David Copperfield* of the 'melancholy waste . . . the ooze and slush' and the 'sluggish ditch depositing its mud' along the walls of the Millbank penitentiary. There is, of course, no resemblance between that and today's one-stop shop for politicians with a message to sell. On a 'Millbank round' they can do half a dozen interviews or more at different newsrooms in less than an hour. Some MPs complain that Millbank has replaced Parliament as the place where politics really happens.

Then it's on to Westminster, where I may go to the daily briefing by the prime minister's official spokesman. In Tony Blair's time these were unmissable. Alastair Campbell was unmistakably his master's voice. If Alastair was cross, you could be pretty sure Tony Blair was cross, albeit rather less so. If Alastair was evasive, you would know that the PM was undecided about what to do. If Alastair praised a minister or failed to defend him, it was certain he was heading for promotion or the chop. Campbell's testosterone-fuelled briefings were inspired by those he had attended as a reporter himself, when Bernard Ingham delivered daily gruff and uncompromising sermons on behalf of Margaret Thatcher.

What began as a daily dose of charm, charisma and a little light sarcasm ended in a spectacular firework display of frustration, petulance and fury. It had to end. David Cameron, like Gordon Brown before him, concluded that the person briefing the media should not be a political ally but a civil servant charged with delivering self-consciously low-octane briefings and focusing on disseminating information rather than highlighting political direction and mood. Even so, the government briefing remains, after the *Today* programme, the next principal morning source of political stories.

At the end of the briefing – and not before – reporters compete to blog or tweet what they've just heard. If the story is big enough, the correspondents from the 24-hour news channels rush on air.

The next critical part of the political editor's day is lunch.

Visit any of the half-dozen or so restaurants closest to Parliament and you will see prominent politicians having lunch with reporters. Journalism depends on contacts, which depend on relationships which, in the Westminster village, traditionally used to depend on a good meal and a nice bottle of wine. When I became a reporter one well-known politician ordered two glasses of champagne at our first meeting and then informed me that when he first entered politics, in the absence of a vote in the Commons or a breaking news story, lunch lasted until, well, dinner. In these more frugal, more work-obsessed and more self-conscious times lunch is more likely to be squeezed into an hour between a minister's meetings and to consist of fish, salad and a bottle of fizzy mineral water.

It is, nevertheless, still the best opportunity to learn what makes politicians tick – what they care passionately about, what's frustrating them and where they see their position on the political greasy pole. Just as importantly, it forges a connection that will guarantee, when you text or call, even at an antisocial hour or an awkward political moment, a reply that might just tell you what is going on behind the scenes.

There was a time when who met whom in Westminster's eateries was kept secret, according to an unwritten code of honour shared by politicians and Westminster journalists. Over the years Downing Street has often demanded, and almost always been refused, the details of a minister's diary. Establishing who he lunched with and when has been Number 10's main method of locating the source of an unhelpful story. If a tale heard over lunch is big enough, rival journalists have been known to out the conspirators, and even to discover – with the assistance of a co-operative waiter – what they ate and drank. I recently found, on leaving a restaurant, that a photograph of my guest and myself had already been posted on the web.

Some see the culture of lunching in Westminster as evidence of a cosy club of politicians and journalists which protects secrets, such as MPs' abuses of their expenses or the smearing of politicians by taxpayer-funded spin-doctors. The unwritten contract may seem clear: the hack feeds the politician, who feeds the hack a story in return, and, as the old saying goes, you don't bite the hand that feeds you. It's certainly true that any specialist journalist has to beware of becoming too close to the people he reports on and starting to see the world as they, rather than the public at large, see it. It's equally true, though, that this era of instant tweeting, freedom of information and Wikileaks makes people more cautious about where they lunch and what they write down. In politics and journalism, just as in any business, there has to be space for things to be said off the record, in confidence – in other words, in secret.

After lunch the Commons press gallery beckons, for a parliamentary statement or PMQs. MPs can be chatted to on their way in or out; there may be a speech or a news conference to attend. My young niece once heard me on the radio and asked me whether all I did was 'burble for a living'. The answer to that is 'yes, but . . .' As well as burbling, I watch and listen and read and talk. What you see in politics is just the tip of the iceberg. The job of the political editor is to fathom out what is hidden below the water.

Tony Blair's relationship with the media began very differently from how it ended. Television loves youth. It loves novelty. It loves informality. No wonder it loved Tony Blair: he delivered all three.

The prime minister he was facing, on the other hand, looked and sounded like what he was, a product of the 1950s. After John Major's surprise victory in the Tory party ballot to replace Mrs Thatcher, his low-key, homespun, reassuring presence on television had at first been seen as a welcome change from the stridency of the Iron Lady. Nowhere was the contrast clearer than in his broadcast to the country at the start of the Gulf War in January 1991. As a military coalition led by the United States, Saudi Arabia, Egypt and the UK prepared to take action to evict the invading forces of the Iraqi dictator Saddam Hussein from neighbouring Kuwait, he told the nation it could be 'proud – very proud' of its servicemen and women. 'Each one of them has Britain's wholehearted support, and the prayers of all of us for their safe return home. And our prayers are also for you, their families. We are no less proud of you. Goodnight and God bless.' It was something a more combative politician would never have dared say, and it moved many voters.

Major was just as gentle with the traditional wartime enemy, the BBC. Invited in the Commons by a Tory MP to condemn reporting that referred to 'British troops', not 'our troops', and what was described as an inability 'to distinguish between good and evil', the prime minister simply replied: 'I believe that what the BBC is doing, in what has already been some remarkable reporting, is trying to keep a proper balance in that reporting – precisely because so much of the world listens to the BBC and because it is important to this country that they continue to do so and to believe what they hear.'

Major was rewarded not only with a shock election triumph in 1992 but by more than 14,000,000 votes, a haul unmatched by any leader before or since. However, as soon as he secured his own mandate everything started to go wrong:

he was struggling with the economy, an unmanageable party divided as never before on Europe and a vanishing parliamentary majority. Just as *That Was the Week That Was* had made Harold Macmillan a figure of ridicule, ITV's brilliant satirical show *Spitting Image* turned the prime minister into an absurd character: a grey-faced, dull, boring man shown eating his dinner with the refrain 'The peas are nice tonight, dear.' And just as Harold Wilson had made Macmillan look like a relic of the past, Tony Blair soon did the same to John Major.

A *Panorama* film I edited soon after his general election victory ended with footage of the prime minister relaxing at home. He was seen putting an easy-listening CD (I don't recall whether it was James Last or Acker Bilk) into a Bang & Olufsen deck before settling into an armchair – I can't be sure, but it may have been a Parker Knoll recliner – to read Stephen Hawking's bestseller *A Brief History of Time*. It was an image that, I suspect, resonated with millions of older voters in the suburbs and the shires. It was, though, I must now confess somewhat guiltily, one that had me, not yet thirty and living in London's trendy Camden Town, sniggering. You don't see much grey hair in current-affairs production offices or TV newsrooms. They were soon lapping up the made-for-television images of Major's nemesis: Tony Blair heading a football with Kevin Keegan, carrying his guitar and, whisper who dares, wearing jeans.

What had first drawn my attention to Tony Blair was not his flair for photo opportunities and soundbites but his willingness to take political risks. After Neil Kinnock had led Labour to their fourth consecutive election defeat the big question was who would be first to tell the party where they had gone wrong and define a route out of their despair.

Whoever it was, I wanted to ensure that he or she did it on the programme I was working on then, *On the Record*. Again and again we bid for an interview with shadow chancellor Gordon Brown. Again and again we were told that he wasn't sure this was quite the right moment. He would, of course, have plenty to say but needed to take time to consider. Growing tired of what it turns out was Brown's characteristic procrastination and in an effort to flush him out, we said we would bid, instead, for Tony Blair. Brown still hesitated. Blair pounced. That difference in their temperaments and their dealings with the media was typical, and the rest, as the saying goes, is history.

In his interview Blair told his party that they had to stop focusing on representing producer interests and become the party that stood up for the consumer. What now feels like a statement of the obvious was at the time considered heresy by some. In the green room afterwards I witnessed a gripping debate between the then BBC political editor, John Cole, and Labour's young pretender. Cole, who was about to retire and probably felt liberated as a result, accused Blair of promoting what he called '*Which?* magazine socialism'. Working people were, he insisted, interested in what they'd always been interested in – their pay and conditions – not, he implied, trendy consumerism. Blair hit back with the argument that voters who'd grown used to choice in their everyday lives would expect the state to be able to offer it to them, too. If only, I thought, this discussion had been on air. It convinced me that Blair was a man who had things to say and was ready to use television to say them.

A couple of years later, when he was the front runner to become Labour leader, he showed again that he was willing to take risks. The contest was necessitated by the sudden death of Kinnock's successor John Smith. Whether or not it was as a result of striking a bargain with Blair, as is widely believed, Gordon Brown had opted not to stand to avoid splitting the pro-modernization vote. I invited Blair to appear in a live TV debate on *Panorama* with his rival candidates for the Labour leadership. As the clear favourite there was every reason for him to refuse (as, sadly, he would when invited to take part in debates as prime minister), and once he had agreed there was every sign that he regretted it bitterly.

When I knocked on his door in one of Blackpool's less than salubrious hotels to warn him that the programme was due to begin, the finest actor on the contemporary political stage emerged white-faced and with trembling hands. Just down the corridor John Prescott was psyching himself up to take on the man whose loyal deputy he would shortly become. 'Fuck off!' he shouted through his door when I knocked. I could hear him rehearsing his lines on the other side. I knocked again. 'Just fuck off, will you?' That was my intro-duction to John Prescott.

At the end of a less than entirely convincing performance Tony Blair ignored the offer of a drink and post-match chatter with Prescott and his other challenger, Margaret Beckett. Instead, he found a quiet corner to make a discreet call. 'Peter. How did I do?' I heard him inquire anxiously. He could not relax until he had the approval of the man already so controversial that he could not be seen to be playing any role in Blair's leadership campaign and was therefore not in attendance that night. Indeed, so controversial was Peter Mandelson, even then, that the Blair team referred to him by a codename, 'Bobby'. It was a name that would not stick. The one that did was the Prince of Darkness.

My relationship with Mandelson in those early New

Labour days was rarely comfortable. Like me he was a former student politician who'd gone on to be a TV producer. Unlike me, he'd decided that politics, not journalism, was his calling. Despite his long and, in his final years, distinguished service in the Cabinet, Peter Mandelson will for ever be branded a spin-doctor. Indeed, he is almost certainly the first person in British politics to have been given that job description. Before the creation of New Labour, spin was a word associated with tops or tumble-dryers. Prior to the 1992 leadership election it was so unfamiliar to British ears I had to write an explanation of what it meant for a documentary I made on how American political campaigning might affect our own.

Some claim that the concept of political 'spin' comes from the phrase 'spinning a yarn', or telling a tale. However, in the US that year I was told it had its origins in baseball and the spin a pitcher puts on the ball. Some believe the 'doctor' bit refers to doctoring a message but my understanding is that it simply denotes someone who's an expert. I suppose we could have had 'spin professors' but somehow that doesn't have quite the same ring to it.

In his effort to end Labour's wilderness years Peter Mandelson didn't just spin, he sought to exert complete control over the media. Sometimes that involved charm. Peter was and still is clever, witty and gossipy. In those days he was also a bully and never more so than when he himself became part of a story. I have only once lost sleep due to anxiety about work, and that was at the beginning of my career as a political reporter after a day on which Peter Mandelson tried to have me fired.

Although only a junior political correspondent in the months leading up to the 1997 general election that swept Tony Blair to power, I appeared regularly on the *Today* programme. It marks the start of the working day not only for many of those who edit newspapers, TV and radio news bulletins but for the spin-doctor, too. His first task is to try to influence the news to which he wakes up and, on this particular occasion, in the summer of 1996, that happened to be what I had to say.

Clare Short – a stubbornly independent member of Blair's shadow Cabinet – had recently given an extraordinary interview to the *New Statesman* magazine in which she had accused 'people in the dark' of transforming Tony Blair from a 'fresh, principled and decent' person into their 'Frankenstein creation – an unprincipled "macho man"'. She didn't name the people in the dark. She didn't need to. Everyone knew she was referring to Peter Mandelson and Alastair Campbell who, she believed, were playing a 'dangerous game which assumes people are stupid' when they acted as if the old Labour party was 'appalling'. It was explosive stuff.

The Prince of Darkness, Peter Mandelson, was clearly not in the ideal position to get Short to unsay what she had just said and she was not in any case the sort of politician who would ever agree to eat her own words. Nevertheless she was persuaded to issue a joint statement with Tony Blair – who was on holiday in Tuscany at the time – designed to dampen speculation that she might be sacked or be about to resign. As the BBC's duty political correspondent that morning I was the one who would get to break the news. Peter Mandelson rang to confirm that the statement was on its way and to tell me something to the effect that 'Clare was just being Clare' and it was all a storm in a teacup.

My home fax machine rang, trilled and whirred with just minutes to spare before the eight o'clock news. I sat in the study scribbling furiously before dialling Broadcasting House to file my report. The *Today* production team were desperately trying to find someone to interview on the breaking story. 'No one will come on,' the editor told me. 'It'll have to be you.' The editor that day was Rod Liddle, who then revelled in causing trouble in the back room and now does it with relish in print.

Having had almost no time to consider what I would say, I was now going to be asked not just to report the facts but to comment afterwards on their significance. As *Today*'s Sue MacGregor began her questions to me, a metaphor popped into my head. I knew it was cheeky, but I couldn't get it out of my mind and besides, I couldn't think of anything else. So I said it. Looking back, I recall the slightly giddy sensation of standing on top of a high wall, resisting the urge to jump, then deciding, to hell with it, and leaping off.

The Blair–Short statement was, I told *Today*'s listeners, the equivalent of an agreement not to get divorced for the sake of the children, in this case the Labour party. The problem, I added, was that, just like any unhappily married couple, they could have another row at any time. If you invited them to dinner you couldn't be sure they wouldn't end up throwing the crockery at each other. Peter Mandelson was, it's fair to say, less than entirely pleased. Moments after I had broadcast the news that Tony Blair and Clare Short would stay together in political sickness and health, I had suggested it couldn't possibly last. I had committed the ultimate sin: not merely relaying his spin but adding some of my own.

I did not have to wait long to feel Mandelson's fury. All I can remember of his call of complaint was the sheer unsubtlety of it. He began by informing me that he regularly went on walking holidays with the BBC's director general, John Birt, an old colleague of his at *Weekend World*. I knew that but I also knew that John, who would himself go on to work for Tony Blair at Number 10, was scrupulous about the distinction between friendships and personal opinions and professional duties and responsibilities.

When I got to the office that morning I had another call. This time it was the man who played soft cop to Mandelson's hard cop: David Hill, Labour's director of communications. By chance my own former colleagues at *Panorama* were filming a documentary in the BBC's Westminster newsroom on the rise of political spin when I picked up the phone. They recorded my end of a tricky conversation and the notes I made of Hill's complaint – 'bizarre terminology . . . not analysis . . . unusual tone'. Somewhat hamming up my defiance for the cameras, I responded:

> I said this was damaging for the Labour party, which it is . . . and that Clare Short had not withdrawn her remarks, which she didn't . . . and that you have not repudiated her comments, which you haven't . . . and I said that the relationship between her and Tony Blair would continue to be difficult. Which it will.

Having picked up that some of my opposite numbers in the press had been told to question my motives, I assured Hill: 'I've had ten years in the BBC and no one has accused me of bias.' I then added, implausibly, that if Labour did so I would 'pursue it'. Looking back I'm not at all sure what I had in mind. I was aware, however, that the *Panorama* recording could serve as an insurance policy in case my bosses at the BBC didn't back me up.

The following evening there was another awkward – although, again, quite minor – story for Labour I was going to have to report. A think-tank was publishing a pamphlet urging Tony Blair to slim down the royal family to a sort of Scandinavian-style, bicycling 'people's monarchy'. In the early hours of the morning the overnight editor of the *Today* programme, Honor Wilson, received a call from Peter Mandelson demanding to know whether the story was being covered and by whom. She quite rightly, but bravely, told him it was none of his business. He retaliated by calling her stupid – three times.

Months later she told me that, put at a disadvantage by the fact she scarcely knew me, she'd been unnerved by his warnings. But he went too far: once he told her that her career could be irreparably damaged if she put me on air, her mind was made up. When the call ended, Wilson told the *Today* team: 'Well, we have to run Nick Robinson now, even if we put him on to discuss what he did in his garden on Sunday.'[1]

At the time my bosses stayed silent – an ominous sign at the BBC. I was convinced that they were deciding whether to back me or to sack me. I have since discovered that in fact they thought it was best simply to carry on as if nothing had happened and certainly not to tell me about the pressure they'd come under. Mandelson had called Samir Shah, then head of BBC Westminster. As it happened they knew each other well, having been at Oxford together and having both gone on to work on *Weekend World*. Samir recalls that their previous friendship did not stop Peter playing the 'I'm close to your boss' card.

'Samir, I've been talking to John . . .' Then, as if he were calling to be helpful, he got to the point: 'You do know that Nick's colleagues are rather concerned about his reporting.' He mentioned that I had been a Conservative supporter at university. Samir invited him to spell out whether he was alleging bias and, if so, what evidence he had. None was produced.

I was just one target in a guerrilla war Labour's spin-doctors were waging against the *Today* programme and the *World at One*. Their aim was clear: to deter the BBC from airing anything that might provoke another of the apparently endless series of complaints from Number 10 or Labour headquarters. This was the time when Labour was taking aim at a somewhat bigger target: the 'Humphrys problem'. After my own run-in with Peter Mandelson I felt bloodied but liberated. I had discovered something: you could survive and indeed prosper as a political correspondent without spending every waking hour or, indeed, the ones when you were meant to be sleeping, worrying about the men in the dark.

After this incident I did still worry about one thing: my colourful metaphor showed no sign of having been on the mark. Far from the divorce I had predicted, Tony Blair and Clare Short appeared to have formed a blissful partnership. By the time she resigned from the Cabinet seven years later, I had long given up hoping. Then Short declared that she was walking out in protest at the Iraq War. I prefer to think it was the seven-year itch. As for throwing the crockery, after leaving the Labour party in 2006 she did go on to accuse Tony Blair of lying to her about the build-up to the war, and to call on the electorate to deliver a hung Parliament. I'd been proved right if, perhaps, more than a little premature.

Although Peter Mandelson did not try again to have me sacked – at least, to the best of my knowledge – we were to clash again. It was a year later and this time it was in public. The occasion was an extravaganza designed to mark the first hundred days of Tony Blair's government. Journalists were

In the early days broadcasters displayed extraordinary deference to politicians but it wasn't to last for long. Clement Attlee (**above**) was once asked by an intrepid man from the BBC if there was anything he'd 'care to say'. His curt reply was: 'No.'

It's quite a contrast with the persistent probing of Robin Day and our contemporary 'big beasts', *Newsnight*'s Jeremy Paxman (**left**) and *Today*'s John Humphrys (**below left**). No wonder politicians much preferred David Frost's sofa schmoozing (**below right**).

BLAIR AND THE BEAST

Tony Blair first tried to tame the media and then was devoured by what he called the 'feral beast'. Reporters on board 'Blairforce One' huddled around the prime minister to quiz him and hear his answers over the roar of the engines (**below**). This flight – bound for a meeting with President Bush – came a week after British and American forces invaded Iraq in March 2003. One mid-flight briefing almost cost Blair his job.

I became political editor of ITV News in the run-up to the war. My leaving present from the BBC was this cartoon (**beneath**) showing Messrs Blair, Campbell and Brown, opposition leaders Duncan Smith, Hague and Kennedy and my opposite number at the Beeb, Andrew Marr.

Tony Blair's face shows the strain as questions mounted about Iraq's missing weapons of mass destruction in June 2003. Days before, the BBC had claimed the government had 'sexed up' intelligence and I reported that ministers did not expect to find any WMD.

This was George Bush's face on a visit to London in November 2003 when I asked him why he appeared to be feared, if not hated, by so many.

Above: BBC staff protest after the Hutton report forced the resignation of the corporation's chairman and director general.

Right: Cherie Blair addresses a last word to the media on the Blairs' final day in Downing Street: 'Bye. I don't think we'll miss you.'

Gordon Brown promised to forge a new relationship with the media when he moved into Number 10. On 27 June 2007, Huw Edwards and I were among those waiting expectantly for the new prime minister's arrival.

It all began to go wrong for the PM when he dithered about whether to call a snap election. In an interview with Andrew Marr at Number 10, he finally called off plans he denied ever making.

After Brown's first news conference with George Bush at a hot and sunny Camp David, the president turned to me and said: 'You should cover your bald head.' As the two leaders walked away I muttered: 'I didn't know you cared.' The leader of the free world looked over his shoulder and replied with a grin, 'I don't.'

Above: Interviewing Brown was always a painful process. Whatever you asked he reacted as if he'd just swallowed a wasp – as brilliantly captured by photographer Martin Argles.

He saw questions – posed here by journalists on a train (**left**) – as traps rather than opportunities. One friend told me he anticipated five negative headlines every time he opened his mouth.

Below: A certain Mrs Duffy from Rochdale got a taste of what it was like when a TV microphone caught the PM referring to her after they'd met as a 'sort of bigoted woman'.

ELECTIONS – THEN AND NOW

Above: Election coverage has changed a little since the first TV election night in 1955 (**inset, top left**), when statistical analysis was done with chalk on a blackboard. Sitting at the centre of the BBC's vast 2010 election studio, surrounded by computers and boffins, was like boarding the Tardis. Our destination – coalition – was as unknown and surprising as many of Dr Who's. One thing stayed constant, of course: a Dimbleby was in charge – Richard then and David now.

Right: Many Tories blame the first-ever leaders' TV debates in 2010 for their failure to win. It had taken more than seven decades after the invention of television for these debates to be staged.

Above: The uprising of young people all over the Arab world, armed only with mobile phones, showed the power of instant communication to shape politics, not just to report it.

Below: Politics may have finally come to terms with TV and radio but it is only beginning to understand the impact of the technological revolution that often has me in knots trying to tweet, blog and broadcast live from Downing Street all at once.

summoned to Labour's Millbank Tower to be told how well it was all going. A crisp white backdrop carried the simple message 'Delivering to the People'. Glossy folders trumpeted the government's achievements.

The prime minister himself couldn't be there. He was on holiday in Tuscany, as he had been when Clare Short attacked the men in the dark. Since he'd been away, things had not been going well, exacerbated by the obvious tension between the deputy prime minister, John Prescott, and Peter Mandelson who, though a mere minister without portfolio, was behaving as if he were Blair's second-in-command. The two men were to host the news conference, which was extraordinarily welcome news to hacks far more interested in examining the dynamics at the top of government than in relaying party political propaganda.

When it was my turn to ask a question I recalled that the prime minister had described himself as the chief executive of UK plc. Was John Prescott, I inquired, deputy chief executive and, if so, what position on the nation's board did Peter Mandelson occupy? The man known for keeping his cool lost it spectacularly. Instead of finding myself the victim of one of Mandelson's icy, withering putdowns I was subjected to a burst of hot anger about the way he was treated by journalists.

The only people who are preoccupied with my role are really preoccupied with it because they are preoccupied with themselves. I have never heard such a stream of vainglorious, self-indulgent questions coming from members of the media about how they are allegedly managed by me. I am sorry if you feel you are not doing your job properly, such that you have to have me write your scripts and fix your headlines.

And all I can say is that I don't really see that sort of performance coming from the rest of the media, who seem to me quite capable of getting on with their own work without interference from me.

The media pack looked on in utter disbelief. John Prescott, who had spent most of the event looking grim-faced, was now smiling. My anxiety turned to hilarity when Peter delivered the final line of his riposte: 'I am sure you will aspire to do better in the future.'

He left the news conference and proceeded to dole out even rougher treatment to Martha Kearney, who was being tried out as a presenter of Radio 4's *World at One*. She has gone on to fill the role permanently and with distinction. A headline in *The Times* a few days afterwards read, apparently without irony: 'Mandelson Accused of Fixing News'. It led one wag to suggest that the paper's next splash should be 'Pope Accused of Being Catholic'. John Prescott later mocked his rival at a photo opportunity on the banks of the Thames, holding up a jar of river water with a crab inside and asking the media pack: 'You know what his name is? He's called Peter.'

Years later, Peter and I would talk or text most days as he did his best to sweeten the sour relationship between Gordon Brown and the media. My reconciliation with the man who tried to have me sacked was one my wife could never understand. By that time, however, he had paid a heavy price for antagonizing both his colleagues and the media. He had been forced out of Tony Blair's Cabinet not once but twice. On the second occasion the person who signed his political death warrant was Clare Short's other man in the dark.

* * *

Alastair Campbell had been signed up by Tony Blair to feed, tame and bully the media beast. His qualifications for the job were that he understood not just the tabloids but the political journalists who worked for them. Recalling his time as a reporter and columnist for the *Mirror*, he said: 'I hold up my hands. I was a biased journalist.'[2] Campbell fought for Labour with the same instinctive tribal passion he deployed to cheer on his beloved Burnley FC. If that meant wooing Rupert Murdoch and the *Mail*'s Paul Dacre while bullying the BBC with equal ardour, so be it.

New Labour followed the lead provided by the man who masterminded the election of their US ally President Bill Clinton. James Carville, Clinton's campaign manager, is best known for his three-word reminder to his team: 'The economy, stupid.' His advice on how to handle the media is less famous but just as influential: 'Feed the beast or the beast will eat you. Give him a cheeseburger or he'll eat your leg.'

Campbell decided to cook up a lot of cheeseburgers, or what Tony Blair would later call 'eye-catching initiatives', to distract the media from their favoured diet of personalities, rows, conspiracies and errors. His aim was to stop the government being knocked off course by feeding the beast. If, however, it didn't behave, he wanted to ensure that the BBC and other broadcasters did not follow the pack.

Most people nowadays get their news from TV and radio and most people say they trust it. Nevertheless Alastair believed, with some justification, that it is the press that often sets the agenda. His explicit objective was to persuade broadcasters not to travel 'in the press's wake . . . As a public sector broadcaster the BBC does have a special duty to give most coverage to the stories and issues that most affect people's lives. This will often mean having a different agenda from newspapers and often going against the flow.'[3]

Campbell's interpretation of this 'special duty' tended, unsurprisingly, to favour the Labour party. In 1995 the Labour leader's speech at the party conference clashed with the much-anticipated verdict in the 'trial of the century', in which former American football star O. J. Simpson was accused of murdering two people, one of whom was his wife. ITN led their bulletins with O. J. The BBC led theirs with Blair's promise to build a 'young country'. It was a decision that enraged many in the BBC newsroom. The anger increased when they learned of a letter that had been sent to TV News by Alastair Campbell.

> Some of your journalists have suggested to us that we are unlikely to get as much coverage for the leader's speech as in previous years because of the O. J. Simpson trial verdict at 6pm. It has even been suggested that there is little chance of Mr Blair's speech leading your bulletins. While of course news judgements must be made in the light of other stories on any particular day, and while I fully appreciate there is much interest in the verdict, I would implore you not to lose sight both of the news value and of the importance to the country of Mr Blair's speech.[4]

Unwittingly Campbell had reinforced concerns among BBC News executives worried about excessive coverage of what they saw as merely an American celebrity crime story. They came to regret the judgement they made and never forgave Campbell for boasting to the press about his ability to shape the news. It was behaviour they would not forget when it came to dealing with him in the future.

Campbell used a speech in 1999 to argue that the BBC

should continue to cover important policy issues like the minimum wage or the 'new deal' for the unemployed even once they were no longer the subject of ferocious political rows. However, that was far from his only agenda. He urged the *Today* programme to drop its hourly newspaper review, 'which is usually just a vehicle for getting in stories not worth reporting in their own right'; he recommended that the BBC's 24-hour TV and radio news channels should stop filling airtime with a 'group of print journalists pontificating'; he suggested that the corporation should 'let democratic politicians speak for themselves'.

His aim was clear. He wanted to decouple the agendas of the BBC and the press and to persuade broadcasters to steer clear of the sorts of stories which can rock governments and drive ministers out of their jobs.

> This is a plea to the broadcasters not always to wait for the leak, the row, the scandal, before deciding to examine a particular government or opposition proposal. Because if they do, like or not, they'll be travelling in the press's wake. That journey is a one-way road to cynicism, and while cynicism is an essential part of politics and journalism, when it dominates most judgements, the media's dominant role becomes the erosion of politics.[5]

Campbell said his objective was to close the 'growing gap between the real agenda and Medialand agenda'. To many it appeared that he simply wanted broadcasters to stop doing what he had pressed them to do when in opposition, i.e. to ruthlessly pursue allegations against ministers.

There was and remains force in some of Campbell's critique but it was fatally undermined by a lack of reflection or candour about his own contribution to media and public cynicism. The man who was seen by most voters as the country's original and most ruthless spin-doctor uttered just one sentence about his own role: '"Spin" never was as important as people imagine and it's even less important now.'[6]

The spin-doctor's lair early in the reign of New Labour was the dimly lit Downing Street basement where Campbell gave his daily briefing for the political journalists in the lobby. The prime minister's official spokesman – the title he insisted we use in reports instead of his name – sat in a large swivel chair like the one on *Mastermind*. On big days his inquisitors from the media could scarcely fit into the room. Some sat on the windowsill, others were forced to squat on the floor at the feet of the man who would spend the next hour or so spinning, mocking and cajoling his way through their barrage of questions. It was usually interesting, often revealing and almost always entertaining – the political equivalent of a post-match news conference with Jose 'the special one' Mourinho. As a new political reporter I would have paid to be there.

Indeed, I confess that I like Alastair Campbell. I'm pretty sure that the feeling is not mutual. We have had several clashes over the years and his diaries contain one or two none-too-flattering references to me but in a world over-populated by grey men with unoriginal views expressed in opaque language he was an invigorating presence.

His greatest value, though, was the daily window he gave us on to the thoughts and frustrations of his boss. He was His Master's Voice, and never more so than when, with a few words, he forced Peter Mandelson out of the Cabinet for a second time. It is an episode that reveals a great deal about the relationship between the media and politics – not all of it good.

It was 24 January 2001, several weeks before Tony Blair was expected to go to the country to seek a second term in office. I headed to Number 10 for Alastair Campbell's morning briefing with some relish. You can tell a story has reached beyond the Westminster village when the policemen who open Downing Street's heavy iron gates or carry out the security checks are talking about it. The question that morning was whether Peter Mandelson could survive or whether he would have to resign again.

Mandelson had been accused of intervening to help obtain a passport for an Indian businessman who'd donated £1 million to his pet project, the Millennium Dome. Srichand Hinduja had been refused a passport once and was, at the time, facing corruption allegations back home. Ever since the allegation had been made in that weekend's *Observer* the government had struggled to get its story straight. Mandelson had issued a statement saying that his private secretary had dealt with the matter but insisting that at no time had he supported or endorsed an application for citizenship. Alastair Campbell had gone further, claiming that the minister had 'refused' to get involved. Both statements were invalidated when it emerged that a Home Office minister said he had spoken to Mandelson about the issue.

Campbell reacted angrily, telling journalists that he had unwittingly made statements to reporters which were 'plainly not true'. As journalists gathered outside the door to Downing Street's basement briefing room everyone knew that Mandelson was being asked to 'pin down' a 'number of areas of fact'. We all assumed that Alastair Campbell would arrive armed with a detailed timeline setting out who had done what and when. On this occasion he didn't. Moreover he looked upset and angry. He then declared: 'Peter Mandelson is at this moment upstairs discussing his future with the prime minister.' It was as good as a death sentence.

I couldn't wait to get out of the briefing and to go on air to say so. As soon as I made it out on to the street I dialled the news desk to tell them I needed to go straight on to the news channel. There was just one problem. For some reason the BBC had failed to send a camera that morning. There was no choice but to dash the half-mile back to our studio. Aware that I am not exactly Westminster's answer to Usain Bolt, I told myself to walk fast rather than run for fear of ending up on screen dishevelled and out of breath. But adrenaline got the better of me and I just couldn't help running as fast as I could.

When I arrived at the newsroom there were people holding open doors and others waiting to propel me in front of a camera and attach a microphone to my lapel. Since the minister had not yet actually resigned – he wouldn't do so for another hour or so – the story depended on my interpretation of what I'd just heard. The second my bottom touched the seat the news channel presenter said, 'Let's join Nick Robinson, who's just run back from Downing Street.' Between wheezy, asthmatic gasps for air, I spluttered out words like 'extraordinary' and 'amazing' as I tried to explain what had just happened. Apparently, this all added to the drama. So much so that that evening's *Newsnight* began its coverage of Mandelson's resignation with my on-air respiratory collapse. Generously, they did not replay the words of the sports presenter who followed my morning report and remarked with a grin, 'Glad those trips to the gym have paid off, Nick.'

Looking back, what really *was* extraordinary was the fact that Tony Blair had sacked a man who was not only his friend but also perhaps his most trusted adviser on the basis of some confusion over a phone call. For after an official inquiry into what had actually happened, Downing Street announced that there had been 'no impropriety, no wrongdoing and no passports for favours'. In his memoirs Blair expresses his deep regret at having let Mandelson go. He concludes: 'It was typical of the way scandals erupt, hot mud is poured over all concerned and the victims are eliminated before anyone quite has the chance or the nerve to wait until the mud is seen to stick or not.'[7]

In truth he'd had the chance but he did not have the nerve. According to Mandelson, he said to the prime minister: 'You're not going to end my entire ministerial career for this, without even knowing the full picture?' Blair replied: 'I'm sorry. There is no other way. It's decided.'[8]

There was, of course, another way. Tony Blair could have waited for the facts, suffered another few days of bad headlines and then opted to keep the adviser and ally who would prove his value when he returned to the Cabinet as deputy prime minister, in all but name, to Gordon Brown.

Why didn't he? His chief of staff, Jonathan Powell, blames it on the fact that the Blair team were 'entrapped by our adherence' to the maxim 'speed kills', which they'd first seen pinned above the desk of President Clinton's adviser James Carville.[9] They believed, in other words, that they had to move faster than their opponents and the media, whatever the consequences. In this case the consequence was the casual discarding of a friend and one of the founders of New Labour. It reminded me of a quip made about another ruthless prime minister, Harold Macmillan. 'Greater love hath no man than this, that he lay down his friends for his life.'[10]

In the days after the resignation Alastair Campbell told a briefing of Sunday newspaper journalists that Peter Mandelson had seemed 'curiously detached'. 'Has Mandy gone mad?' asked the *News of the World*. In my view, all sides had.

There was a third character in the story of New Labour's rollercoaster relationship with the media, someone without whom Peter Mandelson and Alastair Campbell would have been irrelevant. It was, of course, Tony Blair himself. A born actor who loved the stage, he relished the challenge of trying to win over Labour's natural enemies. He was willing to adapt his persona, his language and his image to suit his audience at any given moment. He would tell his party's magazine one day that his favourite dish was fish and chips, while the next confiding to the *Islington Cookbook* that it was 'fresh fettuccini garnished with an exotic sauce of olive oil, sundried tomatoes and capers'. Though much mocked, he gave broadcasters just what they wanted – pithy, engaging soundbites packaged to appeal to their viewers and listeners. Questioning him for ITV News, I used to preface what I wanted to ask him with phrases like, 'Prime Minister, many viewers of ITV *Early Evening News* will be concerned that . . .' in the knowledge that his answer would be pitch-perfect for our audience of housewives and workers home early having their tea. His next answer, to the BBC, would sound subtly but importantly different.

This capacity to judge mood and tone made him the supreme political communicator. So when the news of the sudden and shocking death of Princess Diana was announced in August 1997 it was the new young prime minister who spoke for the nation and to the nation. Cameras were summoned to a village green in Trimdon, County Durham, just before the Blair family attended church in his constituency. 'People everywhere kept the faith with Princess Diana, they liked her, they loved her, they regarded her as one of the people. She was the people's princess and that's how she will stay, how she will remain in our hearts and in our memories for ever.' The tag 'people's princess' may have been Campbell's but the execution was one no other politician could have pulled off.

Pity poor William Hague, the new Tory leader in 1997, a brilliant and natural parliamentary performer but someone who was, and still is, edgy and unconfident when confronted by a camera. Hague did oratory, not empathy. He was at home speaking in the chamber or to a crowd but not to one person watching from his armchair. He was simply no match for Tony Blair. He was not alone. Blair saw off three Tory leaders in all: Iain Duncan Smith and Michael Howard were no more at ease on TV than their predecessor. If Gordon Brown had given him the chance, he might well have seen off the self-styled 'heir to Blair' David Cameron, too.

The death of another princess demonstrated to me Tony Blair's capacity to act for the camera. On board a flight to Sierra Leone in West Africa in February 2002, the news came through that Princess Margaret had just died. I groaned. Not, I confess, out of any feelings of grief, but because I would be forced on arrival at Freetown to stand in front of a camera pontificating about how the prime minister had reacted. It was a very quiet news day. I asked one of Tony Blair's staff to go up to the first-class cabin and ask him for a memory or an anecdote to help me fill the time. Minutes passed and no word came. Only as the seatbelt sign lit up and the wheels dropped for landing did the aide scurry back and say, 'He can't remember anything at all. Sorry.'

On the tarmac a grinning Tony Blair passed the cameras as they were setting up to record his tribute to the princess. Moments later, on cue, he came around the corner, now wearing a black tie and a grave face and intoned that she would be remembered 'with a lot of affection' as she had given 'a great deal of service' to the country. His wife Cherie's recollections were somewhat less warm. In her memoirs she would describe the Queen's sister as 'a stuck-up old slapper' and recall introducing her to a gay MP's partner. 'Partner for what?' asked Princess Margaret. 'Sex,' replied Cherie.[11] I can now picture Tony Blair relaying these stories at the front of the plane and an ashen-faced spin-doctor saying, 'Tell the hacks he can't remember her.'

There were other occasions when getting to ask Blair a question could be a challenge. On the day after the 2005 Budget, the Labour press office informed TV news desks that they were launching a pre-election poster. They made it clear that while cameras were wanted, reporters were not. There would be no opportunity for questions. My bureau chief at ITV, Tim Singleton, smelled a rat. 'Get down there,' he told me, which I did – rather reluctantly, having had a painfully early start interviewing the chancellor, Gordon Brown, who had been very keen to talk about his opponents' policies but far less willing to discuss his own. When I arrived I saw – I could hardly have missed it – a vast, livid-yellow poster, designed in imitation of the warnings carried on the packaging of dangerous chemicals.

'Warning: the Tories will cut £35 billion from public services', it read. This, we would be told later, was 'the equivalent of sacking every nurse, every teacher and every doctor' in the country.

Tony Blair's press officer looked upset that I'd turned up to the event. You do realize, he told me, that there are no questions here. I said I understood that was the plan. My plan, on the other hand, was to shout out a question which would, I hoped, force the prime minister to come to the camera and discuss this issue with me. I had talked about spending both on and off camera with Gordon Brown that very morning, pointing out to him that, much to the disappointment of some of their more radical supporters, the Tories were only, in fact, committed to reducing the rate of increase in public spending, not cutting it. He had made no attempt to correct me. So when Blair and Brown marched towards the cameras I called out: 'Why do you persist in misrepresenting your opponents' policies? You know they are saying they will increase spending but at a slower rate?'

The ploy worked. Tony Blair strode towards my camera and replied: 'I'm actually very pleased you have raised this. That's not what they are saying. We'll give you the quotes from Oliver Letwin about £35 billion less spending.'

'This is not a *cut*, Prime Minister, it's increasing spending at a slower rate.'

'It's a cut over our plans.'

'You can't cut money that hasn't been spent. You're alleging they'll make cuts. But now you're saying they'll spend less. The words are different.'

'They're not different,' he insisted.

Gordon Brown reached into his pocket for a piece of paper, apparently intending to supply Blair with some ammunition. He then put it back again and watched the spectacle with a broad grin on his face. The exchange went on much longer than I expected. I was acutely aware that I had picked a very public fight with the prime minister, but I was damned if I was going to back off now, particularly as he was interjecting responses like 'That's right, Nick' to imply that he'd won me over. What neither of us knew was that the whole exchange was going out live on the TV news channels and being watched all over Westminster. I only discovered this when I returned to my office in the Commons to be greeted by applause from the *Channel 4 News*, *Evening Standard* and *Sun* journalists who shared it with me.

The exchange made good theatre but there was more to it than that. I believed and hoped it would help to explain a complex argument, one that's become very relevant now. The dispute between Labour and the Tories in the Blair years was over the rate of increase in public spending and not about whether to make 'cuts'. Clearly the Tory policy would, over time, if all had gone as they'd wished, have produced a smaller state doing less with fewer people than Labour's system, but that's very different from imposing real cuts – firing staff, closing programmes and squeezing welfare. I persuaded my bosses at ITV News to get our graphic designers to rework Labour's poster to make the point. Our take on it read: 'The Tories plan to spend 2 per cent less than Labour plans to spend in eight years' time.'

Tony Blair told me later that he welcomed the row as it drew attention to his election poster. People would notice what it said more than my attempt to question its premise. I've a horrible feeling that was true.

When Tony Blair delivered his parting shot to the media it was rather lengthier and more closely argued than his wife's one-liner. It was, though, no less heartfelt. It was in this speech, at the Reuters Institute for the Study of Journalism at Oxford University on 12 June 2007, that he coined the 'feral beast' metaphor.

> Scandal or controversy beats ordinary reporting hands down . . . attacking motive is far more potent than attacking judgement. It is not enough for someone to make an error. It has to be venal . . . and the fear of missing out means that today's media, more than ever before, hunts in a pack . . . it is like a feral beast, just tearing people and reputations to bits, but no one dares miss out.

The power of the speech was that it contained some uncomfortable truths. It is certainly the case that Westminster journalists often operate as a pack and love nothing more than sinking their teeth into a possible scandal, particularly when the person at the centre of it is someone as colourful, as controversial and as politically friendless as Peter Mandelson. The way journalists weaken their prey – helped along by opposition MPs – is by posing endless lists of 'unanswered questions'. Newsrooms echo to the sound of reporters swapping views on the latest evidence, searching for inconsistencies justifying new lines of inquiry. When one emerges – as it did in the case of Peter Mandelson – the pack pounces. The prime minister must decide whether to stand by his weakened minister while the full facts emerge or whether to end it, to 'draw a line under the affair', so the government can 'move on'. This feeding frenzy is not a pretty sight. Adrenaline-fuelled young men (and political journalists are still, mostly, men in their thirties and forties) anticipating a kill, albeit only a metaphorical one, never are.

Looking back, I do feel uncomfortable about the speed with

which the scalps were claimed of politicians who often had a good deal to give to public life. Peter Mandelson's resignation followed a pattern that was seen throughout Blair's three terms in office. David Blunkett was another minister who resigned twice and Blair favourites Estelle Morris, Stephen Byers and Beverley Hughes went, too.

Tony Blair was right to observe that reporters are more fearful of being beaten by their competitors than they are about forcing someone from office unnecessarily. However, there are times when individuals do stand apart from the pack pursuing a minister and try their best to explain his or her point of view.

In my own case, one of those was when education secretary Ruth Kelly was hounded for allowing registered sex offenders to be given jobs as teachers. I argued that it was unlikely a mother of four was in favour of paedophiles in the classroom and more probable that she was presiding over a system in chaos. In any alleged scandal reporters can only see the tip of the iceberg and have to guess, and then probe, and then analyse what lies hidden beneath the surface. They should be ready, sometimes, to conclude that the answer is not very much.

However, the great weakness of the 'feral beast' speech was its failure to acknowledge the other side of the argument. As the MPs' expenses scandal would later show, there were plenty of other occasions when journalists didn't pursue questions robustly enough or soon enough. So, too, would the build-up to the Iraq War, which sparked the greatest battle between politicians and broadcasters since Suez.

'A report says President Bush
had to stop Tony Blair
bombing the BBC'

Daily Telegraph, 27 November 2005

8

IT'S WAR

The first step on Tony Blair's road to war with Iraq and the BBC was taken long before the election of George W. Bush as US president, the 2001 attacks on New York and Washington and Saddam Hussein's defiance of the United Nations. It came when Blair deployed British forces for the first time as prime minister, on 16 December 1998. I was sitting in the offices of BBC Radio 5 Live watching Manchester United play Chelsea and waiting to see whether it was safe to go to the station's Christmas party. For days there had been a growing expectation of joint British and American military action against Iraq as punishment for the failure of Saddam to comply with United Nations Security Council resolutions or to co-operate fully with UN inspectors searching for evidence that he was producing chemical and biological weapons. If the action did not start that night I could go to the party as the match would be followed by a football phone-in. If something did happen I was to handle the breaking news.

At 9.23pm air-raid sirens sounded in Baghdad. Minutes

later, Saddam Hussein announced that Iraq was on a war footing. Next anti-aircraft explosions were heard in Iraq's capital city. 'Get in now,' I was told. While running into the studio, sitting in front of the microphone and pulling on my headphones, I recall thinking, I have no scripts, no guests, there are almost no facts and yet I am due to be on air for the next three hours. I learned then the value of the news presenter's sombre and grave tone, which you naturally adopt on occasions like this. It allows you to say not very much at all very slowly while appearing to match the mood of the moment. If you add the odd 'for those just joining us, the news from Baghdad is . . .' before repeating the two facts you have gleaned from monitoring what the cameras are feeding directly on to the TV news channels, you can fill time as the soundless but visibly frantic figures behind the glass in the control gallery find you someone to talk to or something to talk about.

Tony Blair soon filled the space for me by stepping out of the door of Number 10 Downing Street to announce that 'Operation Desert Fox' had been launched and that 'British involvement will be significant'.

> We are taking military action with real regret but also with real determination. We have exhausted all other avenues . . .
> If he [Saddam] will not, through reason and diplomacy, abandon his weapons of mass destruction programme, it must be degraded and diminished by military force.

I reported that night wave after wave of cruise missiles hitting Iraq's capital city. As a result, during the long build-up to the 2003 invasion of Iraq, I never doubted that Blair would be prepared to go to war. As early as the autumn of

1997, his rhetoric in the House of Commons clearly pointed to what he could do later. 'It is absolutely essential that he [Saddam] backs down on this – that he be made to back down. We will, of course, seek a diplomatic solution, but he has to back down because, if he does not, we will simply face this problem, perhaps in a different and far worse form, in a few years' time.'

As we have seen from Churchill's fury during the general strike, Eden's over Suez and Thatcher's throughout the Falklands conflict and the fight against the IRA, government anger with the BBC has always peaked at times of war or national crisis. Prime ministers conflate the national interest with their own personal and political interests. They loathe the fact that their actions are not being presented with the unquestioning deference they believe is due to them at a moment of national emergency and simply cannot under-stand why their enemy's words are given any weight at all. In Tony Blair's war with the BBC Alastair Campbell was more than just the chief protagonist and propagandist. This would be his feud as much as Blair's and it began that night in 1998.

Campbell's diaries covering the four days of the bombing of Baghdad reveal his mindset: 'The BBC was grim with the Baghdad line being swallowed pretty much wholesale.'[1] He called the BBC's head of news to complain of 'an inbuilt bias against us caused by their refusal to match their scepticism of what we said with scepticism of what the Iraqis said and showed them, in an environment where they were TOTALLY dependent on the regime for access and information'.[2]

The following day he noted: 'The BBC was a bit better today, doubtless because of the bullying yesterday.' Two days later, the *Mirror* trumpeted: 'Blair Blasts BBC's War Reports

"Bias"'. One source close to the premier – I wonder who it could have been – told the paper:

> What particularly enraged him is they hardly ever mention there are reporting restrictions and give the impression their reporters are wandering freely around Baghdad reporting the truth. It is absurd to fall for Saddam's propaganda in this way by concentrating so much on damage to Iraqi people. It ends up being almost pro-Iraq, which is a ridiculous position for the BBC to adopt in a time of war. If they are not asking the wounded how they feel about being bombed by the British, they are trying to stir up anti feelings among the Arab and European countries towards Britain's position.

This was the first of five wars* Tony Blair would wage with Alastair Campbell at his side. The second followed in March 1999 in Kosovo. Success there, and the following year in Sierra Leone – where, after nine years of brutality and bloodshed, the British intervened to shore up an ineffectual UN mission and a frail civilian government against the aggression of rebel militia – would convince the prime minister of both the morality and the efficacy of military action. The skirmishes he and Campbell would have with the BBC were preparation for what would later become full-scale conflict – over Iraq again.

Kosovo was a war like no other, a war fought entirely from the air. Its aim was simple: to get the Serb aggressors out of Kosovo and the peacekeepers in, and thereby to persuade the refugees who'd fled in terror to return. All this was to be

---

* Iraq (1998), Kosovo (1999), Sierra Leone (2000), Afghanistan (2001) and Iraq again (2003).

done without the risk of significant losses among alliance forces. The West, though, underestimated the resilience of the Serb dictator Slobodan Milosevic and his allies in Kosovo. Far from withdrawing after the air strikes began, the Serbs actually stepped up their campaign of ethnic cleansing and the NATO attacks appeared to unite them behind their dictator. Inevitably, there was damage to non-military targets and the loss of civilian life. All this handed Milosevic easy propaganda victories.

The BBC, and in particular my colleague John Simpson, the corporation's world affairs editor, became the focus of a Downing Street campaign for daring to point all this out. What he reported from Belgrade was not what they wanted to hear in London.

Alastair Campbell did not always voice his objections directly or in public. On 16 April 1999 *The Times* put the anonymous angry complaints of a senior government official on its front page. Simpson, it was alleged, was 'swallowing Serb propaganda' and failing 'to display scepticism' about the reports of what was referred to as the 'Serb lie machine'. The official was clearly Alastair Campbell, who was reflecting, as he usually did, the frustration of his boss.

When Tony Blair was asked about Simpson at Prime Minister's Questions he replied, diplomatically, that the BBC man should be free to report as he saw fit and the government should be free to speak as it found. Alastair Campbell's diaries show that, as so often, Blair spoke rather more colourfully in private. 'What a precious arsehole,' he said of Simpson. 'Thinks he should swan around criticizing as he pleases but if anyone speaks back it is an attack on civilization as we know it.'[3]

Blair objected not just to Simpson's factual reporting but

what he saw as expressions of opinion. Simpson said the threat – later carried out – to bomb Serb TV stations 'does nothing to persuade this country [Serbia] that the West . . . is any less authoritarian than Mr Milosevic'. The final straw, though, was a column in the *Sunday Telegraph* headlined 'Why This War Isn't Working'.

There was one incident that gave real power to that headline. On 14 April NATO planes had launched two attacks near the town of Djakovica in southern Kosovo. One of the targets turned out to be a column of refugees heading for the Albanian border. As if killing the very people it was meant to be protecting wasn't bad enough, it took NATO another five days to acknowledge the truth of what had happened. On the day after the tragedy its supreme commander, General Wesley Clark, publicly accused the Serbs of an act of extreme brutality, claiming that they had opened fire on the civilian refugees in revenge for a NATO strike on Serb forces north of Djakovica. It wasn't true. Not only had there been a terrible military mistake, it had been compounded by a series of errors in the reports presented to the world. That inaccurate information jeopardized public support for the conflict within and beyond America and Britain, threatening the unity of an alliance nineteen nations strong. It was time to call for reinforcements to fight the battle for public opinion.

After a phone call between President Clinton and Tony Blair, Alastair Campbell was dispatched by Eurostar to Brussels to construct a propaganda machine to rival that in Belgrade. Before then little thought had been given to the fact that a war waged only from the air would leave Slobodan Milosevic almost unchallenged in the battle of the airwaves. His forces had total control on the ground and thus control of the flow of information about the impact of air strikes. NATO's small, inefficient and amateurish media operation was unable to compete. It depended, according to one account, on a German general driving to NATO headquarters in Brussels once a day with the latest information from the military.[4] Campbell replaced it with a new 'media operations centre' which adopted all the techniques he had developed to get New Labour into power: swift rebuttal, 'lines to take', a media grid and a factory to produce newspaper articles under the bylines of NATO leaders. NATO began to admit its mistakes and talk up its successes. After seventy-eight days of bombing – much longer than anyone had expected – victory was declared. Only afterwards did it become clear that NATO's estimates of the number of tanks and artillery pieces destroyed had been overstated.

Victory in Kosovo did more than convince Tony Blair of the moral value of military action against dictators: it established Alastair Campbell as the West's greatest communicator or, as his critics would see it, propagandist-in-chief. General Clark, who became an admirer and friend of Campbell's, concluded: 'The right way to fight a propaganda offensive is not with more propaganda. It's to tell the truth, the whole truth and nothing but the truth, and do it as rapidly as possible . . .' There was, of course, a 'but' and, when it came to Iraq, it would prove to be an important one: '. . . but you need some smart people who can tell you what piece of truth you are looking for.'[5]

The battle lines between government and the BBC had been drawn over Kosovo. Alastair Campbell's involvement in selecting 'the piece of truth' the public would be told about Tony Blair's next war would help to trigger a clash with the corporation that would result in much heavier casualties.

* * *

'*Pro*-hibited – explosives, knives, guns . . .' A stern-faced US marine guard listed the items which could not be taken 'on board' when the media accompanied Tony Blair to his first-ever meeting with George W. Bush – a man he didn't know, who was the enemy of the prime minister's closest ally, Bill Clinton, and with whom he appeared to have little politically in common. We were standing in the snow in woods around sixty miles north of Washington DC waiting to enter the president's country retreat.

'What does he mean, "on board"?' I whispered to an accompanying diplomat.

'What's known as Camp David to you and me is, in reality, "Naval Support Facility Thurmont", he told me, 'and so while not, of course, actually a ship, it is treated like one.'

'. . . grenades, matches,' the marine droned on, 'snuff . . .' *Snuff*? Sadly, I never did get an explanation for why a small pinch of tobacco was regarded as a threat to the leader of the free world. The surprises on this trip, and indeed at every summit with George W. Bush, did not stop there.

That first summit, the beginning of a relationship that would change the world, will be remembered, of course, for two things: jeans and toothpaste. The jeans, officially deemed to be 'ball-crushing', were worn by a nervy prime minister desperate to look relaxed alongside the president. Blair's hands could not quite make their way fully into the pockets, although he was clearly determined to try. The toothpaste, Colgate to be precise, was the bizarre answer the president gave a startled news conference when asked what the two leaders had discovered they had in common.

Like all first meetings between a British prime minister and a US president, this had been the subject of a great deal of forethought, planning and anxiety. It was part summit, part getting-to-know-you. The movie screened at Camp David that night for the Blairs and the Bushes – *Meet the Parents* – could not have been more apt: what the Blair team was undergoing was a turbo-charged version of the panic experienced by most of us on meeting our in-laws for the first time. Just as we can't choose our in-laws, prime ministers can't choose the family of international leaders they have joined. They just have to find a way to get on with them.

The history of the build-up to a war that cost many tens of thousands of lives* and many billions of pounds will be recorded through what was said and not said and by whom at this and the series of Bush–Blair summits that followed. People may talk of the twenty-first century as the age of instant communication – of text, email, Twitter, Facebook and Skype – but international diplomacy is still done face to face and, more often than not, one to one. This poses huge problems for journalists covering these summits – they are not in the room; their sources may very well not be in the room, either, and may manage only to ask their boss fleetingly, 'How's it going?' or, even less helpfully, 'What shall we tell the hacks?' The latter appeal results in a briefing that rarely bears much relation to what is actually going on. On the plane home reporters might get an off-the-record chat with the PM or one of his key advisers but by then the news bulletins have aired and the front pages have been printed.

It is sometimes weeks before the true picture of what took place emerges, bit by bit, and, as has happened with Iraq,

* The actual death toll is disputed. Supporters put the figure at 162,000 while critics insist it was much higher.

multiple official inquiries can be required to establish the whole story.

TV reports of summits are dominated by the body language of the two leaders, the unscripted on-camera exchanges between them and those bits of their news conference that stray beyond the carefully choreographed diplomatic niceties and banalities. Not that much, in short. I accompanied Tony Blair to each of his summits with George W. Bush and sometimes look back with horror at what we didn't know and, therefore, couldn't report.

At one Bush–Blair summit in the countdown to the war their news conference was postponed several times. This seemed significant to me, as the president was known to be obsessed with sticking to schedules and was never late. When the two men appeared there was none of the usual banter or chumminess. The atmosphere was tense. I reported this on air, explaining that while I didn't know the reason, it was clear to me that there had been a disagreement. Weeks later, an official told me they'd argued just before they were due to face the media to talk about the Middle East peace process. Sometimes reporting has to be about informed speculation, not just hard facts.

At that first Camp David encounter, on 23 February 2001, the pictures and the joshing showed how eager Tony Blair was to please and how keen George W. Bush was to 'make nice', as they say on the other side of the pond, with someone he declared would be a 'friend on the end of the phone'. We later learned that the British ambassador to Washington at the time had been given the rather charmless instruction by Tony Blair's chief of staff to 'get up the arse of the White House and stay there'.[6]

Nevertheless the reports of the Colgate summit focused

on answers to questions about what might divide the two men – plans for an EU rapid-reaction defence force and a US missile defence shield – rather than what cemented this unlikely partnership. Just days before they met, British and American planes had bombed Iraqi air defences. At Camp David, Tony Blair promised to use 'whatever means are necessary' to prevent Saddam Hussein from developing weapons of mass destruction. George W. Bush warned that 'appropriate action' would be taken to contain the Iraqi leader. These words went virtually unreported that day. We didn't know how important they would become. It has taught me that the questions designed to highlight problems are not always the ones that reveal the most.

It is said that we all remember where we were on 11 September 2001, the day the Twin Towers were felled in New York by two hijacked passenger planes and war became inevitable. I was standing by the tea bar at the TUC conference in Brighton, chatting to one of the prime minister's advisers about what he would say in his speech that afternoon in preparation for a live broadcast on BBC News 24. The aide's mobile rang. It was a call from the prime minister's hotel suite. 'You can forget your live,' he told me. 'A plane has just flown into the World Trade Center in New York. Apparently, the pictures are extraordinary.' No live, great pictures, someone else's story. That was all I understood at that point.

Nineteen minutes later everything changed as I, like so many others around the globe, watched the second plane hit. This was no accident. It was a devastating terrorist attack sure to provoke a response. Tony Blair has since said that as he saw the pictures in that Brighton hotel he immediately grasped the significance of that moment. Certainly the intense look in his eyes as he left to speed back to London spoke of a man who believed himself a player at the centre of world-changing events, not merely a spectator.

I was outside with a handful of police and security officials waiting for his departure. We stood in virtual silence. There was none of the usual time-filling chatter. What could you say? When the prime minister emerged a colleague shouted a question at him – I forget what – but I do remember that look when he turned towards us.

At this instant – before the full horror of the day's events unfolded; before the horrific death toll mounted in Washington DC and rural Pennsylvania when a third plane careered into the Pentagon and a fourth, bound for the Capitol, crashed en route after passengers bravely tried to wrest back control from the hijackers – one Labour spin-doctor's thoughts were turning to the possibility of releasing bad political news to be obliterated under the rubble of New York. It is still hard to conceive of anyone typing out the words 'This is a good day to bury bad news,' let alone going on to press 'send' to circulate them to colleagues, but this is what one person did. The government already had a reputation for spin but the brutal cynicism of that sentence would sum up for many a culture they abhorred and one that would go on to prove deadly.

Ten days later the prime minister flew to New York to attend the memorial service for the victims of 9/11. On the chartered plane, carrying journalists as well as his officials, were reminders of how the world had so suddenly changed. One was trivial but telling: the in-flight meal no longer came with hijacker-friendly metal knives, forks and spoons. They had been replaced by plastic cutlery. The other was rather more significant. The carefully modulated tones of the

British Airways pilot respectfully requested that passengers refrain from using the onboard phones since the number of lines was limited and 'an important call' was being placed from the first-class cabin. Half an hour later, Tony Blair strode to the back of the plane to talk to the larger than usual pack of travelling journalists. To everyone's astonishment, he announced: 'I have just put down the phone to President Khatami of Iran.'[7]

The president had, he said, condemned the attack on Iran's bitter enemy, normally referred to in his country simply as the 'great Satan'. It was already clear that American military action would follow and that Britain would be involved – but against whom? The suicide pilots, members of the amorphous Muslim extremist terrorist organization al-Qaeda, had been trained and based in Afghanistan but the atrocities of 9/11 had not been perpetrated under the banner of any nation. Blair was asked whether he found it difficult to sleep now that he was on the brink of sending British forces to war again. 'It is a huge and heavy responsibility,' he said, 'but what has heartened me is the understanding that I have found in every other leader I have spoken to of the necessity of not flinching from action here.'

It was also clear that some in the US administration were already connecting the 9/11 attacks with Iraq and Saddam Hussein. The prime minister was asked: 'Where do you see Iraq in all this? Are they in or are they out? There seemed to be some question of the foreign minister yesterday saying that it was nothing to do with them—'

Before the question could be completed Tony Blair interrupted. He wanted to close down a potential gap between London and Washington. 'We have made it clear throughout that we proceed on the basis of evidence.'

Just before the briefing ended I slipped away to try to grab one of the onboard satellite phones before all the lines were taken. Satellite calls don't come cheap, and that day I ran up my biggest phone bill ever as BBC outlets lined up for their turn to hear the news 'live from the prime minister's plane'. The time cannot be far away when it will be taken for granted we'll be able to broadcast from anywhere on the planet – after all, texts have already been sent from the most remote spots in the world, including the top of Everest, and pictures can now be transmitted using a mobile or laptop and a satellite dish that could fit into a satchel. But my broadcast that day was pretty exciting for me and for my colleagues back at base.

The great advantage of flying with the prime minister is the access it provides to aides and advisers, and from time to time the PM himself, during the journey – a sort of international equivalent of standing in Downing Street waiting for someone with something to say to pass by.

Michael Brunson, who was ITN's political editor for many years, described following the prime minister around as like having 'a ringside seat as history is made'. It certainly can be, but sometimes, particularly on foreign trips, it can feel more like being stuck in a tunnel waiting to get into the arena where it's all happening. After speaking at the memorial service in New York, Tony Blair flew on to Washington, where his status as the most popular Brit since Margaret Thatcher or, arguably, Winston Churchill, was confirmed. The prime minister was given a seat in what is known as the 'heroes' gallery' for the president's historic speech to both Houses of Congress. Sitting alongside the mayor of New York, Rudy Giuliani, and the first lady, Laura Bush, he was given two standing ovations as George W. Bush lauded Britain as 'America's truest friend' and thanked him personally.

The visiting journalists, however, were not there to see it. We had fallen victim to one of the drawbacks of flying with the prime minister: having our itineraries dictated by Downing Street. We had been put on a coach to be taken back to the prime minister's plane, known by the media as Blairforce One, waiting at Andrews Air Force Base. We had to be there early so that it would be ready for take-off as soon as the PM's convoy dropped him off at the steps to the plane.

It took some persistence to persuade the coach driver to forgo his football commentary and retune his radio so we could even hear the president and those ovations. On arriving at the base we discovered that incredibly, nobody here, either, was listening to their commander-in-chief. I rather forcibly expressed the view that it really would help if we could at least see this significant moment in world history on television before being expected to report on it. It took the considerable diplomatic skills of the men and women from Number 10 to prevent me from being thrown in the slammer by a marine who didn't much like being lectured by a visiting Brit.

In October America's military response to 9/11 was unleashed. In alliance with the UK, Australia and the Afghan United Front, the US launched 'Operation Enduring Freedom'. Its aim was to destroy al-Qaeda's bases, track down and bring to justice its leader, Osama bin Laden, and to oust Afghanistan's Taliban government in favour of one that would not give America's enemies a hiding place. It turned out to be a rehearsal for the war in Iraq that would follow – both for the military and for Alastair Campbell.

Downing Street's anger with the BBC's war reporting gave a foretaste of what was to come, as Campbell's diary shows:

'BBC were getting more and more outrageous, Taliban claims were being treated pretty much the same as anything we said followed by endless Fergal Keane emoting.'[8]

Fergal Keane, a distinguished war reporter, was not the only colleague whose reporting offended. On the day of the alliance's first significant military victory, the capture of the city of Mazar-e-Sharif, a Taliban stronghold, Campbell wrote: 'I went ballistic about Rageh Omaar's piece, called Sambrook saying it was a fucking disgrace, really lost it with him.'[9]

Richard Sambrook, the head of BBC News, soon grew used to and, immune to, that anger. One fax from Downing Street, entitled 'Catalogue of lies', listed eleven stories giving 'the date, the incident, the allegation' (against the alliance) and what Campbell insisted was 'the fact'. For example, on the second day of air strikes the Taliban had reported thirty-five civilian casualties. There was, said the fax, 'no evidence to support this'. Its aim was to stop the BBC broadcasting the enemy's claims about casualties. When it came to Iraq, Campbell would tell Sambrook that the 'catalogue of lies' originated within his own newsroom.

While George W. Bush and the United States prepared themselves to take on Saddam Hussein, Tony Blair presented himself as a global peacemaker, exporting the lessons he'd learned in the cold and damp of Northern Ireland to the arid deserts of the Middle East and the hot, steamy Indian subcontinent.

My passport was beginning to resemble a dog-eared guide to the world's trouble spots: the Gaza strip, Israel, Jordan, Saudi Arabia and Syria all stamped it in the space of three days in late 2001. In early 2002 India, Pakistan, Bangladesh and Afghanistan were covered, again in three days. I had been puzzled, in the immediate aftermath of 9/11, by Tony Blair's rhetoric about 'the kaleidoscope' having been 'shaken' and his promise to 'reorder the world around us' before the pieces settled again. Now I knew what he meant.

I learned something important myself in those few weeks. It feels good when your country and your prime minister seem to be at the centre of world events. But while he talks about solving global problems that have proved unsolvable for years, if not decades, it's crucial to remember, as you flit from one capital and one leader to the next, that all is not necessarily as he or you might wish it to be, even if he looks you in the eye and insists that behind the scenes things are moving in ways that aren't evident in public.

On one leg of the gruelling Middle East tour I was summoned to the first-class cabin of the 777 chartered by Downing Street to 'have a chat with the boss'. Waiting for me in seat 1A, always his favourite, was Tony Blair. The mood around him was, as it usually was, relaxed, casual and upbeat. There was a real chance of restarting the peace process, he told me.

I recounted what I'd seen on the trip. First there was a memorable news conference with Syria's President Assad. Hailed in advance as a reformer who was backing military action in Afghanistan, Assad had, to Tony Blair's visible dis-comfort, proceeded to condemn the war and to compare those carrying out terrorist attacks on Israel with President de Gaulle's wartime French resistance. Then there'd been news conferences in Gaza with Yasser Arafat, who looked too vulnerable to deliver peace, and in Israel with Ariel Sharon, who looked too inflexible. I don't doubt Tony Blair not only believed that peace was possible but wanted desperately for it to be so. I confess he convinced me it was possible, until I told a BBC correspondent in the region what he'd said. It was nonsense, I was told. And more than a decade on, we're all still waiting.

The trip to Afghanistan should have been the highlight of Blair's post-9/11 travels. He would be the first leader to set foot in the country since the removal of the Taliban and the first to meet Afghanistan's new leader, Hamid Karzai. The journey there, however, was a reminder that this war was far from over. We flew on a Hercules troop carrier, quite a change for the prime minister's entourage from the champagne-and-hot-towels service provided by British Airways. There were no seats, just benches and webbing behind your head to cling on to in the event of turbulence.

Mr and Mrs Blair sat in the cockpit behind the pilots while other passengers had a choice between freezing or sitting under an electric heater that left your throat parched and your head throbbing. The toilet was a bucket, but this being a VIP flight, it had the added luxury of a curtain to screen those going for a pee from their fellow passengers. Women, I'm told, have better bladder control, which was lucky for Cherie, who might have found a trip to the loo less than entirely relaxing. Just to add to the fun we were told that we would be landing in total darkness, to avoid attack by rocket-propelled grenades, using what was described as a 'corkscrew descent', which meant, well, just that – spiralling down on to the runway to make it harder for enemy targeting devices to lock on to us.

On the ground an officer tried to herd the cameramen and reporters and to issue us with safety instructions. He had clearly never worked with journalists before. The pack spotted the waiting Afghan party and sprinted in its direction, cameras running, with the cry 'You're even madder than my bloody squaddies!' ringing in their ears. Karzai and his small group of allies, waiting in the darkness on the edge of the runway, looked for all the world like a bunch of those Second World War resistance fighters spoken of so fondly by the Syrian president. It felt as if we'd been guided in by torch-light to land behind enemy lines – which wasn't, I suppose, too far from the truth.

Having filmed the arrival, the media finally agreed to go where they were told – in the direction of a vast hangar where a press conference would be held. Hamid Karzai, standing at the prime minister's side, displayed one of the greatest strengths of a leader in the television age: he looked serene, even though his mind must have been whirring. Tony Blair declared that he regretted the West had not 'acted sooner' – in other words, before the events of 11 September. Here was a man who now believed in the case for military action to prevent threats rather than solely to respond to them.

From that moment on I felt it was a question of when, not if, there would be a war with Iraq. Over the next year Tony Blair would struggle to reconcile the twin forces working on him – a president who was determined to depose Saddam Hussein, come what may, and a party with grave doubts about his partnership with George W. Bush. He endeavoured to do so by trying to prove that Iraq was a real and immedi-ate danger, to assemble an international coalition of support and to ensure that military action would be seen to be not just necessary and morally justified but legal. Achieving this required him and his ministers to insist both that war was not inevitable and that it was others, and not them, who were talking it up.

In March 2002, defence secretary Geoff Hoon duly told MPs in an emergency debate on Afghanistan that the only people discussing an invasion of Iraq were backbenchers and journalists. It was a scarcely credible assertion. Military preparations were delayed, perhaps unwisely, to ensure no one could say that war was a foregone conclusion. Even when British troops were mustered in Kuwait, pictures of the gathering armed forces did not emerge.

It was in Crawford, Texas, a little less than twelve months before the invasion of Iraq, that the course Tony Blair was set on should have become obvious. George W. Bush had extended the ultimate compliment by inviting Blair and his family to the place where he felt most at home – his ranch, known as the 'western White House'. The president, dressed in buckskin jacket, jeans and boots, collected the prime minister in a pick-up truck at the gates and shouted a cheery 'howdy' at the cameras. Souvenir shops in the main street of the tiny town were selling T-shirts declaring 'United we stand' and 'The British are coming, the British are coming', a prospect hardly seen as a cause for celebration when the phrase was first used in the War of Independence. Now it was seen as a promise, not a threat.

The post-summit news conference was held in a school gym festooned with Union Jacks and Stars and Stripes. After the Bush–Blair family get-together, the president appeared to forget the need to tread delicately around British political sensibilities. 'I explained to the prime minister that the policy of my government is the removal of Saddam and that all options are on the table.' This stark statement of policy produced an intake of breath. British policy was clear: removing another country's leader could never be the goal of military action. Sensing Tony Blair's discomfort, Bush tried to come to his aid. 'Maybe I should be a little less direct and be a little more nuanced and say we support regime change.'[10]

In so doing he merely highlighted that both leaders were talking about the same thing but in a different language. If any gap existed between them, it was not about the goal but the steps they thought politically necessary to get there and how much could be stated explicitly in public.

Bush applauded Blair as a man who didn't need a poll or a focus group to know what was right and what was wrong. It was praise Blair relished after years of withstanding accusations that he was obsessed with image and spin. I now understood what bound together the metropolitan lawyer leading the British left and the Texan oilman pin-up of the Republican right. It was moral certainty.

Once again the headlines that day were not about another step taken towards war with Iraq but a conflict already underway: ongoing Israeli military action in Arab-occupied territories. The Crawford summit was the moment, some believe, when Tony Blair agreed to support military action come what may. Britain's former ambassador to the US, Sir Christopher Meyer, has said that he cannot be sure of the extent of that commitment. 'The two men were alone in the ranch so I'm not entirely clear to this day what degree of convergence was signed in blood, if you like.'[11]

Sir John Chilcot's inquiry into the UK's role in the Iraq War, which would begin seven years later, heard revealing evidence of the prime minister's thinking at this time. In the run-up to Crawford he wrote to his chief of staff, Jonathan Powell:

The persuasion job on this seems very tough. My own side are worried. Public opinion is fragile . . . Yet from a centre-left perspective, the case should be obvious. Saddam's regime is a brutal, oppressive military dictatorship. In fact a political philosophy that does care about other nations – e.g. Kosovo, Afghanistan, Sierra Leone, and is proud to change regimes on the merits, should be gung-ho on Saddam.[12]

'Gung-ho' is a telling choice of phrase and it's not one he would ever have used in public. The prime minister went on to say to his closest aide: 'People believe we are only doing it to support the US, and they are only doing it to settle an old score. And the immediate WMD [weapons of mass destruction] problems don't seem obviously worse than three years ago. So we have to reorder our story and message.' That instruction to 'reorder our story' would cause Tony Blair much grief.

On the plane home from Crawford he came to chat to the travelling media pack. I asked him whether he feared that, like Harold Wilson, his stance towards an American war would make him a figure of hatred in the Labour movement. Did he think that some would refuse to forgive or forget? His non-answer was revealing. He gave me a trademark withering look and said, 'Thanks, Nick.'

I was sitting with my children on a beach in Devon when the call came telling me to get myself not to Texas but to Tony Blair's rather modest answer to the presidential ranch: Trimdon Labour Club in Sedgefield, County Durham.

The prime minister had looked at the polls, which showed widespread opposition to an attack on Iraq, at growing Labour and union hostility and at deepening scepticism in capitals around the globe. He'd decided that now was the time to 'reorder the story' by answering two questions: 'Why Iraq?' and 'Why now?' In a performance that removed any lingering doubt about his willingness to commit British forces to war, he declared that the threat Saddam Hussein posed was 'real and unique' and promised to publish the evidence for this claim, and soon.

That evening the media were invited for a drink at the Trimdon Labour Club bar with Sedgefield's most famous son. Dressed in white jeans and a blue denim shirt, Blair proceeded to order 'a half'. I suggested to him that this made him likely to stand out a little from the normal clientele of a northern working-men's club. With his thumbs tucked behind his belt and using the more earthy language he reserved for private occasions, the prime minister told a group of journalists that the Americans were not prepared to be 'dicked over by Iraq'. That day Saddam Hussein's deputy, Tariq Aziz, had made a vague offer to co-operate with the UN.

Days later another call came with the news that Tony Blair was heading back to Camp David. Blair and Bush would hold what we were told should not be called a 'council of war' as the leaders of France and Germany met to co-ordinate their opposition to unilateral American action.

Midway across the Atlantic journalists once again formed a tight huddle around the prime minister in order to hear his words above the noise of the jet engines. Once again he ratcheted up the warnings. 'I want to emphasize that the threat is very real and it is a threat not just to America or the international community, but to Britain.' He spoke of the danger of Iraq developing nuclear weapons: 'If these weapons are developed and used there is no way that any conflict Saddam initiates using them would not have direct implications to the interests of Britain.'

The Sunday newspaper headlines the following day, 8 September, could scarcely have been starker. 'Saddam poised to strike UK', panicked the *Sunday Express*. 'Blair warns of nuclear threat to Britain', claimed the *Mail on Sunday*. The prime minister had not, in fact, talked of an attack on Britain but about 'implications to the interests of Britain'. I wasn't remotely surprised, though. Moments after Blair had headed back to the first-class cabin, I had watched the Sunday hacks trying to tease out of Alastair Campbell what his boss had meant. Campbell certainly hadn't alluded to any possibility of a nuclear attack on Britain but nor had he done anything to calm the frenzied speculation.

This wasn't the first time this tactic had been used. I'd seen it working once before when a warning about long-range Iraqi missiles being able to hit 'British interests' – a reference, in fact, to UK bases in Cyprus – was interpreted as a threat to the British mainland. Alastair Campbell, now styled director of communications, would, no doubt, argue that it was not he but journalists in search of a headline who exaggerated their reports; that it was they, not he, who were the real spin-doctors. However, he knew exactly what would happen. He watched and understood and did nothing to set them straight. The story had to be 'reordered'.

Meanwhile, President Bush was quoting a report suggesting that Iraq was six months away from possessing nuclear weapons – a claim that caused bafflement among British officials travelling to Camp David and which, even before the war, was contested by the international nuclear watchdog, the International Atomic Energy Agency (IAEA). That didn't trouble Fox News, who flashed up just what the White House wanted to see. The war – the propaganda war, that is – was underway.

Just as the call of the cuckoo is considered the first sign of spring, sneers at the BBC's news coverage are a sure indication that Britain is heading for conflict. A couple of days after returning from the States I was sitting outside a café in Whitehall, sipping my coffee and scanning the anti-war *Daily Mirror*. A Downing Street political strategist wandered past and muttered, 'Ah, I see the BBC's taking its instructions from the *Mirror* again.' He and the rest of the political team knew they had to do something to win back *Mirror* readers and other natural Labour supporters who mistrusted George W. Bush and disliked the idea of Tony Blair acting as his 'poodle', but who, at the same time, feared Saddam Hussein.

The polls showed that widespread opposition to British participation in a war with Iraq would switch to widespread support if the UN were involved and Iraq was seen not to have co-operated.* In the run-up to previous conflicts it had been the pictures that had spoken the loudest. Film and photographs of refugees flooding out of Kosovo had made the case for bombing the Serbs while even memories of 9/11 were enough to convince many of the justice of attacking al-Qaeda's Afghan hosts. In the absence of any such compelling imagery coming from Iraq, Tony Blair and his team put their faith in the picture of risk posed by Saddam as painted by the intelligence.

'If you could see what I can see you'd agree with me' was the argument the prime minister had long used in private. Intelligence has always come wrapped in a certain mystique in

---

* A YouGov/*Independent on Sunday* poll on the day of the Camp David summit showed that 60% of voters – rising to almost two thirds of Labour supporters – said if the US did launch military action against Iraq without UN backing, Britain should play no part. However, 74% said they would support UN military action if the regime failed to let the inspectors return.

Britain and its purveyors have been treated with undue reverence. This is not simply the legacy of James Bond: it is the result of a culture of secrecy which, for decades, meant that it wasn't just the work of the Secret Intelligence Service, or MI6, as most people know it, that was secret. Officially, the existence of the service itself wasn't acknowledged until 1994. Its chief has always been known simply as 'C' and, until recently, his or her identity was never revealed. The first-ever public speech by a 'C' was made in 2010, more than a century after the service was founded. At one Camp David news conference White House officials reserved a seat marked boldly 'Head of MI6'. Well, why not? After all, they had another marked 'Director, CIA'. But it caused panic and consternation among the visitors from Whitehall, particularly when they noticed that I'd asked my cameraman to film the sign.

It was the heads of MI6 and the JIC – joint intelligence committee – who were tasked with producing the fifty-page dossier published at the end of September 2002. As the prime minister prepared to present the report, entitled *Iraq's Weapons of Mass Destruction: the Assessment of the British Government*, to MPs recalled to the Commons for a debate, copies were handed round to the media standing in Downing Street. I arranged with Sky's Adam Boulton that I'd skim-read the second half if he did the same with the first so that we could quickly identify the key points for those watching our respective 24-hour news channels.

The prime minister told the Commons that the intelligence was 'detailed, extensive and authoritative'. In fact there was little in the dossier of which we weren't already aware. One of the few new pieces of information was the claim that Saddam could deploy WMD within forty-five minutes. Both Adam and I highlighted it in our instant summaries of the report. Later, when this statement became the focus of the battle between the government and the BBC, Alastair Campbell would argue that it wasn't a particularly important part of the dossier. That's not how it would have seemed to viewers of that night's BBC *News at Ten*, which led with the headlines:

> The case against Saddam: he has the weapons and he's ready to use them.
> The dossier says he can fire mass-destruction weapons in forty-five minutes.
> Tony Blair tells Parliament he must be stopped before it's too late.

As would soon become clear, there was no definitive evidence that Iraq had any weapons of mass destruction at all, let alone any that could be fired within forty-five minutes – a fact that would lead, once Saddam Hussein had been toppled, to another war, this time between the BBC and the government.

By tradition, the political editors of the BBC, ITV and Sky are given the first chance to put a question to the prime minister or to whichever foreign leader he happens to be meeting. Having left BBC News 24 to become political editor of ITV soon after the Iraq dossier was published, I gained the advantage at this point of routinely being allowed to ask the questions rather than having to listen to others asking them.

I decided to try to compel Tony Blair and his counterparts from elsewhere in the world to venture beyond the carefully scripted, pre-programmed answers worked out by their aides in advance. Often at news conferences it feels as if reporters are simply pressing a button on a sort of rhetorical jukebox.

'Ah, yes,' the prime minister thinks to himself, 'that's answer C3, the one about . . .' and off he goes, trotting out a familiar tune. I believe, like Robin Day, Brian Walden and the other interviewers who inspired me, that forcing politicians to think on their feet can reveal more of what is really going on behind that soundtrack. It entails asking questions that are direct, even blunt. Some would go as far as describing them as rude. I'd dispute that, but there was a war on, after all.

My first chance to put a question to George W. Bush came at a White House news summit in late January 2003, just a few weeks before the invasion of Iraq. The atmosphere was tense. Tony Blair desperately wanted a second United Nations resolution to give military action legitimacy and to swing public and party opinion at home. Bush was just impatient to get on with removing Saddam. 'Mr President, an account of the White House after 9/11 says that you ordered invasion plans for Iraq six days after 11 September – Bob Woodward's account. Isn't it the case that you have always intended war on Iraq and that international diplomacy is a charade in this case?'

Plan of Action was a new book by Woodward, the man who, in partnership with Carl Bernstein, had uncovered the Watergate scandal in the early 1970s. He revealed that just five days after 9/11, President Bush had told his national security adviser, Condoleezza Rice, that while he had to deal with Afghanistan first he was also determined to do something about Saddam Hussein. Seventy-two days after the attacks on the US, he ordered an invasion plan to be drawn up.

President Bush, after a National Security Council meeting, takes Don Rumsfeld [the defense secretary] aside, collars him physically, and takes him into a little cubbyhole room and closes the door and says, 'What have you got in terms of plans for Iraq? What is the status of the war plan? I want you to get on it. I want you to keep it secret.'[13]

Naturally, that is not what President Bush told me but, like him or loathe him, his answer that day, as so often, made the truth pretty plain:

After 11 September the doctrine of containment just doesn't hold any water as far as I am concerned . . . my vision shifted dramatically after 11 September because I now realize the stakes, I realize the world has changed, and my most important obligation is to protect the American people from further harm, and I will do that.

He declared that 'this issue will come to a head in a matter of weeks, not months', a clear signal that war was coming and coming soon. What we didn't know then but do now, thanks to papers released to the Iraq inquiry, is that the president had given the British prime minister a start date for the military campaign. It was 'pencilled in for 10 March. This was when the bombing would begin.'[14]

In fact it was to begin just ten days later.

Before it did there was a massive protest over one weekend in February involving millions of people in up to sixty countries around the world. The march on the streets of London was claimed to be the biggest the city had ever seen, with estimates of the numbers taking part varying from 750,000 to a million. The prime minister put himself up for an unprecedented series of televised confrontations with opponents of the war. On BBC2's *Newsnight* an audience in Newcastle wanted answers to, among other thorny questions,

'Why do the Iraqi people need to suffer?' and 'Do you not agree that most of Britain do not want us to act alone without the United Nations, and do you not agree that it's important to get France, Germany and Russia on board with support to help us?' An edition of ITV's *Tonight with Trevor McDonald* came from the Foreign Office, where the prime minister, overlooked by portraits of Nelson and Wellington, was asked 'How many innocent victims are you going to kill?' and given a slow handclap.

A few days later I took six of the anti-war marchers into Downing Street to put their questions to the prime minister face to face. I was aware of how intimidating it might be for them to speak up in the place that represented the country's seat of power and well aware, too, of how charming Tony Blair could be. I warned them that they'd only get one chance and they would not forgive themselves if they didn't take it.

There was to be none of the sound and fury of the other televised encounters. Instead Tony Blair found himself up against something altogether more testing: the quietly spoken but deeply held fears of people who simply could not understand why he was set on war. We sat in the prime minister's 'den', his office next to the Cabinet room, in armchairs around a coffee table. Joy, on one side of the prime minister, told him that her son had been killed on 9/11 and she didn't want anyone else to die.

'Look,' he replied, 'I don't want to go to war.'

That didn't convince Paul, a student, sitting on his other side. 'You're going to do it anyway,' he rightly predicted. 'France, China, Russia all oppose your path. Why are you ignoring them?' Jane, a Labour supporter who said she felt guilty for not backing her leader, asked what turned out to be the most prescient question of them all. 'You say he's got

WMD. Where are they?' At the end of the recording Tony Blair said thanks, gulped, looked down and blew out his cheeks.

He then did something none of us was expecting. He invited the six protesters to join him in the Cabinet room. They and I assumed they were being offered a quick guided tour. Not a bit of it. He asked them to sit around the Cabinet table and me to leave so that they could say anything else they wanted to say to him in private, away from the cameras. They stayed for more than half an hour. All six emerged feeling no better about the prospect of war but a whole lot better about the prime minister himself. He had, of course, made up his mind to go to war long before he'd met them. What he was pleading for then – and still is now – is acceptance from those who profoundly disagreed with his judgement that his motives were good and his arguments sincere.

At the time I was immensely proud of a moment in which I believed television had enhanced democracy. Looking back, I fear that TV had proved, as it so often does, to be the best medium to capture drama and release emotion but not good enough at the marshalling of facts and cool analysis the build-up to war merited.

There was one more thing Tony Blair required before he could order British troops into action: the support not just of the House of Commons but of his own parliamentary party. A victory delivered by the votes of pro-war Tory MPs would, in truth, have amounted to a crushing political defeat. On the eve of the vote Robin Cook, who had been foreign secretary at the time Blair first bombed Iraq, resigned from the Cabinet in protest at a decision he'd fought. His doubts had been known for days but he'd remained silent in public. He was determined that the House of Commons would be the first to hear his reasons. In his powerful resignation speech he declared that 'history will be astonished' at 'the miscalculations' that had led to war. 'Tonight the international partnerships most important to us are weakened. The European Union is divided, the Security Council is in stalemate. Those are heavy casualties of a war in which a shot has yet to be fired.'

It was a speech greeted not by the usual 'hear, hears' or waving of order papers but by a standing ovation from anti-war MPs. Some of those backing the military action heard for the first time the case against it from someone in their own party they respected and wondered if they'd got it horribly wrong. Few dwelled on Cook's description of the evidence that Saddam had weapons of mass destruction as merely 'suggestive'. It was too late not just to change MPs' minds but to make any impact on public opinion.

The Labour whips in the Commons had arranged business to ensure that Robin Cook's speech would be delivered as late as possible, just before the night's main news bulletins. By then those bulletins were reporting Saddam Hussein's words of defiance and the final ultimatum to him about to be delivered by President Bush. I was still editing my report for ITV when Cook spoke. To my huge regret, I neither saw his speech nor found room for a clip. The BBC managed to squeeze in less than fifteen seconds.

The next day, 18 March 2003, Tony Blair gave his own final pre-war speech which sought to sweep away the doubts and reassure the doubters. Action could be taken with a 'clear conscience and a strong heart', he declared. There was one more day before hostilities would begin. Time aplenty for a few pot shots at the BBC.

On the eve of the launch of the campaign Tony Blair wrote to the corporation's director general, Greg Dyke,

> I believe, and I am not alone in believing, that you have not
> got the balance right between support and dissent; between
> news and comment; between the voices of the Iraqi regime
> and the voices of Iraqi dissidents; or between the diplomatic
> support we have, and diplomatic opposition.

Alastair Campbell fleshed out this complaint in a letter to
Richard Sambrook – just one of thirteen he sent between
2001 and 2003. It reads like a long shopping list of grievances
rather than a serious attempt to get any particular aspect of
the coverage changed. He began by claiming that the BBC
had quoted out-of-date polls, focused on the wrong parliamentary rebellion and that Radio 4's newspaper review had
highlighted the wrong story before adding, 'put all that to one
side'. He didn't seem to realize that by this time he had
alienated the people he was trying to persuade. Campbell
then cited five on-air reports to which he objected. His
targets included John Humphrys, foreign correspondent
Rageh Omaar and a man it was clear he already loathed:
'Andrew Gilligan said on the *Today* programme today that
"innocent people will die here in the next few hours".' Not,
perhaps, the most contentious thing ever voiced on the eve of
war, but it was a cause of fury at Number 10.

Campbell's letter concluded with a weary note of defeat-
ism. 'I know you will try to justify this. You always do. But it
is wrong.'[15] And there was a warning shot across the bows: 'If
the BBC reporting continues as it is this will become a public controversy which I am sure neither of us particularly
want.'

It was one of the most accurate predictions Alastair
Campbell ever made.

The Times, 26 June 2003

9

WHERE IS HE? WHERE ARE THEY?

'Where is Saddam? Where are those arsenals of weapons of mass destruction, if they indeed were in existence?'

A fortnight after Saddam's statue in Baghdad was hauled down by American troops, with the tyrant himself ousted and, for the moment, nowhere to be found, those two questions were causing the British prime minister considerable embarrassment. Never more so than when they were put to him not by a reporter or an anti-war protester, but by the Russian president, Vladimir Putin, speaking at a joint news conference at his residence just outside Moscow. Often there is simultaneous translation on such occasions. Not this time, which meant, rather unnervingly for Tony Blair, Russian speakers got to hear – and to laugh at – Putin's answer to his own question long before his guest did. As the deadpan translator read out the joke the discomfort of the visitor from London visibly increased.

'Perhaps Saddam is still hiding somewhere underground in a bunker, sitting on cases containing weapons of mass destruction, and is preparing to blow the whole thing up.'

This was, perhaps, the last time that that question would seem remotely funny. Even Alastair Campbell smiled. He often did when his boss was in most trouble, as if he were thinking, you're on your own now. See how you get on.

Just the day before Blair and Campbell had been warned by the intelligence services of the possibility that no weapons would be discovered. They were asked how big a problem it would be if it turned out none were found. Campbell's diaries record the answer: 'Very difficult.'

Now that the mission had been accomplished and Saddam had fled; now that weapons inspectors could work unhindered, Tony Blair could no longer reach for the Donald Rumsfeld defence. A year earlier, when challenged on the lack of proof that Iraq had WMD, the sardonic US defense secretary had said that 'the absence of evidence is not evidence of absence'. It was now.

A visit a few weeks later to Saddam's former summer palace on the banks of the Tigris should have been much easier. The carved wooden staircases, the gold taps, the vast electronic gates, the swimming pools and the tennis courts all highlighted the luxurious lifestyle enjoyed by the dictator while his own people suffered. Now the temporary home of the Desert Rats, it also demonstrated that 'the good guys' had won the war. In one of the palace's opulent rooms an Iraqi barber had set up shop. Above a small mirror I saw photographs of squaddies with a variety of brutal army haircuts. Since the barber spoke not a word of English his customers simply pointed at the style they wanted. One had clearly decided that this establishment needed a shop front and had made a sign using a bit of card and a felt pen. It read: 'Barnet Butcherer of Basra'.

The Downing Street spin-doctors had, wisely, decided not to include the Barnet Butcherer of Basra among the day's photo opportunities, to which they'd clearly given considerable thought. Dressed in chinos and a white shirt with his sleeves rolled up, Tony Blair visited a school, where he was photographed holding a bunch of flowers and a young Iraqi boy who planted a kiss on his cheek. At the palace he addressed a group of soldiers dressed in combat fatigues. To convey the perfect image when they posed for photographs, some stood behind him against the backdrop of a view of the Tigris and the city of Basra. He told them: 'When people look back on this time, and on this conflict, I believe they'll see this as one of the defining moments of our century.'

It was a defining moment for a reason no one could then know. Andrew Gilligan, a reporter for the BBC Radio 4's *Today* programme, had just dropped a journalistic bombshell by claiming that, a week before publishing their dossier outlining the threat posed by Iraq's WMD, Downing Street had ordered it to be 'sexed up'. Specifically, according to 'one of the senior officials in charge of drawing up that dossier . . . the government probably knew that that forty-five-minute figure was wrong even before it decided to put it in'.

I had learned of the broadcast from the ITV News foreign desk as the wheels of the prime minister's plane touched down at Basra airport. Aware that the report viewers would see at 10.30pm that night would have to be filed hours before then, I wanted a heads-up on what was being said at home. I had two instant reactions. First, the story was unsourced and I was not prepared to report something that controversial second-hand. Secondly, I did not trust Andrew Gilligan. He was someone with good contacts who'd exposed costly and dangerous failures at the Ministry of Defence and he was a great generator of headlines, but I had found that his stories didn't always stand up to thorough examination. I was far from alone. The BBC's evidence to the subsequent Hutton inquiry showed that Gilligan had already been warned by his bosses to be more careful with his choice of words and less loose with his use of 'facts'.

However, it was immediately clear that the BBC were throwing their full weight behind this story. Jeremy Bowen, a reporter I greatly admire, twice tried to get Tony Blair to answer a question about the missing WMD as he moved from one photo opportunity to another. The BBC's bulletin would focus on Gilligan's allegation while mine would come uncomfortably close to what Alastair Campbell must have been hoping for. It was not a position in which I much liked finding myself but in the weeks and months that followed I never once regretted my decision.

At Saddam's palace, Alastair Campbell, surrounded by reporters, poured scorn on a story written by a journalist for whom he had particular contempt. He regarded Andrew Gilligan as someone who'd taken the cavalier attitudes of Sunday newspapers to the BBC. And indeed, Gilligan had been hired by an editor of the *Today* programme, Rod Liddle, whose motto was (and remains, in his current job as a newspaper columnist) 'The only point is to get up people's noses.' Campbell especially objected to Gilligan's reporting for the programme from Baghdad – on one occasion, he had dismissed claims made by America's military HQ as yet 'more rubbish' and asserted that the average Iraqi was in more danger than he had been before Saddam was deposed. But despite his public bluster about the story, Campbell, prone to bouts of depression, was privately deeply anxious. He wrote in his diary that day: 'It's grim for me.

It's grim for TB and there is this huge stuff about trust.'[1]

In his memoirs, Tony Blair claims: 'There could hardly have been a more inflammatory or severe charge. Mistaken intelligence is one thing. Intelligence known to be mistaken but nonetheless still published as accurate is a wholly different matter. That is not a mistake but misconduct.'[2]

The row between the government and the BBC did not, though, explode straight away. Andrew Gilligan was not the first person to have raised questions about the missing WMD. Indeed, just the day before, Donald Rumsfeld had suggested that the weapons would probably never be found and that Saddam might not actually have had any before Iraq was invaded. The absence of evidence was, doubters of the war now believed, the evidence of absence. Robin Cook, who'd resigned from the Cabinet before the war, was already demanding an inquiry into the missing WMD. Clare Short, who'd been persuaded not to resign with him, had now done so. She covered her embarrassment by angrily denouncing Tony Blair, claiming that she and the country had been spun into an unnecessary war by the prime minister she had once attacked as the creature of 'people in the dark'.

Tony Blair, meanwhile, had moved on from Iraq, travelling first to Poland, then to Russia and, finally, to Evian in France for a summit of world leaders. The questions about missing WMD followed him every step of the way. He remained calm and, outwardly at least, confident, urging 'those people who are sitting there saying, "It's going to be proved to be a great big fib got up by the security services, there'll be no weapons of mass destruction" . . . to be patient about this'.

This comment, made to Adam Boulton in an interview for Sky News, completely contradicted what I had been told on the plane to Evian by one of the prime minister's advisers.

'Do you guys really think you'll find anything?' I'd asked.

'Well,' he said, 'we might not actually find a bright shiny warhead attached to a missile.'

I tried to hide my astonishment as he conceded that the evidence the world was waiting for might come simply in the form of Iraqi papers and interviews with scientists.

ITV News led with my report that night, in which I stated: 'It's what many suspected but until now the government had denied. Government sources have told me that weapons of mass destruction may never be found in Iraq.' Downing Street's press office instantly issued a flat denial to the Press Association. I was furious. They knew who I'd been speaking to, yet they had refuted something they knew to be true and made sure that no paper followed up the story. I had a glimpse of what they were willing to do to kill a story they didn't like. I learned, too, how much harder it is to make an impact on ITN, brilliant though it often is.

In the meantime Alastair Campbell's bubbling anger had boiled over into uncontrollable rage when he saw what was in the Sunday press. The *Mail on Sunday* – one of the growing number of papers he detested – published on 1 June an article by Andrew Gilligan which went further than his original broadcast. It named the man allegedly responsible for the 'sexing up' of the WMD dossier. 'I asked my intelligence source why Blair misled us all over Saddam's weapons. His reply? One word: Campbell.'

Just in case that wasn't provocative enough, Gilligan's conclusion made it clear that he was accusing the government of lying.

Some say none of this is important. All that matters is that a tyrant was toppled, a people were freed. But the dossier saga touches on an even more important goal than the freeing of oppressed foreign peoples. That is, that your words should be credible, and your own people should be told the truth.

Deliberately or not, Gilligan had created what was to prove a deadly cocktail by mixing together the long-hated *Mail* with the long-resented BBC, stirring in a personal attack on Alastair Campbell and topping it off with an allegation that the prime minister had lied. Tony Blair appeared on camera again to deny that 'we doctored intelligence reports' and to state categorically: 'I stand absolutely 100 per cent behind the evidence, based on intelligence, that we presented to people.'

This was, though, now only partly about the evidence – or lack of it – which had led to the invasion. It was now about a war Alastair Campbell wanted to wage against his tormentors in the media. In his diaries he wrote: 'I hated these people. The BBC/Mail link was now beyond the pale.'[3]

Tony Blair might have been able to stop him. He did try at times to restrain him but, just as he had with George Bush, he chose to stand shoulder to shoulder with him, believing that what was at stake was his place in history. Britain had clearly gone to war on what turned out to be a false prospectus but he was determined to rebut the claim that the country had gone to war on a lie.

The point of no return came when Campbell, against his boss's advice, decided to accuse the BBC of lying in televised evidence given to a Commons select committee. Up to that point he'd rarely been seen speaking in public. In an unsuccessful attempt to keep himself calm, he kept jabbing a pin into the palm of his hand, drawing blood. He told the MPs that he would keep 'banging on' until the BBC apologized.

Two days later he marched uninvited, and barely under control, into the studios of *Channel 4 News* for one of the most extraordinary broadcast interviews ever seen. He told a stunned Jon Snow that the corporation 'just have to accept for once they have got it wrong'.

Campbell was determined that if more blood was to be spilled it would not be his. In his campaign against the BBC he needed evidence that Gilligan's story was wrong. A call from the Ministry of Defence convinced him that he'd got what he needed. A government WMD expert, Dr David Kelly, had come forward to admit to his employers that he'd talked to Andrew Gilligan, although he insisted that he could not have been Gilligan's primary source. Advised that Kelly had long worried about Iraq's weapons programme, Campbell concluded that he was the source but that Gilligan must have misrepresented what he'd said. If he could reveal Kelly as the source he would, as he put it in his diaries, 'fuck Gilligan'. Campbell and Tony Blair believed that they had to identify Kelly to Parliament. They agreed that while they couldn't give his name to the media, they could do everything but. It was inevitable that his identity would come to light. Kelly was now to become a weapon in their battle against Gilligan.

A shy, softly spoken scientist, David Kelly was simply not equipped to cope with being thrust into the firing line. It was painful to watch his appearance, on 15 July 2003, before the same Commons committee that had cross-examined Campbell. One MP, tipped off by Gilligan, asked whether he'd been the source of another, more carefully worded, BBC report about Iraq's WMD, broadcast on *Newsnight*. David Kelly lied. He had been but he denied it. The MPs concluded, wrongly, that he was not the source of Gilligan's story. One told him that he was 'chaff' put up to distract them and dubbed him a 'fall guy'. Kelly's face betrayed his deep anxiety.

For a long time Gilligan's bosses at the BBC didn't realize what he'd got them into. Since the invasion of Iraq, they had received repeated complaints from Alastair Campbell whereas ITV News hadn't had one. So when Campbell wrote to take issue with Gilligan's report they regarded it as just another in the long line of obsessive gripes. The editor of the *Today* programme, Kevin Marsh, who had replaced Rod Liddle the previous year, wrote in an email to his boss: 'I started to look at this point by point but it's all drivel and, frankly, it'd be easy to get as confused as Campbell is. The man's flapping in the wind.' In another email, Marsh commented: 'I am more convinced than I was before that he is on the run or gone bonkers or both.'[4]

This contempt was the product of years of being on the receiving end of Campbell's constant bombardments. But there was another reason why Kevin Marsh and his presenter, John Humphrys, stood behind Gilligan. They'd had lunch with the two top men at MI6, Sir Richard Dearlove and Nigel Inkster, who had told them that Iraq and Saddam had not posed an imminent danger and appeared to suggest that Iran and Syria gave greater cause for concern. It was their words Humphrys recalled on air when a government minister challenged him for reporting on the disquiet of 'rogue elements' in the intelligence services. 'I myself have spoken to senior people in the intelligence services who have said things, that the government has exaggerated the threat from Saddam Hussein and his weapons of mass destruction.'

Despite Campbell's apoplexy and the BBC's weary defiance,

the battle over whether the government had 'sexed up' the case for war still might have subsided if it had not been for what happened on the night of 17 July.

All was quiet on board the plane taking Tony Blair from Washington DC to Tokyo. Up front the prime minister was sleeping soundly after being officially declared an American 'hero' by the House of Representatives, which had voted to award him the Congressional Gold Medal of Honor for his 'outstanding and enduring contributions to maintaining the security of all freedom-loving nations'. His speech had been interrupted by no fewer than seventeen standing ovations. Back in the cheap seats, the journalists accompanying him were snoring away. Just two of us were awake. Patrick Hennessy, then of the *Evening Standard*, was writing his copy for the first edition and I was suffering from food poisoning and being mothered with dry toast and black tea by one of the British Airways cabin crew.

Hennessy called his news desk using the onboard satellite phone to check if there was anything he needed to know. It was a conversation that changed from chatty to grave in a second. He turned to me and said, 'You're not going to believe this. David Kelly has gone missing.' The police had mounted a search for him. As we talked about what this might mean colleagues began to stir. Another call a little while later brought the news that Kelly's body had been found in woods near his home. One wrist had been slashed and it would later be confirmed that he had taken an overdose of painkillers.

By now the plane was in a frenzy. Every journalist was calling his or her news desk to get the latest details. The gaps in what we knew were filled with a mixture of wild speculation and gallows humour. Where was Alastair Campbell? someone asked. He'd been in Washington but had then flown back to London. He couldn't have, could he? It was instantly clear that a prime minister confronting accusations that he'd led his country to war on a lie would now face the charge that he'd driven the source of that story to take his own life. Worse still, the conspiratorially minded would hint darkly at officially sanctioned murder.

Normally on these trips journalists can wander freely towards the front of the plane to catch the eye of a friendly official or to pass forward a note asking someone to come back for a chat. Not today. The curtain between economy and business class had been firmly velcro-ed in place from floor to ceiling. No one, we were told, could talk to us. But they knew they would have to say something before the plane landed and the reporters rushed on to camera or to file their copy.

In first-class Tony Blair had been woken with the news. He was shattered and knew instantly how serious this would be for him. Revealingly, even writing many years later, he blamed the media for the scandal Kelly's death would cause.

> Of course in the rational world, it would be a personal tragedy. It would be explained by the pressure on him. It would be treated as an isolated event. I knew there was not the slightest chance of that happening in our media climate. It would be treated as a Watergate-style killing.[5]

As the Boeing 777 began its descent into Tokyo there was a growing clamour from those in the back for some response to what had happened. Despite the dispatch of a steady stream of urgent messages there was still not a word from a government spokesman, let alone the prime minister himself. I had already broadcast from the plane but knew I would have to go straight on to camera when we reached the ground. The clunking sound of the plane's wheels being lowered for land- ing could be heard and still there was nothing.

Finally, Alastair Campbell's deputy, Godric Smith, pulled aside the curtain to announce that the prime minister would be setting up an inquiry chaired by a judge (later named as Lord Hutton) into 'the circumstances surrounding the death of Dr David Kelly'.

On the tarmac the media and their cameras were held aboard the plane so that no one could catch sight of, still less throw a question at, the prime minister, who was rushed off to his hotel. Later a single camera, but not one journalist, was summoned to record a carefully worded statement from Tony Blair. 'I am profoundly sad for David Kelly and his family. He was a fine public servant. He did immense service for his country and I am sure he would have done so in the future.' The inquiry should 'be allowed to establish the facts' and in the meantime, 'all of us, politicians and media alike, should show some restraint and respect. That's all I'm going to say.'

That, of course, could not possibly be all he would say. He still had many days of his trip to go and he was travelling with a large group of journalists for whom, whether we were in Japan or China or Korea or Hong Kong, there was only one story.

Prime ministers have come to detest and fear being accom- panied on foreign trips by the media pack – twenty or more hacks from television, the press and the news agencies. As well as travelling on the same plane, they stay in the same hotels and turn up everywhere the PM goes, but all too often they are not remotely interested in what is preoccupying him.

He is worrying about how to forge a relationship with president A or premier B and remembering the names of his family, his favourite sports team or the time he came to London as a student, reading diplomatic advice on what to say and what not to say at all costs and calibrating a negotiating position.

Meanwhile, the media pack – which eats, sleeps and writes together and can at times become mildly hysterical due to a mixture of jet lag and lack of contact with the real world – may have decided that a story brewing at home is much more important and interesting than a handshake and a trade deal with a leader few have heard of in a faraway country nobody knows much about. To make matters worse, every leader expects a news conference with his honoured guest, providing the media with a daily opportunity to quiz the prime minister on a subject he may wish to avoid.

It is hard at the best of times, and this wasn't the best of times.

Our moment to pursue the topic at the top of everyone's agenda came at a news conference hosted by a startled-looking Japanese prime minister and an ashen-faced Tony Blair. I had been told that I was to ask the first question. I spent a long time weighing up in my mind what it should be. My first thought was 'Have you got blood on your hands?' but I rejected that as too crude, too lacking in respect for the man who'd died and a prime minister who, whatever else his detractors thought he was guilty of, was not a murderer. I asked instead whether he accepted any personal responsibility for Dr Kelly's death. He looked close to tears.

Jonathan Oliver of the *Mail on Sunday* had told me that if he didn't get picked to put a question he'd shout one out anyway. I tipped off the TV cameras. He got to his feet and called out the question I'd chosen not to ask: 'Have you got blood on your hands?' before adding, for good measure, 'Are you going to resign?' Tony Blair stood fixed to the spot, unsure, it seemed, whether to reply or simply to turn and leave. He had to be ushered off the stage by Japanese officials. I am still approached by people who think I was the one who asked that question.

A curious footnote to that day is provided by the prime minister's next assignment, a speech – virtually ignored at the time and since – in which he said that British entry to the Euro could, in the right circumstances, provide a huge boost to our economy and implied that he hoped the pound would be scrapped after the following election. It was a speech that might have been historic if he'd pursued that theme.

The next stop was South Korea. Here, amid the tension and the drama, I found myself at the centre of a rather surreal and comic diplomatic row which illustrates the clash between the demands of diplomacy and those of journalists on a mission and a deadline. The prime minister's news conference with President Roh came as the BBC was preparing to confirm that Dr David Kelly had, indeed, been Andrew Gilligan's source. It was to be conducted by a master of ceremonies, a rather imposing man much taller than most Koreans and dressed in tails and white gloves. By the time he called me to ask a question I knew that my booking for the satellite feed back to London had already begun. So I asked Tony Blair whether he was telling the country that he didn't believe the government had done anything wrong and, as he began to answer, started to walk away towards my camera, writing my script as I did so (the pictures and the prime minister's response would be combined with my words back in London). I was interrupted by the MC booming, 'You have no question for our president?'

It was not so much an invitation as an order, but I was pre-occupied by what Tony Blair had just said and was, in any case, under the impression that a colleague from the BBC was going to ask about Korea. It turned out he wasn't, either. So I mumbled that no, thanks very much, I did not have a question and continued in the direction of the satellite dish. As I did it dawned on me that not only had I just given grave offence but, worse still, I had caused the leader of the country in which I was a guest to lose face on live television.

As soon as I'd finished my news report I ran back to find the man in the white gloves and apologized profusely for the terrible faux pas I'd committed. He drew himself to his full height and barked out: 'I no accep your apology!'

I half-expected him to take off one of his gloves and slap me in the face with it before presenting me with a choice of pistols for a duel. Instead he bowed, turned on his heels smartly and marched away. A hapless Downing Street official was then summoned to the presidential palace to be given a dressing-down for the behaviour of the wicked British media.

It was not the war with Iraq that almost cost Tony Blair his job, nor the allegedly 'sexed-up' dossier, nor the missing WMD. What he feared would force him from office were the words he uttered on the back of the plane en route to his final port of call, Hong Kong. Even though the media had travelled many thousands of miles with him, attended speeches and photo opportunities and stayed in the same hotels, they had been successfully kept at arm's length and had up to now had no direct contact with the prime minister.

His officials had realized that they would have to allow

reporters at least one opportunity to talk to him before we were all back in London if the weekend 'news in focus' pieces and post-trip columns were not to be full of descriptions of a prime minister too scared to face questions. When they decided the moment was right we were given just a minute or two's notice to push aside our food trays and form a huddle around the space where we were told Tony Blair would stand.

Often such moments have been a chance for a relaxed chat, to hear first hand and off the record what the PM has thought of the other leaders he's met, how he sees some problem at home, and for him to joke about how the hacks spent their last night away. On this occasion, however, a tetchy and drawn Tony Blair spoke only for the record, with his words taped and transcribed later. Some reporters had to clamber over seats and crane their necks to hear what was being said above the noise of the engines.

It was a man from the *Mail*, Paul Eastham, who cut straight to the chase. 'Why did you authorize the naming of David Kelly?'

'That is completely untrue,' Blair shot back immediately. 'And why, again, as I say, don't you wait for the inquiry? . . . You should just wait for the inquiry to have a look at it.'

At a normal news conference the prime minister is in control. He can insist on only one question per reporter. His staff can decide whether or not you will be heard as they are handling the microphone. This was different. Tony Blair was standing just inches away from a pack that smelled political blood. They were determined not to let him get away without answering their questions, and Alastair Campbell was not there to protect him. Again and again he was asked, 'Did you authorize anyone in Downing Street, or in the MoD, to release Dr Kelly's name?'

What followed appeared to be a complete denial, despite the mounting evidence that this was precisely what had happened. 'Emphatically not. I did not authorize the leaking of the name David Kelly.'

This was the statement that would be used against Tony Blair by the Tory leader, Michael Howard, at Prime Minister's Questions. It took all Blair's training as a lawyer to construct a defence of those words that was consistent with the facts. He had not authorized the *leaking* of the name, merely the *confirmation* of it to journalists who asked the right question. The Hutton inquiry learned later that one reporter – armed with the official hints that the man in question was an MoD official who'd worked as a UN weapons inspector – had put twenty-one names to a press officer before reaching that of David Kelly and having it confirmed. In his memoirs Tony Blair defends himself and Alastair Campbell against what he calls 'brutal media allegations' by arguing that 'we would have been at risk of a charge of concealment ... had we known the source of the leak and refused to say'. He also blamed the BBC for staying silent until after his death on whether Kelly had been their source.

From that day on tape recorders and notebooks would be banned from all mid-air conversations with Tony Blair or his successors. In journalistic jargon, such conversations would be 'on background' – that is, used to enhance understanding but not quotable in any way. Which, to you and me, means they are deniable.

That extraordinary 19,000-mile trip had one last twist. Blairforce One was hit by an incoming typhoon on the runway at Hong Kong airport as we prepared to fly home. The pilot aborted take-off once and considered abandoning any attempt to fly that day altogether. In the event, battered by ferocious winds and driving rain, the prime minister made it back to London shaken, a little scared but unscathed – just as he would be after Lord Hutton's inquiry.

Hutton's verdict – which was widely denounced as one-sided or a 'whitewash' – came as a shock. It should not have done. The cross-examination of the prime minister and the director general of the BBC, and the judge's attitude, should have been enough of a signpost to the likely outcome.

Tony Blair was handled with great deference. His insistence that he had acted 'in good faith' was never challenged. His evasive responses on his role in the naming of David Kelly went untested. The director general of the BBC, on the other hand, was treated with disdain. The judge peered at Greg Dyke over his gold half-rimmed spectacles and greeted his answers with the long drawn-out 'Yerrrsss' which I had come to understand as his shorthand for 'And you really expect me to believe that?'

When Andrew Gilligan was cross-examined he was forced to accept that his central allegation, that 'the government probably knew the forty-five minutes figure was wrong', was 'not sufficiently supported' by what Kelly had told him. It was, in other words, not an accurate report of what his source had told him, but his own interpretation. Kevin Marsh, the editor of *Today* at the time, told me in Radio 4's *Battle for the Airwaves* that 'to misquote and misattribute' his single, anonymous source was 'journalistically criminal'.

Hutton found the government not guilty on all charges, in particular of 'sexing up' their Iraq dossier or having a 'dishonourable, underhand or duplicitous strategy' to leak Dr Kelly's name to the media. He found the BBC guilty of making 'unfounded' allegations, their editorial processes to have been 'defective' and criticized the governors for not properly investigating Downing Street's complaints before standing up for the corporation's independence.

The chairman of the BBC, Gavyn Davies, resigned instantly. The following day Greg Dyke would go, but not before delivering an emotional speech to over a thousand BBC staff who regarded him as their champion. On being told in a phone conversation with an old friend in BBC management that Dyke had not in fact resigned but had been sacked by the board of governors, I had to make a snap decision about what to say in my imminent report for the ITV evening news – which was even more imminent than I'd anticipated. The link to Television Centre had gone down and my report, originally scheduled for later in the bulletin, suddenly became the top story. There was no time to make any check calls or to warn my bosses, but I knew how many governors had been ready to back him and how many had wanted him out, and the information came from a reputable source. So I said it: Greg Dyke had effectively been sacked.

I had cause to reflect afterwards that if Lord Hutton had cross-examined me about this story I would have had to have admitted that I could not be certain of it at the moment I broadcast it, explaining that this was how live broadcast journalism worked. I suspect he might not have been convinced.

The reaction was almost instant. The BBC issued a denial. My somewhat startled editor rang to ask me whether I was sure I was right. After some hours, as others pursued the story, the BBC released a new statement saying that the governors had not actually held a vote. That was confirmation that the story was true. It is what we hacks call a 'non-denial denial': they were denying that a vote had taken place but not denying that the number of governors who had wanted Dyke to go had outweighed the number wanting him to stay.

Alastair Campbell had resigned from Downing Street before Hutton reported. He had, though, lost none of his anger or his appetite for revenge: 'What the report shows very clearly is this: the prime minister told the truth, the government told the truth, I told the truth. The BBC, from the chairman and the director general down, did not.'[6]

He expressed his hope that 'the media will learn lessons from this report' and would adopt a 'more honest' approach in future. There was no hint of any lessons he might have learned. Campbell had declared in advance that he wanted a 'straight win' and not a 'messy draw'. Now he'd got it he was determined to seal his victory.

When I had the chance to interview him I asked him whether he was proud of having done to the BBC what even Margaret Thatcher and Norman Tebbit had failed to do during their clashes with the corporation in the 1980s. I could have pointed out that in fact no other politician had ever done it. It was not a question he liked. The atmosphere between us quickly soured. I persisted and ended the interview with a question I should not have asked. 'Why haven't you apologized to the Kelly family?' I forget his reply. All I can recall is the venom with which he uttered it. The interview ended, the cameras were switched off and Alastair Campbell told me he would never speak to me again.

I had clearly touched a very raw nerve. A friend who was with him explained that he had, in fact, apologized to the Kelly family, but in private, not in public. I decided immediately that I would not run that part of the interview. I then wrote a letter, which I delivered to Campbell's house, explaining that I'd been mistaken and making my own apology for a question that had clearly caused him real hurt. If there is one lesson I take away from the Gilligan/Kelly/Hutton affair it is that the pain a journalist may feel making a swift apology when he gets something wrong is much more bearable than the agony of having it dragged out of him later.

The report by Andrew Gilligan that kicked off this whole saga will be remembered for one expression: 'sexed up'. It was, of course, a phrase without real definition but most of the public would have taken it to mean spun, exaggerated or embellished. There can surely now be no doubt at all that the intelligence presented to the public on Iraq had, indeed, been 'sexed up'.

Lord Hutton did not examine the prewar intelligence but a later inquiry, led by Lord Butler, did. It concluded that 'more weight was placed on the intelligence than it could bear', that judgements had stretched available intelligence 'to the outer limits' and it criticized the forty-five-minute claim in the government's dossier as 'unsubstantiated'. Tony Blair's assertion in the Commons that the intelligence against Iraq was 'extensive, detailed and authoritative' was somewhat at odds with Butler's description: 'sporadic and patchy'.

So the intelligence was wrong, but who had done the sexing up? Hutton heard a great deal of evidence that Alastair Campbell and his team of press officers had commented on the draft dossier. He also heard, however, that any suggested changes had been approved by the joint intelligence committee. This did not, however, apply to a last-minute amendment 'prompted' not by Campbell but by the prime minister's principal political adviser, his chief of staff, Jonathan Powell.

After the JIC signed off the dossier for the last time, Powell wrote an email to John Scarlett, its chairman, telling him that there was 'a bit of a problem' and suggesting he should 'redraft' the paragraph that stated: 'Intelligence indicates that as part of Iraq's military planning Saddam is prepared to use chemical and biological weapons if he believes his regime is under threat.'

This implied that the danger from Saddam's WMD would exist only if the British and Americans attacked him. The final dossier contained something rather different: 'Intelligence indicates that as part of Iraq's military planning Saddam is willing to use chemical and biological weapons.'

Scarlett admitted that he had been 'prompted' to make the change but insisted that it was all his own work and that he had acted under 'delegated authority' as the JIC chairman. In doing so he was making himself a human shield that protected Powell, Campbell and Blair from the charge that they had 'sexed up' the dossier. Even Lord Hutton acknowledged this:

> The possibility cannot be completely ruled out that the desire of the prime minister to have a dossier which, whilst consistent with the available intelligence, was as strong as possible in relation to the threat posed by Saddam Hussein's WMD, may have subconsciously influenced Mr Scarlett and the other members of the JIC to make the wording of the dossier somewhat stronger than it would have been if it had been contained in a normal JIC assessment.

In short, then, the head of the JIC may have 'sexed up' his own intelligence in response to being 'prompted' by his political masters: Blair, Powell and, of course, Alastair Campbell.

Nevertheless it is also clear that Gilligan 'sexed up' his own report. The claim in his original early-morning broadcast, that 'the government probably knew that forty-five-minute figure was wrong even before it decided to put it in', was not what he had been told by his source. Gilligan's explanation to the Hutton inquiry was that this was a mistake, 'the kind of mistake that does arise in live broadcasting . . . but it was a live broadcast, and once the words are out of your mouth, the . . . you know, I did not go back and look at the transcripts'.

His later broadcasts were more judiciously worded but they were still wrong. He not only misquoted David Kelly and overstated his role in drawing up the dossier; he also persistently claimed that information had been 'inserted against the wishes of the intelligence agencies'. It had not.

Mistakes are, as I've shown, all too easy to make in live reporting. They can also be made in carefully scripted broadcasts. In one sense journalism is rather like intelligence: you can never be 100 per cent sure of your report, you have to suspect your sources, you should always seek to check and you should be careful to admit the limits of what you do and do not know. Whether you're a hack or a spook, there's no excuse for not going back and correcting something that you know to be wrong. Yet Gilligan consistently reassured his bosses at the BBC, including the director general himself, that his story was 'an absolutely accurate reflection' of Kelly's views. Their mistake was to believe him.

Some argue that Gilligan's story has been proved right by the fact that no WMD were found, the 'forty-five-minute claim' was shown to be exaggerated and the dossier was, as we've seen, 'sexed up'. I disagree. Gilligan was on to something very big. He had a very good source and could have had

a great scoop if he'd handled it properly. That the BBC director general and chairman stood up to government bullying
and for the corporation's independence is admirable. Sadly,
they chose the wrong man to stand up for and the wrong
story to defend the BBC's reputation for accurate and impartial reporting. The reasons they did so are clear.

The BBC had grown so weary of Alastair Campbell's endless complaints and personal attacks that they no longer
distinguished between those which had merit and those that
were merely vexatious. They were misled by Andrew
Gilligan but did not do enough to test his story once the row
with Downing Street began.

Greg Dyke saw himself less as the BBC's editor-in-chief
than as its defender-in-chief, leading the resistance to Alastair
Campbell's onslaught. Campbell and Dyke now abhor each
other but they have quite a lot in common. Both are Labour
men, both are defined by their directness, both are ardent
football fans and both commanded the undying loyalty of
those with whom they worked, thanks in large part to their
passion in fighting their corner. Neither was interested in a
diplomatic solution or a fudge. They both wanted to win at
all costs.

Speaking outside Television Centre on the day he resigned,
Dyke said he was 'not a political animal'. He and some of
those cheering him seemed to regard this as a badge of pride.
It might, perhaps, be thought to disqualify someone from
running a public-sector organization with a budget of over
£2 billion which is the country's dominant news-provider.

Throughout the crisis Gavyn Davies stood by his director
general and staff as some previous BBC chairmen have failed
to do. Tony Blair believes that Davies' Labour connections –
he was a lifelong supporter of the party and his wife, Sue

Nye, was Gordon Brown's closest aide – made him more determined to ignore the outcry from his own side. In a surreal twist, the former BBC director general John (by now Lord) Birt drafted one of the letters of complaint to his old organization in his new role as an adviser to Tony Blair. It is impossible to know if Blair is right but what the episode does highlight is the dangers inherent in mixing party politics and broadcasting. They led to Davies resigning, as politicians once did, to take responsibility for the faults of others.

Ironically, Lord Hutton's verdict of guilty on all charges and the decapitation of the BBC's leadership did not damage the corporation's reputation. The inquiry was seen as a whitewash by many and silenced those who claimed that the BBC was effectively run by the government. Trust in the corporation, though dented by the affair, was quickly restored.

Tony Blair, on the other hand, is still struggling to restore the trust he could once take for granted. He did go on to win another election – an historic third consecutive Labour win – after Iraq but his relationship with his party had been permanently damaged. Pressure on him from Gordon Brown to step aside could no longer be resisted and finally, in June 2007, he formally resigned as both prime minister and party leader and handed over the reins to the chancellor.

Six months earlier, another trip to Washington DC had given me a glimpse of the stress being felt by the two men who had launched the invasion of Iraq. Now back with the BBC, I was there as their political editor at a time when powerful voices in America were demanding a rethink of the country's approach to a war that was going tragically wrong. George Bush had recently made a visit to London, amid the protests of thousands of demonstrators on the streets, and I had rattled him by asking why so many seemed to fear or even hate him. He had reacted simply by praising democracy. On this occasion, my question was prompted by a study he'd commissioned, published the previous day, which highlighted just how bad things were on the ground in Iraq.

'Mr President, the Iraq Study Group described the situation in Iraq as grave and deteriorating. You said that "the increase in attacks is unsettling". That will convince many people that you're still in denial about how bad things are in Iraq, and [make them] question your sincerity about changing course.'*

'It's bad in Iraq,' was the president's terse and tetchy response. 'Does that help?' He giggled nervously.

'Why did it take others to say it before you've been willing to acknowledge for the world—'

'In all due respect, I've been saying it a lot,' he interrupted. 'I understand how tough it is . . .'

My persistence had not improved his temper, and facing his controlled fury was not a comfortable experience, especially as he was standing just a few feet away from where I was sitting. When he called me 'sir' he did so in a tone that really didn't sound as if he meant it at all respectfully. '. . . Make no mistake about it,' he concluded. 'I understand how tough it is, sir. I talk to families who die.' While answering questions from others he would sometimes turn in my direction and say, 'And you, sir, should recognize . . .' This confrontation between the leader of the free world and the

* 7 December 2006. Interestingly, the transcript on the White House website inaccurately records the question as 'That won't convince many people that you're still in denial,' which changes its meaning somewhat.

man he remembered as 'that bald guy from the BBC' was not to be the last.

A few weeks later, at the end of December 2006, Saddam Hussein – who had been captured three years earlier – was executed for crimes against his own people. It would be another three years before British forces were withdrawn and the Americans were there until December 2011. No weapons of mass destruction were found. The absence of evidence had, by then, become the evidence of absence. Almost ten years after the atrocities of 9/11, Osama bin Laden, hiding in a private residential compound in Pakistan, was killed by US special forces during a covert operation. An 'exit strategy' endorsed by NATO is being pursued in Afghanistan but at the time of writing, British troops remain in the country.

Since leaving office Tony Blair has continued to behave as if all that was wrong with the now infamous WMD dossier was the flawed intelligence. He claims that it was not about making the case for war against Iraq and that there was no disquiet among the intelligence services about it. Both views are very hard to square with what we now know. In his memoirs he blames the whole saga on 'today's craving for scandal'.

The intelligence was wrong. We admitted it. We apologized for it. We explained it, even. But it was never enough, in today's media, for there to have been a mistake . . . A mistake doesn't hit the register high enough. So the search goes on for a lie, a deception, an act not of error but of malfeasance. And the problem is, if one can't be found, one is contrived or even invented.

He makes no apology for involving political appointees and press officers in the presentation of intelligence or the grave damage it did to the reputations of those involved.

Blair's reluctance to comment more than he has may be rooted in a fear that the media would turn any comment he does make into the headline he has always been determined not to see written: 'Blair says sorry for Iraq.'

He has said that he is sorry for the loss of life and for the faulty intelligence. He is not sorry for the decision to go to war or the way in which the case for it was made.

Not all who were around him then agree. Since the war Alastair Campbell's deputy, Tom Kelly, has commented that the government should have admitted the scope for reasonable doubt about the existence of WMD, concluding that Downing Street put the importance of being in control above that of being open and honest. Jonathan Powell argues, however, that the media would have ignored the subtleties of a more candid position and that the prime minister had to be an advocate – making the best possible case he could.[7]

The relationship between Tony Blair's government and the BBC was broken before the invasion of Iraq. The fall-out from the decision to go to war shattered it beyond repair. The prime minister's director of communications and BBC news executives no longer spoke, they merely exchanged faxes. Angry and unfocused complaints were followed by defensive and defiant responses. Trust, empathy and understanding had long since disappeared. The death of David Kelly, though completely unforeseeable and a cause of heartfelt and deep regret on both sides, was the tragic consequence.

2 October 2007

10

'I JUST CAN'T COMMUNICATE'

'It's not normal to call prime ministers liars, is it?' Gordon Brown's words were uttered in cold fury at the end of a tense dialogue. Interviews with Brown were never easy but this was definitely my worst.

It was the summer of 2009, the deficit was soaring and I had pressed the prime minister to admit that whoever formed the next government would need to make significant public spending cuts. At the time many in his Cabinet, not least his chancellor, Alistair Darling, were imploring him to abandon his plan to present the choice facing the country as one between 'Labour investment' and 'Tory cuts' and to start admitting that spending cuts were inevitable under any party. He saw this not just as a political trap but as a diversion from the economic priority to stimulate growth.

In our interview he said the government was ready to make 'efficiency savings' and 'asset sales' but would not acknowledge the need for spending cuts. He said that I was not living 'in the real world'. I asked him whether he was being straight with the British public. 'What people will notice is what you're not saying, Prime Minister.'

He replied tetchily: 'What I have said, and *just listen to me, Nick*, is it's all about getting growth.'

Alistair Darling would later acknowledge in an interview that, if re-elected, Labour would make cuts deeper than those imposed by Margaret Thatcher.

My exchange with the prime minister was typical of many of Gordon Brown's dealings with reporters and presenters. In one series of interviews at the Labour conference in 2009, he lost his temper repeatedly. He complained to Sky News's political editor, Adam Boulton, that he was not being given the chance to talk about the economy and accused him of being obsessed with 'personality' as opposed to policy. Afterwards he attempted to walk off, even though he was still wearing a microphone on his lapel and was expected to remain in his seat to talk next to BBC *Breakfast*'s Sian Williams. She, too, was chastised for the nature of her questions and when, at the end of her live interview, the prime minister stood up to leave, he blocked the camera she was speaking to. On his return to his hotel suite his staff gave him a 'proper bollocking'.[1]

Interviewers came to believe that Brown was stonewalling legitimate inquiries. He came to believe that interviewers were impugning his honesty and pursuing their own agenda or, as he put it to his aides, asking 'Tory questions'.

Brown's spin-doctor, Damian McBride, describes these rounds of TV interviews in his autobiography, *Power Trip: A Decade of Policy, Plots and Spin*, as 'never far from a Demolition Derby . . . On a bad day, after each political editor had finished, Gordon would want to scream a string of foul-mouthed abuse in his face.' In between each interview

McBride ushered his boss out of the room to calm him down, telling him: 'It was fine, it was good, you dealt with it well, it's all OK. And, I know he's a bastard – he's a Tory, he can f*** off the next time he asks us for a favour – but let's just do the next one and get through it. The same routine. After every single interview. Every single time.' McBride has written of his love for Brown. Perhaps he convinced himself that he alone could understand and control the Prime Minister's barely containable temper – rather like some who continue to express their devotion to an abusive wife or husband.

Unlike Tony Blair, the quick-witted, self-confident lawyer used to thinking on his feet, Brown was a cautious, calculating former university lecturer who had always painstakingly prepared his public presentations. Blair treated questions as a launch pad for what he'd come to say. Brown saw them as getting in the way of or, worse still, competing with the message he'd long planned to put across. In opposition, and then as chancellor, he had strictly rationed his media appearances and before being interviewed sometimes spent days or even weeks planning how to answer the difficult questions he foresaw. As someone who'd been for a few years a TV journalist himself, he developed the skill of self-editing his answers as he was speaking to avoid falling into whatever trap he thought had been set for him. His friends say that the moment he opened his mouth to respond to any question, he would see five potential bad headlines in his head.

What had been his strength in opposition and as chancellor became his weakness as prime minister, once he was forced to take questions, often on a daily basis, on a vast and unpredictable range of subjects. Tony Blair's approach to a tricky inquisition was to try to answer 'yes' before swiftly adding a 'but', which gave both interviewer and listener the impression that he was engaging with the question. Brown, by contrast, sought simply to ignore or parry questions by asserting 'what people want to know is . . .' or 'what I am focusing on is . . .', signalling that what he had been asked was somehow illegitimate or unfair. Interviewers reacted by repeatedly asking variants of the same key question in order to either force an answer or expose the fact that none was forthcoming.

None of this can have been very satisfying for viewers or listeners. Nor was it comfortable for the journalists who should have relished the privilege of interviewing the country's leader but came to loathe it. Those who interviewed Brown regularly grew accustomed to him tearing off his microphone at the end before storming out of the room or, more awkwardly, forgetting to remove it and having to be saved from tripping up or garrotting himself by the very people from whom he was so determined to escape.

At the end of my worst interview ever the prime minister had nowhere to go to since we were filming on a train. Unable to repress his anger, he started to upbraid me as the cameraman filmed some editing shots. I had, he complained, made the interview about his honesty rather than economics. I replied that I had asked the questions that were currently at the heart of the political debate. This was a conversation which should have taken place once the cameras and the microphones had been switched off. If the tape had been fed back to the busy newsroom as usual, our exchange would have been heard by everyone there and quite possibly leaked to a newspaper. Another prime minister, John Major, had once been caught out this way when confiding in ITN's Michael Brunson about the 'bastards' in his Cabinet.

Since Brown clearly didn't intend his comments to be

broadcast and I needed to maintain a professional relationship with him, I told my cameraman and producer to ensure
that only the interview itself could be heard in London and
requested that they keep the original tape out of the BBC
library. No other fragments of 'private' conversations are
revealed in this book, but since this one took place on camera
it is technically 'on the record' and I am including it because
it helps to explain, I hope, both Gordon Brown's anger with
the media and the media's frustration with him.

Anthony Seldon and Guy Lodge, Brown's biographers,
believe that the media reporting he endured was 'poorer than
for any recent premiership'. That is saying something, given
that Seldon is also the biographer of John Major, who got a
dreadful press, though at least had good relations with
broadcasters.

Brown's disastrous relationship with the media raises an
important question for the future. In this media age can only
the masters of the slick answer, the shameless photo opportunity and manufactured empathy succeed? Does history
belong to those Professor Peter Hennessy has dubbed
'plausible tarts'? To answer it we must first examine how and
why things went so wrong for the man who wanted so badly
and waited so long to become prime minister.

Television holds a mirror up to the faces of those in public
life. Only individuals with superhuman reserves of confidence, control over their emotions and the hide of an ox can
cope with what they see. Gordon Brown had none of these
traits.

When Brown re-embraced Peter Mandelson to help turn
around his premiership he admitted to his old political
enemy that he 'wasn't a politician for the television age',

explaining: 'I've got all the policy, all the ideas. I just can't communicate.'[2] He added gloomily: 'It seems that you can be a good prime minister or a popular one, preferably both. But I'm neither.'

During the many dark days of the Brown premiership people would ask me, 'Doesn't he realize how badly it's going?' The answer was that he knew precisely how badly, and that just made his problems worse. He exacerbated them still further by brooding endlessly on them, working ever-longer hours, sleeping less and succumbing more frequently to angst.

I interviewed Gordon Brown in the Cabinet room at Downing Street on one of those dark days, in September 2008, as one of the many plots to remove him was being hatched. The former home secretary Charles Clarke had just predicted that Labour was 'destined for disaster' and Brown's air of despondency seemed to have sucked all life from the building. I had come to talk to him not about his premiership but about his predecessors: he had kindly agreed to be inter-viewed for a radio series I was making about former prime ministers. Perhaps for this reason, with the pressure off, it turned out to be one of the most revealing conversations I ever had with him.

Brown told me that his hero Clement Attlee, the taciturn, uncharismatic Labour leader who'd ousted Churchill after the war, could never have achieved what he had if he'd faced the demands of the modern media. 'If, in 1945, they'd had to have daily press conferences, or weekly briefings, or had to have the visits all over the country, I think it would have been a very different atmosphere.'[3]

He related the story of how Attlee's government decided in 1948 to devalue the pound. They did so over many months, in secret, without a word ever emerging to trouble the markets. The chancellor, Stafford Cripps, was ill and recuperating in a sanatorium in Switzerland. The Cabinet decided someone had to go and see him there to discuss the idea with him in person and return to report his views in further consultations. Making any decision at that sedate speed would be impossible today. Brown was lost in his own thoughts, making no eye contact with me. I wondered if, after all, this interview was actually about him as well as Attlee. I said: 'You must rather envy that?'

The tape records his wistful answer. No words, just a low murmur of assent. I recall him looking into the middle distance – perhaps pondering that if he'd been born a few decades earlier he could have succeeded where he was now clearly failing.

Brown was unlucky. Not only had he become prime minister at a time when the press was tiring of the Labour party and the global economy was grinding to a halt in a way few had foreseen, he also faced the first Conservative leader since Margaret Thatcher who was a TV natural. David Cameron attributed his rise to the top of the Tory party to his television performances. His notes-free leadership pitch to the party conference in 2005 had caught the public eye but it was the launch of his campaign, at which he effortlessly fielded questions on a wide range of topics, that first attracted the attention of political reporters. Cameron was determined to use television to convince the public that his party had changed, most memorably on a trip to the Arctic to highlight his green credentials. It became famous for the sight of the Tory leader being pulled through snow by huskies.

What is less known is that the image-conscious Cameron

was adamant he would never be seen in a hat, even when the temperature dropped below minus 25 degrees centigrade. His team believed only losers were filmed wearing hats. John Major had been ridiculed after being snapped in a turban on a trip to India and William Hague for an ill-judged flirtation with a baseball cap. Tony Blair's aides claimed he had never been pictured in a hat. It was an unequal contest with a prime minister who – as well as having struggled to look dignified in a Biggles-style flying helmet – had to be told to brush his hair, remember not to use jargon and, above all, to try to be nice.

The signs of the problems Gordon Brown would encounter were visible long before he entered Number 10. In January 2007, I'd found myself in Bangalore with the man by then destined to be our next prime minister, who was scheduled to speak at the Confederation of Indian Industry conference.

Every political editor had had the same call. Gordon wants you to come on this trip, we were told. It'll be a kind of dress rehearsal for those he does when he's PM, his aides said, and it's a good chance for everyone to get to know each other better. They were more right than they realized.

The chancellor had written a weighty and worthy speech about the creation of a new world order in which remodelled international organizations would deliver justice and security for all. His agenda was typically ambitious, taking in the reform of the UN, the G8, the IMF, the World Bank and NATO – all of which were, he claimed, designed for the world of 1945 and not the twenty-first century. There was a coded message in the speech: those who'd hated Blair and Bush's unilateralism now had to show that multilateralism could work. It was all very interesting but I was searching the text in vain for a clear and pithy soundbite or a sentence not swamped by the alphabet soup of international acronyms. As I listened to Brown delivering his words my despair grew. He was chomping his way through them like a cow relentlessly chewing on grass, barely pausing to look up. This story was going to be a hard sell.

The Indian media weren't even listening. They were obsessed with the somewhat less cerebral British opinions emanating from the *Celebrity Big Brother* house, where Shilpa Shetty, a Bollywood actress, was being taunted by several of her fellow contestants on Channel 4's reality show. They'd made jibes about her cooking, suggested that she was dirty, imitated her accent and asked whether she lived in a shack. One, Jade Goody – a 'celebrity' by virtue of the fact that she had come fourth in a previous edition of the non-celebrity version of the show – had renamed her Shilpa Poppadom and, even more charmingly, Shilpa Fuckawallah. This was big news. The headline in the *Times of India* on the day Gordon Brown arrived read 'Big(ot) Brother bullies Shilpa'. Effigies of the programme's producers were being burned on the streets. There was no way Indian journalists were going to let Britain's next leader pass through their country without making a comment.

After his speech and talks with the Indian trade minister, a baffled-looking Brown emerged to be confronted by a couple of dozen TV news crews representing India's extraordinary number of rolling-news channels. Advised by the British high commissioner that there was a real threat to diplomatic relations, Brown declared the comments of Jade Goody to be 'offensive' and said he wanted Britain 'to be seen as a country of fairness and tolerance'.

I rang my news desk to tell them what he'd said and then

to discuss how I planned to turn the chancellor's thoughts on the future of the world into a compelling piece of television. I drafted a script for my piece on a plane to New Delhi. On arriving I was met by a man from the BBC. Forget that future-of-the-world stuff, he told me, you're on the *Big Brother* row now. So it was that in the early hours of the morning I ended up on the streets of the Indian capital talking about Gordon Brown's views of a programme I, and surely he, had scarcely seen.

> It is a tale of our times, of how a heady mix of celebrity and race, and reality television, and our imperial past, have dragged politicians, both here in India and back home in Britain, into one of the most curious rows either side can ever remember. Gordon Brown had little choice but to soothe Indian feelings today. That was the diplomatic advice. Tonight he's left wondering how a row about reality TV got in the way of, well, reality.

The next evening it was back to the new world order. I was invited to meet Gordon for a drink and a chat in the hotel bar. One of his aides brought over a bottle of champagne. No one mentioned what we were celebrating but I assumed it was his imminent rise to the highest office in the land: that day he'd publicly acknowledged for the first time that he would be succeeding Tony Blair. Gordon, ever self-conscious, looked rather uncomfortable. So did I. I was afraid he would want to know what I was going to ask him in an interview for the following morning's *Today* programme. But the champagne soon flowed and so did the conversation.

Brown explained the thinking behind his speech. I encouraged him to find more accessible language to talk about it.

When he removed a large black felt-tip pen from his pocket to make notes of what I'd been saying I decided it was time to change the subject. We talked about another of his favourite themes, Britishness, and about how our very different roots made us see the country. He told me that seven generations of Browns had lived in or near the area he now represented as an MP. He was intrigued by my own very different story of a German Jewish mother who'd married an Englishman, from an army family, she'd met in Switzerland. After more than an hour of conversation I felt we'd made a connection that would last. It didn't, in fact, last until the following lunchtime.

When I awoke the next morning I was given a fax of the morning papers. All of them headlined the words uttered by the man who was now officially our next prime minister as he laid flowers on the tomb of Mahatma Gandhi. Speaking under the shade of a tree to the journalists travelling with him, Brown had declared Gandhi to be not just someone he admired but his inspiration. The father of the Indian nation had had, he said, 'the strength of belief and willpower to do what is difficult and right for the long term, even when there are easier short-term options on offer'.

He had insisted that he wasn't comparing himself with Gandhi but few listening doubted that he was inviting the media to do just that. Sure enough, the *Sun* and the *Guardian* ran, side by side, photographs of both Gordon and Gandhi.

I decided I could not possibly do an interview on the rather heavy subject of global institutional reform without a little mention of the man dubbed by the *Mirror* 'Mahatma Gordi'. Teasing him gently, I suggested that some listeners might be spluttering into their cereal at the thought of him as Gandhi's spiritual successor. He was not, however, amused. Indeed, he was clearly furious, even when I moved on to such embarrassingly soft questions as 'What do you mean by "new world order"?'

He began to respond with what his allies referred to as the 'wall of sound'. This was a Brown tactic which involved talking for as long as possible to eat up time and avoid what he called a 'gotcha' question. The more he talked, the more determined I became to ask a question. After the interview Gordon complained. I maintained I'd behaved perfectly reasonably. As he stomped out of the room one official scurried up and, rather surprisingly, congratulated me for standing up to him. 'Not enough people talk to him like that,' he said. It didn't do much to cheer me up. The champagne that had been meant to seal a good working relationship between the BBC's political editor and the next prime minister was by now leaving a rather sour aftertaste.

I was resolved, however, to find a way to unlock on camera the Gordon Brown whose company I'd enjoyed in that hotel bar in India. I came up with the idea of filming him in Kirkcaldy talking about the roots we'd discussed. We stood in the church where his father had given the rousing sermons he had written out, memorized and delivered without notes, a skill his son always envied.[4] I read from a selection of the Reverend Brown's injunctions to his flock which the family had published. The titles of the sermons made it apparent that Gordon had been brought up by a man who set very demanding standards. 'Making the best use of time' was followed by 'Towards set objectives', with its instruction to 'not trifle because we think we have plenty of time ahead of us'. The Reverend Brown spoke repeatedly about the importance of having a 'moral compass', a figure of speech his son would adopt and, occasionally, be haunted by. Being a 'son of the Manse', Brown said, meant 'the spotlight is always on you . . . it's noticed if you don't behave'.

This rather shy man had spent all his life on public display. The boy who went to secondary school at the age of ten and university at sixteen had always carried the burden of other people's expectations. I asked him whether he would finally feel he'd lived up to what the Reverend Dr John Brown had expected of him when he reached Number 10. His eyes moistened.

Later he took me to the school rugby pitch where, at the age of sixteen, he'd had the accident that had left him blind in one of those eyes and partially sighted in the other. It would affect him not just physically but psychologically for the rest of his life. For six months after the accident he lay in hospital with his eyes covered and never lost the fear he felt then of losing his sight altogether. 'I knew I wasn't going to play football or rugby again. You have to think again. What are you going to do with your time? I think I became more focused on what I had to do.'

It was typical of Gordon Brown that he was reluctant to talk about what was a pretty serious handicap and, when he did, that he presented it as a strength rather than a weakness. What he called 'focused' others would call obsessive. One of those closest to him told me he thought Gordon woke every day thinking, 'Is today the day I lose my sight?' This, he concluded, was what fed a tendency to paranoia.

Gordon Brown was hesitant, nervous and unsure even where to stand when he delivered his first speech as prime minister on 27 June 2007. When he emerged from Number 10 the photographers, perched on their tall ladders, shouted at the country's new leader to move so that they could get the famous black door into their shots. That, though, was not the style of a man who had launched his bid for the premiership half-obscured by a glass autocue screen. It was clear that the Brown years were going to be very different from Blair's.

They started with a lack of polish and slickness and with a modesty that came as a relief to many. He pledged simply to uphold the motto of his old school in Kirkcaldy: 'I will try my utmost. This is my promise to all of the people of Britain. And now let the work of change begin.'

That promise of change would, journalists were told, apply, above all, to the way Downing Street handled the media. The era of spin was declared to be over. A civil servant, not a Labour party spin-doctor, would run government communications. MPs would hear announcements before listeners to the *Today* programme or readers of the morning papers. For a short while that really did happen. Journalists had to go to the House of Commons press gallery to hear what the prime minister was going to say. There was no briefing, no interviews in advance, no quiet word in the ear. Brown duly appointed a Treasury official as his spokesman and briefings were straight, factual and non-partisan.

The worse events were in the real world, the better they were politically for Brown. He was to be tested by terrorist attacks on London and Glasgow, floods that killed thirteen and forced many more to leave their homes, and by the return of foot-and-mouth disease. His aides joked that next up would be a plague of locusts. What would actually follow was, arguably, worse – a banking crisis like of which had not been seen since the 1930s. In the face of all these challenges Gordon Brown's media appearances seemed to many to be, well, prime ministerial.

I filmed him chairing a COBRA meeting on how to handle the floods. The word COBRA, sounding as it does rather more dangerous and exciting than most government acronyms, has acquired a curious mystique which evaporates somewhat when people remember that all it stands for is Cabinet Office Briefing Room A – a room in the bowels of Downing Street where ministers and officials usually meet to handle emergencies. Brown came over to many as a reassuring figure; strong, decisive, a man who gave it to them straight. Labour's new ad team at Saatchi and Saatchi summed up his image with the slogan 'Not flash, just Gordon'.

That, however, was before the election that never was.

On the first day of Gordon Brown's first party conference as Labour leader I faced an 'unenviable task'. That, at least, is how it was described by the *Today* programme's Sarah Montague. At 8.25am, Sarah and I were squashed together with the prime minister in a bedroom at Bournemouth's Highcliff hotel (temporarily converted, I ought to add, into a radio studio). Brown repeatedly evaded Sarah's questions about whether he would call an early general election to capitalize on his political honeymoon and secure for himself a personal mandate. As he did so I wondered what on earth I should say when it was my turn to comment. Before the interview I had joked that I was journalism's equivalent of an ice-skating judge and would be giving marks for content and presentation. Now that crack didn't seem quite so funny. I was going to have to give the prime minister very low marks for being straight about the question that was obsessing the political classes. What's more, I would have to do it with him sitting across the table from me. The word 'unenviable' didn't quite do the situation justice.

Asked to rule out calling a snap election, Brown suggested

– as he often did – that this was the wrong question: 'What people want me to talk about today is not some inner speculation.'[5]

The day before, Andrew Marr, on his Sunday-morning television show, had asked the prime minister whether his aides were advising him to go to the country within the next few weeks. He had replied: 'No. I'm actually getting on with the job. My focus is on the work ahead.'

We now know that Brown had instructed his team to talk up the possibility of an early election in order to destabilize David Cameron and the Tories. He would authorize the printing of 5 million election leaflets at a cost of over £1 million, in addition to the recruitment of extra staff, and sign off the party's manifesto.[6] At the time I had been unaware of this. What I did have to go on were endless conversations with those close to the prime minister who delighted in teasing me about their knowledge of the 'will he or won't he' question. My on-air assessment was:

> The curiosity is the prime minister has been going round say-
> ing people shouldn't be talking about this. I'm afraid – and
> the prime minister knows this – I've had to suppress more
> than a grin, almost a laugh because it's his aides, his advisers,
> his Cabinet ministers who can talk of little else to journalists.
> This is not one of those games that journalists are playing on
> politicians, it's a game politicians are playing, via the media,
> to try and unsettle their opponents and to give him [Brown]
> the option and see if he might give it a go.

I did my best not to look at the prime minister at this point. Gordon Brown left the room without responding anyway. One of his aides called me later and said he'd demanded to know 'Who's been talking to fucking Nick Robinson?'

Two days later the question came up again on the conference stage, raised by Brown's own choice of friendly interviewer, Mariella Frostrup. His coquettish reply was, 'Charming as you are, Mariella, I think the first person that I would have to talk to is the Queen.'

The following week he tried to intensify his opponents' discomfort by visiting Iraq and distracting the media's attention from the Conservative conference. While in Basra – and not, it should be noted, in Parliament – he announced that 1,000 British troops would be brought home by Christmas. This led to a rare but wounding attack by former prime minister John Major, who told BBC News: 'What is pretty unattractive is the nods, the winks, the hints, the cynicism, the belief that every decision is being taken because it is marching to the drumbeat of an election rather than to the drumbeat of solid, proper government.'

Brown's plan was beginning to go badly wrong. The shadow chancellor, George Osborne, had unveiled a political game-changer: a hugely popular promise to cut inheritance tax (which he would, of course, never be able to keep). David Cameron, apparently nerveless in the face of universal predictions that he was heading for certain defeat, challenged the prime minister to 'call that election'. Finally, at the end of the Tory conference, a poll showed that in marginal seats, if not the electorate as a whole, the Conservatives were, in fact, ahead,* with Labour on course to lose their overall majority. Although Gordon Brown had never actually privately made a decision to hold an early election, he was

* ICM/*News of the World* marginals poll: Conservative 44%, Labour 38%.

now forced to go through the ignominy of publicly calling it off. The way he did so turned a mistake into a calamity.

I was lying on my sofa with a box of tissues and a bucket of self-pity recovering from post-conference 'man flu' when I received a curious call. A very senior Conservative wanted to know if I'd heard what Brown was doing. The prime minister was apparently about to tell the BBC – in a pre-recorded interview for the *Andrew Marr Show* – that there would, after all, be no election. There was something rather embarrassing, if not mortifying, in having to admit that I was completely in the dark.

Marr and his production team had been asked to slip into Number 10 discreetly on a Saturday afternoon to record the interview for transmission the following morning. Brown's team wanted to avoid a whole series of tough inquisitions at the hands of different broadcasters or a bombardment of hostile questions at a news conference. Like the strategy of talking up an early election, this was a disastrous mis-calculation. Sky's Adam Boulton had also had a tip-off. Furious that such important news was being given exclu-sively to the BBC, he headed to Downing Street to break the story and describe it as 'an abject humiliation'. Marr then emerged from the door of Number 10 to announce to the world that the prime minister had told him he was not going to have an election that year or, probably, the following year, either. I lay on my sofa watching, sniffing and, I confess, sulking.

The reason Brown gave in his interview for not going to the polls made matters even worse. 'Yes, we could have had an election based on competence . . . but what I want to do is show people the vision that we have for the future of this country.'[7] On that night's late news I concluded that 'he would have had much more chance of being believed' if he'd said that before the polls turned against him.

> One of the most powerful weapons that any prime minister can wield in this country is the power to call an election when you like. Somehow Gordon Brown has turned that weapon upon himself – damaging his reputation, ending his political honeymoon as prime minister and damaging the morale in his party.

At a Downing Street news conference on Monday 8 October, Brown decided to 'take responsibility . . . take the blame', but he tried to dodge what he, no doubt, regarded as the 'gotcha' question that was put to him again and again: 'Surely you changed your mind because you thought you might lose. Why can't you admit that?'

I pressed him: 'You ordered your civil servants, you ordered your ministers and your party to be ready for an election. At the last minute when the polls turned, you turned?'

'That is not correct, Nick,' he replied. 'I said to you that I did consider an election. My first instinct was always to keep on with the business of governing, to set out my vision of what the country should be like for the future.'

Was Gordon Brown the victim of a malevolent media bent on tripping him up rather than eliciting answers? He probably wonders to this day what on earth he was meant to say when he was first asked whether he was planning to call a snap election. He would have feared that answering 'yes' would have led to breaking news flashes that Britain was 'on standby for an election'; 'no', on the other hand, would have been a lie and quickly exposed as such. And what of those questions about whether the polls had influenced his decision to call it off? 'Yes' to that would have allowed reporters to say 'Brown admits: "I cancelled election I was set to lose"', whereas 'no' would have been another absurd untruth.

The real problem was not his evasive answers, let alone hostile questions. It was his failure to make a decision either to announce an election or call it off in enough time to retain control of events. He could still have made his route out of the mess easier by deploying a little disarming candour. For example, he could have said at the outset something like: 'There are people urging me to have an election because they think it would be good for the country if the government got a new mandate for the changes we want to make. I am not convinced but I promise to make my decision and end the uncertainty soon . . .'

After scrapping it he would have won respect if he'd simply laughed when asked about the polls and agreed, 'Well, yes, they did help me make up my mind.'

The public both respects and understands politicians who admit they've yet to make a decision, or have changed their minds, or now realize they have made a mistake. As it was, after the phantom election Gordon Brown found himself the butt of jokes. At the next Prime Minister's Questions the Tory leader David Cameron taunted: 'He's the first prime minister in history to flunk an election because he thought he was going to win it!'

In one fell swoop Gordon Brown had undermined his own reputation for competence, for putting the national interest first and, above all, his claim to have abandoned spin to be straight with the public.

As prime minister Brown had already confronted a series

of national and international crises over which he had very limited control and there were more to come – the credit crunch, the MPs' expenses scandal and developments in the ongoing war in Afghanistan, which the West was beginning to lose. It is ironic, then, that again and again, what damaged him most was not these but avoidable crises all of his own making.

The Times, 29 April 2010

11

SPEAKING IN A FOREIGN LANGUAGE

Most prime ministers find solace in foreign travel. Abroad they are treated with a reverence they rarely experience at home. They are driven around in convoys accompanied by motorcycle outriders and greeted by military bands playing national anthems; they can discuss global challenges free, for a fleeting few days, from any sort of challenge from their opponents and concerns about managing their party.

Yet Gordon Brown rarely looked comfortable on the world stage. As chancellor he had proved to be a skilled inter-national negotiator. As prime minister he was ill at ease with the personal and yet very public diplomacy now required of him. As ever, the travelling media pack ensured that his domestic troubles followed him wherever he went. Increasingly the prime minister responded to questions reporters regarded as fair and legitimate as if he were being hunted by a gang hell-bent on humiliating him. The private chats on board his plane made matters worse, not better. Increasingly, Gordon Brown and those of us who followed him were speaking to each other in a foreign language.

Brown walked a tightrope at his first summit with the US president George Bush in July 2007. He tried to signal to people at home that the Brown–Bush relationship would be very different from the Blair–Bush partnership, while striving to reassure the Americans that nothing fundamental had changed. Those travelling with him were told that this would not be the backslapping, gag-cracking, occasionally wince-inducing kind of summit we'd grown used to when Tony Blair was in power. Brown's wife would not be accompanying him. What was more, even though the summit was at Camp David, the president's country retreat, where he could relax and get to know his guest, the two men would wear suits – a dress code that was the subject, it has since emerged, of intense negotiations between Downing Street and the White House.

Bush respected his guest's wishes, left his cowboy jacket and boots in the wardrobe and dressed up for the occasion but he couldn't resist getting his revenge. Collecting the prime minister in a golf buggy, he spun it towards the TV cameras to reveal a surprised expression on Gordon Brown's face that said 'This wasn't in the script.' The president looked relaxed. The prime minister looked anything but.

At their news conference, held outside, in the baking Maryland sun, the president repeatedly referred to his guest as Gordon or Gordon Brown and praised him as 'a principled man who really wants to get something done'. The prime minister, for his part, didn't use his host's first name once, sticking with President Bush or Mr President throughout. The reporter chosen to go first was a man whose birthday it was, which allowed Bush to unsettle his inquisitor by wishing him a happy birthday and declaring the USA to be an 'amazing country' in which you could question the president before you were forty years old. Brown tried and failed to join in with the joke by pointing out that six of his Cabinet were that age or younger. Bush replied with a less than helpful quip: 'You must be feeling damn old, then.'

Few people, as I was to discover, can outquip George Bush, a man who is sharper and more intelligent than most assume. As I wiped the sweat from my reddening forehead at the end of the news conference he made a crack for which I suspect I will be remembered long after any report I have broadcast has been forgotten.

'You should cover your bald head.' The advice was not altogether friendly. Perhaps he was recalling our spat over whether he was in denial about the Iraq War. Grinning at his little jest, Bush shook hands with Brown and both men strode purposefully towards Marine One, the president's official helicopter.

Acutely aware that I was being stared at by the assembled journalists, diplomats and politicians, I muttered, 'I didn't know you cared.' My confidence that both leaders were well out of earshot was misplaced. Bush glanced over his shoulder and called back, 'I don't.'

By the time Gordon Brown next visited the president, on 17 April 2008, the sun was no longer shining on the prime minister, though it was, as George Bush remarked, another beautiful day. After their news conference in the Rose Garden of the White House, he was looking forward to serving his guest a 'nice hamburger – well done'. He and Brown had been holding talks about the credit crunch, Afghanistan and Iraq and Brown had earlier been introduced to the two leading candidates to be the next president: former first lady Hillary Clinton and a man called Barack Obama.

Bush was in a relaxed and playful mood. 'Nick, you need a

hat, my boy, you need a hat,' he said when it was my turn to ask a question.

Brown was very far from relaxed. He knew that the journalists travelling with him were all focused on the extraordinary revelation that the prime minister had interrupted his visit to the leader of the free world to call a Labour MP few of us had ever heard of before. Angela Smith, the member for Sheffield Hillsborough, was a parliamentary private secretary – a ministerial bag carrier – who was threatening to resign as evidence mounted that a tax cut Brown had made a year earlier, in his last Budget as chancellor, was being paid for by some of the poorest people in the land. Labour MPs had just begun to realize that more than 5 million people could be worse off as a result of the scrapping of the 10p rate of income tax to pay for a headline-grabbing 2p cut in the standard rate.

On this occasion it was Tom Bradby of ITV News who asked the awkward question. 'A member of your government appears upset enough tonight about the abolition of the 10p rate to consider resigning. Isn't it time for you to at least consider unravelling that particular change?'

It produced a textbook Gordon Brown response which began badly and got worse. 'You asked also about our economic policies . . .'

In a reply that lasted well over two minutes, he did not once refer to Angela Smith and simply dismissed the growing number of Labour MPs who shared her concerns. 'Where the 10p rate has affected people, whether it be low-paid workers or pensioners, or whether it be families with children, we have acted to see that we could do the best by people in our country.'

George W. Bush could only look on sympathetically as his guest ground his way through his lengthy answer, which took in child tax credit and pensioners' winter allowances but did nothing to address the growing political revolt he faced at home. Afterwards Brown's aides recall the president trying to make light of what had happened. Bush sat on his desk in the Oval Office, swinging his legs like a small boy and handing out gum. Why, he joked, were the Brits so interested in Tempe, Arizona? Brown was not amused. He was still muttering away angrily like Muttley, the cartoon dog in *Wacky Races*.

On the plane taking him to his next stop, Boston, his displeasure became all too apparent. All I remember of his mid-air conversation with journalists is his fingers digging deeper and deeper into the headrest of one of the seats as he faced question after question on what he would do about the victims of his tax change.

Less than a week later, after dozens of Labour MPs joined the protests, Brown finally agreed to allow Alistair Darling to make a U-turn and bring forward emergency measures to compensate at least some of the losers. But he could not bring himself to admit that he'd changed his mind when threatened by a revolt on his own backbenches.

'What changed between last week, when you told me you wouldn't move? Again and again you have told your MPs you wouldn't move, but in the face of a defeat, you move?' I asked him.

'What I said was I wouldn't change the decision to abolish the ten pence rate.'

Another week on, in an interview for the *Today* programme, he finally conceded that his policy had been flawed. 'We made two mistakes. I'll be honest about it: we made two mistakes.' The mistakes were to not compensate low-paid workers and certain pensioners. In his memoirs, Alistair Darling estimates the cost of the compensation that was finally paid as £6 billion – an extraordinary sum.

Even many of those close to Brown believe that he cut income tax in his last Budget before moving to Number 10 to impress the right-wing press and Rupert Murdoch. At the time questions were asked about where the money to pay for it was going to come from. Darling later gave his verdict on the affair: 'If something appears to be too good to be true it probably is.'[1]

Polls show that few voters think politicians tell the truth. Most political journalists are, believe it or not, less cynical. We might spend our working lives detecting evasions, diversions and half-truths, but we generally expect those we deal with not to tell us something they know to be untrue. Indeed, a decent working relationship with the politicians on whom we report depends on it. Gordon Brown's handling of the election that never was and the 10p tax saga corroded his credibility with journalists. Increasingly, he found himself treated with a mixture of contempt and ridicule.

It was a simple enough question. Anyone could have answered it. Well, almost anyone. Nicky Campbell, the presenter of Radio 5 Live's *Breakfast* programme, knew that there was one person who would be unable to do so: Gordon Brown.

'When you woke up this morning what was, truthfully, the very first thing that came into your head?'

It was April 2008. The prime minister was on the last leg of the hated 'morning round' – a relentless series of interviews which had today begun on the breakfast TV sofas and was ending in a BBC studio, where he was being switched from one radio network to another. The very best political communicators keep their message constant but adapt their style to suit the interviewer they're facing and the programme's audience. Not Gordon Brown.

'Well, we heard about house prices, didn't we, because I was talking only a few days ago about the problems people face about fuel bills and because food bills . . .'

It was exactly the sort of answer Nicky Campbell was prepared for. He had his follow-up ready. 'When you woke up – that's the commitment you have to the job – that's what you thought of?'

Around the country people eating their toast or brushing their teeth or driving their car to work got the joke instantly. Brown, on the other hand, was driven by his mental autopilot straight into the hole that had been dug for him. 'I was thinking of what we can actually do about first-time buyers who are finding it difficult to get mortgages . . .'

'That's quite something for a first thought in the morning . . . if I'd asked Tony Blair, he probably would have said, "A cup of coffee." '

The reason Brown had missed one of the 'gotcha' questions that so obsessed him was that it focused on his personality, not his policies. He simply hadn't seen what was coming.

Campbell quipped that listeners might have expected a more 'human answer' before suggesting that people found 'the lack of connection' with the prime minister difficult. It was an exchange that summed up the daily agony Brown encountered as premier. He believed he was taking 'the right long-term decisions for Britain' but instead of being allowed to talk about these, he constantly found himself in the psychiatrist's chair.

There was worse to come. Campbell went on to list the self-inflicted wounds that had weakened the government in the preceding weeks: the confusion about whether Brown would attend or boycott the opening ceremony of the Beijing Olympics in protest at the Chinese government's suppression of human rights; his painfully awkward decision to allow the Olympic torch to be paraded up Downing Street by aggressive Chinese security service operatives while refusing to touch it himself, for fear the controversy might somehow rub off on him; the U-turn on his refusal to be seen signing the Lisbon Treaty, which resulted in the humiliating experience of arriving after other EU leaders had left and being forced to sign it alone. Was all this, Nicky Campbell asked, evidence of 'ruthless ambition married with incompetence'?

Brown's reputation for competence rested on one foundation stone: his handling of the economy. Throughout the decade he'd spent as chancellor the electorate and the markets had put their faith in his constantly repeated promises of prudence, stability and 'no more boom and bust'. When the economy turned, as it did so drastically at the start of his premiership, Brown was once again reluctant to face reality and paid a heavy price for denying in public what others were all too ready to concede in private.

The economic storm clouds began to gather soon after the Budget of March 2008, although few had the faintest clue at first how bad things would get. Long before public anxiety focused on deep spending cuts or tax rises, worries were centred on the immediate impact of the 'credit crunch': falling house prices and the drying up of business loans.

I was invited to film the prime minister visiting a nurse who'd benefited from a government housing scheme and to travel back with him afterwards to Number 10 and interview him in the Cabinet room. Sitting in the back of the official Daimler as it sped through central London, listening to Gordon Brown surveying and analysing the forces at work in the global economy, was to see him at his best. His knowledge, experience and international contacts made him uniquely well qualified to confront the challenges the country faced.

I explained to him that the news that day would focus on the latest figures showing the fastest drop in house prices since the early 1990s and suggested that the public were looking for some acknowledgement that difficult times lay ahead. Interviews should not be plotted out in advance with their subjects but I thought I would get better answers if Brown had some idea of where I was coming from. It made little difference.

I began with what I thought was a simple invitation to speak directly to the public about the problems confronting the economy. 'People see house prices falling, mortgages being refused, they see loans ending for small businesses. They fear they're in for a truly dreadful time economically.'

Brown reacted with an assertion that he could be trusted. 'I'm always vigilant. The record is over the last ten years we've maintained a course of stability, always, at very difficult times.'

Having tried once or twice to get him to tackle the issue, without success, I suggested: 'People might begin to wonder whether the government is in denial about how bad things might become.'

This visibly irritated the prime minister. 'I think it's quite the opposite.' He went on to list the government's initiatives to support the housing market and small businesses and to secure international stability.

The suggestion that he was 'in denial' had become a theme of the Brown premiership. It was flourishing in the gulf between the prime minister's optimism and the gloom that was rapidly overtaking the Treasury. As chancellor, Brown, egged on by his adviser, Ed Balls, had regarded officials at both the Treasury and the Bank of England as too cautious and too conservative. He had wanted to make Balls his chancellor but had been talked out of it. The two old allies now grew increasingly frustrated as they watched Alistair Darling, the man who had got the job, adopt the 'Treasury view'.

That summer Darling was warned by his top official that public borrowing could top £100 billion – a shocking prediction but one that in fact turned out to be a significant underestimate. Darling told the *Guardian* that the economy faced the worst storm in sixty years. He was promptly forced to give a humiliating TV interview in an effort to 'correct' the headlines he'd generated and was ruthlessly briefed against by Brown's spin-doctor, Damian McBride. Darling later complained that 'the forces of hell' had been unleashed on him for simply telling the truth. The problem was that Gordon Brown simply did not accept that it was the truth. He assured journalists travelling back with him from the Olympic Games that there'd be an economic recovery within six months.

'Whatever it takes' was always Brown's answer to those who asked what he'd do to avoid economic disaster. No one, not least him, could have predicted that that would mean part-nationalizing the British banking system and committing an eye-watering £400 billion of public money – around a third of what the entire economy produces in a year – to doing so.

It had to work, and it did. It saved the banks and the City, and saved the British economy from an even greater disaster, but not from a long and deep recession from which we have yet to emerge. Other countries followed Britain's example. The history books will give Gordon Brown great credit for this.

The prime minister believed his next task was to persuade world leaders to take internationally co-ordinated action to boost confidence. He spoke passionately and persuasively about the need to avoid the mistakes of the 1930s, in particular the abortive London Economic Conference of 1933 which brought the representatives of sixty-six nations together only for them to fail to agree how to fight global depression. He decided to stage his own London summit, seizing the opportunity provided by Britain's turn in the chair of the G20, until then a largely insignificant organization but invaluable now since it brought together the world's richest economies with fast-developing nations like Brazil, India and Indonesia.

The first person Brown had to get on board was the man everyone wanted to be at the front of the queue to befriend: the new president of the United States, Barack Obama. The first world leader Obama invited to visit him at the White House was the prime minister of Japan, a decision that fuelled a sustained bout of navel-gazing within a government living in constant fear that its country's 'special relationship' with the US might be revealed to be not so special after all. The early signs were not good. Obama, it was said, thought the future lay in Asia, not Europe (an undeniable fact of life). He recalled the brutal British suppression of the uprising in his father's native Kenya. Worst of all, he had returned the bust of Churchill that George Bush had kept proudly on his desk in the Oval Office.

The fact that Gordon Brown was the first European leader to visit President Obama in March 2009 did little to reassure. Every journalist travelling with the prime minister had instructions from his or her news desk to take the temperature of the special relationship and report back. The reply was cool, if not downright chilly.

This may have had something to do with the fact that we were kept outside the locked gates of the White House for over an hour and a half in the snow and freezing temperatures while British and American officials haggled over who could come in. The White House had decided there would be no news conference with the president and the prime minister. In its place would be what the Americans call a 'pool spray' and we Brits know as a 'grip and grin' – a handshake and a smile for the cameras and, if we were lucky, a banality or two from the host and his guest. Most reporters and cameramen wouldn't even make it into the grounds. This wouldn't do. Every travelling hack knew the first question he'd be asked when he got home: 'What was he like?' And if he hadn't been to the White House before, the second would be 'What was it like?' The media party huddled together for warmth on Pennsylvania Avenue quickly concluded that Britain didn't matter any more.

After much pleading by Downing Street officials we were all let in. White House officials had simply wanted to avoid setting a precedent for every foreign visitor but they knew when they were beaten. Once in the Oval Office the questions focused on whether our oldest ally still really cared for us. I went first.

'Mr President, it's often been said that you, unlike many of your predecessors, have not looked toward Europe, let alone Britain . . . Can you comment?'

'This notion that somehow there is any lessening of that special relationship is misguided,' Obama replied. 'Great Britain is one of our closest, strongest allies and there is a link, a bond there, that will not break.'

There followed an excruciating attempt at banter by a president known as 'the Vulcan', after Mr Spock in *Star Trek*, who had no emotions, and a prime minister who just couldn't do cod small talk.

'I'd like to think that our relationship is terrific. And I'm sure he won't dispute that, in front of me, anyway,' joshed Obama.

'I don't think I could ever compete with you at basketball. Tennis,' countered Brown.

'Tennis. You gotta game.'

'We maybe have a shot,' said Brown. 'I think you'd be better.'

The special relationship was safe, officially at least. But then came news of the gifts the men had exchanged. Gordon Brown's team had gone to huge trouble to find a suitable replacement for Churchill's bust. They'd chosen a pen-holder, but it was no ordinary desk ornament. It was made of wood from HMS *Gannet*, the sister ship to the *Resolute* whose timber had been used to make the presidential desk in the Oval Office, a gift from Queen Victoria. In return, the White House had chosen a box set of American movies, available on Amazon for $17.99. The angst about the special relationship began all over again. The word 'snub' started to make its way into newspaper reports. It wouldn't be the last time.

Gordon Brown's team were furious at what they regarded as the media's self-regarding obsession with trivia. They were frustrated that the fuss was overshadowing a hugely successful speech the prime minister had given the following day to the US Congress, which had been greeted by no fewer than seventeen standing ovations. If they'd watched TV instead of reading press cuttings faxed from home they needn't have been. My report for the BBC's *News at Ten* that night gave him the write-up he would have wanted.

America has long behaved as if it wished Tony Blair was still prime minister. Not any more . . . Gordon Brown's reception here suggests that he's no longer regarded as that guy who isn't Tony Blair. He believes he can build a real partnership with Barack Obama and that he is getting a hearing for his views.

Just a few weeks later, Brown toured three continents trying to drum up support for his G20 summit in the face of many who questioned the value of a couple of dozen world leaders meeting for just a few hours and wondered whether the words in their communiqué would mean anything. His answer was that the very existence of a summit would focus minds, force people to talk and, in some cases, to act.

The prime minister was by now at odds with both Alistair Darling, who had told the *Daily Telegraph* that ministers had to show humility and admit the mistakes made in the run-up to the recession, and the governor of the Bank of England. In Brown's absence Mervyn King raised his voice to warn against a further economic stimulus, making it clear that the government had reached the end of its capacity to spend and borrow its way out of trouble. These were words that wrote the script for reporters travelling with the prime minister in exchanges that continued to be fractious.

In São Paulo, where Gordon Brown agreed to do a string of TV interviews, his aides decided to put me last in the queue, once again, figuring that the other travelling correspondents might annoy him less. They were wrong. The prime ministerial temper was soon under severe strain.

To save time on occasions like this the broadcasters share or 'pool' two cameras so that the PM can keep his seat while reporters from different channels take it in turns to sit in the interviewer's chair. Just before I walked into the room one of Brown's aides wrote a note for him and handed it to him discreetly and out of view of the cameras. The prime minister ignored the signals and held the note up close to his working eye so that he could read it properly. It was now visible to anyone who cared to look, and right in front of the cameras. 'Stay calm,' was the gist of it, as 'Nick Robinson gets under your skin.' The terrified aide leaped across the room to grab the note from a bemused prime minister with the agility of a fly-half diving for the try line. As it happens, on that occasion my interview was rather more serene than those that preceded it.

The lead-up to the London summit may not have augured well but it turned out to be Gordon Brown's greatest triumph. Twelve presidents, eleven prime ministers and a king arrived for a kind of Oscar night for world leaders. The star of the show was, of course, President Obama. Every overseas leader had wanted to be the first to welcome him to their country and the prize had gone to Gordon Brown. His limousine was so big and his cavalcade so long that it couldn't actually fit into Downing Street.

Brown was rewarded not just with memorable pictures but with words of praise from the most popular man on the planet. 'You're to be congratulated because you've shown extraordinary energy and leadership, and initiative in laying the groundwork for this summit. All of us owe Prime Minister Brown an extraordinary debt of gratitude.' Obama had what he called 'an important message' for those worrying about spending more: 'Don't short-change the future because of fear in the present.'

Brown had inspired, chivvied and bullied fellow leaders into promising a trillion dollars in increased funding for the International Monetary Fund and for a new package to finance world trade. Even President Sarkozy of France, who'd threatened to boycott the summit, was impressed. Some weeks later, at a dinner at the Elysée Palace, he stunned the British prime minister and his closest aides with the candour of his assessment: 'You know, Gordon, I should not like you. You are Scottish, we have nothing in common and you are an economist . . .'

Diplomats and civil servants were, I'm told, fidgeting nervously at this point, wondering where the president's remarks might be leading. They need not have worried. '. . . but somehow, Gordon, I love you.'

This expression of Gallic ardour so unsettled the Scot known for never showing his emotions that Sarkozy added hastily, if perhaps unnecessarily, 'But not in a sexual way.'

The G20 may have impressed world leaders, leader writers and even political editors but it failed to make much of an impression on the public. Brown could not translate the language of international summits into that spoken by most ordinary humans. He would occasionally suggest that it was the duty of political journalists to find a way to explain it. His wider economic argument – about the need for growth and an economic stimulus – was, however, to be fatally undermined by the opposition of both the Treasury and the Bank of England.

Within days the headlines had moved on to the subject of leaked emails indicating that the spin-doctor Brown had brought with him from Number 11 had been planting highly personal stories in the press in order to smear his boss's opponents. Damian McBride was clever, amusing and like-able if he didn't regard you as a threat. If he did, though, he could be vicious. Blairites referred to him as McPoison or McPrickface. Whenever Brown had been warned about McBride's behaviour he'd told insiders that they were 'too nice'. The emails revealed that McBride had discussed plac-ing on a new Labour-supporting website called RedRag tales concerning a gay Tory MP and rumours that a leading Conservative was suffering from a sexually transmitted disease while the wife of another allegedly had mental problems.

Thanks to McBride's own recently published mea culpa we now know that this was the tip of a very large and very ugly iceberg. Smearing Gordon's enemies was what his spin-doctor thought he was in business to do. Those close to Brown at the time now insist that they knew nothing about what was going on. They risk sounding like the chief of police in the movie *Casablanca* who exclaimed that he was 'shocked, shocked' to be told what was going on in his town. Yet when Peter Mandelson was asked to join Gordon Brown's Cabinet he demanded that McBride be moved from Number 10. When Mandelson discovered that the spin-doctor had simply been moved next door to the Cabinet Office he was told that the Prime Minister regarded his personal Machiavelli as 'indispensable'. Then and now voters were reminded that, as even his friends used to say, there was a 'bad Gordon' as well as a 'good Gordon'.

What really ended the G20 effect, though, was the greatest scandal to hit Parliament in decades: a scandal over duck houses and dog food. Gordon Brown had proved himself a skilful co-ordinator of global economic action. His handling of the MPs' expenses scandal was little short of calamitous.

'Nick?' asked the voice on my phone. Whoever it was – he didn't say – was shouting to make himself heard over the din of what sounded like a crowded bar. In the background I could make out the sound of glasses clinking above loud chatter and the odd guffaw. 'I'm calling from Strangers',' the voice went on. It was now recognizably that of a well-known

Labour backbench MP calling from one of the Palace of Westminster's most frequented bars. 'We just thought you'd like to know' – he was beginning to sound rather pleased with himself – 'that we've tabled an EDM [Early Day Motion] calling for *your* expenses to be published.' There was a roar in the background before the line went dead. I can only imagine what happened next but it's not hard to guess. Glasses will have been refilled amid shouts of 'That'll bloody well teach him!'

Sure enough, the next day a motion duly appeared on the Commons Order Paper entitled 'The Reporting of Mr Nick Robinson', calling on the BBC to publish 'a full itemized account of the expenses of Mr Robinson, in the name of transparency and the accountability of public funds'.

An EDM is, at best, Westminster's equivalent of a letter sent to a local paper. At worst, it's a form of parliamentary graffiti which allows MPs to sound off under the spurious authority of a motion that will never actually be debated. Nevertheless, the sight of the names of seventy-eight MPs representing all the big parties was, I confess, a little un-settling. I soon realized, though, that this was a case of those with something to hide trying to humiliate the messenger before shooting him. Worse things had happened to reporters in the chequered history of the relationship between Parliament and journalists. The motion was tabled in February 2008, more than a year before the *Daily Telegraph* published, day after painful day, the receipts of MPs who'd claimed for moat-cleaning, giant flat-screen TVs and phantom mortgages.

What became a fully fledged political scandal had begun with a Freedom of Information request for a handful of MPs' expenses claims, including Gordon Brown's. If the Commons had gone along with the ruling of the information commissioner, which agreed that expenses could be published under headings – travel, subsistence and so forth – the scandal might have been avoided. As it was, the Commons authorities decided to appeal against the decision only to find themselves ordered to produce every receipt, producing a crisis which eventually saw four MPs and two lords sent to prison. Gordon Brown's failure to grasp what he was dealing with and his concern with soothing his own backbenchers rather than the public did him enormous damage.

When the questions about MPs' expenses first began, he insisted that it wasn't a matter for him. MPs' pay and rations were set, he pointed out, not by the government but by the House of Commons. After the first whiffs of skulduggery emerged he decided it was a matter for an inquiry that would report after the next election. As the affair mushroomed he said that the inquiry should be speeded up. Then, as panic set in, he pre-empted the whole thing with his now infamous broadcast on YouTube proposing yet another approach. Those three minutes of internet footage deserve to be the subject of a doctoral thesis, summing up as they do so many of the problems of Gordon Brown's premiership and his strained relationship with the press and broadcasters.

The film opens with the prime minister speaking to camera in front of a marble fireplace at Number 10. What catches the eye, though, is not the background but the incongruous wide grin on Gordon Brown's face as he tells viewers: 'Going around the country, I've been struck by the comments made by young people when I meet them about what jobs they want to do when they grow up.'

His point was that, while the aim of many was 'to make a difference', none of them told him they wanted to be an MP. It was important to attract young, committed people into politics but the issue of expenses was, he said, casting a cloud over the whole of Parliament, which was why it was right to try to establish clearer, simpler rules for claiming expenses. Then there it was again – another grin, once again utterly unrelated to what he was actually saying. It was as if someone was throwing a switch at random moments to change the expression on his face.

John Prescott would later say, believe it or not in an attempt to be helpful: 'I have worked with Gordon Brown for an awfully long time. He must have the worst bloody smile in the world.' Nevertheless, he added 'the man has got the ability and the intellect to get on with the job'.

But to many the smile smacked of at worst, insincerity and at best, insecurity and it exposed Gordon Brown to yet more painful ridicule. Since this is what the YouTube broadcast is now known for, few recall that it would have been controversial anyway. In it he proposed that MPs be paid a daily attendance allowance – £150 a day – instead of having to make itemized expense claims. MPs quickly objected to the idea of a 'clocking-in' fee and the public was resistant to what sounded like a daily bonus for simply turning up to work.

Neither MPs nor journalists could cross-question Brown on his proposal as he had not made it to Parliament or in a news conference or interviews. He'd recorded the clip in a hurry in order to claim credit for a strategy another minister was due to unveil later that day. The policy was still being debated, it was the day before the Budget and he had not had time to review it.[2]

The whole point of direct messages posted on YouTube was to bypass the 'mainstream media' which Brown's team and, in particular, his wife Sarah thought had written him off. This medium gave Number 10 total control of not just the content but the presentation of what the prime minister said. The problem, of course, was that the content was flawed and the presentation was dire. Over 4,000 hostile comments were posted on this one broadcast before Downing Street switched off the feedback. Politicians are always keen to find new ways to talk directly to voters. They are less keen, though, when voters talk back.

A few days later broadcasters were invited into Downing Street to interview the prime minister about his latest initiative on expenses – he had, by now, abandoned his YouTube idea. It was another unhappy occasion. As Brown did one interview in his study those of us awaiting our turn sat in the Cabinet room next door. The end of each interview was marked by the sound of raised voices followed by the exit of a white-faced hack who'd been upbraided for daring to question the prime minister's integrity. An equally distressed-looking aide would pass in the other direction in the hope of calming down the boss before the next confrontation.

The madness of it all was that Gordon Brown had volunteered for a set of interviews when he had little new to say while refusing to do them when he had. If he'd set out his daily allowance proposal in interviews reporters would have asked about how the scheme would work. Now, instead, they were asking him why he'd made such a mess of the whole thing.

Ever since the election that never was the Labour party and the Cabinet had agonized about whether to remove Gordon Brown. Over lunch with one minister after another I would hear the calculations. A senior minister who has never been outed as an anti-Brown plotter reminded me how Anthony Eden had waited years to replace Winston Churchill. He was, he quipped, 'like a racehorse trained to win the Derby in about 1938 but who didn't come out of the stalls until 1955'. The parallel did not need spelling out.

Labour was doomed to defeat if they kept their leader; almost anyone would be better at connecting with the electorate; David Miliband or Alan Johnson could comfortably command the Cabinet; Brown would not go quietly, he would fight to stay on and, if forced out, would poison the party's future. Thus ran the partial plots and incomplete conspiracies. At different times and at different levels of involvement they included the majority of the Cabinet, everyone from Brown's deputy, Harriet Harman, who invited his enemies to discuss what to do over a dinner of roast goose at her Suffolk country cottage, to his former acolyte Douglas Alexander, who switched his allegiance to David Miliband after being unfairly blamed for the prime minister's catastrophic indecision over whether to go to the polls, and Jack Straw, who had never forgiven himself for not confronting a previous failing Labour leader, Michael Foot. When I once named on air those wrestling with their doubts and outlined their deliberations I was attacked for shoddy journalism and for accusing ministers of what Stalin called 'thought crimes'. Voters, in my view, had a right to know.

In the early summer of 2009 the Cabinet got their chance to ditch the man they believed was driving them at high speed over an electoral cliff. They chose not to take it. Their decision sealed the fate of Gordon Brown and the Labour government.

On Thursday 4 June Britain went to the polls to vote in local and European elections. No one was waiting for the results. They were already entirely predictable: Labour would get a pasting. What people were anticipating was the fall-out. In the two days before the elections, first the home secretary, Jacqui

Smith, and then communities secretary Hazel Blears, both of whom had faced embarrassing revelations about their expenses claims, had announced their resignations. It looked to some voters like a conspiracy to unsettle or unseat the prime minister. The truth was more mundane but just as worrying for Brown: the party had been overtaken by a collective despair that contained the seeds of political action.

On the eve of polling day, at Prime Minister's Questions, Gordon Brown failed to back Alistair Darling to stay in his job in the reshuffle everyone knew would follow the election results. That night, in Downing Street, one of those closest to the prime minister emerged from the door of Number 10 and confirmed to me, off the record of course, that Brown's mind was made up: Darling was to be replaced. The chancellor, however, was resisting the offer of a move to the Home Office or, indeed, any other department. The welfare secretary, James Purnell, had been sounded out about a move to Education, which would free Ed Balls to move to the Treasury. Balls had even organized a leaving party at his department.

I had spent polling day talking on camera to those Labour backbenchers willing to trigger a leadership ballot and privately to the many ministers who were not ready to go public. One of those I most wanted to speak to did not answer his phone and ignored my texts. Silence is often as revealing as conversation in journalism. The question not answered, the call not returned, the offer of support ignored. However, its significance is also difficult to report. It was always possible, after all, that the minister had lost his phone or there had been a family crisis.

My failure to get hold of James Purnell was still gnawing away at me as I edited my report for the *Ten O'Clock News*. At five to ten my phone went. It was the political editor of the

Sun, George Pascoe Watson. 'You need to know about our "splash",' he said. Purnell was resigning and calling on Brown to go. So that was why he hadn't been answering his phone. He'd been writing his resignation letter and briefing the two journalists with whom he regularly played golf, George at the *Sun* and Phil Webster of *The Times*, and Patrick Wintour of the newspaper that had already shocked Brown by calling on him to quit, the *Guardian*.

Rushing off to my live position on a balcony overlooking Parliament, I shouted at my news desk to warn the studio that there was breaking news and to get pictures and started to phone ministers for their reactions. As the lift doors shut another call came through – this time, it was James himself. I told him I had less than two minutes before going on air and I needed to know very quickly why he'd resigned, what he intended to do now and who else might follow him. Then the lift cut the signal so I had to ring him back as the soundman put an earpiece in my ear and the music of the opening titles began. An email arrived with the text of his resignation letter. I yelled down the line to the studio: 'I've got the letter, I've spoken to him, just throw to me,' or perhaps something to that effect but rather less coherent.

Huw Edwards' headlines and my cue were now, like my video report, out of date. 'Tonight more ministers have come out in support of Gordon Brown,' Huw said, before adding: 'But there has been a dramatic development in the past few minutes, so let's join Nick Robinson at Westminster . . .'

Like most television journalists, I am an adrenaline junkie, addicted to those moments when your pulse races, your heart pounds, your throat goes dry and you have to take a deep breath and try to convey the drama while retaining your judgement. I kicked off by reading out Purnell's letter:

Dear Gordon,

We both love the Labour party. I have worked for it for twenty years and you for far longer. We know we owe it everything and it owes us nothing. I owe it to our party to say what I believe, no matter how hard that may be. I now believe your continued leadership makes a Conservative victory more, not less likely . . . I'm therefore calling on you to stand aside to give our party a fighting chance of winning. As such, I'm resigning from the government.

If it appeared that night as if Purnell's action had dramatically changed the odds on Gordon Brown remaining prime minister, it soon became clear that the minister was operating alone. He had hoped his resignation would protect his friend David Miliband from accusations of plotting but he had assumed that Miliband and others in the Cabinet would follow his cue. As it turned out, while they agreed with Purnell's analysis, they were not ready to nail their colours to the mast. When one of Brown's fiercest critics, John Hutton, did resign from the Cabinet the next day, he told me in his resignation interview that his decision was personal and not political. This took me by complete surprise given what I knew of Hutton's feelings about Brown.

In September 2006, when I was chronicling the angry fall-out of the bid by Brown and his allies to force Tony Blair to name the date he would leave office, Hutton had called me in fury from his car. His words imprinted themselves on my brain long before I could scribble them in my notebook: 'It would be an absolute fucking disaster if Gordon Brown was prime minister and I'll do anything in my power to fucking stop him.' Before ringing off, he declared: 'And you can use that in any fucking way you like.'

Although I could have named him on air I decided to treat his outburst as off the record – perhaps hoping that more might come my way – and quoted him simply as a Blairite minister. The press began to work their way through Blairite ministers in an attempt to identify my source. Years later Hutton outed himself, but before he did, one likely candidate, John Reid, decided to make it clear that it wasn't him. At that year's TUC conference he marched up to me in a crowded bar and shouted at the top of his voice: 'It's only because I swear too effing much that everyone effing thinks I was the effing source for your effing quote and you know I effing wasn't.'

Had Hutton, Reid, Purnell and Miliband ever joined forces, the prime minister would have gone. As it was, a wounded Brown was able to stagger on even though he lacked the political strength to carry out the reshuffle he'd planned. Gracelessly and grudgingly, he summoned Alistair Darling to his study and told him, 'OK, you can stay.' The pair did not exchange another word.

Downing Street was now occupied by two former friends who'd fallen out catastrophically but felt forced to stay together for the sake of their party. Increasingly, they disagreed not just about economic policy but about political strategy, too.

In September 2009 Gordon Brown returned to the United States for another meeting of the G20 and to attend a UN summit. At a Downing Street briefing before the trip one journalist asked officials to list the other leaders the prime minister would be meeting for one-to-one talks. President Obama was not among them. The White House then disclosed that the president was due to meet the Chinese and

Russian presidents and the Japanese premier. The *Sun* and the *Daily Mail* suggested that Brown was being snubbed.

It was a story that could have been stopped in its tracks. There was a perfectly good reason for Obama choosing to meet leaders with whom he'd not yet had bilateral talks, rather than entertaining the prime minister again. After all, they'd already had two meetings, one in the White House and one at Downing Street. It could also have been pointed out that the French president and German chancellor had no meetings planned, either. Instead Brown panicked and demanded that his officials find a way for him to sit down formally with the president.

When the visiting press pack landed in Washington they heard from diplomats and others of the lengths to which Number 10 had gone to kill the snub story. They'd even offered to make a last-minute change to government policy on swine flu immunization in Africa to bring it into line with America's. At home the 'S' word was all over the next morning's front pages and one incoming phone call was all it took to stand up the story for me.

The call was from the White House, as the voice on the line announced. Not recognizing the name of the man I was being put through to, I mouthed it to the BBC's US producer, who waved his hand in the air to indicate that he was very senior. The official wanted to assure me of the deep respect the president had for the prime minister. He said that the White House had been asked by Downing Street to help kill the snub story. I dutifully wrote down what he was saying before querying, 'Are you telling me that the prime minister did not ask for a meeting with the president?' My caller was evasive, merely repeating his expressions of warmth for Gordon Brown. In the absence of any denial from the White

House, I followed up the story, quoting on air 'one diplomatic source' who said that Number 10 had been 'frantically trying to arrange formal talks' between the two leaders.

Equally frantic to kill the story, Number 10 let it be known that Brown and Obama had had a 'brush-past', or 'walk and talk' – a chat on the move between meetings rather than a formal bilateral. It soon emerged that the brush-past had taken place in the kitchens of the UN building ('Gordon's Kitchen Nightmare' yelled the *Sun*). The prime minister was more angry than I'd ever seen him. So too, apparently, was the White House. The president's outspoken chief of staff, Rahm Emanuel, told one member of Brown's entourage: 'Your press are fucking criminals. What do we have to do to convince them of our special relationship? Do they want pictures of Gordon banging Michelle in the Oval Office?'

On the plane home I had a long heart-to-heart with a civil servant working for the prime minister. Our discussion about why this damaging story had unfolded as it had began with us both defending the way we'd behaved and ended in agreement that the snub story was a pretty worrying reflection of the dreadful state of relations between the media and Gordon Brown. It was not Number 10's finest hour, or mine.

When it came to the 'C' word, there was method in what seemed to many to be Gordon Brown's political madness. He believed that by conceding the need for cuts he would be playing on his opponents' chosen territory. Labour could win a debate about growth versus austerity, he told his colleagues, but were certain to lose one in which the choice was 'nice cuts' from Labour and 'nasty cuts' from the Tories.

In his memoirs Peter Mandelson describes how he and Alistair Darling eventually persuaded the prime minister to use the 'C' word in his speech to the TUC conference in 2009: 'Labour will cut costs, cut inefficiencies, cut unnecessary programmes and cut lower-priority budgets.' In fact, he used it no fewer than eight times. Backstage afterwards he tore into his advisers. 'Well, are you satisfied, all of you? We should not be in this place! We have got to move to growth!' If only they had a fair press, he said, he was certain he would win the argument with the public. 'Now it's useless. The Treasury will be turning the screw. They and the others have set the terms of this argument which has followed them. We should not have gone down this course . . . Cuts versus cuts will just kill us . . . Don't give me all this stuff about spending cuts.'[3]

The irony is that Brown's reluctance to confront the country with the choice it faced ensured that the electorate never had the debate it should have had. His argument about the need for a stimulus and a growth plan was never fully heard. The questions that went untested were how much government should be cutting, how fast it should do it and, crucially, which programmes should face the axe and which should be saved from it.

A little over a week after his U-turn on cuts Gordon Brown was suffering again. With the champagne on ice for News International's annual party at the Labour conference, which Cabinet ministers were planning to attend, the *Sun*, whose support Tony Blair and Alastair Campbell had been so proud to secure, switched to backing the Tories on the eve of the prime minister's keynote speech. Although the *Sun*'s endorsement was of limited value, this desertion symbolized the end of the New Labour era. It was also a personal blow to a man who had invested as much in his relationship with newspaper editors and media moguls as Tony Blair ever had.

Gordon Brown and Rupert Murdoch were surprisingly close. Both men shared a dislike for the English establishment and a Presbyterian hunger for hard work. Their children played together while they discussed politics and economics. The Browns attended the wedding of the woman Murdoch entrusted with his British newspaper interests, Rebekah Brooks, and Sarah Brown asked her to a 'slumber party' at Chequers. The Browns were also close enough to Paul Dacre, the editor of the *Daily Mail*, to invite him to the funeral of their baby daughter, Jennifer. No broadcaster was anywhere near as intimate with Gordon Brown. Like Blair, he believed that TV and radio all too often took their cue from the press.

The *Sun*, however, had been targeting Brown for months over what they alleged was his betrayal of 'our brave boys' fighting in Afghanistan. Day after day the paper had protested, 'Don't they know there's a bloody war on?' After Remembrance Sunday they stepped up their campaign, accusing the prime minister of failing to bow his head after laying his wreath at the Cenotaph and castigating him over a letter of condolence he had written to the mother of a fallen soldier, which she described as a 'disgraceful, hastily scrawled insult'. He'd not only misspelt Jacqui Janes' surname but appeared to have crossed out and corrected the name of her twenty-year-old son, who'd died after suffering gruesome injuries on the front line.

This was hardly fair. Anyone familiar with Gordon Brown's handwriting knew that it always looked like that. Its untidiness was emphasized by the thick, black felt-tip pen he used for the same reason as he had his speeches printed in 36-point type: so that he could read them with his one half-good eye. Yes, there were mistakes in the letter, but someone on Brown's staff should have pointed those out to him. I said as much on the news, irritating *Sun* executives and confounding those in Downing Street who claimed the BBC simply followed the trail of the press pack.

The next day Brown held a news conference. Dressed in a dark suit and sombre tie, his voice deeper and more gravelly than normal, suggesting he'd had even less sleep than usual, and his damp eyes occasionally glistening in the camera lights, he sought to limit the damage created by the carelessly written letter. His tone was painfully personal as he strove to demonstrate the emotional connection modern politics demands but with which he was so obviously uncomfortable. After describing himself as 'shy', he insisted that he did 'feel the pain of those who'd lost loved ones'. Without directly referring to the death of his own baby daughter, he said, 'I'm a parent who understands the feelings when things go dreadfully wrong.'

Few recognized the problems Gordon Brown's poor eyesight caused him. His confidence was corroded by the ever-present worry that he would be unable to read an autocue or fail to recognize someone he ought to know. His advisers sought to be at his side at all times to guide him to the right place or person. One recalls his panic when he was accidentally left alone at the beginning of an international meeting. On another occasion, filming behind the scenes with the prime minister, I was travelling with his entourage on a small private plane taking him to visit President Sarkozy in Paris when he tripped heavily over an unseen obstacle while walking up the aisle of the aircraft. Although I assured his advisers that I had no desire to embarrass him and wouldn't make use of the footage, the pall of anxiety was palpable. Only later did I learn that for a few days Brown had believed the fate he'd always dreaded was coming to pass: that he was going completely blind. Thankfully, it had just been an infection in his one functioning eye. But he lived in constant fear not simply of losing his sight but of being considered no longer fit to do his job as a result.

It should, perhaps, have come as no surprise. The moment when many concluded that Gordon Brown's re-election hopes were at an end combined an awkward appearance on camera, a misjudged encounter with an ordinary member of the public and a failure to control his temper. It was a made-for-television blunder by a man hopelessly ill-suited to the medium.

The woman who unwittingly exposed these limitations in one stroke was a sixty-six-year-old grandmother from Rochdale, Gillian Duffy. She was steered towards Gordon Brown by his most trusted aides in their eagerness to show the prime minister connecting with the public. Mrs Duffy had a lot to say and wasn't going to let this opportunity pass. 'My family have voted Labour all their lives. My father, even when he was in his teens, went to Free Trade Hall to sing "The Red Flag". And now I'm absolutely ashamed of saying I'm Labour.'

Instead of asking her why she was ashamed, Brown listed all the reasons she should be proud of the government. This only encouraged her to plough on. 'How are you going to get us out of all this debt, Gordon?'

Next came her views on welfare – 'there's too many people now who aren't vulnerable but they can claim, and people who are vulnerable can't claim, can't get it' – before she tackled the subject shown by all opinion polls to be the public's main concern but which politicians were loath to address. 'You can't say anything about the immigrants . . . but all these Eastern Europeans what are coming in, where are they flocking from?'

Ironically, given the firestorm that ensued, Brown in fact handled her surprisingly well, praising her 'good family' and telling her, 'It's very nice to see you. Take care.' After he'd moved on, Mrs Duffy returned the compliment, informing reporters that the prime minister was 'very nice' and that she would, after all, be voting Labour. That was before she heard what Gordon Brown had said about her after getting into his official car. He was still wearing a radio microphone, provided by Sky News at Labour's request, which he had forgotten to turn off.

Normally, sound recorded in a private location would be regarded as just that – private. But Sky judged it to be in the public interest to ignore that convention and broadcast what their camera had recorded. Whether or not it was in the public interest, it was certainly of interest to the public or, to put it another way, a bloody good television story.

'That was a disaster,' Brown was heard complaining to his aides. '[You] should never have put me with that woman . . . she was just a sort of bigoted woman who said she used to be Labour.'

Every stage of this political horror show was to be relayed on television. The tape of what Brown had said about her was played to Mrs Duffy while a camera captured her appalled reaction.

I'm very disappointed. I'm very upset. He's an educated person, why has he come out with words like that? He's going to lead this country and he's calling an ordinary woman who's just come up and asked him questions that most people would ask him . . . and he's calling me a bigot . . . What was bigoted in that what I said? I just asked about national debt. I am quite shocked. Very shocked.

By this time Brown was taking part in a scheduled interview with Radio 2's Jeremy Vine, who had been warned just before going on air about what had happened with Mrs Duffy. The BBC was still debating whether to follow Sky and use the tape. In the meantime, the programme's producer was inundated with calls demanding that Vine stop questioning Brown on the economy and start asking about the 'bigoted woman' comment. He took the phone off the hook. Towards the end of the interview, the BBC made its mind up that the tape could be aired.

Brown listened in agony to what he had been caught saying. Even though he was in a radio studio, his interview was being filmed and transmitted live, so his reaction, too, was recorded on camera. He covered his face with his hand as he heard himself bad-mouthing a voter and blaming his staff. He insisted that he hadn't meant to insult Mrs Duffy – it was just that 'it was a question about immigration that was annoying'.

Half a century after the first-ever television election, this was the day that showed just how far TV's influence on politics had gone. First cameras filmed an encounter staged for their benefit. Then a microphone recorded the prime minister's private reaction to it. Next they filmed Mrs Duffy's response to that reaction. Then Gordon Brown's reaction to that response. News correspondents were soon broadcasting live from outside Mrs Duffy's house as she awaited the arrival of a contrite prime minister, who begged her to appear on camera outside to show that she'd accepted his apology. Fittingly, she refused.

It was, the columnist Charles Moore wrote later, 'a political snuff movie' and encapsulated perfectly how the modern media work. 'There is no agenda that [they do] not dictate, no time to think, no privacy, no respect, no mercy, no escape. New Labour was born by understanding this and manipulating it so it is entirely fitting that it should now be dying by mishandling the same phenomenon.'[4]

It certainly wouldn't have happened to Clement Attlee.

Gordon Brown never mastered the slick answer, the shameless photo opportunity or the contrived empathy. He faced a much more hostile media corps than Tony Blair ever had. By the time he came to power the press had already turned against New Labour and soon they turned against Brown personally. Their attacks hurt him deeply. The legacy of spin, sleaze and splits made the electorate cynical and produced journalists who were too ready to play to the gallery rather than to challenge that cynicism.

That said, Brown's fate cannot be blamed on the media. Ever since the invention of radio at the beginning of the twentieth century, prime ministers have been obliged to try, with varying degrees of success, to capitalize on the power of broadcasting to convey their message and their own qualities to the electorate. Brown could have made good use of TV and radio to speak directly to the country about the three huge challenges he confronted: the global economic crisis, the MPs' expenses scandal and the mounting death toll in Afghanistan. Leadership involves finding the words to reassure, to persuade, to lead. Brown never found them, nor did he develop a prime ministerial style of his own. Too often this reflected the fact that he had not forged the underlying policies.

Historians will debate whether Gordon Brown was suited to be prime minister in any age. What is beyond doubt is that he was not suited to the job in the age of television.

12

THE BATTLE OVER,
A NEW ONE BEGINS

It was in the back of a people carrier in a car park in my home city of Manchester that I first had the thought. I was surrounded by empty cardboard cups, a banana skin and a half-eaten chocolate bar, the remnants of frequent refuelling to replace the adrenaline my body was pumping out. This was a moment we'd dreamed of, talked about incessantly and planned for endlessly. The thought was – and I really had no time for it then – is this really it?

If you'd stumbled across the car park that night you would have struggled to make sense of the sight of a perhaps vaguely familiar bald man in glasses screaming at the two other people in the vehicle, then leaning through the open window to shout at two more people in another car parked alongside it and to shove scraps of paper into their hands.

This was 15 April 2010: the night of Britain's first-ever live TV election debate, one of three to be broadcast by ITV, Sky and the BBC respectively. My task was simple enough. Watch the politicians speak, pick out the most interesting bits, write a few pithy words around them and put it all on the telly. After all, it's what I do day in, day out. If only. This report was to be different. It not only had to capture the essence of a moment of history and to be scrupulously fair to everyone concerned; it also had to be on air one minute after the debate ended. Normally a TV news report takes at least an hour to edit. If I want it to be really good, or the story is particularly complex, I sometimes allow an hour's editing for every minute on screen, which means a four-minute report takes four hours to cut.

On this occasion I, or rather, we – my producers Thea and Lindsay, videotape editors Vik and Rob, and me – had to watch, listen, pick, write, edit, measure for duration and examine for fairness all at the same time without a minute, let alone an hour, to pause or think or change our minds or look back at what we'd done. Of course, TV sports reporters do this all the time but, if they'll forgive me, no one accuses them of bias in choosing which goals, fouls or controversies to show. The equivalents of those events in the game of politics are always hotly disputed. So it was that I found myself in the back of that car with a set of headphones clamped to my head (hence the shouting), monitoring the debate on one screen, tapping my words on to another, pointing at a third, where my team were editing the pictures, and scribbling down ideas for the best clips for the second team in the car next door to find, edit and measure for duration. And then shouting some more.

Earlier on that day, David Cameron had been filmed nervily gripping the hand of his wife, Samantha. Asked how he was feeling, he replied edgily that he was 'Oh, just taking it easy . . . ish', before adding tellingly, 'What do you think?' Perhaps he had just realized that, as the front runner, he had everything to lose. And lose he did. The clear winner was the

Liberal Democrat leader, Nick Clegg. More than 9 million people watched Gordon Brown try to woo him – 'I agree with Nick' was the phrase that came to define the opening of the 2010 campaign. It was a sentiment which, it was soon clear, a large number of viewers shared. The party's average poll rating jumped from 19 per cent before the debate to 29 per cent afterwards.

When, to everyone's surprise, the Lib Dems lost rather than gained seats in the election, it became fashionable to say the debates had, in fact, changed nothing. I do not believe that. Certainly Cleggmania had subsided before polling day: the party's rating had dropped again to around 25 per cent, and it's impossible to gauge how it would have done without the debates but with the higher profile it normally enjoys during election campaigns. However, I agree with the psephologist Peter Kellner, and many Conservatives, who argue that the debates may have helped rob the Tories of a straight victory and a clear parliamentary majority and smoothed the path to the first coalition government since the Second World War. They sucked the oxygen from a conventional campaign which would have focused on the choice between David Cameron and an unpopular Gordon Brown and the country's economic crisis. They boosted the profile of Nick Clegg, making the idea of a coalition with him as deputy prime minister much more sellable than it would otherwise have been. David Cameron, having failed to win the election, felt compelled to turn to him to secure a working parliamentary majority. The electorate had rejected Labour, forcing Gordon Brown to retire. He was replaced, as expected, by a leader called Miliband – but not the one most had expected. Ed beat his brother David, showing a degree of ruthlessness he will need at the next election.

Watching my debate piece back now is strangely deflating. Just another set of talking heads, well, talking. To me it conveys none of the drama, the buzz, the sense of our national story being written that I hoped it would. My feeling now about those ground-breaking election debates is just a deeper version of my feeling in that car park on the night the first of them was broadcast. Is this it? There have been so many skirmishes in the war to win the right to report what our elected representatives say, to cover elections, to ask politicians questions that hold them to account, to see and hear them speaking in the House of Commons and, finally, to have proper, full-length election debates before the entire British public. Could there possibly be any left to fight?

Over half the adult population – more than 22 million people – saw at least some of the three broadcasts, the sort of figures even *The X Factor* struggles to match. Millions discussed what they'd seen, millions went on to vote – many of them for the first time, and most more informed and more engaged than before. Yet just at the moment when British politics at long last came to terms with the most powerful communications medium known to man, it was becoming clear that there is a much bigger battle to face on a new front: the battle to convince people that all the politics they can now watch and hear is not a pointless, irritating and destructive distraction from the challenges of real life, pursued by identikit politicians all in it for themselves and out of touch with ordinary folk. It's a view you hear routinely in the office or the pub or on radio phone-ins. I believe it's profoundly mistaken and, worse, dangerous.

Sitting in Court 73 of the Royal Courts of Justice over the summer of 2012 I watched prime ministers past and present take the stand at the Leveson inquiry into the culture, practices and ethics of the press. One by one they turned their evidence into a trial of the media. I relived my past as they relived theirs. I absorbed their pain and frustration and anger at the way they'd been treated. Each made it plain that it is the media he blames, at least in part, for the widespread contempt in which politicians are held.

It was the first time I'd seen Tony Blair in a long while. Once scarcely a week had passed without me being in the same room as him. As he waited to be called to give his evidence he caught my eye, smiled and said a cheery 'Hi, Nick!' Always a sucker for the Blair charm, I replied somewhat goofily, 'Nice to see you. How are you?'

'Well . . .' the master communicator said. He spotted the obvious hazards of giving an honest reply in front of a group of journalists sitting with pens poised over their notebooks. So my question went unanswered.

On the stand Blair entered one guilty plea – failing to take on the media – but insisted he was not guilty of the two other charges often made against him: doing a deal with Rupert Murdoch and presiding over a spin operation that bullied journalists. He fleshed out his description of the media pack acting like a 'feral beast', moving from one victim to the next. As with his original speech, a powerful critique was somewhat diluted by an unwillingness to acknowledge his own role in the breakdown of trust between the media and politicians.

When Gordon Brown came to court it was I who caught his eye and smiled. I got no acknowledgement. He seemed to look first at me and then at two sketch-writers who regularly tormented him, Quentin Letts of the *Daily Mail* and Ann Treneman of *The Times*. We were, I sensed, a wholly unwelcome reminder of days he'd rather forget. When the

Right Honourable member for Kirkcaldy and Cowdenbeath gave his evidence anger and anguish were etched on his face. He spoke about newspapers' 'licence to deceive', declaring that they 'sensationalize', 'distort fact and opinion and mix them together' and focus not on 'policy difference but [on] an issue of motive, an issue of intentions, an issue of character, an issue of personality, an issue of evil practice'.

He spoke of how the *Sun* had accused him of not caring when young soldiers were killed or maimed in Afghanistan and of how they'd revealed that his baby son had a serious illness and then claimed they'd done it with his approval. It was powerful and moving testimony. But when he went on to deny he had known about the regular, persistent and malicious briefings by his aides against Tony Blair, Alistair Darling and many others, the journalists present could scarcely believe what they were hearing. Brown's period in the wilderness had not, it seemed, brought him great self-knowledge.

In the Blair years a Downing Street spin-doctor once asked me for advice on how to rebuild relations with the media. I told him to put a note above his desk reading 'Don't insult their intelligence'.

It was, surprisingly, Sir John Major, so often mocked for his dated and stilted speaking style, who proved to be the most eloquent at Leveson. In large part this was because he was willing to address his own mistakes. I was 'much too sensitive from time to time about what the press wrote', he said. 'God knows why I was, but I was.' He described reading the newspapers each morning as a 'source of wonder' – and he clearly didn't mean that in a good way – as he discovered 'what I thought that I didn't think, what I said that I didn't say, what I was about to do that I wasn't about to do'.

When it came to David Cameron's turn to give evidence interesting historical reflections were clearly not on the agenda. He was fighting for his personal and political reputation in real time. Every word he uttered, every expression on his face and every evasion he made would not just be broadcast live but subject to instant analysis on Twitter. I was struck that day by the contrast he must be feeling between the warm and comfortable embrace of Downing Street, where doors open magically for him, people address him as 'Prime Minister' and he is in charge, and the cold, bleak Court 73, where he faced five hours of cross-examination by a barrister who called him plain Mr Cameron in front of a judge even the prime minister must stand up for when he enters court.

It wasn't meant to be like this. David Cameron had asked Sir Brian Leveson to investigate why the press, the police and politicians had failed to recognize the widespread use of phone hacking by the press until they were forced to do so by public outrage in the wake of the revelation that the *News of the World* had illegally accessed the voicemails of the murdered teenager Millie Dowler. At the time the prime minister can never have imagined that his inquiry would force him to reveal relationships with media executives that all his predecessors had been able to keep secret.

It was not just a matter of answering questions about which media figure he'd met when, but also of having to bear the exposure of mortifyingly chummy text exchanges with Rebekah Brooks, until recently the most powerful woman in the British press. The woman who had made friends with both Tony Blair and Gordon Brown had befriended a third prime minister – no matter that the three agreed on precious little. Cameron saw Brooks most weekends when he was 'in the country' for parties, 'country suppers' and horse-riding.

In my job you see political leaders moved to sadness, anger and defiance, but rarely do you see them embarrassed to the degree David Cameron was when Brooks' text to him on the eve of his party conference speech was read out: 'I am so rooting for you . . . as a proud friend . . . Speech of your life? Yes he Cam!' The longer it went on the more uncomfortable he looked, although he was, perhaps, relieved not to be asked to confirm that he used to sign off messages 'LOL', believing the abbreviation to mean 'lots of love' and not, as it does to most texters, 'laugh out loud'.

Cameron repeatedly stressed that television, rather than the written press, was the way to communicate with voters and that television had therefore been his top priority. This seemed somewhat at odds with the catalogue of meetings with media folk disclosed to the inquiry. At one point during his evidence a list of them was projected on to the screens in the court. Again and again the names of members of the Murdoch family, Brooks and the editors of their newspapers appeared. I was somewhat alarmed when I noticed my own name among them, mentioned four times on a single page, and heard Robert Jay QC, lead counsel to the inquiry, remark, 'There are a lot of references to Nick Robinson on this page and elsewhere.'

I looked down at my notebook, feeling strangely uncomfortable even though my appointments with the prime minister – for two interviews and two TV filming trips – were hardly in the same league as country suppers, cosy lunches or business breakfasts. Jay went on: 'He's someone that you keep in contact with for obvious reasons?' The prime minister paused briefly then replied with one word, 'Yes,' and the questioning moved on. The records, incidentally, show that I had one so-called 'social' meeting with Cameron – a dinner – in seven years, and that was when he was in opposition. In comparison his diary listed ten meetings with Rupert Murdoch, fifteen with his son James and nineteen with Rebekah Brooks, not counting occasions on which they simply happened to bump into each other.

The truth is that, however important TV might be in reaching the electorate, David Cameron had long since abandoned the view taken by his team when he first became Tory leader that there was 'no need to suck up to Murdoch'. In 2007 he'd hired as his director of communications the man Murdoch had hand-picked to edit his biggest-selling paper, the *News of the World*. Andy Coulson had resigned when phone hacking at the paper was first revealed but remained on close terms with both Murdoch and Rebekah Brooks. Their very public trials have once again shone a spotlight on the wisdom of David Cameron's choice of advisers and friends. He has always insisted that they never influenced his decision-making over, for example, Murdoch's attempt to take over BSkyB. Indeed, I was made aware of the prime minister's intense frustration with my reporting of his Leveson appearance. He believed that he had conclusively knocked on the head any suggestion of a conspiracy between him, his ministers and the Murdoch empire and couldn't understand why that was not the focus of my report. What I believed then, and believe now, is that the whole affair had raised important questions about why those close to David Cameron had decided that it was right, after all, to 'suck up' to the Murdoch empire, and why it clearly wanted to suck up to him.

The Leveson inquiry acted very successfully as a form of truth and reconciliation commission. It gave a public airing for the first time to the torment experienced by those who found themselves unwittingly and unwillingly caught and then trapped in the media spotlight, inspiring screenwriters of TV hits like *Broadchurch* to add journalists to the list of on-screen villains. It highlighted the impotence felt by the apparently powerful. It forced newspapers to examine and confront malpractice.

What it did not do was build a consensus around how to stop it happening again. In part this was because there was no agreement on what 'it' was. If 'it' was phone hacking, the newspapers were able to point out that this was already illegal. If 'it' was invasion of privacy, then Leveson was being asked to solve a problem that had defied resolution by a generation of lawyers and politicians. Or was 'it' the power of Murdoch and other media moguls? Ever since Rupert Murdoch took on and defeated the print unions that had closed *The Times* for a year the world had been split between those who thought he was the saviour of British newspapers and those who objected to the unaccountable power and influence of a foreign citizen over British public life. All too rarely was anyone willing to admit that it was perfectly possible to hold both views at the same time.

To make matters even more difficult, subtle and complex arguments about public policy quickly boiled down to a simple question: whose side are you on? Are you with the victims or the press? Reeling from the fallout of hiring Coulson and befriending Brooks, David Cameron announced that the test of any new system of press regulation was whether it would satisfy the victims. This ignored the fact that the experiences of 'ordinary people' like Kate and Gerry McCann or Chris Jefferies (the victim of terrible character assassination when he was briefly and falsely suspected of a vicious murder) were very different from those of their celebrity spokesman Hugh Grant. What linked them was an effective new lobby group called Hacked Off. Its campaign so infuriated the newspapers that it united a group of proprietors and editors who rarely agree on very much. One reason for the months-long impasse in cross-party attempts to find a better way to regulate the press has been that they have all feared being accused of 'letting down the victims' which, in practice, makes them wary of disagreeing with Hacked Off. At the same time the prime minister, like all his predecessors, has been very wary of making permanent enemies of the *Mail*, *Telegraph* and News International titles whose proprietors and editors will never forgive him for setting up Leveson. I never agreed with those who thought that broadcasting regulation provided a model for the news-papers. In this country radio and TV has always been treated very differently – the final chapter of this book will examine why I think things should stay that way.

Much of broadcasting is publicly funded and all of it is required by law to be fair and balanced. It would be intoler-able to impose similar obligations on the free press and the public would, in any case, soon miss the combination of robustly independent and raucous newspapers with the more trusted, more balanced and inevitably blander world of tele-vision and radio.

Though Leveson only examined the behaviour of news-papers his inquiry highlighted the impact of the media as a whole on politics. The prime minister likened politics in the 24/7 media age to 'fighting a sort of permanent battle' in which issues are 'thrown at you hour by hour, where responses are demanded incredibly quickly, and it can, if you're not careful, take up all your energy in dealing with that, and that is hopeless'.

It would be easy and soothing to argue that the critiques made by all modern prime ministers have nothing to do with television and radio journalism. That would be complacent. When it comes to the reporting of politics, we all, press and broadcasters alike, swim in the same sea. If it is polluted we all suffer.

The phone-hacking scandal is, however, a reminder of how different broadcast journalism in Britain is from newspaper reporting, first and foremost because of its legal obligation to be impartial. The afterword to this book examines whether that will be sustainable in the face of technological change. In his 'feral beast' speech Tony Blair was right to observe that new technology has driven not just a speeding-up of the news cycle but a constant search for impact from media outlets struggling to maintain shrinking readerships and audiences.

Let's address that change for a moment. When I first became a reporter in 1995 most people had the choice of just four terrestrial TV channels. Sky TV had been launched but as yet had very few subscribers. Television current-affairs programmes still often set the news agenda. ITV alone had three of them, *World In Action*, *TV Eye* (formerly *This Week*) and Brian Walden's *Weekend World*. There was no BBC News channel or website. The worldwide web had, in fact, only just been invented – in 1991 it had been unveiled as a way of allowing 'high-energy physicists to share data, news and doc- umentation'. Blackberries and Apples were what you put in pies. If you pasted anything on to your wall it was because you wanted something more interesting than a coat of Dulux. There was no Facebook, no Twitter and there were no blogs.

Newspapers had just been through what they saw as their computer revolution – the shocking innovation of journalists being required to put their own copy on to the page instead of using typesetters to line it up, letter by letter, in little blocks of metal type. They had no idea that they were about to face a much greater challenge from the computer's capacity for communication.

Contrast the speed and scale of the developments over the past two decades with other similar periods. Over the 1950s and 1960s, or the 1960s and 1970s, we've seen how politics, culture and broadcasting evolved. However, the fixed points – the daily newspapers and the evening news bulletins – did not change at all. Now they are both being pressurized by instant news. This has had a real impact not just on the pace but on the tone of political reporting.

Consider one of the first stories I broke, or rather, as you'll see, merely confirmed. In March 1996 someone I knew in Downing Street rang to tell me about a very odd conversation he'd just had. He'd bumped into Michael Heseltine, then deputy prime minister, on his way out of a meeting and warned him about an awkward story that was about to break. 'Forget it,' said Hezza, assuring my source he need not give it another moment's thought. In fact, the deputy prime minister continued, he might as well take the rest of the day off. When he saw what was coming out the next morning, his story wouldn't matter a damn, but no, no, Heseltine protested, he wouldn't, indeed couldn't, say what it was.

What could it possibly be? I racked my brain. I called the most senior BBC news executive I knew. We decided that it had to be the long-rumoured royal divorce, the final split between Prince Charles and Princess Diana. Royal correspondents were put on standby.

Having done my duty, when I awoke the next morning and switched on the radio I had quite forgotten the call the day before. Until, that is, I heard the newspaper review. It included a report that hadn't been on the news and hadn't been discussed on the *Today* programme. The *Daily Mirror*'s front page claimed the government was about to reveal that BSE, a cattle disease, could spread to humans. Its headline was a bit more hysterical than that: 'Mad Cow Can Kill You: Government to Admit it Today'. That's it, I thought, that's the bloody story. But that was all I knew about it. I didn't have the *Mirror* delivered, I couldn't read it online and there was no such thing as tweets. In fact, to all intents and purposes, it wasn't news at all except to readers of the *Mirror*.

I dialled the number of a man I knew at the Department of Health, whose minister would announce the link, and copied a trick I'd once seen in a film. It had looked pretty implausible then and I couldn't imagine it would work now. 'I know you can't tell me anything,' I said, 'but the *Mirror*'s right, isn't it? I'm going to count to ten before putting down the phone and if you don't stop me I'm going on air to say it's true.' Suddenly ten seconds felt like a very long time indeed. Or, rather, nine and a half did.

'I didn't stop you,' my acquaintance said helpfully.

Within minutes I was on the radio reporting that although ministers had been telling us for years that British beef was safe – one had even force-fed his daughter a burger for the cameras – it wasn't. A week later, there was a worldwide ban on all British beef exports that was not fully lifted for another four years.

Imagine that happening now. The report would be on the 24-hour news press reviews the night before the *Mirror* reached the news stands, perhaps even ahead of the ten o'clock news on the main channels. Experts would be interviewed, politicians asked to comment, viewers and listeners invited to phone in, text and email. The story would start to trend on Twitter. Provided just one reporter was able to stand it up, as I was, others would repeat it without needing to bother to establish the facts for themselves (which is what happens when the giveaway words 'media sources' appear at the foot of the screen on Sky News a minute after a story breaks on the BBC). Government ministers would be dragged out of dinners or woken at home and told by press officers, 'We've got to have something to say . . .' Every paper would change its front page. And all this before a single copy of the *Mirror* had been picked up by a single reader.

The next day they'd all need something new. An account of what the minister said in the Commons when he confirmed the link between BSE, the disease in cattle, and CJD, the human illness, would already have been seen live on news channels and analysed on the main bulletins. Some political journalists would start to look for a fresh angle. Why was the bad news revealed on the day it was? Was it an attempt to bury other bad news? Had there been a cover-up? Was the agriculture minister now under pressure to resign? Hacks would compete to come up with a witty hashtag (for non-tweeters, that's a way of labelling messages so you can search for others on the same subject) to capture the mood – #madasacow, probably, or #cowgate.

What about the many very busy people who don't follow Twitter, or watch 24-hour news, or read a paper regularly, or just didn't have time that day; those who missed the TV or radio news because they had to take the kids swimming or sing in their local choir; those who were typing emails or shopping online? They would miss the carefully chosen words of advice from the scientist or the minister. When you hear politicians complain about the speeding up of the news cycle, the increase in competition and the search for impact amid all the noise, this is what they mean. They've got a point, and the change is far from over.

Twitter has created a world of instant, cost-free news and comment from anyone prepared to condense their thoughts into 140 characters. It also allows its users to recommend and pass on links to full-length articles, web pages and photographs to anybody anywhere. I used to share David Cameron's view that 'too many tweets make a twat' (although, unlike him, I knew that four-letter word would offend). His point seemed to have been made when Ed Miliband proclaimed to the world his love of the TV quiz show *Blackbusters* (not, as he meant to say, obviously, *Blockbusters*). Someone in his office crudely joked that it was lucky he wasn't a fan of *Treasure Hunt*. George Galloway, the newly elected MP for Bradford West, couldn't blame a typing slip when he tweeted on election night that he was 'happy after the Blackburn triumph'.

When disciples of so-called social media predicted that the 2010 election would be the 'Twitter election' I was scathing. I was proved right: television, as we've seen, made much more of an impact. Thirty thousand people commented on the TV debates by tweeting; as many as 300,000, it's estimated, may have read those tweets.[1] That's a big number but still only a fraction of a television audience of millions.

But that was then. Twitter was only four years old and 2010 was the first election for which it had existed. By 2012 there were more than 10 million active Twitter users in the UK. Even I now have an account. As one disciple, Clay Shirkey, puts it: 'Here comes everybody.' Comics, pop stars and football players have millions following their utterances.

Even hacks like me can build up – the last time I looked – around 100,000. BBC's *Question Time* regularly prompts in the region of 50,000 tweets a show. Instead of simply watching the politicians and public figures the BBC has picked to debate the issues of the day, or shouting at the telly or arguing with your family, you can now sound off to hundreds of thousands of people you don't know watching all around the country. There's even a pub in Hackney, east London where customers can view *Question Time* together, tweet together and, believe it or not, dance the 'Dimble-dance' to the theme music.

The 'Arab spring' of 2011 convinced many of the political might of Twitter. I suspect that in truth it was the mobile phone – whether used for texts or emails or tweets – that empowered the protesters on the streets of Tunisia and Cairo. Unless they are prepared to turn off the web and mobile phone network entirely, dictators can no longer easily control the flow of information to their people. It's all very different from my trip as a student to East Berlin, where I vividly recall how travelling a hundred yards from one side of the wall to the other took you into an entirely different world, one where there was no advertising on the streets, no foreign newspapers, no television beyond the officially sanctioned propaganda about five-year plans and tractor-production targets. The idea that a mere physical barrier could separate people so completely is almost impossible to convey to my children's generation.

Twitter also showed its power as a source of news when a Pakistani IT consultant from Abbottabad, who'd gone up into the mountains for a bit of peace and quiet, unwittingly tweeted a running commentary on the operation that led to the killing of Osama bin Laden. 'Helicopter hovering above

Abbottabad at 1AM (is a rare event),' he tweeted. His first reaction was irritation at the noise. 'Go away helicopter – before I take out my giant swatter.' Then he realized something much more serious was happening. 'A huge window shaking bang here in Abbottabad Cantt. I hope its not the start of something nasty.' Those who have followed false twitter rumours about the death of a host of world leaders, from Nelson Mandela to Mikhael Gorbachev, will know it's not always so valuable.

Some now claim that we are seeing the death of 'old media' or 'mainstream media' (MSM) and the rise of a new 'citizen journalism'. Clay Shirkey has written about the 'mass ama-teurization' of journalism and politics. John Prescott, who has found a new lease of political life tweeting to his 143,000 followers, claims that 'Twitter is OUR media . . . It's given me a voice and a connection to millions of people that the distorted prism of the mainstream media denied.' Prescott may have struggled to get a fair hearing in the press, but the idea that a man who was deputy prime minister for a decade and is now a peer of the realm represents a fightback of the people against the establishment may be stretching things a bit.

I welcome the fact that reporting is becoming more and more open to all – the antithesis of the old closed shop of the parliamentary lobby. The gradual shift from broadcasting, one person talking to many, to many speaking to many; from transmission to communication; from media tailored to a mass audience to media tailored for me, is all very exciting but – and it's a big but – it comes at a cost.

All too often what appears in tweets and on blogs is not reporting but opinion, not fact but comment, not analysis but prejudice. Its strength is also its weakness. It can do simple but not complex, black and white, not shades of grey, instant but not considered. What's more, it reinforces the media's pack mentality. If a reporter wants to know what his rivals think he doesn't need to wait until he reads their paper or watches their report or bumps into them in the corridors of the press gallery or the lobby coffee bar. He can read it instantly on his phone.

As a result, journalists sitting in the House of Commons press gallery, who once closely followed Prime Minister's Questions in the chamber below them, now have one eye on a handheld screen to see what their colleagues are saying about who has won and who has lost. Once a group view has formed, it takes a brave hack to say, 'That's not how it seemed to me.'

Scarcely has a policy been announced, let alone understood or analysed, before it has been labelled, mocked and a campaign has begun to reverse it. Take George Osborne's 2012 Budget, which quickly became known as an 'omnishambles' after Ed Miliband used this term – which he'd picked up from a leaked report of a meeting of Downing Street aides – invented by the brilliant BBC political satire *The Thick of It*. Thanks, in part, to that buzzword spreading on Twitter, various unpopular taxes were soon labelled, again thanks in part to Twitter, the 'pasty tax', 'caravan tax' and 'charity tax'. The chancellor made U-turns or semi-U-turns on them all. Let's take as an example what became known as the 'granny tax', which in fact he didn't U-turn on. This was the Treasury's proposal to reduce a planned increase in tax-free allowances for pensioners. It doesn't involve anyone, whether a granny or a granddad, paying a penny more in tax. It does, however, mean that in future less of their money than they expected will be tax-free and that the amount anyone can earn before paying tax no longer depends on how old you are. Complex that, isn't it? 'Granny tax' is so much simpler.

By 2pm on Budget day the hashtag had taken off on Twitter. The chancellor had finished delivering his Budget speech less than half an hour earlier. By 4.30pm it was the biggest-trending Twitter topic on the planet. John Prescott's attack on it was re-tweeted – copied and passed on by others – over 1,000 times. Overall there were over 200,000 tweets in twenty-four hours about the Budget. By the next day the policy was universally known, and referred to in the news-paper headlines, as the granny tax. Government spin-doctors tried in vain to get out the message that in fact no granny would pay any more tax, but it was already much too late.

My point is not whether the policy is a good or a bad one, or that it would, before Twitter, have been uncontroversial. Any policy that involved the Treasury's Budget balance sheet showing a saving of over a billion pounds a year from pensioners, and which affected more than 4 million people, many on modest incomes, was sure to cause a fuss. It is that the sheer speed of the modern news cycle meant the govern-ment had lost the argument over whether this was the right way to raise money before they'd ever really made it, and certainly before the alternatives were examined.

Incidentally, I did tweet myself during the Budget speech that 'pensioner tax "simplification" could raise a lot of £s for government'. Few re-tweeted that gem. It lacked the punch of the two key words 'granny' and 'tax'. What works on Twitter is stuff that makes you laugh and stuff that makes you angry, not stuff that makes you pause and think.

Young people receive more and more of their political information online. Increasingly, they don't read one news-paper or watch one television bulletin. They scavenge as they surf, as any parent observing a teenager scanning his hand-held device while watching TV, eating or brushing his teeth can tell you. Twitter may be the biggest source of breaking news but it is not where most readers spend most of their time. That is on social media sites. Many referrals to articles or videos produced by the mainstream media reach them this way.

These personalized media make it easier for people to confine themselves to news that fits in with their pre-existing view of the world. If you only follow people who think like you do, it is very easy to kid yourself that everyone thinks like you do. In this sense technology has shrunk the world rather than opened it up. In politics we have seen a sort of re-creation of the culture of eighteenth-century London. Back then it was coffee houses that spawned the chattering classes, giving people of all backgrounds somewhere they could go to discuss the news and read the papers which, though their circulations were low, were becoming ever more influential – papers like the forerunner of today's *Spectator* magazine which has, appropriately enough, named its excellent blog 'Coffee House'. In the 1740s there were over 550 coffee houses in London. Like the hundreds of political blog sites produced by MPs, activists and commentators, each attracted a particular clientele: Tories and Whigs, wits and stock-jobbers, merchants and lawyers, booksellers and authors. Charles II later tried to suppress them as 'places where the disaffected met, and spread scandalous reports concerning the conduct of His Majesty and his Ministers'.[2]

The King's description could just as easily be applied to one of the most-read and most anti-politics of all blog sites, 'Guido Fawkes'. It is gossipy, can be witty and occasionally breaks news (the emails that forced Gordon Brown's adviser

Damian McBride to resign were published here). What appears to fuel it, though, is a belief, or if you prefer, a prejudice, that those who are elected to govern us are all stupid, venal and hypocritical.

Blogs, and much of what is churned out on Twitter, like the coffee houses, are still the preserve of the self-selecting few. Beyond the big-name celebrity feeds their readerships are still tiny compared with the audiences for TV and radio programmes. They matter, and they're growing, but this is not broadcasting. It is narrowcasting.

The 'mass amateurization' of reporting has produced another danger: the confusion of news with comment and of reporting with reacting. Before the advent of the internet and 24-hour news it used to be said that an empty newsroom was a good newsroom. It is all too easy these days to convince yourself, sitting at your desk in your office, tapping away on your keyboard, that you are reporting. You have to remind yourself that this isn't reporting at all. Reporting is getting out of your chair, on to your feet, going to a place where something is happening, looking with your own eyes, listening with your own ears, asking your own questions, forming your own impressions and telling the story of what you found. Of course, we can't all do that all of the time. Resources are tight, deadlines loom, the 24/7 news beast has to be fed. But you can phone, send an email, tweet – it doesn't matter how you do it – and find something out from someone who knows. Reporting is not passive. It is active. It is inquiring, it is inquisitive and – as my mentor Brian Redhead once described himself – it is nosy.

A big question hanging over the Leveson inquiry was how on earth you make money from good, old-fashioned reporting. Hundreds – yes hundreds – of local newspapers have closed or merged in the space of a couple of years. National papers are sustained by the energy and open wallets of a handful of family businesses: the Murdochs (*Sun*, *Times*, *Sunday Times*), the Barclay brothers (*Telegraph*), the Lebedevs (*Independent*, *i* and *Evening Standard*), the Beaverbrooks (*Mail*, *Mail on Sunday* and *Metro*) and Richard Desmond (*Express* and *Star*). Pearsons, the owner of the *Financial Times*, was also for many years a family business. They do it in the pursuit of power and prestige, rather like the owners of football clubs. The question politicians will soon have to answer is: if you don't want family A to own paper B, who exactly would you like to sell it to, or would you rather it closed altogether? In other words, how do you ensure media plurality without simply having fewer newspapers?

Over the time I have been a reporter a crisis of trust has developed, first in politics and then in the media. Belief in politics has been wounded not only by anger about spin – in particular over the Iraq War, sleaze, the MPs' expenses crisis and the never-ending headache of party funding – but also by a sense pervading the public that politicians are unwilling or unable to confront powerful global forces, whether they be the banks and the markets or Europe and mass immigration. The press faced a crisis focused not just on phone hacking and payments to the police for information but on their contempt for privacy and calculated grooming of those in power. And then there was the BBC.

When I first wrote this book the BBC's traumas – whether involving the sexing up of allegations about the sexing up of the case for war, or the naming of the *Blue Peter* cat, or the prank calls of Messrs Ross and Brand – appeared to have been put firmly behind it. However, history should teach us that there is always another waiting around the corner. My colleague John Simpson described the crisis that began soon after the first edition came off the presses as the worst in the corporation's history. The Savile affair was so grave not simply because the BBC had failed to protect its staff and visitors from the predatory sexual abuse perpetrated by the DJ and presenter Jimmy Savile (a fault replicated, as it happens, in the NHS and Her Majesty's prisons). It was made worse by the fact that BBC News had been alerted to but had failed to report on the allegations when they were first made.

Arguing over which crisis sits where in the league table of grimness is probably pointless but I don't share Simpson's view. Savile raises very serious questions with which the BBC and a number of independent inquiries have wrestled and continue to do so. The BBC lost not only a director general and several senior editors. We also lost some of our hard-won reputation for integrity and forfeited the audience's trust. However, unlike many of the crises described in this book, this one did not threaten the corporation's very existence. I spoke to both the prime minister and the leader of the opposition early on and it was clear to me that neither wished to exploit the Savile affair to attack, less still to undermine, the BBC.

I never believed, and nor did the independent Pollard inquiry produce any evidence to suggest, that there was a cover-up of Savile's behaviour in order to protect the BBC's reputation, let alone to protect a Christmas special tribute programme. Some not familiar with the BBC were baffled by the organization's failure to communicate with itself – in particular, the apparent coyness with which the then head of news told the then head of television about *Newsnight*'s investigation into Savile's sexual activities. As an insider I didn't find it surprising at all. BBC News is given direct control of its own budget, airtime and agenda precisely so that channel controllers or people in its entertainment arm cannot influence its journalism. There are plenty of occasions on which BBC journalism has not suited the wider interests of the BBC – for example, the investigation into the business activities of Sir Alex Ferguson's son that led the manager of the most popular team in the land to boycott *Match of the Day* or *Panorama*'s interview with Princess Diana, which made life a lot harder for those dealing day-to-day with Buckingham Palace.

It was, though, deeply frustrating to watch my organization get things so badly wrong despite spending vast amounts of time and energy creating new systems and procedures to ensure 'compliance' with rules and guidelines. It was a reminder to me and, I believe, to many at the top of the corporation that what matters most is judgement and leadership. It was also a warning to pause and think before writing breathless scripts about the failure of this or that politician or business leader to 'get a grip' during a crisis. This was a moment to learn that saying it is much, much easier than doing it.

In the wake of all these crises of trust there is a danger that politicians and the media will become trapped in a vicious circle where all are competing to look good simply by making someone else look bad. This would create a world in which journalists search out anything which smacks of corruption, hypocrisy or self-interest and politicians line up to offer up synthetic outrage in the hope of surfing the public's anger rather than being subsumed by it.

Looking back over my time as a political journalist, I can't help feeling that too much of it has been spent reporting on the three 'S's – spin, sleaze and splits. Not enough has been devoted to the war of ideas – or a fourth 'S', substance. There is a complex series of reasons for this. It's not just that the three 'S's are easy to write about and make for lively broadcasts and newspapers people want to read. It is also that, in the era after the fall of the Berlin Wall and the death of ideology, the public has sometimes struggled to distinguish between the behaviour and the beliefs of the big political parties. More recently mainstream politicians have seemed to many people incapable of grasping the problems that affect such a large number of lives.

The scandals that have hit politics and the media have shown the failings of the establishment, the need for journalists willing to challenge it and the fact that public cynicism can sometimes be fully justified. They have, if you like, proved the need for destructive as well as, if not as a precondition of, constructive reporting. However, it will soon be time to build again.

That's where the other lesson comes in. I may have clashed with politicians in my time but I believe in the political process as the way to make decisions. This book, and my career if you like, has been inspired by a faith in the power of radio and television to widen interest in and deepen understanding of the struggle for power in Britain and the means used by those we elect to address the big questions of peace and war, freedom, prosperity and fairness. What was the point of all those battles for the right to report what is being done in our name if a growing number believe politics is, at best, irrelevant and, at worst, an establishment plot to do down ordinary, hard-working people?

In my view, trust will only be rebuilt if people are convinced that the country is having serious debates about the fundamental issues that affect the quality of their lives: how to get the economy growing again and deliver fairness while dealing with Britain's debts; how to reform the welfare state and immigration system in a way that restores confidence; how to resolve Britain's internal and external tensions, in particular the relationship between Scotland and the rest of the Union and the UK and the EU.

People crave to be told of clear positions, clearly stated, and to have their opinions heard. This requires politicians to be more willing to speak plainly, to be more honest about their past mistakes and more open about their uncertainties and the limits of their power. It requires the media to be prepared to give politicians and others a little more space to think aloud about possible solutions to the country's problems before they are condemned by their opponents.

While the web gives politicians the room they so desperately need, it rarely supplies the audience. Perhaps we should invite leading politicians to spell out their views in short, authored films or radio essays to stimulate debate? During the miners' strike of 1984–5 *Channel 4 News* invited Arthur Scargill of the National Union of Mineworkers and Ian MacGregor, the head of the National Coal Board, to do just that. It made for memorable and informative TV. Maybe we should do a few more news items allowing one politician or one party to spell out their positions in greater detail rather than encouraging them to serve up a steady stream of carefully market-researched, heavily scripted and highly partisan soundbites? That would make delivering impartiality more challenging, but so be it. Maybe reporters' 'two-ways' with presenters should concentrate a bit more on what was just said and what it means, and a bit less on ascribing motive?

It is perhaps time to remember some words of wisdom from one of the great, late practitioners of the art form of the interview. Brian Redhead used to say that if the *Today* programme had invited someone into the studio they clearly thought he was not a fool and had something worthwhile to say. He should therefore be allowed to put his point across.

The ideas raised here are more questions than answers: as potential solutions, they all contain flaws thrown up by the way politics has been transformed. While the media revolution has been going on, plenty has changed in politics over the last couple of decades. Since I became a political reporter we've seen the creation of the Scottish Parliament and Welsh and Northern Irish assemblies; the election of a government committed to Scottish independence; elected mayors and now elected police commissioners and the introduction of an often baffling array of voting systems. The two political Goliaths, Conservative and Labour, have been getting fewer and fewer votes and there has been a rise in the popularity of smaller parties: we now have a Green MP and a Respect MP in our own Parliament, plus UKIP and BNP representatives in Europe. We have witnessed the creation of the first stable peacetime coalition government and there are plans to have elected lords or senators in the upper House.

Politics is no longer the simple, two-way battle between a government and an opposition preparing to govern. Television and radio can no longer consider broadcasting the views of one side and then the other to be the extent of their responsibilities. Giving fair yet engaging coverage to all these political forces is a huge challenge.

I speak from bitter personal experience as the producer of the only prime ministerial interview in history to be censored by a court. It was back in 1995, when I was at *Panorama*. Just a few days before my wife gave birth to our first baby, I took a call at home from the head of press at the BBC. Without pausing even to say hello, let alone 'How are you?', he demanded to know if I had written a certain memo, firing off quotes from it to jog my memory. 'You might want to think hard,' he said, 'because the political editors of three national newspapers are all on hold and they say they've got a copy of it.'

The memo that had been leaked to them was indeed mine. I had written to the head of BBC current affairs complaining that I'd been told to produce an interview with the prime minister, John Major, which was clearly part of a carefully calculated fightback campaign just weeks before local elections in England and only a matter of days before Scotland went to the polls. This, I suggested, raised some difficult questions of political balance.

A few days earlier a senior Tory minister had launched a campaign against BBC bias and the press were, quite understandably, putting two and two together and viewing my note as evidence that the BBC was bowing under pressure from Number 10. My memo was going to be front-page news. If that wasn't bad enough, it soon became apparent that the opposition parties in Scotland, led by the SNP, would use this as an excuse to take legal action against the BBC to prevent the interview being broadcast. I was told that our lawyers were confident we'd win so we went ahead and recorded the interview. Some hours later we heard that we had lost.

The programme was now subject to an interdict – the Scottish legal equivalent of an injunction – which led to another difficult call. I had to phone the prime minister's press secretary and explain why Mr Major's interview would not be shown in Scotland. It wasn't only Scotland that would be affected, either. Since TV transmitters do not respect national boundaries, viewers in the north-east of England and Northern Ireland, whose transmitters covered parts of Scotland, also faced a blackout. If, in future, parties do not think they are getting a fair deal, be in no doubt that they will resort to the law.

Likewise, no one should assume that because we have had the first live prime ministerial debates on television more are certain to follow. There was a gap of sixteen years between America's first presidential debate, featuring Nixon and Kennedy, in 1960, and the second, involving Gerald Ford and Jimmy Carter, in 1976. They have been irregular, too, in Australia and Canada.[3] Many Conservatives believe that it was a bad idea for David Cameron, as the front runner, to take part in those 2010 debates. They gave Nick Clegg a huge boost and the hullabaloo that surrounded them diverted the spotlight from where the Tories wanted it to be: on Gordon Brown's record. Some close to Cameron take the view that he should not make the same mistake twice. Why now risk giving a platform to Brown's successor, Ed Miliband, to establish himself in the public mind as a potential future prime minister? The PM has already agreed to another set of debates in principle but could easily scupper them by failing to reach agreement on the format, the timing or on dealing with the difficulties presented by the prospect of two coalition partners debating with each other, or any legal threat posed by the Scottish Nationalists or UKIP claiming the right to participate even though they do not have significant representation at Westminster or the prospect of forming the next government.

Whether or not these debates continue it is vital to ensure that television news and interviews do the job of testing politicians' promises and exploring the matters they would rather not talk about. In 2010 there was little coverage of the issues that went on to dominate the months and years that followed: the creation of a coalition, NHS reforms and the scrapping of tuition fees.

Indeed, looking further back, campaign reporting has often failed to foresee what lay ahead: the poll tax, which would help force Mrs Thatcher from office, in 1987; Europe, which went on to split the Tories, in 1992; the possibility of war with Iraq in 2001 or the need to curb public spending in 2005. It is what I call Robinson's law of elections: they are never fought on the issue which dominates the Parliament that follows. Of course, some events – the 9/11 attacks in 2001 and the banking crash of 2008 – simply could not have been predicted. However, it's a list that will make me pause and think before the next time. In the run-up to the 2010 election the most memorable TV interview was Piers Morgan's soft-soaping of Gordon Brown. We can and should do better than that.

It is the job of reporters to cover the political debate as it is and not to create the one we wish we had. We shouldn't overstate the public's appetite for what we think is good for them – the broadcast equivalent of 'eating your greens', or become nostalgic for an era of high seriousness which, like any supposed 'golden age', probably never existed.

Nevertheless, I will always remember the reverence with which my grandfather listened to the greeting 'This is London'. It didn't promise the truth and nothing but the truth. That's too grand a claim for any reporting. It did promise that this was as close as we could get to the truth today and that tomorrow we would try to get closer still. That is what broadcasting live from Downing Street should do, too.

A last word

BIAS AND THE BEEB

I t didn't look good. Believe me, I do know it didn't look good. Not when it appeared on YouTube – 40,000 hits and counting – or when it appeared in glorious Technicolor on the front page of the only paper my kids read every day, the *Metro*. Certainly not when it was shown in prime time on *Have I Got News For You*. It was the moment I 'lost it' with a protester wielding a home-made cardboard sign on a pole demanding that the government 'Bring our troops home now' and 'Cut the war, not the poor'. If you managed to miss all those opportunities to see the BBC political editor's moment of shame, let me tell you what happened. I stamped on the pole and broke it in two, unaware that my 'placard rage' was being filmed by the protester's pal. Until, that is, he shoved his camera in my face, saying, 'You should be ashamed of yourself, mate. You should be ashamed.' My response was less than entirely conciliatory. 'I'm not remotely ashamed of myself. Why should I be ashamed of myself?'

In truth, I am now a tad regretful about what was, I hope, a rare loss of cool. However, that's not how some see it. They used my tantrum as evidence of bias – proof that the BBC's political editor was in favour not just of war but also of cuts for the poor. I've tried telling my critics that my anger stemmed from the fact that it was very off-putting having a placard waved within inches of my head during a live broadcast on one of the most significant stories of the year, the first announcement of spending cuts by the new coalition government. The protesters had gone to the trouble of finding an enormously long pole in order to reach me as I stood on top of a podium some ten or twelve feet above the ground. I've pointed out that George Alagiah, who was posing the questions to me, said on air, 'Well done for trying to get away from that person behind you.' I've insisted that I would have been just as irritated if the sign had read 'Two pizzas for the price of one', or, for that matter, 'Give Nick Robinson a pay rise'. I've even argued that in our democracy there is no shortage of times and places to make the case against wars or cuts. Just behind my head during the *Six O'Clock News* is, I contend, neither the time nor the place. But I might as well have saved my breath. For some, my actions were, and remain, proof that I have an agenda.

This is far from the only time I've been accused of bias. My reports regularly trigger complaints that I've been too hard or too soft on the government or ignored this or that strand of opinion. When Gordon Brown was prime minister any blog I wrote seeking to explain his thinking produced comments alleging that I was a craven apologist for what those taking issue with me called 'Nu Labour'. He, on the other hand, might well have agreed with the Facebook campaign which called for me to be sacked because of my allegedly pro-Tory views.

The BBC has, of course, always faced these sorts of

accusations. As we've seen, the loudest to complain have often been the holders of the highest office in the land. Churchill's doctor claims that the great man grumbled to him not just about his stroke or the 'black dog', the bouts of depression he suffered, but about the BBC being riddled with communists. Eden agreed and could not forgive the corporation for its failure to act as a national cheerleader during his ill-fated invasion of Suez. He wondered, 'Are they enemies or just socialists?' Wilson came to believe, with some foundation, that the security services were out to get him and, with very little justification, that the BBC was part of this right-wing plot. He complained about 'the prejudice of the BBC compared to the meticulous impartiality of ITV'. Margaret Thatcher was convinced that the national broadcaster was offering succour to the nation's foes – Irish terrorists, the Argentine junta, the Libyan dictator Colonel Gaddafi and those she dubbed 'the enemy within'. Tony Blair came to behave as if he shared this analysis. David Cameron has yet to demonstrate similar fury but his government shows some warning signs of frustration and irritation.

These complaints – and, indeed, those faced from time to time by ITV, Channel 4 and Sky* – all have one thing in common. They are rooted in the claim, a very big claim, made by broadcasters that their reporting is impartial. Impartiality is not only a founding principle of broadcast news in Britain, it's a legal obligation. But it is now under threat from technological change, commercial pressures and the conviction of some on both left and right that it is, in fact,

* The BBC receives more complaints than its competitors because it is the national broadcaster, is paid for by a compulsory levy and airs a far wider range of programming – current affairs, debate and discussion as well as news – than its rivals.

a cloak used by the establishment to impose their views and values on the rest of the population. It is, however, an idea I believe is worth fighting for.

For decades the worlds of impartial and partial journalism have been separate. Broadcasting offered one, print the other. You could have news, or news plus views.

Now, though, these worlds are converging. Broadcasters offer text on their websites, newspapers video on theirs. In my home BBC and Sky 'impartial' news channels co-exist with American news-and-views channels (Fox News and MSNBC), the Qatari-based Al Jazeera and English-language news services funded by the Chinese, Russian, French and Iranian governments. On my iPad – and pretty soon on smart TVs – one brush of my finger is enough to switch between these and hundreds of independent sites supplying news, opinion and information. Yet they are all regulated in different ways and they are not all under an obligation to be balanced and impartial.

This leads some to argue that television and radio news should go the way of print. It should be free of controls and customers should pick the product that suits them best. Rupert Murdoch's son James, when he was still chairman of BSkyB, used the media industry's most prestigious annual lecture to launch an all-out assault on a system of regulation which he described as 'authoritarianism'.

How, in an all-media marketplace, can we justify this degree of control in one place and not in others? So why do we continue to assume that this approach is appropriate for broadcasting – especially as one communications medium is now barely distinguishable from another? Would we welcome a world in which *The Times* was told by the government how much religious coverage it had to carry? In which there were a state newspaper with more money than the rest of the sector put together and 50 per cent of the market? The effect of the system is not to curb bias – bias is present in all news media – but simply to disguise it. We should be honest about this: it is an impingement on freedom of speech and on the right of people to choose what kind of news to watch.[1]

Murdoch's ire was directed at Ofcom, the media regulator which sets and polices the rules on impartiality, taste and decency for commercial broadcasters in the way the BBC Trust does for the corporation. Before the 2010 election he lobbied the Conservatives hard to dismantle the regulator he found so irksome. A senior Tory minister has told me that had the party secured a majority it was his expectation that the regulator would have been weakened, the Murdoch company News Corp would have taken full control of BSkyB and James Murdoch would have got his way and turned Sky News into a channel to challenge what he saw as the BBC's innate liberal bias.

Rupert Murdoch told a House of Lords hearing in 2007 that Sky News would be more popular if it were more like his US television channel, Fox News, and 'a proper alternative to the BBC'.[2] He is reported to have dubbed Sky 'BBC lite' and, when asked whether he wanted to make his British channel more like his American one, to have replied 'I wish.'

So Britain might have got a kind of Fox News lite, a channel which, like the original Fox News in America, called itself 'fair and balanced', meaning 'not like the establishment TV networks'. Since the Tories did not get a majority, Ofcom has not been dismantled, Sky News remains robustly committed to impartiality and the Murdochs are a little distracted by other concerns, it would be easy to think that this argument has gone away. It hasn't.

In December 2011 I organized a seminar to discuss the future of impartiality. To my surprise, and that of many of his own staff, the BBC's then director general, Mark Thompson, backed some of James Murdoch's arguments and declared that the corporation's competitors should be as free as newspapers to express their own opinions.

> In the future maybe there should be a broad range of choices. Why shouldn't the public be able to see and hear, as well as read, a range of opinionated journalism and then make up their own mind what they think about it? The BBC and Channel 4 have a history of clearly labelled polemical programmes. But why not entire polemical channels which have got stronger opinions? I find the argument persuasive.[3]

Thompson argued that impartiality could in future be the BBC's unique selling point in a world of competing news-with-views.

A new Communications Act will soon be drawn up to bring the law up to date with ever-changing technology. Parliament may face a choice: whether to stick with the model of impartial broadcasting we've always had or allow viewers and listeners to be free to choose from news-providers with competing opinions, as they are in any newsagent or on the web, or, perhaps, a mix of the two – 'impartial TV' with opinionated video news provided by what we used to call newspapers.

* * *

It has been a very long time since British newspapers laid claim to impartiality. In the 1640s the *Mercutius Civicus* carried the subtitle: 'Truth impartially related from thence to the whole Kingdome to prevent mis-information', while London's *Daily Courant* boasted of 'delivering Facts as they come related, and without inclining to one side or the Other'.[4] Press impartiality was, however, more honoured in the breach than in the observance. In the 1740s Samuel Johnson's pride in the neutrality of his parliamentary reports for the *Gentleman's Magazine* was tempered by his confession that he 'took care that the Whig dogs shall not have the best of it'.[5]

Come the 1920s, though, newspaper proprietors were reassured by the idea that the BBC should be unbiased since they regarded comment on the great issues of the day as their territory and theirs alone. They wanted to be sure that they, not the BBC, would offer views – full-bodied, red-blooded and high-octane – as well as news. As we saw in Chapter 2, the BBC wasn't ordered to be impartial when it was formed. It chose this path, which reflected the lofty ideals of its founder, John Reith, offered protection from commercial attack, political disapproval and interference and minimized the threat of its licence being revoked by the government. Reith also believed that an impartial broadcasting company would offer its audiences a unique alternative to the one-sided views of the world provided by the press, enabling them to form opinions for themselves.

When Reith dared to suggest that the BBC might need to touch on matters concerning politics, religion and industry, the newspapers reacted with alarm. The *Morning Post* warned of 'a vista of horrible possibilities. The average man or woman, when at leisure with the world, has not the slightest desire to be plunged into disputes on any of these subjects.'[6] The *Daily Telegraph* urged 'much caution', *The Times* insisted that 'balance must be kept'. Only the *Guardian* hailed the idea of 'the clash of opinions'.

Impartiality was underpinned by an unwritten deal between the BBC, the politicians and the press. The broadcasters would be left alone, free of government control and censorship, provided they were cautious, expressed no opinions themselves and ensured balance when they broadcast the opinions of others. This was formalized in a motion of the House of Commons on 22 February 1933, which stated that 'it would be contrary to the public interest to subject the corporation to any control by Government or by Parliament', and reminded the BBC: 'Only by the exercise of the greatest care in the selection of speakers and subjects can the function of the corporation be fulfilled and the high quality of the British broadcasting service be maintained.'[7]

The father of BBC impartiality showed that the idea had its limits, however. John Reith might have fought to avoid a government take-over during the general strike of 1926 but he was also clearly on the side of ministers. He blocked requests to broadcast from the Labour party and union leaders, helped redraft his friend the Tory prime minister's script and made a broadcast himself welcoming the end of the strike:

> Our first feeling on hearing of the termination of the general strike must be one of profound thankfulness to Almighty God, who has led us through this supreme trial with national health unimpaired. You have heard the messages from the King and from the prime minister. It remains only to add the conviction that the nation's happy escape has been in large measure due to a personal trust in the prime minister.[8]

Reith later boasted to his staff that 'we were able to give listeners authentic impartial news of the situation to the best of our ability'. However, in his private diaries, he noted, after his tussle with the government, that 'they know they can trust us not to be really impartial'.[9] The BBC's chief engineer during the strike wrote more openly about his concerns. 'It was not so much that the news was altered as given bias by elimination.'[10]

This 'bias by elimination' was to be seen again. In the years that followed, opposition to Neville Chamberlain's prewar policy of appeasement went virtually unheard. Winston Churchill was prevented from broadcasting his criticisms of Chamberlain's stance, thanks to both Reith's practice of allowing the parties to pick their own speakers and his own personal animus. Ironically, Churchill would later benefit from the BBC's instinctive deference to authority. The corporation followed the press in not reporting the serious stroke that incapacitated the prime minister in 1953. This record is used to support the arguments of those who claim that the BBC has always been the creature of the establishment.

Soon after I was appointed as the BBC's political editor in 2005 I bumped into Tony Benn, the veteran left-wing politician and irrepressible campaigner. 'Congratulations,' he said, 'on becoming an embedded reporter.' What, I asked him, somewhat naïvely, did he mean by describing me as 'embedded', the jargon usually applied to reporters who live alongside military units in times of war. 'Well,' he remarked with a chuckle, 'you're embedded in Downing Street. You go in the door of Number 10 to be told what they think and then you come out and tell us.' It was a view, albeit a jaundiced one, which I did and do take seriously because of my experience in, and during the build-up to, the Iraq War.

Night after night, in late 2002 and 2003, when I'd been doing the same job for ITV News, I had spent time speaking to people inside Downing Street, if not always crossing the hallowed threshold of Number 10 itself, as Benn suggested. Night after night I relayed the latest thinking of those in power on the looming war, diplomacy and the state of opinion within the government and in Parliament. I also reported on the opposition of the Liberal Democrats and the nationalist parties in Parliament, the dissent among the public at large and demonstrators on the streets and the doubts of Clare Short and Robin Cook in the Cabinet. However, the more it became clear that war would not be stopped by its opponents, the more time I spent reporting on what those in power were trying to do, why they were trying to do it and how one could judge their success. That is a crucial part of my job but I do now accept there's a danger that I – and my colleagues doing similar jobs – looked as if we were indeed 'embedded'.

Let's be clear, this was no playful Bennite tease. In the run-up to war Benn claimed in the press: 'The BBC is just a war-propaganda machine for the government.' I've little doubt he took the same view of ITV and Sky's coverage. His argument has been taken much further by the founders of Medialens, a website that claims that balanced reporting amounts, in reality, to 'a lethal bias'. It contends that even those it sees as the 'best' UK media (the *Guardian*, the *Independent* and *Channel 4 News* as well as the BBC) are, in fact, 'cheerleaders for government, business and war'.

I have always found the site's founders, David Cromwell and David Edwards, as charming as Tony Benn, even when I have read their assertions that BBC journalists like me are complicit in mass murder. That is the claim they made in the lead-up to the war in a letter to Richard Sambrook, head of BBC News at the time.

> We believe you are a sincere and well-intentioned person . . . but you are at the heart of a system of lethal, institutionalized deception. Like it or not, believe it or not, by choosing to participate in this propaganda system, you and the journalists around you may soon be complicit in mass murder. As things stand, you and your journalists are facilitating the killing and mutilation of thousands, perhaps hundreds of thousands, of innocent men, women and children.

Cromwell and Edwards argue in their writings not just that there can be no media neutrality and no objectivity, but that the attempt to achieve them is 'morally abhorrent'.[11] 'It doesn't matter that all the media professionals in the world refuse to recognize the myth of "objective" echoing of power – the real world of cause and effect, of lies and manipulated public support, of moral responsibility for death nevertheless does exist.'[12]

It is absurd – not to mention offensive – to suggest that journalists who report both the case for war and the case against it are morally responsible for those who die in it. But is there something in the concern they express that 'balanced reporting' can allow those in power too much control over the terms of debate, particularly when there is no division between the leaderships of the governing and opposition parties?

Tony Blair spent months refusing to debate the case for and against war, insisting that he was pursuing a diplomatic solution. During that time there was extensive reporting of the exchange of views between the rival diplomatic approaches of France, Germany and Russia and the USA–UK axis but the argument was still one based on the premise that Saddam Hussein had weapons of mass destruction, was a threat and had to be confronted. The question was essentially one about when the time for diplomacy elapsed and the time for military action began. With the benefit of hindsight there was not enough scepticism about the value and reliability of intelligence material and, therefore, not enough questioning of the underlying premise shared by most opponents as well as supporters of the war – that Iraq posed a threat at all.

The number of MPs who opposed war at all costs and were willing to say so was relatively few and mainly confined to the smaller parties. ITV News, the BBC and Sky did broadcast interviews with outright critics of military action, including Tony Benn and the former UN weapons inspector Scott Ritter, and indeed, an entire BBC *Panorama* programme was made examining the case against it. However, I now believe that too much of the prewar debate on television news was dominated by the theatre of the prime minister facing those who'd taken to the streets to protest against him and too little time was given to questioning and examining in detail the facts behind the justification for war and the likely consequences of the fall of Saddam.

The build-up to the invasion of Iraq is the point in my career when I have most regretted not pushing harder and not asking more questions, but I reject the idea that I and my colleagues were either the willing slaves of a government hell-bent on propaganda or naïve dupes.

What I have discovered in my job is that people with very strong views simply cannot understand why you are not as angry as they are. They watch a report and wonder why you don't just come out and say that certain politicians are war criminals or crooks or liars. They assume that the reason you don't is bias. They believe there can be no neutrality in a battle in which the stakes are high; that those who don't join the struggle must, in truth, be fighting for the other side. They see the BBC as part of an establishment which is undermining the opinions and values of most ordinary people like them. Interestingly, this applies as much on the right as the left.

Paul Dacre, not just the editor of the *Daily Mail* but its beating heart, reminds its readers most days of the BBC's alleged failings. In a rare public appearance, he argued that the corporation was 'imposing its own world view . . . under the figleaf of impartiality' and accused the BBC of being 'sympathetic to Labour, European federalism, the state and state spending, mass immigration, minority rights, multiculturalism, alternative lifestyles, abortion and progressiveness in the education and the justice systems'.

And the list goes on. The corporation is, according to Dacre, 'hostile to Britain's past and British values, America, Ulster Unionism, Euroscepticism, capitalism and big business, the countryside, Christianity, and family values'.[13]

Dacre is by far the most successful editor of my lifetime. He has presided over a newspaper wooed by politicians who are afraid of it because it has tapped into the hopes, and above all the fears, of what has become known as middle England. The catalogue of charges above reflects the view of Dacre and the *Mail* that decent British people and their beliefs and opinions are under assault from those who want to take and spend their money, order them what to do and how to behave and belittle and undermine their values.

The BBC's former director general Mark Thompson seemed to confirm this critique when he told the *New Statesman*: 'In the BBC I joined thirty years ago there was, in much of current affairs, in terms of people's personal politics, which were quite vocal, a massive bias to the left. The organization did struggle then with impartiality. And journalistically, staff were quite mystified by the early years of Thatcher.' Critics of the BBC usually neglect to quote his next sentence: 'Now it is a completely different generation. There is much less overt tribalism among the young journalists who work for the BBC.'[14] Perceptions of whether the BBC is right-wing or left-wing have remained steady in recent years. A clear majority see it as neither one nor the other and roughly equal numbers consider it biased against their viewpoint.

I am not one of those who thinks – and there are too many who do – that if the BBC is being attacked by both sides it must be in the right place. It is perfectly possible, and indeed it has often been the case, that there is some merit in the criticisms of people who hold opposing views. The BBC appointed a Europe editor to improve its coverage after both Eurosceptics and Euro enthusiasts complained, rightly, that its EU reporting was unsatisfactory.* Those who have complained about the BBC's handling of the build-up to the war in Iraq or mass immigration have something in common. They believe their views were treated as marginal or extreme, only to be seen later as mainstream. Mark Thompson

---

* A panel headed by former Cabinet secretary Lord Wilson found no evidence of deliberate bias in the BBC's reporting of Europe but concluded there was a 'widespread perception' of 'certain forms of cultural and unintentional bias' which had to be corrected. The inquiry reported 'an institutional mindset' at the BBC when it came to the EU and a tendency to 'polarize and over-simplify' issues.

observed: 'Views which start off as extreme can become the prevailing view inside five years.'[15]

There are examples of this on both left and right and others that don't fit neatly into the political spectrum. Monetarism and the economic theories of Milton Friedman were seen by many in politics and the media as eccentric, right-wing and foreign until they were absorbed into the Treasury's bloodstream in the late 1970s and taken up by both major parties. Green politics followed the same path. So, too, did gay rights.

There is a link between these issues. It is the decision of the leaderships of the main political parties to adopt an idea which all too often marks its shift from the margins to the mainstream. This brings with it dangers. As one idea becomes the accepted norm, opposition to it is all too easily deemed marginal. According to a major BBC review of 2007, 'Safeguarding Impartiality in the 21st Century',

> recent history is littered with examples of where the main-stream has moved away from the prevailing consensus . . . Euroscepticism was once belittled as a small-minded, blink-ered view of extremists on both left and right: today it is a powerful and influential force which has put pro-Europeans under unaccustomed pressure. Multiculturalism was for years seen by many in Britain as the only respectable policy for managing the problems posed by immigration – over the past two years it has been much harder to find people in public life who support it.[16]

Down the ages political parties have tended to dismiss those who don't share the conventional wisdom of the time as being on the fringe, extreme, or even loopy. Broadcasters have to be wary of following that lead, particularly when a significant proportion of public opinion is with the dissenters. The BBC's review concluded, rightly, that impartiality 'is not necessarily to be found on the centre ground'.

Immigration has been the subject both mainstream politics and broadcasting have been least good at discussing, and for the same reason – a fear that the debate will play into the hands of extremists. Mark Thompson conceded that the BBC had been 'rather nervous about letting that entire debate happen . . . there was an anxiety [about] whether or not you might be playing into a political agenda if you did items about immigration'. The BBC's former head of news Helen Boaden has spoken of the 'deep liberal bias' she detected when she began her job in 2004.

Their words are a reflection of the fact that, albeit slowly, the BBC saw that it had a problem and dealt with it. Their 2006 review adjudged that 'impartiality in programme-making is often achieved by bringing extra perspectives to bear, rather than limiting horizons or censoring opinion'. That is why, controversially and in the face of protests, the BBC invited Nick Griffin, the leader of the British National Party, who had just been elected to the European Parliament, on to *Question Time*, and why the issue of immigration was raised by broadcasters in the 2010 election even when none of the main parties wanted to debate it.

A more recent review of the BBC's output, published in 2013, suggested that an over-dependence on politicians – and, in particular, on the spokespeople of the big parties in Westminster – as sources of news and contributors to programmes made matters worse. It carries the risk that, if Westminster isn't buzzing about something, we programme-makers will assume there's no debate going on or, worse still, that when the government and opposition leaderships agree there will be what the report's author, Stuart Prebble, called 'an assumed consensus' on an issue.

Having repeatedly berated itself for failing to recognize the growing concern about immigration and the EU, the BBC now needs to look ahead to identify future pitfalls. We should be particularly wary of embracing new conventional wisdoms. Consider those that have emerged on gay rights, the NHS or public ownership.

The legalization of gay marriage raises a danger that broadcasters may treat social conservatives or those with strong religious convictions as being on the 'wrong side of history', but this is a debate like any other – both sides should feel their voice is being heard.

As predictions mount that the NHS faces a massive financial black hole – estimated by its chief executive to be in the region of £30 billion – there is a risk of casting those who argue that health care could be organized and funded in a different way as somehow unBritish. Even before Danny Boyle's extraordinary tribute in the opening ceremony of the 2012 Olympics in London, Nigel Lawson had dubbed the NHS Britain's only national religion. I recall Nick Clegg's bemusement when he learned that a thanksgiving service was to be held at Westminster Abbey to mark sixty years of the NHS. Clegg, who has a Dutch mother and a Spanish wife and has lived in Munich, Helsinki and Brussels, recognized that there are alternatives for Britain beyond a stark choice between either our beloved NHS or a US-style model driven by the health of a patient's bank balance. Even as I write these words I am aware that they will be seen by some as a form of heresy.

Equally, those who believe railways should be renationalized are often asked questions implying that they are dinosaurs, even though their views would be regarded as mainstream in most Western European countries. Gordon Brown infuriated some in the Treasury when, at the height of the financial crisis, he resisted taking ownership of the failing banks. He was afraid of what was known as the 'n' word – nationalization.

The BBC should not fear any debate and should be suspicious of those who want us to censor views they happen not to share. There are lessons here from the BBC's history. Churchill's warnings about German rearmament and the dangers of appeasement were not heard on the BBC after 1935. They were not part of the 'assumed consensus' and did not emanate from a frontbench politician. The debate that should have taken place about the right way to deal with the Nazi threat never happened. Let's be clear: Nick Griffin is no Winston Churchill but the BBC's primary responsibility is to ensure that it is the national forum for discussions about the country's future. Thus broadcasters have to avoid narrowing the debate by deciding that certain views are mainstream and others are not and should therefore not be heard. We do, however, have to remind people that just because they feel strongly about something or are out of favour with their party leadership, it does not necessarily mean that they are the next Churchill, with escape from their wilderness years dependent on being allowed to broadcast at will. This is why broadcasters apply a policy of 'due impartiality', which enables them to take account of how much support someone has and the evidence underlying his or her arguments before deciding how much coverage he is entitled to.

The biggest cause of viewers and listeners feeling any broadcaster is biased is not hearing views from people like themselves. Quite naturally, they assume that the reason they don't is that their views are deemed unacceptable.

A survey carried out for the BBC in 2006 found that more than half of respondents thought broadcasters often failed to reflect the views of 'people like me'. Those most likely to say this were middle-aged 'C2DEs' (in marketing speak, the lowest of three socio-economic categories), those without access to the internet and those with least interest in news and current affairs. The group with the lowest level of agreement were middle-aged 'ABC1s', the highest category, readers of 'quality' newspapers, and supporters of the Liberal Democrats.*

This is one reason why since then programmes have placed a much greater emphasis on inviting and airing direct comment from their audiences, whether it is made by phone, text, email or Twitter. It is a fact of life that the people who work in newsrooms – at the BBC, ITN, Sky or most newspapers – tend to be younger, more urban, better educated, higher paid and more socially liberal than many of those for whom they broadcast or publish. All broadcasters have rightly worked hard in recent years to ensure that their newsrooms reflect the ethnic make-up of Britain. There are still important efforts being made to ensure that women are promoted, both off and on screen. We should also look at wider issues of representation.

In my early days I worked on *Brass Tacks*, a current-affairs programme based in Manchester, whose team included a former merchant seaman with a broad Scouse accent and arms covered in tattoos. He understood the lives of the people we were making programmes about, as well as those who watched them, much better than I did. I have worked with few like him in TV since. The best-known member of my current

* Ipsos–Mori survey, 26–30 October 2006.

team is a man who is rarely seen but often heard. Paul Lambert – or 'Gobby', as everyone calls him – is the man who stands in Downing Street shouting questions at those going in or coming out of Number 10. If a politician is in serious trouble, Gobby will turn up outside his or her house demanding to be told, 'Are you going to resign?' Listen hard and you'll notice something else. He doesn't speak with the rootless received pronunciation of many in broadcasting but in the Estuary English used by millions.

My former colleague Jeff Randall, who was the BBC's first business editor and now presents for Sky News, was once told by an earnest young producer that he couldn't possibly wear his Union Jack cufflinks on screen. 'Why on earth not?' inquired Jeff. It would look, he was told to his astonishment, as if he were supporting the BNP. Jeff pointed out that this was the flag that was flying outside the building and kept his cufflinks on.

Impartiality means not just reporting without prejudice and debating without limits, but making sure that viewers can see and hear people like them – whether that is men and women with tattoos or accents or even, Jeff, those who wear Union Jack cufflinks.

All this assumes that reporting can actually be wholly objective. It's an idea that Nick Davies, in his brilliant polemic *Flat Earth News*, calls a 'great blockbuster myth', since no journalist can claim to record the objective truth. News necessarily involves selecting which stories to report and the angle from which to approach them. Davies, the driving force behind the *Guardian*'s tireless and ultimately successful efforts to expose phone hacking in the Murdoch press, argues that too much modern journalism accepts and parrots conventional wisdom and the views of the wealthy, the powerful and the well-connected rather than challenging them, and that impartiality is a cover for this culture.

> Neutrality requires the journalist to become invisible, to refrain deliberately (under threat of discipline) from expressing the judgements which are essential for journalism. Neutrality requires the packaging of conflicting claims, which is precisely the opposite of truth-telling. If two men go to mow a meadow and one comes back and says 'The job's done' and the other comes back and says 'We never cut a single blade of grass', neutrality requires the journalist to report a controversy surrounding the state of the meadow, to throw together both men's claims and shove it out to the world with an implicit sign over the top declaring, 'We don't know what's happening – you decide'.[17]

Davies is confusing impartiality with mere balance. An impartial journalist should do what any decent journalist should do: dig out the facts for himself. He should go to the meadow and report whether the grass has been cut and, better still, film or photograph it so his audience or readers can see it for themselves, too. Impartial journalists are not interested in balance for its own sake. We need to move beyond 'he said, she said' and ask 'what is?' We should start by searching for the truth, approach subjects with an open mind and seek to be fair, even-handed and conscious of our own vantage point on a story as well as the limits of what we can know.

So how would the BBC have covered the debate referenced in the title of Davies' book over whether the earth was flat? How might a seventeenth-century BBC *News at Ten* have covered Galileo's persecution at the hands of the Church after he stated that the evidence showed the earth was round and circled the sun? Critics of impartiality fear that the BBC news might, at best, have run a soundbite from Galileo followed by one from the Papal Nuncio or, at worst, refused to run the heretical view at all. That, of course, won't do.

There is a much more recent test of this argument: the debate over global warming. Some contend that the sheer weight of scientific opinion that global warming is happening and is man-made should silence the minority contrarian view. The BBC recently commissioned Professor Steve Jones of Imperial College, London to conduct a review of its own science coverage. He concluded that the BBC too often put fringe views on a par with well-established fact, producing what he called 'false balance'. It was like, Jones said, broadcasting a debate between a mathematician and a maverick biologist about what two plus two equals. Interestingly, and I believe rightly, the BBC Trust responded by saying that they would not allow 'bias by elimination' and would continue to broadcast the voices of those Jones labelled 'climate-change denialists'.

The vast majority of scientists do believe that man-made climate change is a reality. However, there are important dissenting voices asking questions about how climate change research has been carried out and reported and the way doubts about it have been repressed. In addition, regardless of whether or not you believe in the scientific consensus, there is an important debate to be aired about what the correct policy response should be. Some argue that governments should adopt the 'precautionary approach' and spend large sums on green energy. Others maintain that Western governments are set on a course which will suppress growth in their own countries without saving the planet.

Impartiality is, then, far from as easy as it sounds. There is, of course, an alternative. Rival TV channels, like rival newspapers, could take different views. Would an informed public debate have been more likely if one channel was running a campaign to stop global warming and another ran one to combat the 'climate doom-mongers'? Would debate on the war with Iraq have been improved if those who supported it watched a channel which reflected their views back to them while those opposing it chose a different channel that shared and reinforced their own opinions? These are not hypothetical questions. Broadcasting might be like that in future. In America, it already is.

American TV news used to be pretty much like ours. That, though, was before Fox News arrived, proclaiming that it was 'fair and balanced', unlike what it derided as the 'liberal' television news provided by the big three networks – NBC, ABC and CBS – and the pioneer of 24-hour news, CNN. According to one Fox executive, these old stations all behaved as if they believed 'America is bad, corporations are bad, animal species should be protected, and every cop is a racist killer. That's where "fair and balanced" comes in. We don't think all corporations are bad, every forest should be saved, every government spending program is good.'[18]

Fox News insists that it is impartial, proclaims that 'we report, you decide' and has been extraordinarily successful. For over a decade it has been America's leading news network with ratings that exceed the combined figures of all its news channel rivals. The key to its dominance has not been biased news reporting – much of it is very good – but outspoken, provocative and very biased talk shows. Rupert Murdoch is said not to be very comfortable with much of their content but he and his shareholders are very comfortable with the vast sums of money it has made for News Corp.

The inspiration behind the network is the brilliant TV producer turned political propagandist Roger Ailes, who helped to sell Richard Nixon, Ronald Reagan and George Bush senior to the American public and knows intuitively how to tap in to the hopes and fears of his compatriots. His fellow Bush aide, Lee Atwater, once described Ailes as having 'two speeds – attack and destroy'.

Has what's been good for Mr Ailes and Mr Murdoch, for Fox News and News Corp, been good for the quality of political debate in America? Not according to one critic, who claims that Fox News has helped to create an 'alternative reality' with 'a whole alternative knowledge system, with its own facts, its own history, its own laws of economics'.

Those are the words not of a wishy-washy liberal Obama-lover, but of David Frum, a former speechwriter for George W. Bush, who describes a world in which

> conservatism has evolved from a political philosophy into a market segment. An industry has grown up to serve that segment – and its stars have become the true thought leaders of the conservative world. The business model of the conservative media is built on two elements: provoking the audience into a fever of indignation (to keep them watching) and fomenting mistrust of all other information sources (so that they never switch channels).[19]

Fox News has some excellent news reporters but its presenters, as Frum points out, are paid to make people angry and to make them disbelieve what they're told on other channels.

On a trip to Washington in the lead-up to the Iraq War I saw this for myself as I sat in my hotel room watching a Fox News discussion on the link between Iraq and 9/11. It should have been a brief one as there isn't and wasn't any evidence of any link. When the programme's expert guest pointed this out his hosts looked less than happy. 'Sure,' one of them said, with a forced grin, 'but Saddam and Bin Laden both hate America and want to hurt us, right?' The expert paused briefly, perhaps to contemplate the possibility of never being booked to appear on Fox News again. He smiled wanly before weakly assenting to this preposterous assertion. Research later found that two thirds of Fox viewers believed the US had 'found clear evidence in Iraq that Saddam Hussein was working closely with the al-Qaeda terrorist organization'.*

When the United States grappled with reforming its extraordinarily costly healthcare system a bevy of Fox News presenters urged their viewers to defeat the president's bill. Glenn Beck told his viewers that the healthcare proposals would be 'the end of America as you know it' while his colleague Sean Hannity called it 'the most irresponsible piece of domestic legislation in our lifetime'. When the Tea Party movement campaigned against government and for lower taxes, Fox News didn't merely report on it – its presenters advertised it, promoted it and spoke at its rallies.

Why not, you might ask, provided people can also watch alternative views on another channel? Such a liberal news channel does exist – it's called MSNBC. In 2008, the year

---

* Program on International Policy Attitudes, *Political Science Quarterly*, winter 2003–4. This compared with lower, though still very high – around 50% – figures for the other networks. It may, of course, be attributable not to Fox's coverage but to the fact that people holding those views tend to watch that channel.

Barack Obama put himself forward as the candidate to change America, the liberal network advertised itself using images of JFK and Obama, telling viewers, 'Watch MSNBC . . . and experience the power of change.'

The audiences for these news channels may be relatively low – Fox News rarely reaches more than 2 million at any one time – but a huge proportion of politically active voters access their news from partisan channels. In the US presidential election of 2008 approximately two thirds of MSNBC and CNN audiences said they would vote for Barack Obama compared with fewer than one in ten Fox News viewers.[20]

The danger is that a growing number of the most politically committed voters on both the right and the left are living in what David Frum called an 'alternative reality' where there is no shared information, no agreed facts and therefore no common starting point for any public debate. If there is no forum in which viewers have their own prejudices challenged then debate risks being based increasingly on anger, mistrust and allegations of bad faith.

It wasn't always like this. Broadcasters in the USA were, as they are in Britain, not only committed to being impartial but also legally obliged to be so. For decades after the creation of American TV news broadcasts in 1948, journalists were required to present controversial issues of public importance in a manner that was 'honest, equitable and balanced' in accordance with what was called the 'fairness doctrine'.

Less restrictive than British media regulation, this did not stop the development of outspoken radio talk-show hosts – what later became known as 'shock jocks'. It did, though, ensure that a single network could not broadcast from a single perspective, day after day, without presenting opposing views. The Supreme Court upheld the fairness doctrine even when it was challenged as an assault on First Amendment rights to free speech. In one case, the court ruled that someone attacked by a Christian radio programme had a right to reply since the First Amendment did not give the radio station the exclusive rights to the airwaves on which they broadcast.*

However, in the Reagan era the regulator, the Federal Communications Commission, turned against the very idea of regulating and scrapped the fairness doctrine in 1987 on the grounds that it 'restricts the journalistic freedom of broadcasters ... [and] actually inhibits the presentation of controversial issues of public importance to the detriment of the public and the degradation of the editorial prerogative of broadcast journalists'.

Twice since then Congress has passed bills calling for it to be reinstated. Twice President Reagan vetoed them. Conservatives mocked the doctrine as, in the words of the veteran politician Newt Gingrich, 'affirmative action for liberals'. Even President Obama has resisted calls to re-introduce it, no doubt aware that going to war with Fox News might not be good politics.

Under current British law there can be no channels like Fox News or MSNBC. Broadcasters are required to show due impartiality, and those who have tried to replicate US-style talk shows have often been frustrated by the intervention of the regulators. Richard Littlejohn, the *Daily Mail* columnist, is known and loved by his readers for his attacks on what he and they see as an out-of-touch establishment. In the 1990s he had a compelling morning radio programme on

* Red Lion Broadcasting Co. v. FCC 1969.

London's LBC station which daily lambasted John Major's failing government. When LBC lost its broadcasting licence, Sky News tried to transfer his trenchant opinions from the pages of the press to the airwaves, but Littlejohn complained that it was impossible for him to say into a microphone what he was perfectly within his rights to write because the regulator's idea of balance 'equates to one set of politicians telling one set of lies followed by another set of politicians telling a different set of lies. The truth doesn't enter the equation.'[21]

The regulator, Ofcom, does allow programme presenters to 'express their own views' but states that they 'must not use the advantage of regular appearances to promote their views in a way that compromises the requirement for due impartiality . . . [and] alternative viewpoints must be adequately represented'.[22]

The current head of Sky News, John Ryley, has shown no sign of wanting to turn his channel into a British version of Fox News. He resisted Rupert Murdoch's hopes that it would follow this route, and when James Murdoch condemned the authoritarianism of British media regulation in 2009, he insisted that Sky was impartial 'not because Ofcom tells us to, but because it's what our audience expects of us. In simple terms, it's good business for us to be impartial.' However, aware perhaps of who pays the bills for Sky News, he added: 'We should trust journalists to exercise editorial judgements and we should trust viewers to choose the news that they want to consume.'

Many of Sky's staff have previously worked at the BBC or ITN. To Rupert Murdoch's frustration, they often share the same values and professional culture. The market they are operating in is very different from that of the United States.

Fox News grew out of the long tradition of radio talk shows that were high-octane, controversy-rich and not for faint hearts. It developed as a reaction not just to the established 'liberal' TV news networks but also to a press which, unlike that in Britain, proclaims its impartiality and is often bland. Nevertheless there will be many pressures for change here in the UK – commercial, political and legal.

A scandal-hit News Corp may be less influential than it was but the arguments James Murdoch made will not go away. Newspaper groups struggling to find ways to survive in the digital age will want to examine any way in which they can make money from news, something Fox News does in bucketloads. This wouldn't have to mean turning Sky News into Fox Lite. We could, for example, see the creation of a new network, let's call it Sky Talk, which carried Sky News in addition to outspoken talk shows. News Corp has already experimented for a year with Sun Talk, an online radio off-shoot of the newspaper which dubbed itself 'the home of free speech'.

There are leading Tory figures who would relish the creation of a channel they would see as a counterbalance to the broadcasting establishment and a way of dealing with the traditional frustration governments feel with the BBC. They will urge their leader or his successor to learn from Rupert Murdoch's jaundiced observation about the prime ministers he has known: 'They all hated the BBC; they all gave it what-ever it wanted.'[23]

Another source of pressure could be the dwindling audiences for TV news among the young and ethnic minorities. Polling suggests that it is precisely these groups who value and believe in impartiality less than others. 'New News, Old News', a report into the way TV news will look in the future, recommended 'a variation in the impartiality rules' for 'channels of minority interest' as part of efforts to attract those groups to watch more news.[24] Another report argued on the same grounds that 'there will be a role in the future for polemical channels . . . [to] widen the diversity of voice in British broadcasting'.[25]

Finally, the law, in the form of the Human Rights Act, may begin to chip away at the restrictions placed on broadcasters. An unlikely alliance of TalkSport radio host Jon Gaunt and the civil liberties campaigning group Liberty went to the High Court to claim that his human rights had been violated when he was sacked after a broadcast in which he called a councillor who had banned smokers from adopting children a 'Nazi'. Although Gaunt lost the case the judge found that this was, indeed, protected 'political speech' and declared that freedom of expression should be accorded a high degree of protection which was capable of extending to offensive expression.

The judge ruled that Gaunt's interview breached broadcast regulations not because of the use of the word 'Nazi' but because the interview was 'abusive, hectoring and out of control'. In future a court may be asked to determine where the line is between speech which is deemed to be political and that which is out of control.

So how should policy-makers respond to these pressures for change? Without fear, argues Mark Thompson, since 'in a world of internet-fuelled plurality and saturation in a global sea of opinion, much of it extreme, I believe the premium on impartiality has grown and will grow further'.[26] He argues that provided every household in the land has access to impartial broadcast news which is properly funded and independent, no risk will be posed by other channels following a different route.

Some worry, though, that there are dangers in allowing any change to the rules requiring all broadcasters to be impartial. The first concern usually expressed is that even a little bit of opinionated broadcasting might pollute the well. The success of Fox News in America forced other TV news outlets to change their approach. CNN became more populist and more focused on domestic news; MSNBC was turned into a liberal alternative to Fox – just as opinionated but coming from the left rather than the right. Would BBC and ITV news be unaffected if a new British opinionated channel changed the terms of trade?

Another source of disquiet for some is that comment which, as we all know, is cheap, might be used as a substitute for first-hand reporting and specialist analysis, which is expensive. In newspapers we are already seeing the rise of freesheets that survive on a mix of celebrity gossip, press releases and stories lifted from Twitter, television and the web. Their 'serious' content consists, in the main, of news agency reports and opinion. It is possible to envisage a TV news equivalent combining opinion – preferably as provocative and partisan as possible – and pictures bought in from news agencies. If that were to come about, we might look back at the choice of broadcast news we have now and reminisce about how lucky we were to have three news-providers, the BBC, ITN and Sky, that were respected around the world.

Finally, some fear that in Britain it wouldn't necessarily be a channel with right-wing views that would be first to take advantage of any change in the law. It might be one of religious intolerance that promotes hatred of the West and encourages extremism. That is how Press TV, a channel funded by the Iranian government and controlled from

Tehran, is regarded by many. Until its recent closure by Ofcom, it advertised itself, just as Fox News does, as reaching those parts other networks simply don't reach. Its website declares that it does this by 'heeding the often neglected voices and perspectives of a great portion of the world; embracing and building bridges of cultural understanding; encouraging human beings of different nationalities, races and creeds to identify with one another'.

This 'embracing and building bridges' did not extend to the people of Israel. One of Press TV's regular presenters used to be George Galloway (before his return to Parliament in 2012 in the Bradford West by-election). Galloway was found to be in breach of broadcasting rules by Ofcom after describing Israel as 'a terrorist gangster . . . miscreant, law-breaking, rogue, war-launching, occupying state' and declaring that 'if I was running Iran I would build a bomb because Israel is aiming hundreds of nuclear weapons at me'.

Ofcom's ruling was not made because Galloway's views of Israel can be censored but because they were delivered unchallenged and without any balancing opinions. The London headquarters of Press TV defended their actions by explaining that editorial decisions were ultimately not taken by them but in Tehran. Ofcom responded by removing their broadcasting licence in January 2012.

This is, perhaps, the best test of your standpoint on the future of broadcast impartiality. Do you see the removal of Press TV's licence as an unacceptable attack on freedom of speech, or as a reassuring sign that the airwaves are regulated so that they cannot be used for propaganda? Should television and radio allow people to choose from a range of channels with views that suit them best, or will that allow people to occupy an 'alternative reality' which fosters narrow, sectarian, intolerant attitudes?

With my background, it is hard to remain impartial about impartiality – though I must, as one day I may have to report on this debate. These, though, are the questions I would ask if I were in charge of shaping the future of broadcasting in this country which, thankfully, I am not.

I cannot write about impartiality without asking myself, am *I* biased? It's a question that is sometimes asked by others because of a fact that's well known inside the Westminster village, less so beyond it. Before I covered politics as a journalist I was involved in it. I confess that I was one of those sad young people who, rather than enjoying myself drinking beer and playing pool, spent far too long in earnest debates and electioneering. A quarter of a century ago, when it was not exactly fashionable, I was chairman of a now largely forgotten organization called the Young Conservatives. The YCs, as they were known, used to have lots of members in the sort of prosperous leafy villages I was brought up in. They were rather better known for their dances and discos than their political campaigns.

They were not the same crowd, incidentally, as the rather less lovable Tory students who earned a bad name in the early 1980s when some of their members called for Nelson Mandela to be hanged on the grounds that he was a terrorist. They were led by a chap called Bercow. You may have heard of him. These days he's to be found shouting 'Order, order' and telling MPs to calm down. Twenty-five years is, as someone should once have said, a long time in politics.

My political involvement raises another important question. Is it really possible for someone who has held strong political views in the past to become an impartial reporter? In my case it's up to others to make the judgement. I look at the many people I know who had clearly expressed political views before going on to report with distinction and answer, yes.

My predecessor as BBC political editor, Andrew Marr, has owned up that he was a schoolboy Maoist who ordered copies of the Chinese leader's *Little Red Book* to give to his schoolmates. He tells me that his politics had been moderated somewhat by the time he reached Cambridge, though he remained to the left of Labour. Before moving to the BBC Andrew wrote many brilliant political columns for *The Economist*, the *Independent*, the *Observer* and the *Express* spelling out his attitudes on many of the key issues of the day. He once joked: 'The first thing that happens to you as a BBC journalist is that you're taken down into a dank basement to have your trousers pulled down and your organs of opinion removed with a pair of secateurs by the director general and popped in a formaldehyde bottle. You're told you're allowed them back when you leave.'

Nevertheless the *Daily Mail* greeted his appointment with an aggressive personal campaign attacking his alleged bias. Marr responded in the only way he could; the only way anyone in his position can: by the simple and yet difficult technique of winning the trust of the *Mail*'s readership. The attacks stopped.

I'm sometimes asked whether it's really possible to switch your own political views on and off. The glib answer, though there's a good deal of truth in it, is that after twenty-five years of looking at both sides of an argument I don't really have many views left. Besides, those I had are somewhat out of date. It's a point I once tried to make to Tony Blair. When I first became a reporter, Alastair Campbell couldn't resist heralding my arrival for a meeting with his boss with the announcement, 'Prime Minister, the chairman of the Young Conservatives.' Having anticipated such a welcome, I had a response ready. 'Prime Minister,' I said, 'at the time of my life when I was involved in politics you had long hair and were playing the guitar with the Ugly Rumours.'

Blair reacted instantly. 'Yes, Nick, but I wish I still was.'

We had both made our choices when we left university. The difference between them was that he chose to get involved in politics, and I chose to have no more to do with it and become a journalist instead.

The more serious answer is that no one is born impartial. Broadcasters are not a breed apart. From the moment we arrive in the world we, like everyone else, are shaped by our upbringing, our surroundings and our background. We all quickly form opinions, attitudes and prejudices. We soon discover ideas that move us and others that leave us cold, people we warm to and those we dislike. Many broadcasters were involved in campaigns or in party politics before they appeared in front of the microphones or the cameras.

Prejudices are much easier to leave behind when they're openly acknowledged. In my experience, the journalists who are least impartial are those who pretend to have no views at all. They discount the arguments of others as extreme or marginal or absurd with the confidence of people who have only ever known or mixed with people who think the same as they do.

As broadcasters we agree to leave our opinions at the door when we go to work. For most of the colleagues I have worked with at the BBC and ITN, and those I know at Sky News, this is no mere contractual or legal obligation. They do not say, 'We're required to be impartial.' They say, 'We are impartial. That's what the BBC/ITN/Sky is.' It is a belief based on the recognition that the privilege of broadcasting the news to a mass audience comes with a responsibility to provide people with the information they need to make up their own minds, not to tell them what they should think.

The problem with the idea of impartiality, say some, is that it has no objective meaning. What I think is impartial you might think is biased, and vice versa. Impartiality is, in other words, like beauty – in the eye of the beholder. It is at best, the critics argue, a pretence and at worst bias in disguise. Some on the left denounce the BBC for promoting the monarchy, the market and the military. Others on the right condemn it for advocating European federalism, mass immigration, multiculturalism, state spending and minority rights.

The BBC, on the other hand, has tended to behave as if impartiality is like virginity – something you've either still got or you've lost. For years the corporation was inclined to react with shock and indignation if anyone so much as dared to suggest that it might have surrendered its virtue.

My view has always been that impartiality is rather more like marital bliss – something to believe in and strive for but which you must accept you will almost certainly never quite achieve. When you fail it's best to say sorry and try harder in future. My wife may not find this parallel altogether reassuring.

As we've seen, delivering impartiality comes with problems aplenty. The public seems to get that it is both a worthy goal and one that is almost impossible to attain. The last major poll on this issue suggested that the vast majority (84 per cent) agreed with the proposition that broadcasters must try very hard to achieve impartiality while almost half (44 per cent) acknowledged at the same time that it was impossible to do so as there was no such thing as impartiality.*

There is an inherent and proper tension between politicians and broadcasters. Ours is like a forced marriage. We have no choice but to spend a great deal of time together. We are, in many ways, dependent on each other. Unable to break free we grumble, complain and, occasionally, fight but, so far at least, divorce has been avoided.

It is a relationship which, at one and the same time, has proved to be both deeply flawed and yet functioning. And for the past quarter of a century it is a relationship I have had the pleasure and sometimes the frustration to be a part of. I am, after all those years, prepared to confess to one bias – a belief that British broadcasting, though far, far from perfect, has always proved to be greatly superior to the alternatives.

* Ipsos–Mori poll for the BBC review 'From Seesaw to Wagon Wheel: Safeguarding Impartiality in the 21st Century', 2007.

SOURCE NOTES

1: 'I spy strangers'

1 Quoted in Andrew Sparrow: *Obscure Scribblers: A History of Parliamentary Journalism*, Politico's Publishing, 2003.
2 Quoted in Sparrow, op. cit.
3 John Gay: *Fifty One Fables in Verse*, 1727.
4 Jeremy Black: *Walpole in Power*, Sutton Publishing, 2001.
5 Quoted in Sparrow, op. cit.
6 Quoted in Sparrow, op. cit.
7 Quoted in Sparrow, op. cit.
8 Quoted in Sparrow, op. cit.
9 David Brown: *Palmerston: A Biography*, Yale University Press, 2010.
10 Spencer Leigh Hughes: *Press, Platform and Parliament*, Nisbet & Co. Ltd, 1918.
11 Quoted in Sparrow, op. cit.
12 Quoted in Michael Cockerell, Peter Hennessy and David Walker: *Sources Close to the Prime Minister: The Hidden World of the News Manipulators*, Macmillan, 1984.
13 James Margach: *The Anatomy of Power*, Star, 1981.
14 Sparrow, op. cit.
15 Quoted in Sparrow, op. cit.
16 James Margach: *The Abuse of Power: The War Between Downing Street and the Media*, W.H. Allen, 1978.

2: A Titanic opportunity

1 Asa Briggs: *The BBC: The First Fifty Years*, Oxford University Press, 1985.

2 Ibid.

3 Lord John Reith: *The Reith Diaries* (ed. Charles Stuart), HarperCollins, 1975.

4 Briggs, op. cit.

5 Robert Wood: *A Word in Your Ear: The Broadcasting of an Era 1923–1964*, Macmillan, 1979.

6 Geoffrey Cox: *Pioneering Television News*, Luton University Press, 1995.

7 Briggs, op. cit.

8 David Dilks: *Neville Chamberlain*, Vol. 1 1869–1929, Cambridge University Press, 2002.

9 Peter Hill: 'Parliamentary broadcasting – From TWIW to YIP', *British Journalism Review*, Vol. 4, No. 4, December 1993.

10 J. A. Ramsden: 'Baldwin and Film' in Nicholas Pronay and D. W. Spring (eds.): *Propaganda, Politics and Film 1918–45*, Macmillan, 1982.

11 *The Reith Diaries*, op. cit.

12 A. H. Booth: 'British Hustings 1924–50', quoted in Pronay and Spring, op. cit.

13 Philip Williamson and Edward Baldwin: *Baldwin Papers: A Conservative Statesman 1908–1947*, Cambridge University Press, 2004.

14 Ibid.

15 Stanley Baldwin: speech during Westminster St George's Division by-election, March 1931.

16 Philip Williamson: *Stanley Baldwin: Conservative Leadership and National Values*, Cambridge University Press,1999.

17 Quoted in Briggs, op. cit.

18 John Reith: *Broadcast Over Britain*, Hodder & Stoughton, 1924.

19 Briggs, op. cit.

20 Reith, *The Reith Diaries*, op. cit.

21 Quoted in Michael Tracey: 'The BBC and the Reporting of

the General Strike' (paper and CD Rom), University of Colorado, 2005.

22 The Crawford committee, quoted in Briggs, op. cit.

23 Quoted in Asa Briggs: *The History of Broadcasting in the United Kingdom*, Vol. II: *The Golden Age of the Wireless 1927–1939*, Oxford University Press, 1995.

24 Briggs, *The BBC: The First Fifty Years*, op. cit.

25 Leonard W. Connolly, *Bernard Shaw and the BBC*, University of Toronto Press, 2009.

26 Martin Gilbert: *Churchill – A Life*, Minerva Press, 1992.

27 D. J. Wenden: 'Churchill, Radio and the Cinema' in Robert Blake and William Roger Louis (eds.): *Churchill: A Major New Assessment of his Life in Peace and War*, W.W. Norton & Co., 1992.

28 Martin Gilbert: *Winston S. Churchill: The Coming of War, 1936–39*, Companion Vol. V, Part 3, Heinemann, 1982.

29 Paul Addison: *The Road to 1945: British Politics and the Second World War* (revised edition), Pimlico, 1994.

30 Quoted in Wenden, op. cit.

31 Cox, op. cit.

32 Marista Leishman: *My Father – Reith of the BBC*, Saint Andrew Press, 2006.

33 Quoted in Briggs, *The History of Broadcasting in the United Kingdom*, Vol. II, op. cit.

34 Briggs, *The BBC: The First Fifty Years*, op. cit.

35 Asa Briggs: *The History of Broadcasting in the United Kingdom*, Vol. III: *The War of the Words*, Oxford University Press, 1995.

36 James Curran and Jean Seaton: *Power Without Responsibility: The Press and Broadcasting in Britain*, Routledge, 1991.

37 Wood, op. cit.

38 Peter Hill: 'Almost in the Field of Human Conflict', in *The House* magazine, 28 March 1994. Quoted in Mark D'Arcy (ed.): *Order, Order!: 60 Years of Today in Parliament*, Politico's Publishing, 2005.

39 Quoted in D'Arcy, op. cit.

40 Ibid.

3: 'Why do we need this peep show?'

1 Briggs: *The BBC: The First Fifty Years*, op. cit.
2 Michael Cockerell: *Live From Number 10: The Inside Story of Prime Ministers and Television*, Faber and Faber, 2005.
3 Grace Wyndham Goldie: *Facing the Nation: Television and Politics 1936–1976*, Bodley Head, 1977.
4 Cockerell, op. cit.
5 Quoted in Goldie, op. cit.
6 Quoted in Goldie, op. cit.
7 Herbert Nicholas quoted in Briggs, *The BBC: The First Fifty Years*, op. cit.
8 David Butler: memo to Nuffield Conference, 1958.
9 Cockerell, op. cit.
10 Goldie, op. cit.
11 Ibid.
12 Robert Dougall: *In and Out of the Box*, Collins and Harvill Press, 1973.
13 Richard Lindley: *And Finally ... The News from ITN*, Politico's Publishing, 2005.
14 Sir Robin Day: Foreword to Geoffrey Cox: *Pioneering Television News*, op. cit.
15 Peter Hill: Obituary of Roland Fox, BBC parliamentary correspondent, *Daily Telegraph*, 28 December 2000.
16 D. R. Thorpe, *Supermac: The Life of Harold Macmillan*, Chatto & Windus, 2010.
17 Cockerell, op. cit.
18 Goldie, op. cit.
19 Ibid.
20 Harold Macmillan: *The Macmillan Diaries* (ed. Anthony Howard), Vol. II: *Prime Minister and After, 1957–1966*, Macmillan, 2011.
21 Goldie, op. cit.
22 Asa Briggs: *The History of Broadcasting in the United Kingdom*, Vol. V: *Competition, 1955–1974*, Oxford University Press, 1995.

4: 'The hot, pitiless, probing eye'

1 Charles Williams: *Harold Macmillan*, Weidenfeld & Nicolson, 2009.
2 Cox, op. cit.
3 Quoted in Cockerell, op. cit.
4 Sir David Butler's private papers.
5 Cox, op. cit.
6 Ibid.
7 Dominic Sandbrook: *Never Had It So Good: A History of Britain from Suez to the Beatles*, Abacus, 2005.
8 BBC Annual Report 1958.
9 Cox, op. cit.
10 *The Prime Ministers*, BBC Radio 4, 17 May 2011.
11 Quoted in Martin Rosenbaum: *From Soapbox to Soundbite: Party Political Campaigning in Britain Since 1945*, Palgrave Macmillan, 1997.
12 Ibid.
13 Marcia Williams: *Inside Number 10*, Weidenfeld & Nicolson, 1972.
14 Ibid.
15 Cockerell, op. cit.
16 Wilson to Professor Neustadt, quoted in Ben Pimlott: *Harold Wilson*, HarperCollins, 1992.
17 Cox, op. cit.
18 Cockerell, op. cit.
19 Briggs, *The History of Broadcasting in the United Kingdom*, Vol. V, op. cit.
20 Cockerell, op. cit.
21 Edward Short: *Whip to Wilson*, Macdonald, 1989.
22 Quoted in Dominic Sandbrook: *White Heat: A History of Britain in the Swinging Sixties*, Abacus, 2007.
23 Ibid.
24 Richard Crossman: *The Crossman Diaries* (ed. Anthony Howard), 1979, entry for 27 February 1969.
25 Cockerell, op. cit.
26 *The Prime Ministers*, op. cit.

27 Cabinet meeting minutes (CAB 128/41), July 1966.
28 Cabinet meeting minutes (CAB 128/42), November 1967.
29 Marcia Williams quoted in Briggs, *The BBC: The First Fifty Years*, op. cit.
30 Robert Mackensie quoted in Cockerell, op. cit.
31 Marcia Williams, op. cit.
32 Lance Price: *Where Power Lies: Prime Ministers v The Media*, Simon & Schuster, 2010.
33 *Radio Times*, 10 June 1971.
34 Tom McNally: quoted in Cockerell, op. cit.

5: The lady who was for turning

1 Clive James in the *Observer*, quoted in Cockerell, op. cit.
2 Barry Day, quoted in Rosenbaum, op. cit.
3 Rosenbaum, op. cit.
4 Margaret Thatcher: *The Path to Power*, HarperCollins, 1995.
5 Cockerell, op. cit.
6 www.dailymail.co.uk/news/article-438281/Revealed-Red-Army-Colonel-dubbed-Maggie-Iron-Lady-changed-history
7 Margaret Thatcher: speech to Finchley Conservatives, 31 January 1976.
8 Thatcher archives, THCR 2/6/2/134: 9 May 1979. The archives are accessible online at http://www.margaretthatcher.org
9 Thatcher archives, THCR 2/6/2/134.
10 Rosenbaum, op. cit.
11 Thatcher archives, INGH 2/2/1: 8 June 1979.
12 Thatcher archives, THCR, 2/6/2/123/f31.
13 Thatcher archives: memo, 13 March 1980.
14 Thatcher archives, http://www.margaretthatcher.org/document/112175: 31 August 1979.
15 Thatcher archives, http://www.margaretthatcher.org/document/112259: 9 November 1979.
16 Minutes for Cabinet meeting of 8 November 1979 (CAB 128/66/20).
17 Michael Leapman: *The Last Days of the Beeb*, Coronet, 1987.
18 Lawrence Freedman: *The Official History of the Falklands Campaign*, Routledge, 2005.

19 Quoted in Cockerell, op. cit.
20 Thatcher archives, www.margaretthatcher.org/document/104934
21 ITN's David Nicholas, quoted in Cockerell, Hennessy and Walker, op. cit.
22 Cockerell, Hennessy and Walker, op. cit.
23 Bernard Ingham: *Kill the Messenger*, HarperCollins, 1991.
24 Margaret Thatcher: speech to the American Bar Association, 15 July 1985, Royal Albert Hall.
25 Cockerell, op. cit.
26 Norman Tebbit's description of the job of Marmaduke Hussey.
27 Nicholas Jones: *Shafted: The Media, the Miners' Strike and the Aftermath*, Aldgate Press, 2009.

6: 'Anything else you'd care to say, Prime Minister?'

1 *Guardian*, 21 April 1997.
2 *Frost on Sunday* website.
3 Memo quoted in Paul Donovan: *All Our Todays: Forty Years of the Today Programme*, Jonathan Cape, 1997.
4 Donovan, op. cit.
5 Charles Nevin: *Daily Telegraph*, 21 June 1986.
6 *Desert Island Discs*, BBC Radio 4, 6 January 2008.
7 Quoted in Steven Clayman and John Heritage: *The News Interview: Journalists and Public Figures on Air*, Cambridge University Press, 2002.
8 Jeremy Paxman: *The Political Animal: An Anatomy*, Penguin Books, 2007.
9 *Kebabbed*, BBC Radio 4, 16 April 2000.
10 John Birt: speech in Dublin, February 1995.
11 Quoted in Donovan, op. cit.

7: Tony tames the beast

1 Tim Luckhurst: *This is Today*, Aurum Press, 2001.
2 *British Journalism Review*, June 2000.
3 Alastair Campbell: 'Broadcasting Politics', speech to Fabian Society, 1999.

4   'The BBC, Labour's Fax and Blair's Speech'. *Evening Standard*, 4 October 1995.

5   'Broadcasting Politics', op. cit.

6   Ibid.

7   Tony Blair: *A Journey*, Hutchinson, 2010.

8   Peter Mandelson: *The Third Man: Life at the Heart of New Labour*, HarperPress, 2010.

9   Jonathan Powell: *The New Machiavelli: How to Wield Power in the Modern World*, Bodley Head, 2010.

10 Jeremy Thorpe: after 'the night of the long knives', a brutal Cabinet reshuffle.

11 Cherie Blair: *Speaking for Myself*, Little, Brown, 2008.

8: It's war

1   Alastair Campbell: *The Alastair Campbell Diaries*, Vol. 2: *Power & The People 1997–1999*, entry for Hutchinson, 2011, 21 December 1998.

2   Ibid.

3   Ibid., entry for 21 April 1999.

4   Ed Stourton: 'How the Kosovo War was Spun', *Sunday Telegraph*, 17 October 1999.

5   Ibid.

6   Sir Christopher Meyer: *DC Confidential*, Weidenfeld & Nicolson, 2005.

7   Prime minister's briefing to the press en route to New York, 21 September 2001, available at http://tna.europarchive.org/20070205135013/ http://www.pm.gov.uk/output/page1602.asp

8   Alastair Campbell: *The Alastair Campbell Diaries*, Vol. 4: *The Burden of Power: Countdown to Iraq*, Hutchinson, 2012.

9   Ibid.

10 Press conference, Crawford Summit, April 2002.

11 Meyer, op. cit.

12 http://www.iraqinquiry.org.uk/media/50751/Blair-to-Powell-17March2002-minute.pdf

13 Bob Woodward: *Plan of Action*, Simon & Schuster, 2004.

14 Memo from David Manning, foreign policy adviser to the

prime minister. Quoted in *The New York Times*, 27 March 2006.

15 http://the-hutton-inquiry.org.uk/content/bbc/bbc_4_0131to0135.pdf

9: Where is he? Where are they?

1 Alastair Campbell and Bill Hagerty (eds.): *The Alastair Campbell Diaries*, Vol. 4: *The Burden of Power: Countdown to Iraq*, op. cit., entry for 29 May 2003.

2 Tony Blair, op. cit.

3 Alastair Campbell and Richard Stott (eds.): *The Blair Years: Extracts from The Alastair Campbell Diaries*, Hutchinson, 2007, entry for 21 July 2003.

4 Emails submitted to Hutton inquiry.

5 Blair, op. cit.

6 Campbell and Hagerty, op. cit., entry for 28 January 2004.

7 Jonathan Powell: speaking at an Institute of Government seminar, 8 March 2011.

10: 'I just can't communicate'

1 Anthony Seldon and Guy Lodge: *Brown at 10*, Biteback Publishing, 2010.

2 Mandelson, op. cit.

3 Gordon Brown in an interview for *The Prime Ministers*, op. cit.

4 Author interview with Guy Lodge.

5 *Today* programme, 24 September 2007.

6 Peter Watt: *Inside Out: My Story of Betrayal and Cowardice at the Heart of New Labour*, Biteback Publishing, 2010.

7 *The Andrew Marr Show*, 7 October 2007.

11: Speaking in a foreign language

1 Alistair Darling: speaking on *Your Money and How They Spend It*, BBC2, 30 November 2011.

2 Seldon and Lodge, op. cit.

3 Mandelson, op. cit.

4 *Daily Telegraph*, 3 May 2010.

12: The battle over, a new one begins

1 Nic Newman: #*UKelection2010: Mainstream media and the role of the internet: how social and digital media affected the business of politics and journalism* (pamphlet), Reuters Institute, July 2010.
2 *An historical and chronological deduction of the origin of commerce, from the earliest accounts*, printed at the Logographic Press by J. Walter, 1787.
3 Ric Bailey: *Squeezing Out the Oxygen – or Reviving Democracy? The History and Future of the TV Election Debates in the UK* (pamphlet), Reuters Institute, February 2012.

A last word: Bias and the Beeb

1 James Murdoch: 'The Absence of Trust', McTaggart Lecture 2009.
2 Lords Communications Committee minutes, September 2007.
3 'Future of News and Current Affairs: BBC, Fox or Third Way?', Institute for Government seminar, 16 December 2011.
4 Mitchell Stephens: *A History of News*, Harcourt Brace & Co., 1997.
5 Quoted in ibid.
6 Quoted in Briggs, *The History of Broadcasting in the United Kingdom*, Vol. II, op. cit.
7 Quoted in the report of the Ullswater committee, 1935.
8 Ian McIntyre: *Reith: The Expense of Glory*, HarperCollins, 1993.
9 Reith, *The Reith Diaries*, op. cit.
10 P. P. Eckersley: *The Power Behind the Microphone*, Jonathan Cape, 1941.
11 David Edwards and David Cromwell: *Newspeak in the 21st Century*, Pluto Press, 2009.
12 David Cromwell and David Edwards: *Guardians of Power*, Pluto Press, 2005.
13 Paul Dacre: Cudlipp Lecture, 22 January 2007.
14 Mark Thompson: *New Statesman* interview, 2 September 2010.

15 Mark Thompson: speech at the Institute for Government, 16 December 2011.

16 'From Seesaw to Wagon Wheel: Safeguarding Impartiality in the 21st Century', BBC, 2007.

17 Nick Davies: *Flat Earth News*, Chatto & Windus, 2008.

18 John Moody, Fox News Channel's senior vice-president for news and editorial, in *Brill's Content* magazine, October 1999.

19 David Frum: 'When did the GOP lose touch with reality?', *New York Magazine*, 20 November 2011 (GOP stands for Grand Old Party, a nickname for the Republican party).

20 http://newbusters.org/blogs/noel-sheppard/2008/08/07/mccain-backers-watch-fox-obamas-watch-cnn-msnbc-nets#ixzz1tLOxnkpi

21 *British Journalism Review*, Vol. 13, No. 3, 2002.

22 Ofcom Broadcasting Code, rule 5.9.

23 Rupert Murdoch: evidence to the Leveson inquiry, 25 April 2012.

24 'New News, Old News', Hargreaves and Thomas, ITC/BSC, 2002.

25 'New News: Impartial Broadcasting in the Digital Age', Tambini and Cowling, 2002.

26 Institute for Government seminar, 16 December 2011, op. cit.

PICTURE ACKNOWLEDGEMENTS

Every effort has been made to trace the copyright holders of photos reproduced in the book. Copyright holders not credited are invited to get in touch with the publishers.

Line drawings and cartoons in the text:

2   'The Diviner' by Arthur Norris, *Punch*, 3 May 1916.
52   *Idol-Worship or The Way to Preferment*, anonymous print, 1740. Satire on Robert Walpole showing him as a colossal figure at the entrance to St James's Palace bending forward with his naked backside exposed for an ambitious young man to kiss; another man holds a petition and bowls a hoop lettered, 'Wealth', 'Pride', 'Vanity', 'Folly', 'Luxury', 'Want', 'Dependance', 'Servility', 'Venality', 'Corruption' and 'Prostitution', through Walpole's legs towards an arcade whose arches are labelled, 'Saint [James's P]alace', 'The Treasury', 'The Exchequer' and 'The Admiralty'.
86   'Sir John Reith' by David Low, *New Statesman*, 11 November 1933.
126 'Look, How Conservative Freedom <u>Works</u>!' by Vicky (Victor Weisz), *Daily Mirror*, 8 August 1955. The figure depicted is Charles Hill, the Tory postmaster general, later asked by Harold Wilson to 'sort out' the BBC as its chairman. Mirrorpix.

PHOTOGRAPHS

Conservative Party poster, 1958: Getty Images; Robin Day interviewing Harold Macmillan, 2 October 1958: PA/PA Archive/Press Association Images; Dwight D. Eisenhower and Harold Macmillan, Downing Street, 31 August 1959: AP/Press Association Images; Harold Wilson at home, 1964: ITV/Rex Features; Robin Day, Richard Dimbleby and Harold Wilson, pre-General Election, September 1964: © BBC Photo Library; David Frost and Lance Percival, *That Was The Week That Was*, 13 November 1963: *Daily Mail*/Rex Features.

Margaret Thatcher at a farm, Willisham, 22 April 1979: Gamma-Keystone via Getty Images; Robin Day interviews Margaret Thatcher, 9 April 1984: Getty Images; Brian Walden interviews Margaret Thatcher, 28 October 1989: PA/PA Archive/Press Association Images; Geoffrey Howe speaks in the House of Commons, 13 November 1990: PA/PA Archive/Press Association Images; Denis Thatcher and Margaret Thatcher leave Downing Street, 28 October 1990: © Trinity Mirror/Mirrorpix/Alamy; Margaret Thatcher leaves the Grand Hotel, Brighton, 12 October 1984: PA/PA Archive/Press Association Images; *Daily Mirror* front page, 13 October 1984: Mirrorpix.

Brian Redhead in the *Today* studio: © Graham Turner/the *Guardian*; Brian Redhead, July 1987: © TopFoto/UPP/TopFoto.co.uk.

Section two
Clement Attlee returns to Downing Street from Washington, 1950: Brian Harris/*The Times*/NI Syndication; Jeremy Paxman and Tony Blair, 6 February 2003: Jeff Overs/BBC; John Humphrys, August 2007: Jeff Overs/BBC; David Frost and Tony Blair, 12 January 1997: Getty Images.

Reporters and Tony Blair, March 2004: © Nick Danziger; Tony Blair, Evian, 2 June 2003: Stefan Rousseau/PA Archive/Press Association Images; George Bush, London, 20 November 2003: PA/PA Archive/Press Association Images; demonstration, Television

Centre, Wood Lane, London, 5 February 2004: Matthew Fearn/PA Archive/Press Association Images; Cherie Blair, Downing Street, 27 June 2007: Getty Images; cartoon by Martin Rowson: courtesy the artist.

Nick Robinson and Huw Edwards, Downing Street, 27 June 2007: Jeff Overs/BBC; Gordon Brown and Andrew Marr, Downing Street, January 2009: Jeff Overs/BBC; Nick Robinson and Gordon Brown, April 2010: courtesy Martin Argles; Nick Robinson and Gordon Brown on the train to Weymouth, 27 April 2010: courtesy Lindsay McCoy; Gordon Brown talks to Gillian Duffy, 28 April 2010: Getty Images; Gordon Brown and George W. Bush, Camp David, 30 July 2007: Charles Dharapak/AP/Press Association Images.

Robin Day (second from left) and others in the Operations Centre in the basement of Broadcasting House, 26 May 1955: © BBC Photo Library; election studio, BBC, 2010: © BBC Photo Library; Nick Clegg, David Cameron and Gordon Brown, TV election debate, 15 April 2010: Rob Evans/AP/Press Association Images.

Protesters, Tahrir Square, Cairo, 25 November 2011: © Monique Jaques/Corbis; Nick Robinson, Downing Street, May 2010: Jeff Overs/BBC.

INDEX

INDEX